Yamada-kun
THE
en Witches

6

MIKI YOSHIKAWA

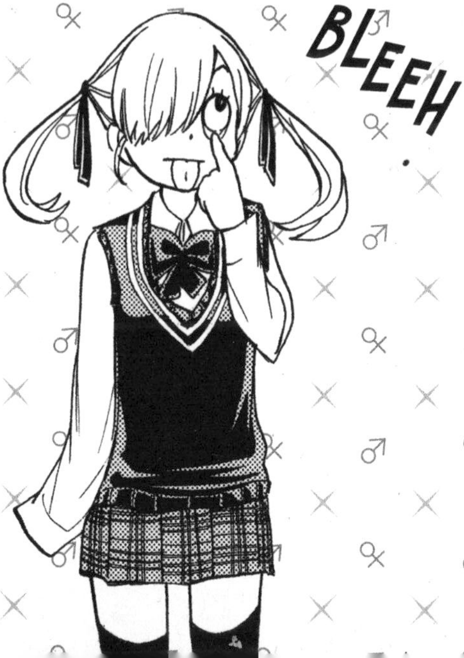
BLEEH

CONTENTS

CHAPTER 44: Annoying and gross.

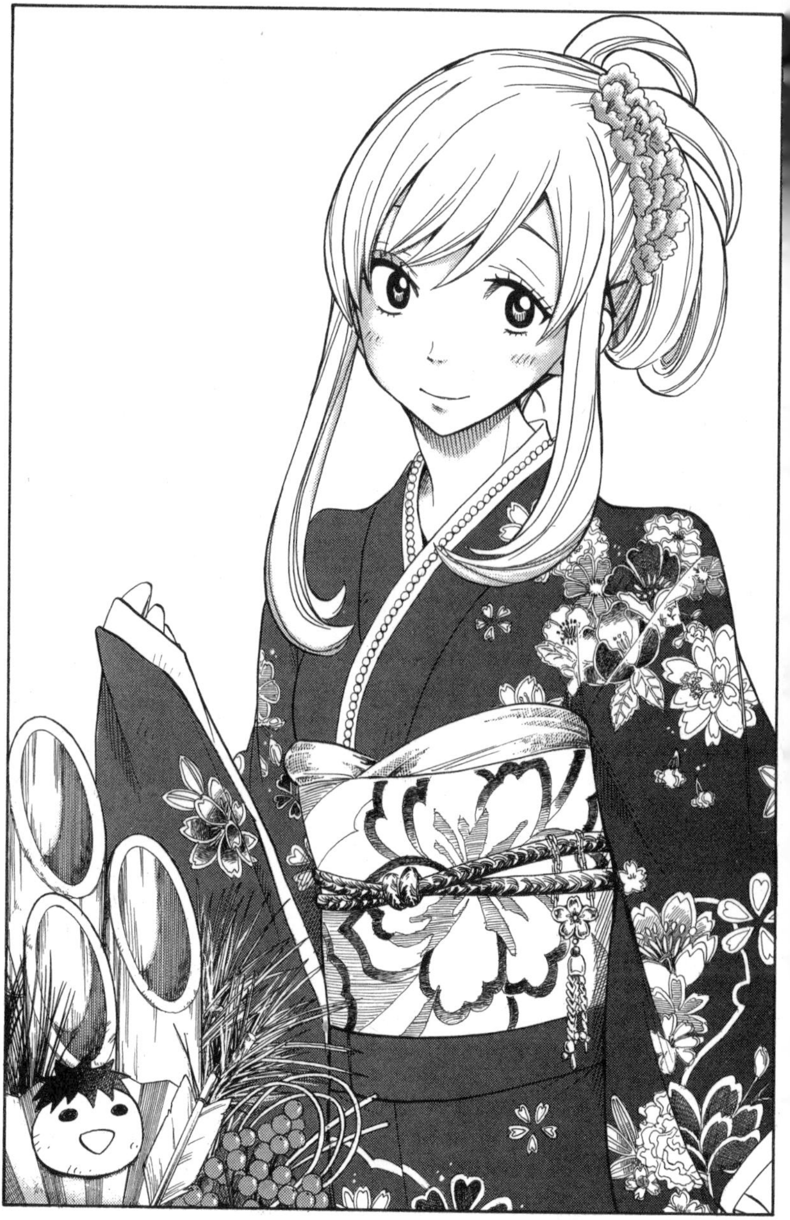

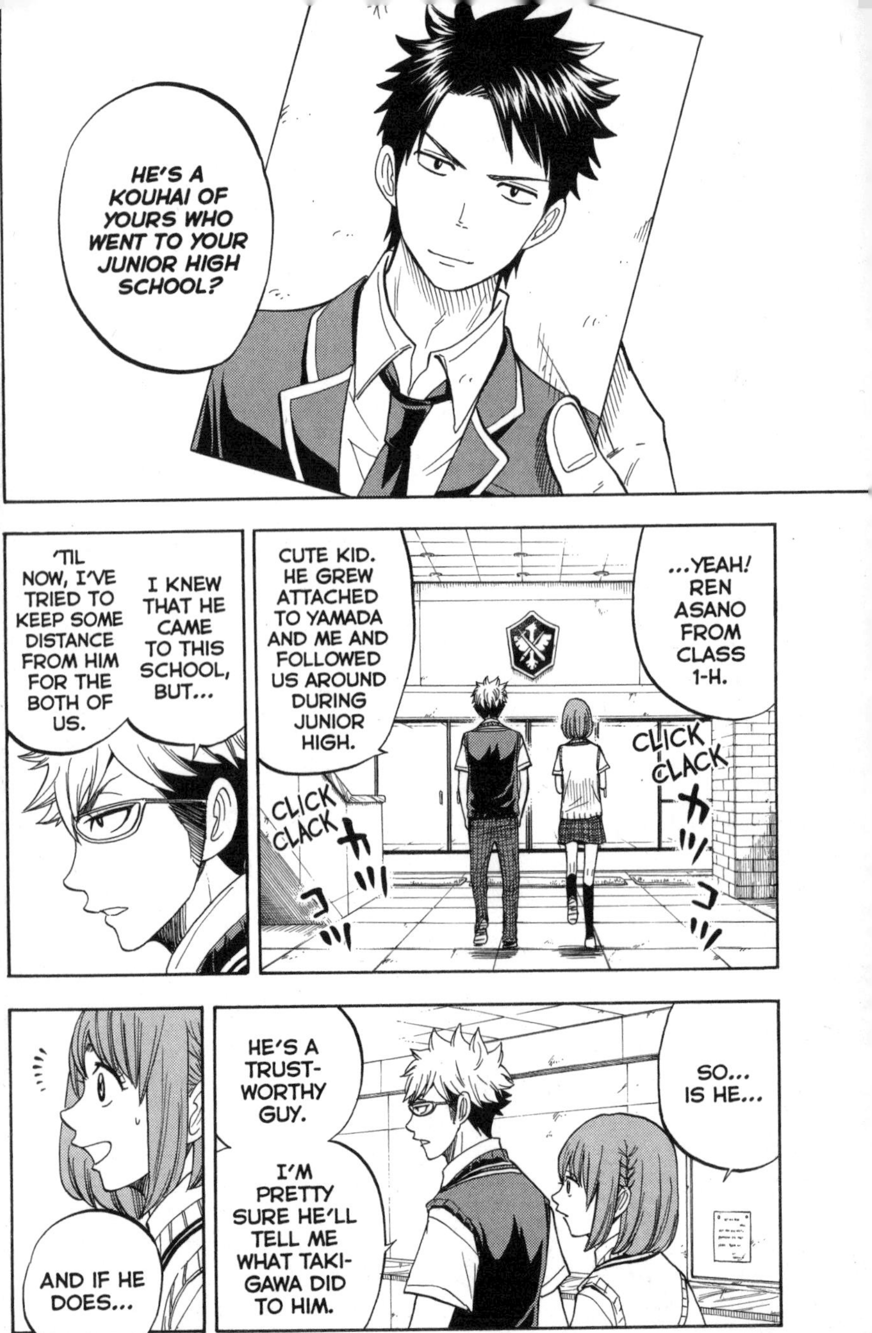
HE'S A KOUHAI OF YOURS WHO WENT TO YOUR JUNIOR HIGH SCHOOL?
...YEAH! REN ASANO FROM CLASS 1-H.
CLICK CLACK
カッ コッ
CUTE KID. HE GREW ATTACHED TO YAMADA AND ME AND FOLLOWED US AROUND DURING JUNIOR HIGH.
CLICK CLACK
カッ コッ
I KNEW THAT HE CAME TO THIS SCHOOL, BUT...
'TIL NOW, I'VE TRIED TO KEEP SOME DISTANCE FROM HIM FOR THE BOTH OF US.
SO... IS HE...
HE'S A TRUST-WORTHY GUY.
I'M PRETTY SURE HE'LL TELL ME WHAT TAKI-GAWA DID TO HIM.
AND IF HE DOES...

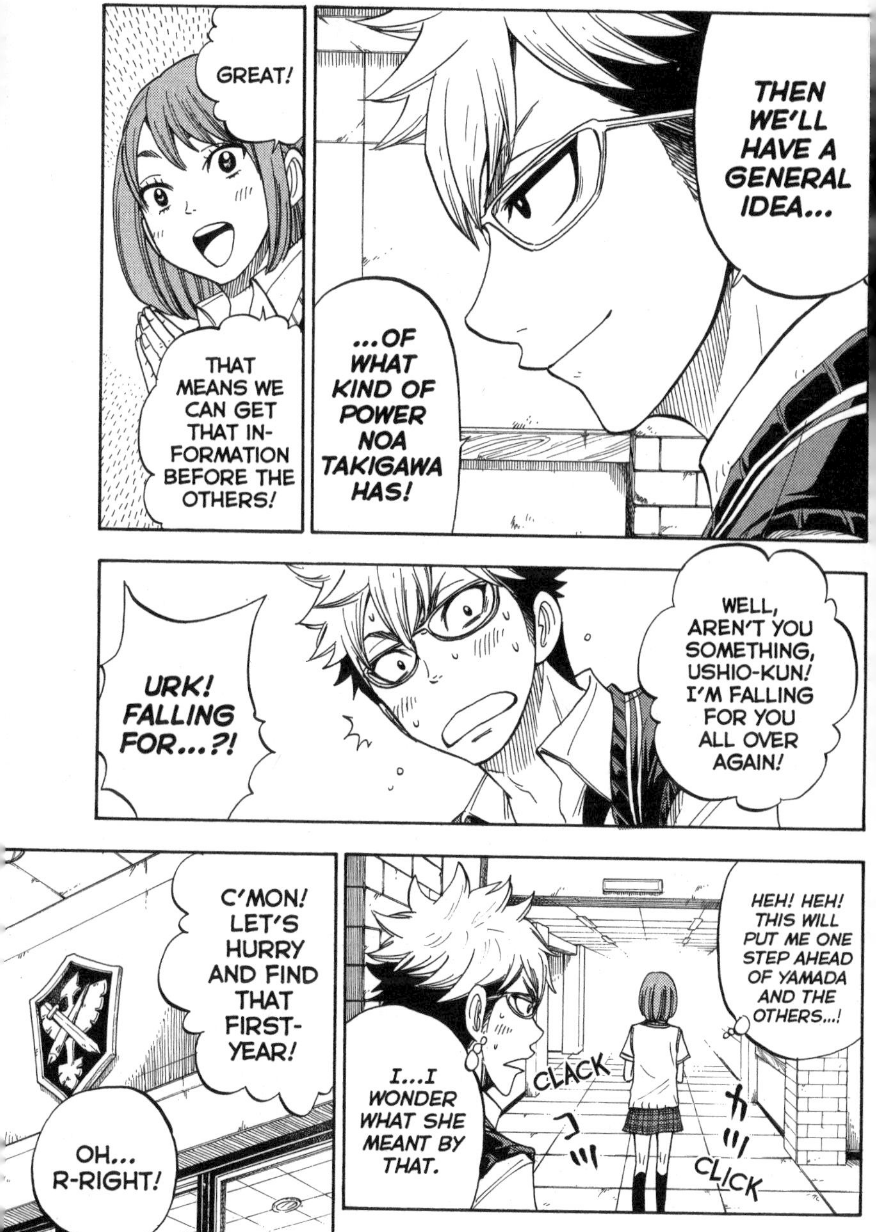
THEN WE'LL HAVE A GENERAL IDEA...
...OF WHAT KIND OF POWER NOA TAKIGAWA HAS!
GREAT!
THAT MEANS WE CAN GET THAT IN-FORMATION BEFORE THE OTHERS!
WELL, AREN'T YOU SOMETHING, USHIO-KUN! I'M FALLING FOR YOU ALL OVER AGAIN!
URK! FALLING FOR...?!
HEH! HEH! THIS WILL PUT ME ONE STEP AHEAD OF YAMADA AND THE OTHERS...!
CLICK
CLACK
I...I WONDER WHAT SHE MEANT BY THAT.
C'MON! LET'S HURRY AND FIND THAT FIRST-YEAR!
OH... R-RIGHT!

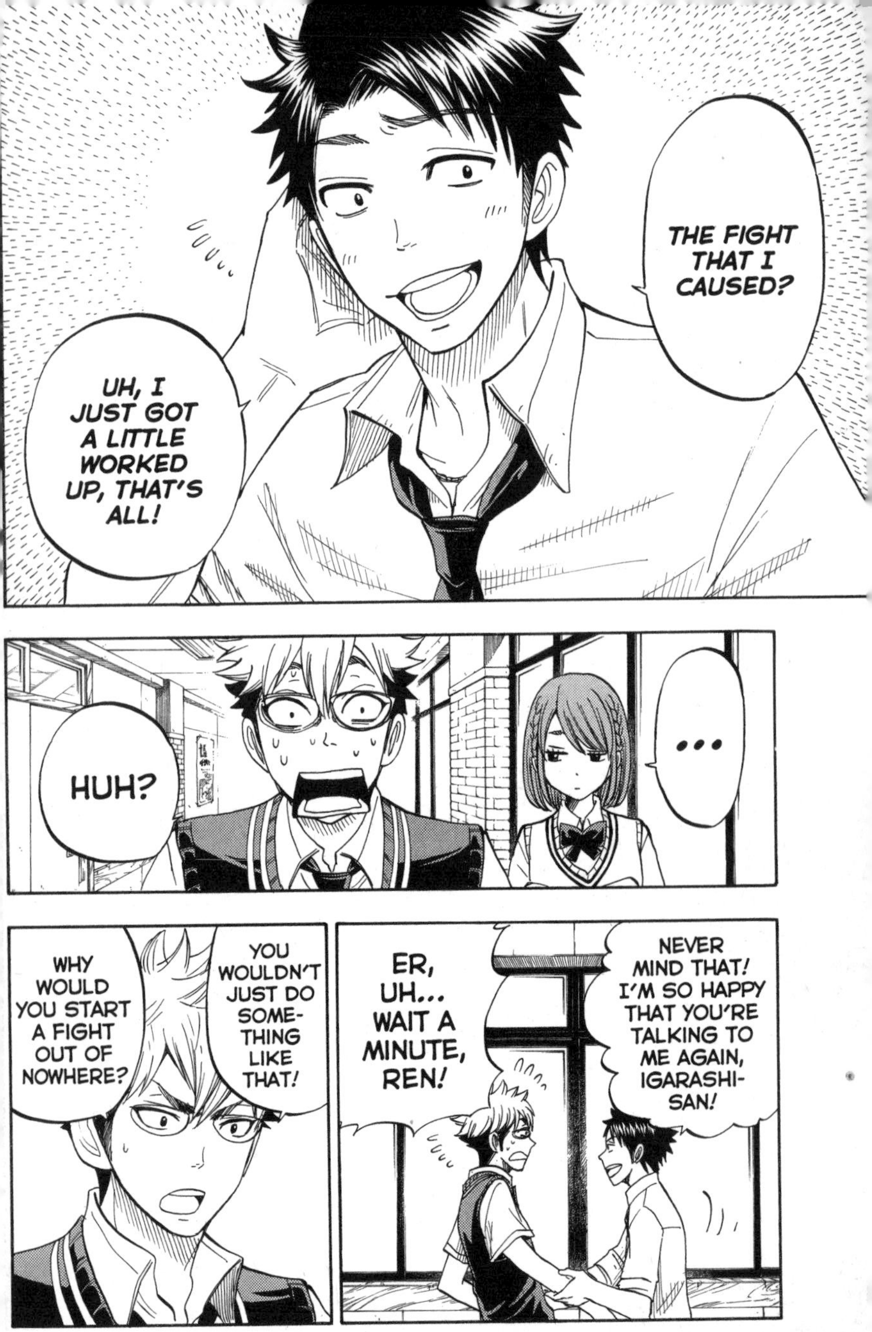
THE FIGHT THAT I CAUSED?
UH, I JUST GOT A LITTLE WORKED UP, THAT'S ALL!
...
HUH?
NEVER MIND THAT! I'M SO HAPPY THAT YOU'RE TALKING TO ME AGAIN, IGARASHI-SAN!
ER, UH... WAIT A MINUTE, REN!
YOU WOULDN'T JUST DO SOME-THING LIKE THAT!
WHY WOULD YOU START A FIGHT OUT OF NOWHERE?

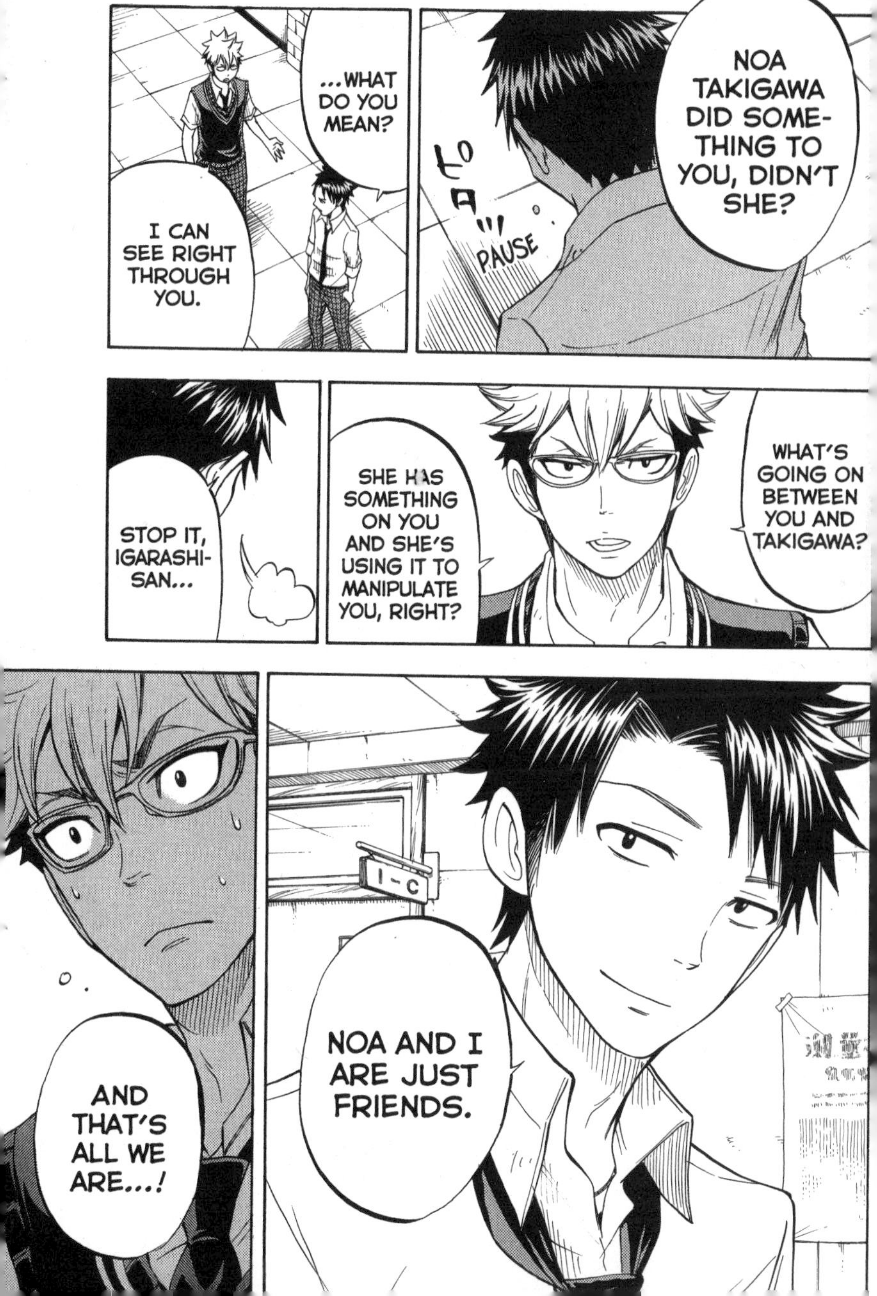
NOA TAKIGAWA DID SOME-THING TO YOU, DIDN'T SHE?
PAUSE
...WHAT DO YOU MEAN?
I CAN SEE RIGHT THROUGH YOU.
WHAT'S GOING ON BETWEEN YOU AND TAKIGAWA?
SHE HAS SOMETHING ON YOU AND SHE'S USING IT TO MANIPULATE YOU, RIGHT?
STOP IT, IGARASHI-SAN...
NOA AND I ARE JUST FRIENDS.
AND THAT'S ALL WE ARE...!

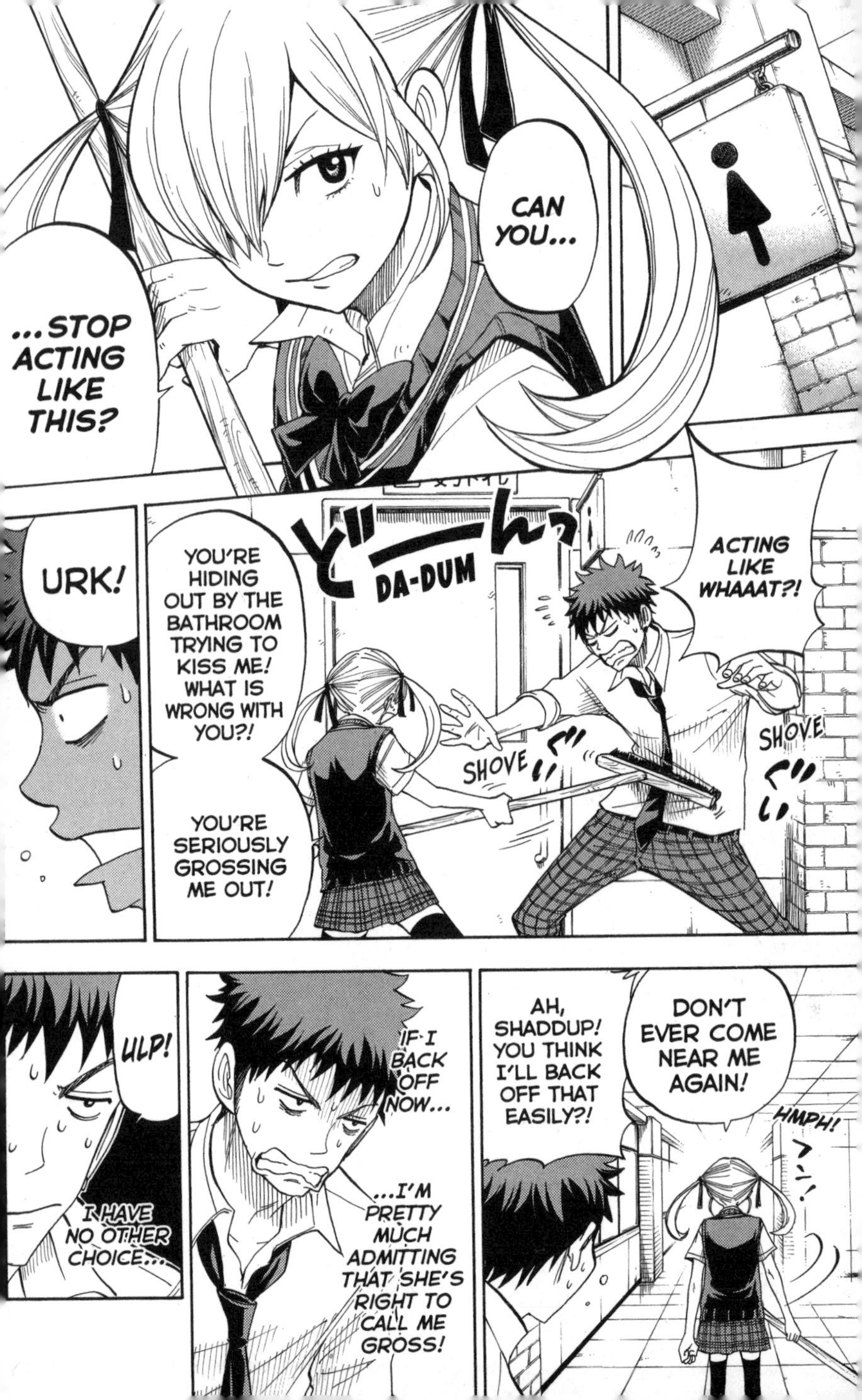
CAN YOU...
...STOP ACTING LIKE THIS?
ACTING LIKE WHAAAT?!
どーんっ
DA-DUM
YOU'RE HIDING OUT BY THE BATHROOM TRYING TO KISS ME! WHAT IS WRONG WITH YOU?!
SHOVE
ぐい
SHOVE
ぐい
YOU'RE SERIOUSLY GROSSING ME OUT!
URK!
DON'T EVER COME NEAR ME AGAIN!
AH, SHADDUP! YOU THINK I'LL BACK OFF THAT EASILY?!
HMPH!
IF I BACK OFF NOW...
...I'M PRETTY MUCH ADMITTING THAT SHE'S RIGHT TO CALL ME GROSS!
ULP!
I HAVE NO OTHER CHOICE...

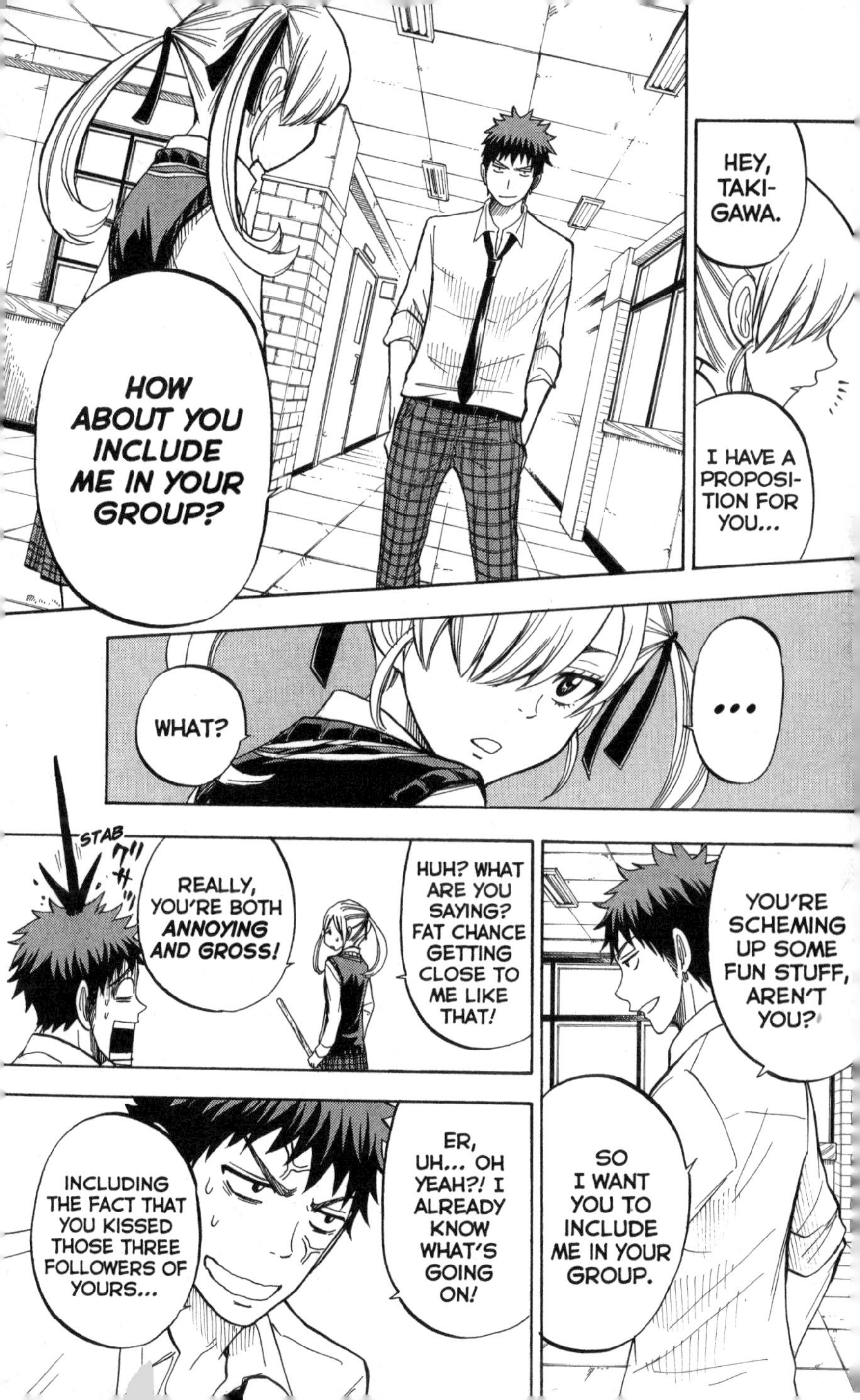
HEY, TAKI-GAWA.
I HAVE A PROPOSI-TION FOR YOU...
HOW ABOUT YOU INCLUDE ME IN YOUR GROUP?
...
WHAT?
YOU'RE SCHEMING UP SOME FUN STUFF, AREN'T YOU?
SO I WANT YOU TO INCLUDE ME IN YOUR GROUP.
HUH? WHAT ARE YOU SAYING? FAT CHANCE GETTING CLOSE TO ME LIKE THAT!
REALLY, YOU'RE BOTH *ANNOYING AND GROSS!*
STAB
ER, UH... OH YEAH?! I ALREADY KNOW WHAT'S GOING ON!
INCLUDING THE FACT THAT YOU KISSED THOSE THREE FOLLOWERS OF YOURS...

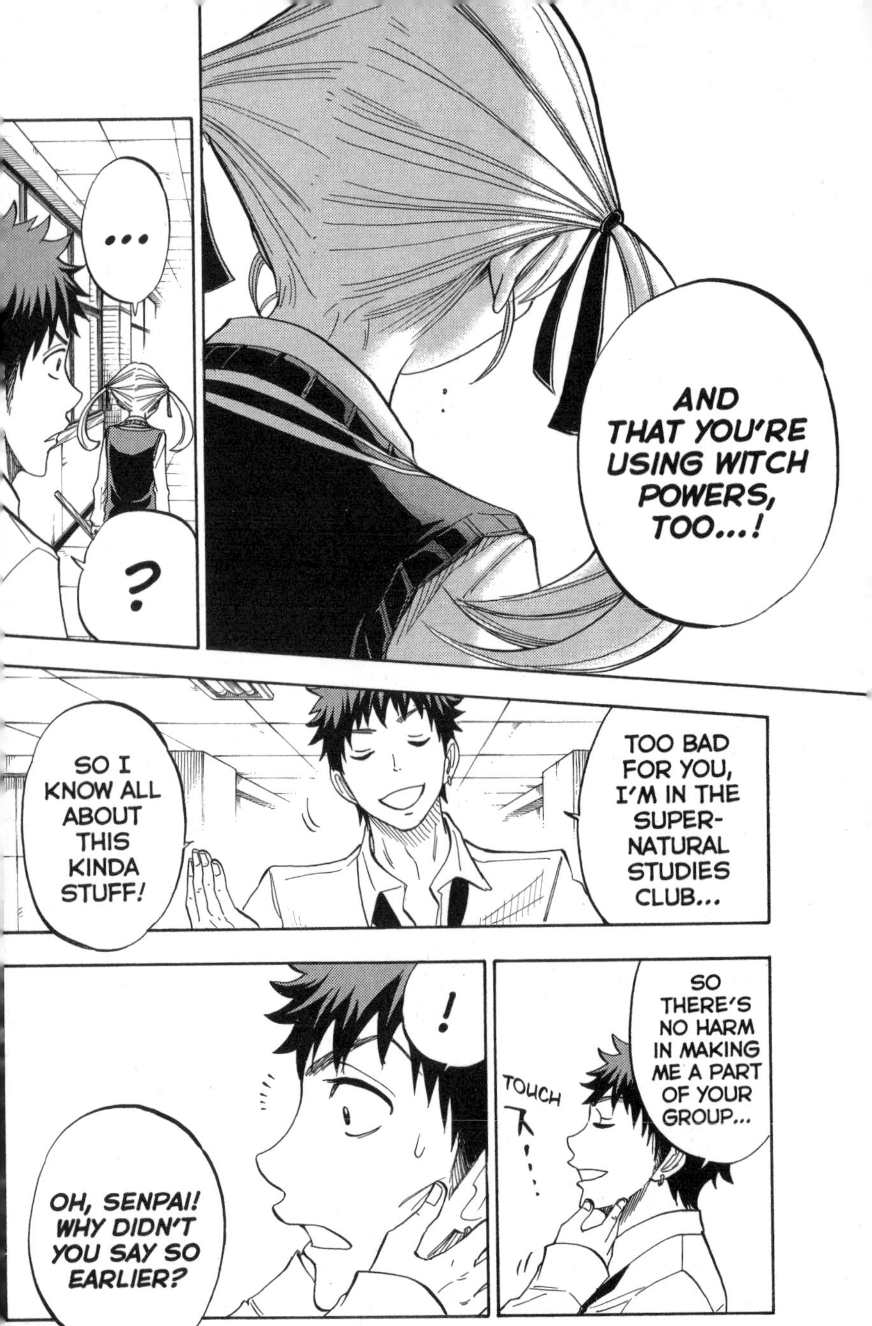
AND THAT YOU'RE USING WITCH POWERS, TOO...!
...
?
TOO BAD FOR YOU, I'M IN THE SUPER-NATURAL STUDIES CLUB...
SO I KNOW ALL ABOUT THIS KINDA STUFF!
SO THERE'S NO HARM IN MAKING ME A PART OF YOUR GROUP...
TOUCH
!
OH, SENPAI! WHY DIDN'T YOU SAY SO EARLIER?

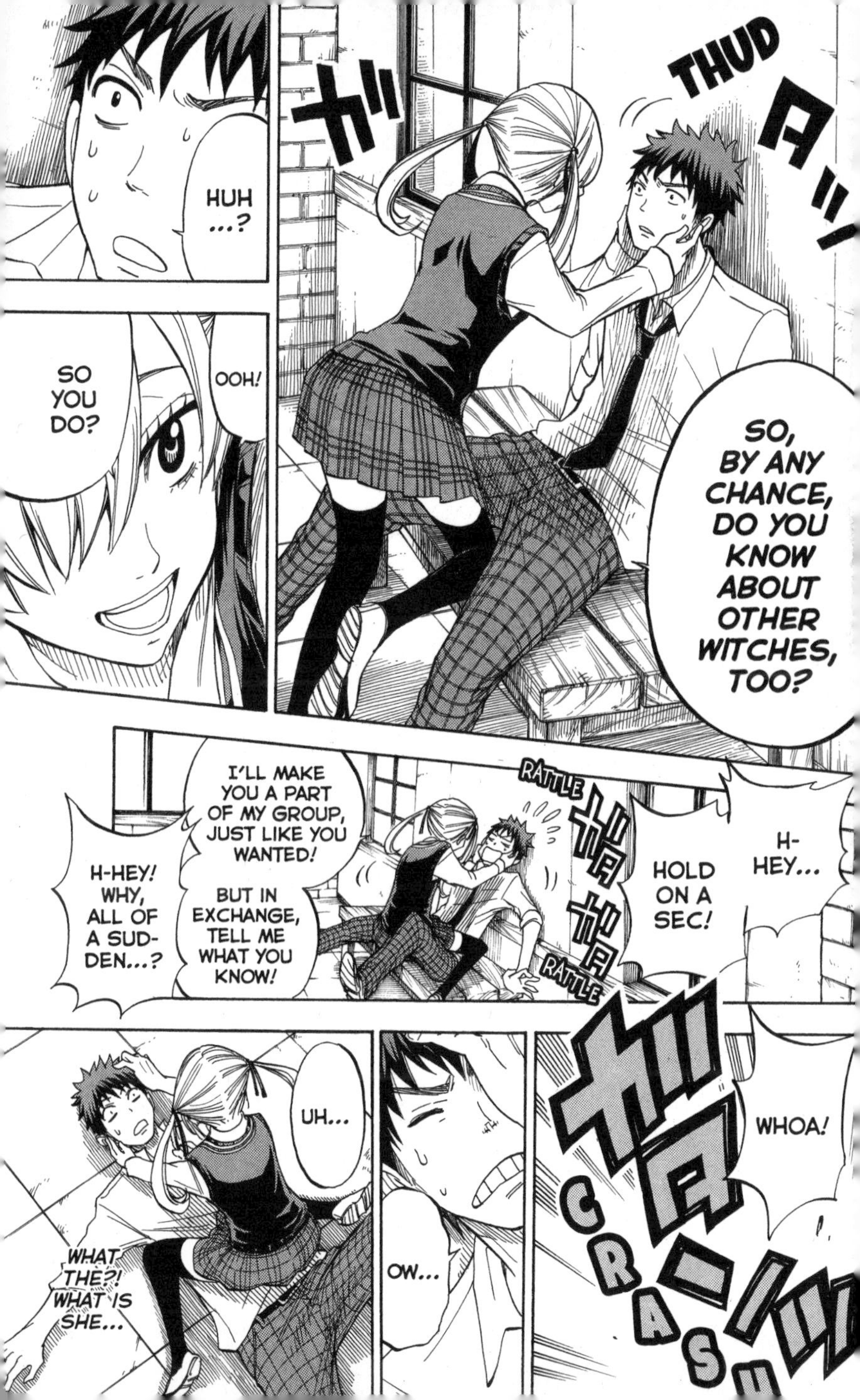

THUD
SO, BY ANY CHANCE, DO YOU KNOW ABOUT OTHER WITCHES, TOO?
HUH ...?
OOH!
SO YOU DO?
H- HEY...
HOLD ON A SEC!
RATTLE
RATTLE
I'LL MAKE YOU A PART OF MY GROUP, JUST LIKE YOU WANTED!
BUT IN EXCHANGE, TELL ME WHAT YOU KNOW!
H-HEY! WHY, ALL OF A SUD-DEN...?
WHOA!
CRASH
OW...
UH...
WHAT THE?! WHAT IS SHE...

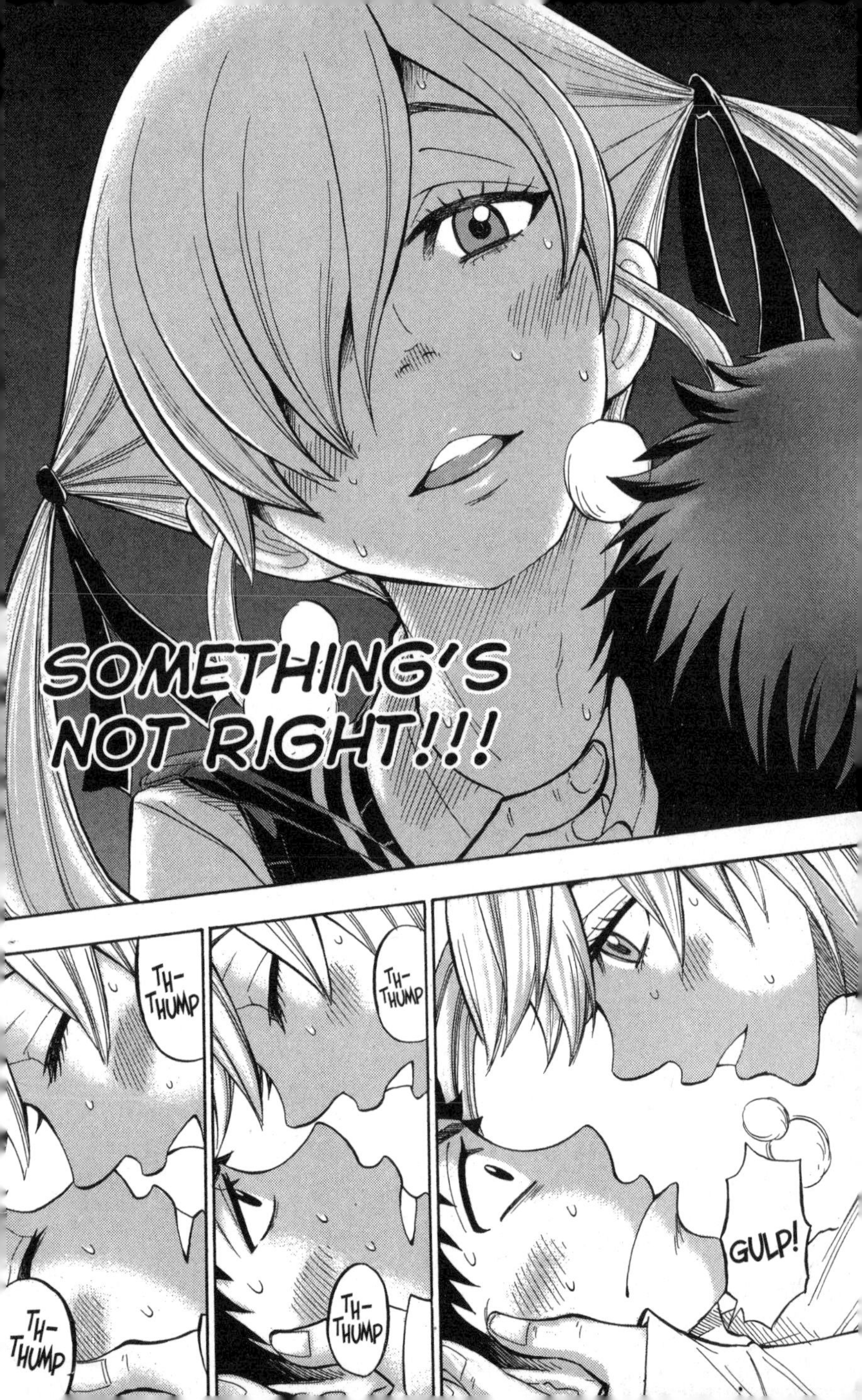
SOMETHING'S NOT RIGHT!!!
GULP!
TH-THUMP
TH-THUMP
TH-THUMP
TH-THUMP

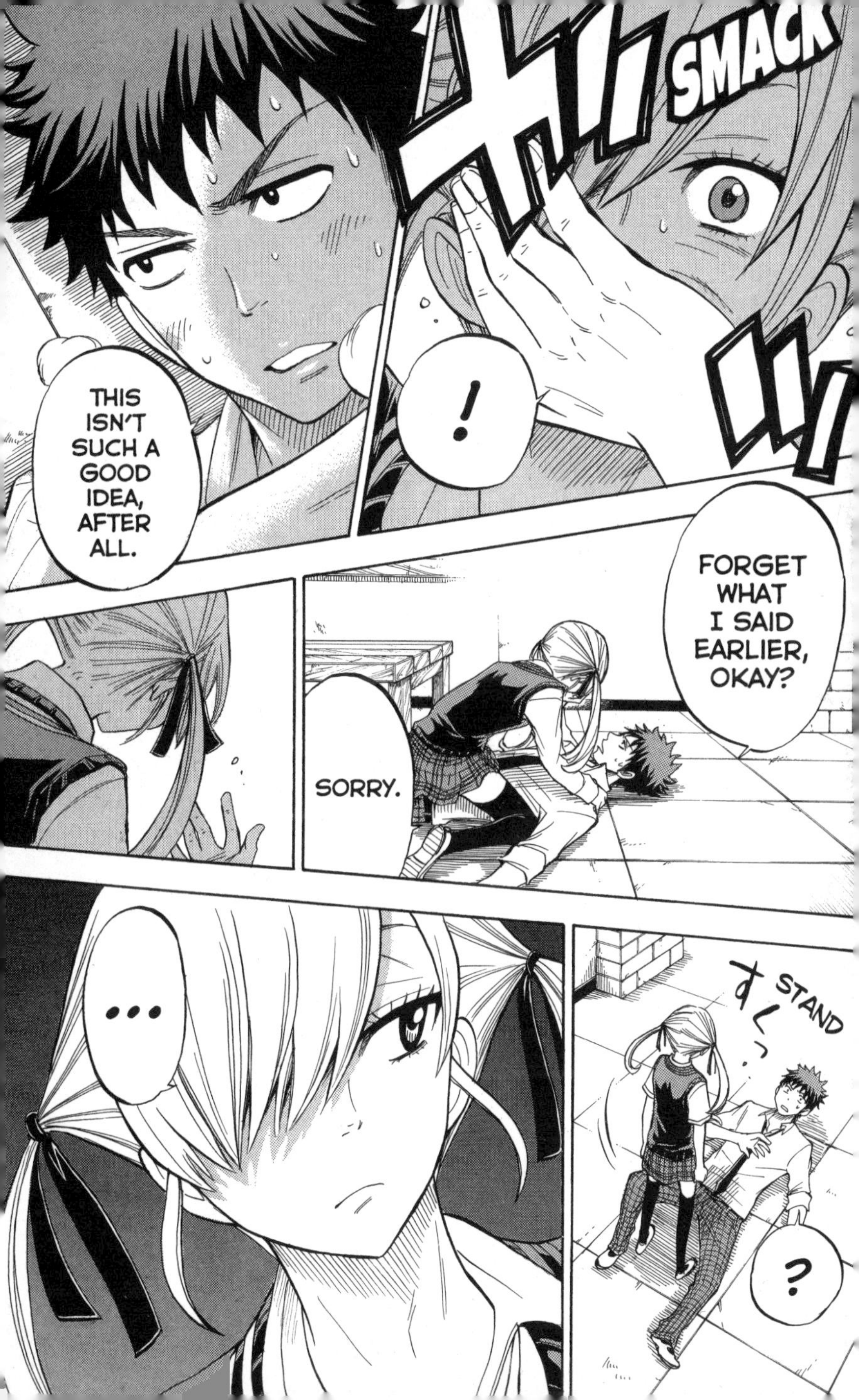
SMACK
!
THIS ISN'T SUCH A GOOD IDEA, AFTER ALL.
FORGET WHAT I SAID EARLIER, OKAY?
SORRY.
すくっ
STAND
?
...

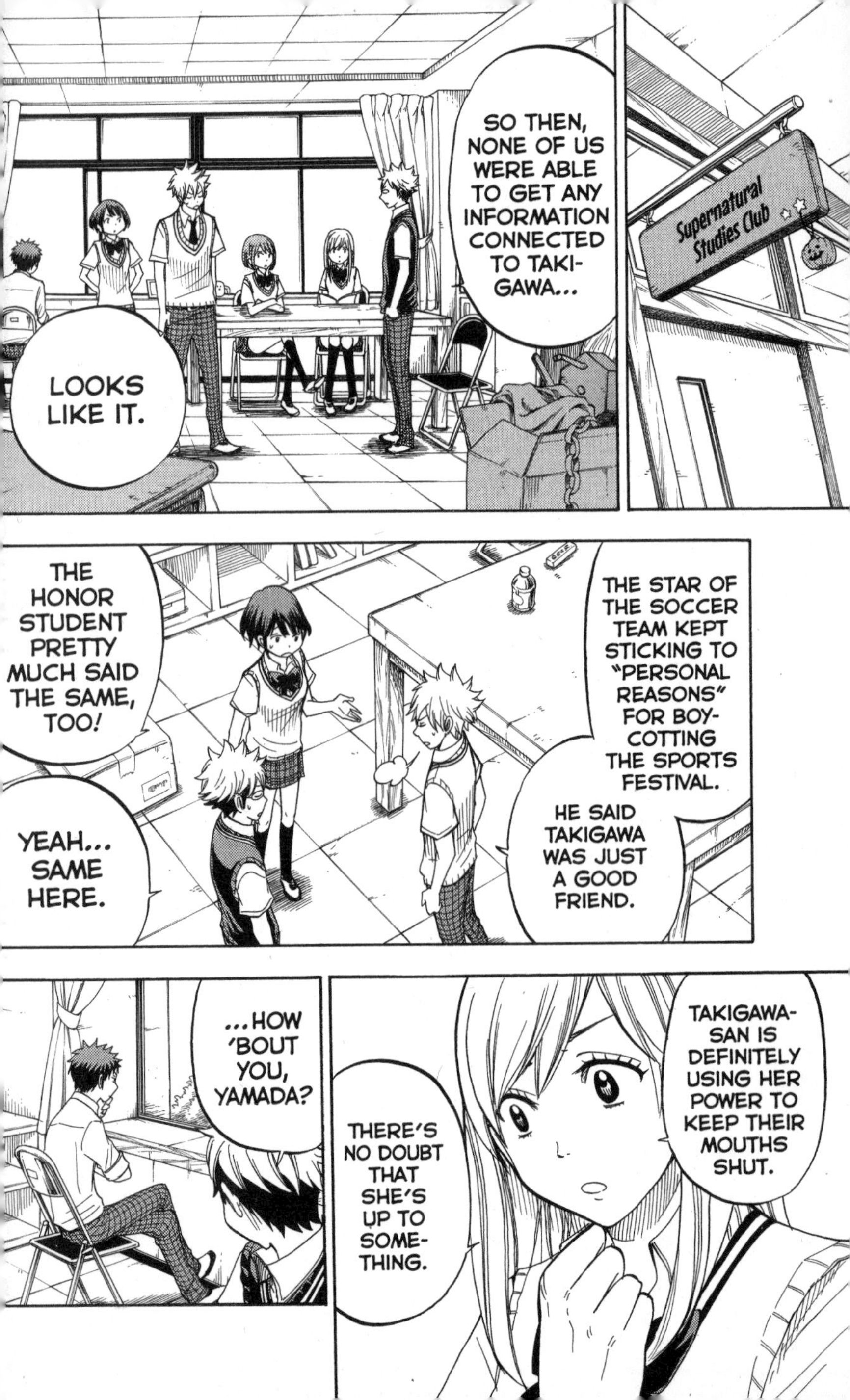
Supernatural Studies Club
SO THEN, NONE OF US WERE ABLE TO GET ANY INFORMATION CONNECTED TO TAKI-GAWA...
LOOKS LIKE IT.
THE STAR OF THE SOCCER TEAM KEPT STICKING TO "PERSONAL REASONS" FOR BOY-COTTING THE SPORTS FESTIVAL.
HE SAID TAKIGAWA WAS JUST A GOOD FRIEND.
THE HONOR STUDENT PRETTY MUCH SAID THE SAME, TOO!
YEAH... SAME HERE.
TAKIGAWA-SAN IS DEFINITELY USING HER POWER TO KEEP THEIR MOUTHS SHUT.
THERE'S NO DOUBT THAT SHE'S UP TO SOME-THING.
...HOW 'BOUT YOU, YAMADA?

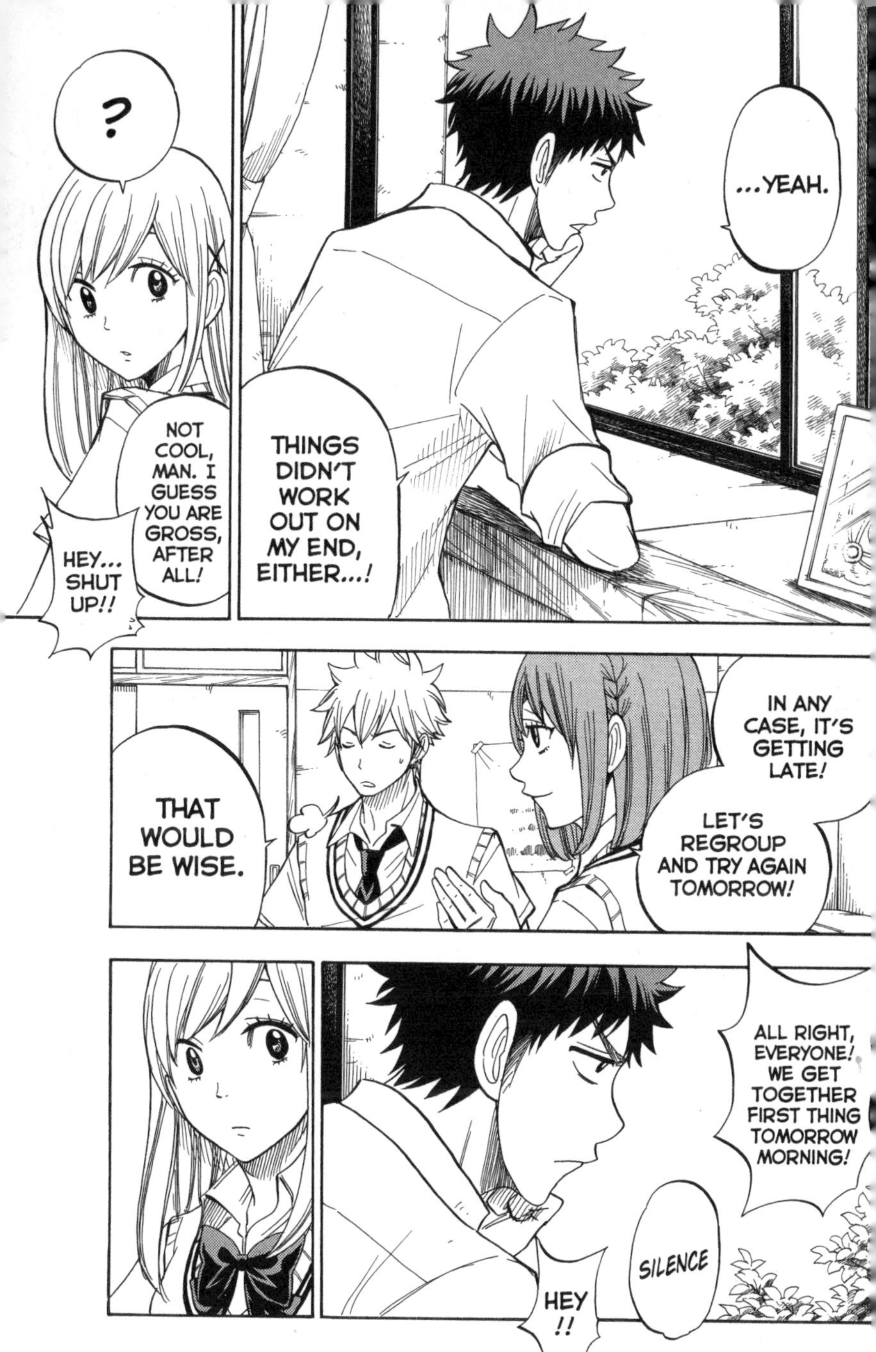
...YEAH.
THINGS DIDN'T WORK OUT ON MY END, EITHER...!
?
NOT COOL, MAN. I GUESS YOU ARE GROSS, AFTER ALL!
HEY... SHUT UP!!
IN ANY CASE, IT'S GETTING LATE!
LET'S REGROUP AND TRY AGAIN TOMORROW!
THAT WOULD BE WISE.
ALL RIGHT, EVERYONE! WE GET TOGETHER FIRST THING TOMORROW MORNING!
SILENCE
HEY!!

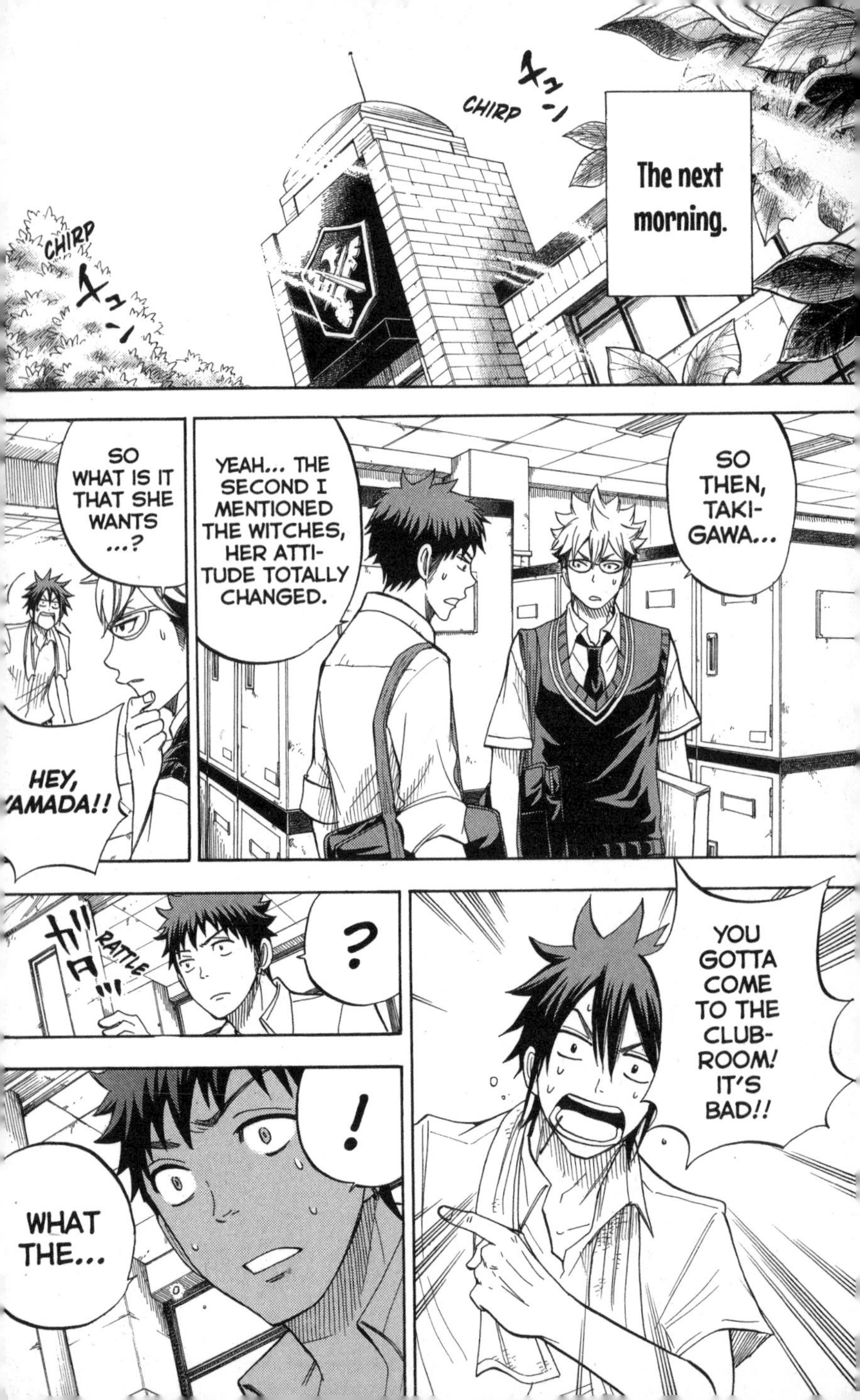
The next morning.
CHIRP
CHIRP
SO THEN, TAKI-GAWA...
YEAH... THE SECOND I MENTIONED THE WITCHES, HER ATTI-TUDE TOTALLY CHANGED.
SO WHAT IS IT THAT SHE WANTS ...?
HEY, YAMADA!!
YOU GOTTA COME TO THE CLUB-ROOM! IT'S BAD!!
RATTLE
?
!
WHAT THE...

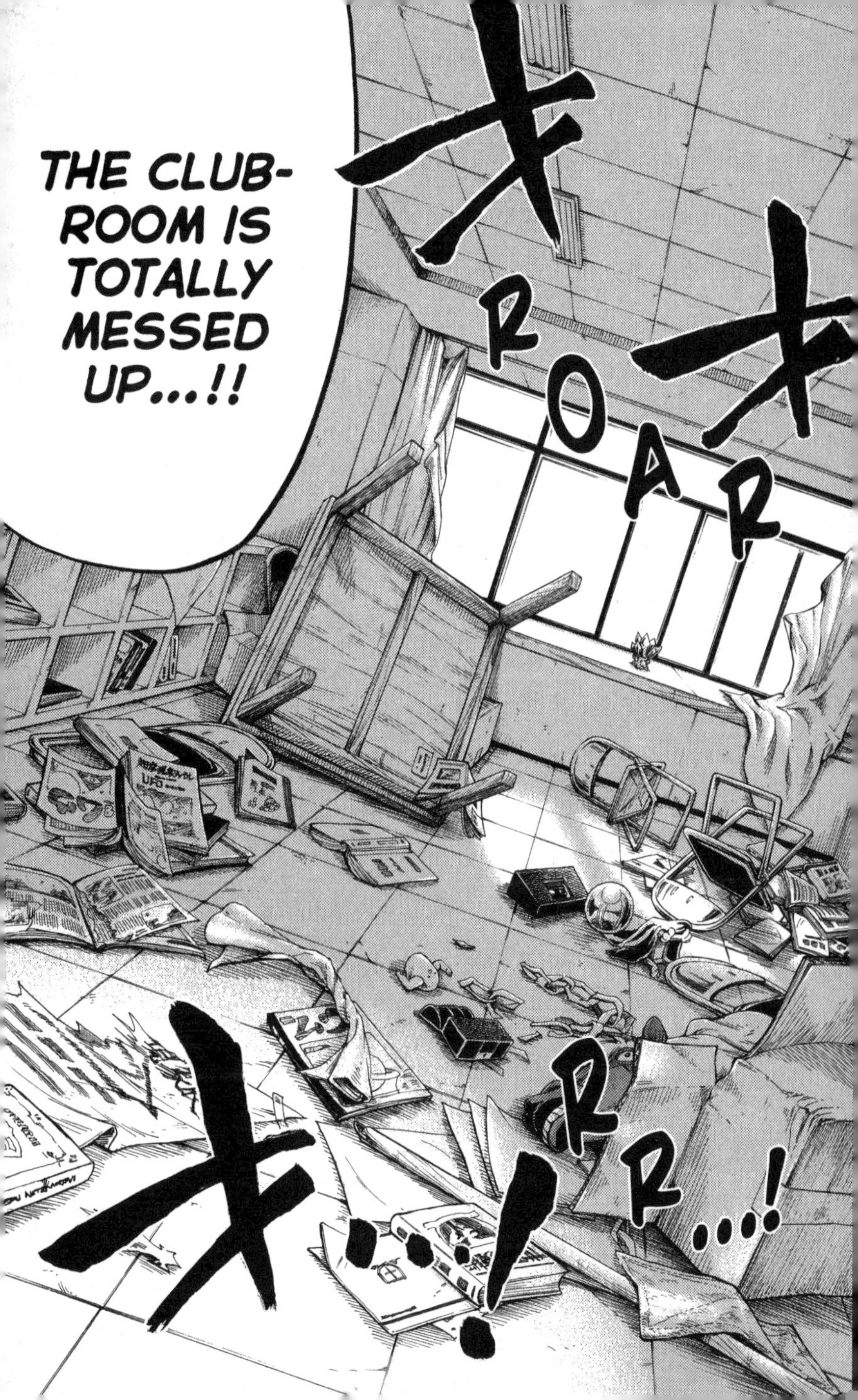
THE CLUB-ROOM IS TOTALLY MESSED UP...!!
ROAR
RR...!

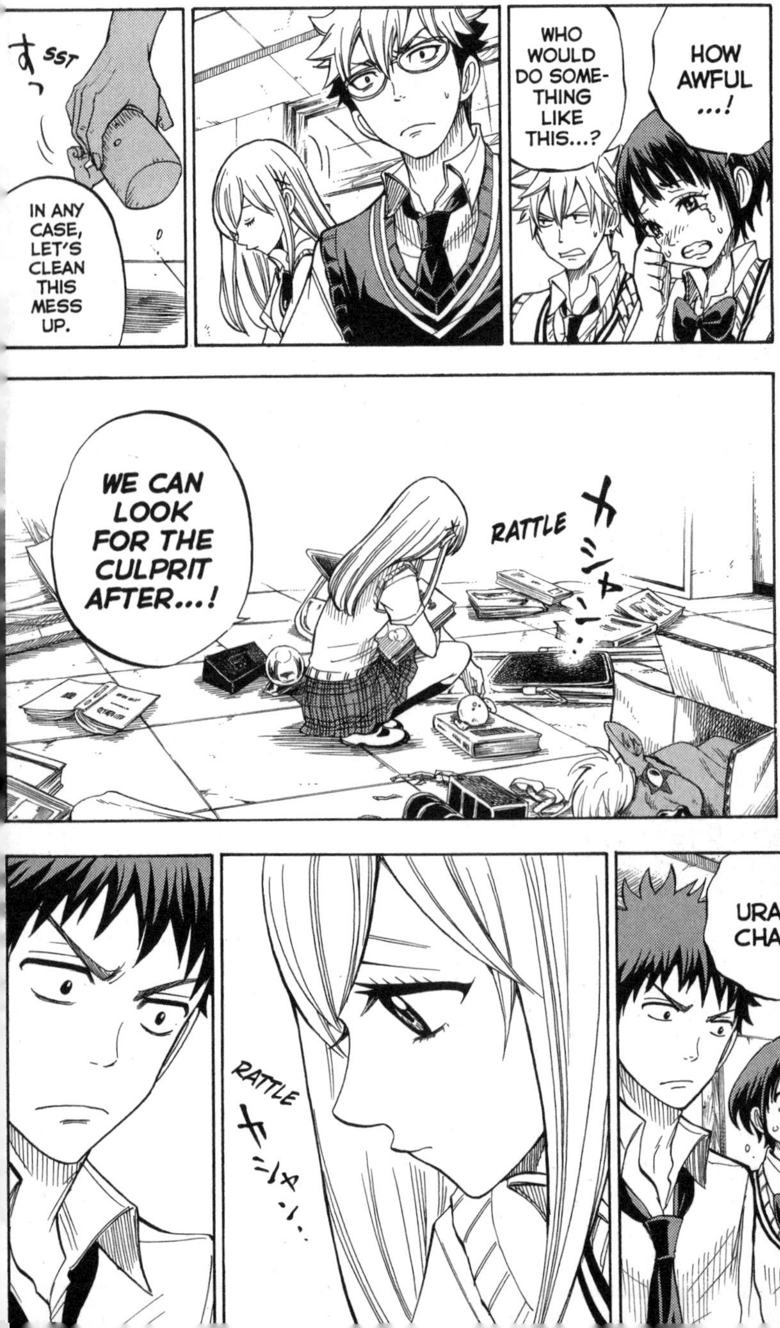
HOW AWFUL ...!
WHO WOULD DO SOME-THING LIKE THIS...?
すっ SST
IN ANY CASE, LET'S CLEAN THIS MESS UP.
RATTLE
WE CAN LOOK FOR THE CULPRIT AFTER...!
URARA-CHAN...
RATTLE

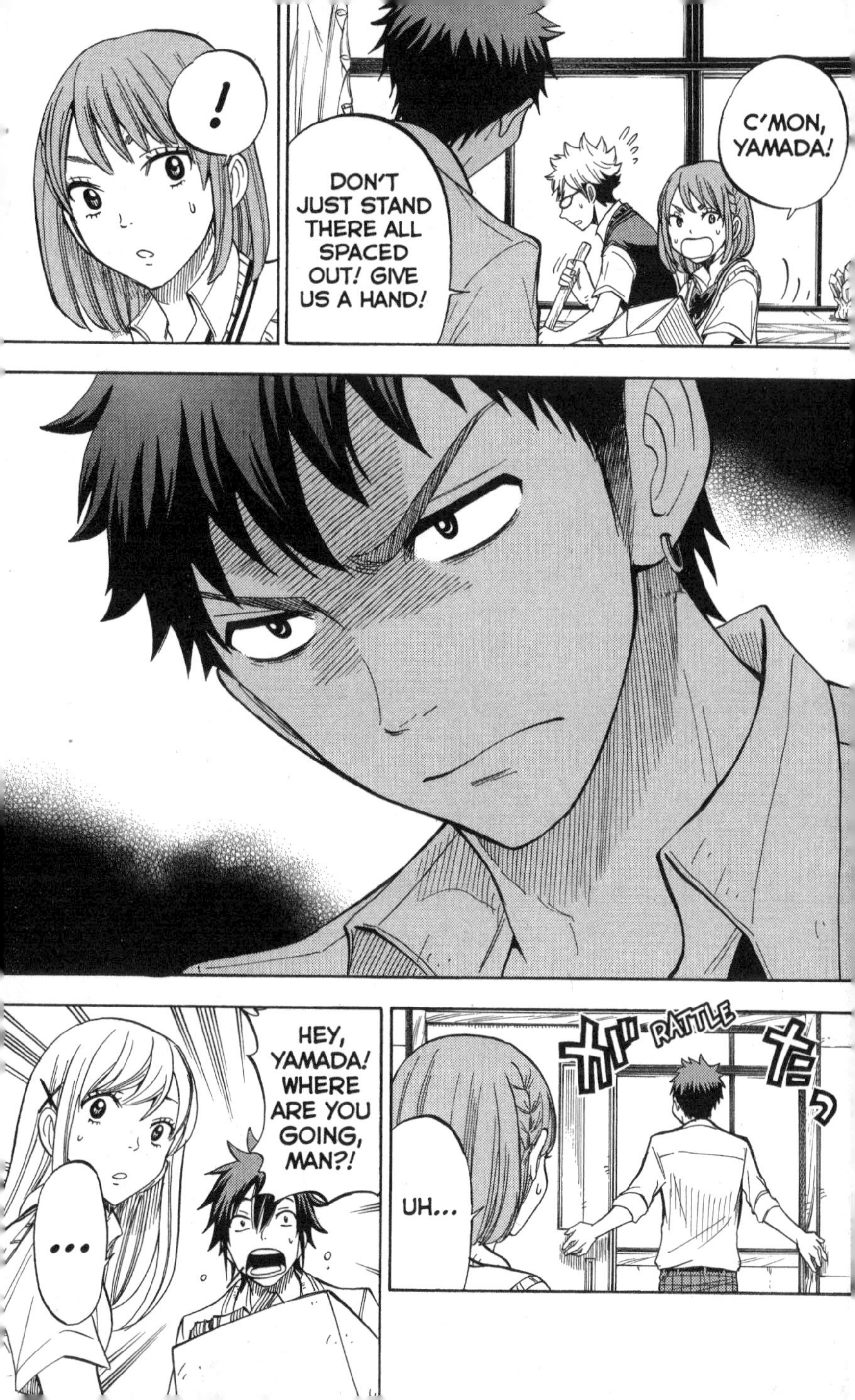
C'MON, YAMADA!
DON'T JUST STAND THERE ALL SPACED OUT! GIVE US A HAND!
!
RATTLE
UH...
HEY, YAMADA! WHERE ARE YOU GOING, MAN?!
...

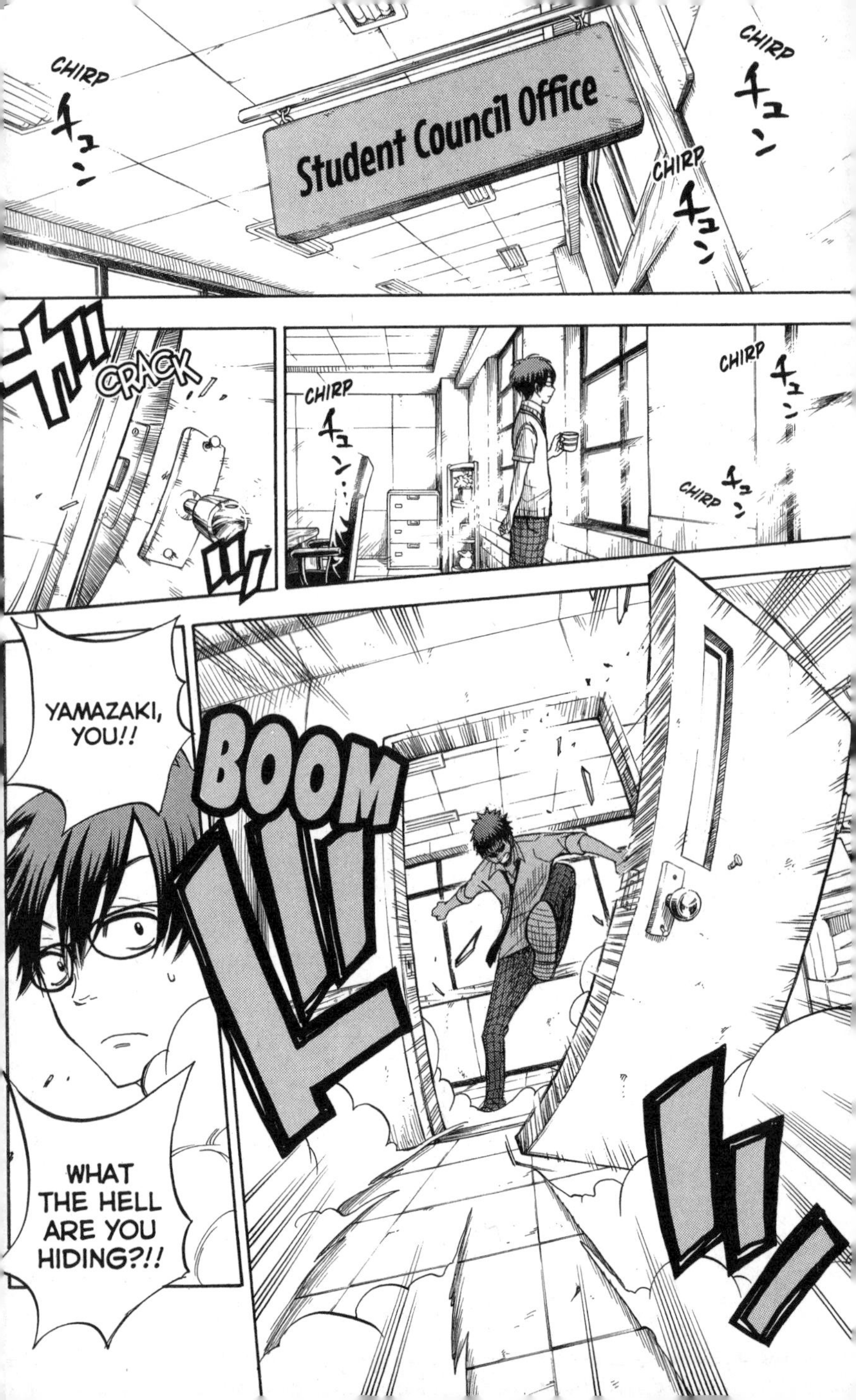
CHIRP
チュン
Student Council Office
CHIRP
チュン
CHIRP
チュン
CHIRP
チュン
CHIRP
チュン
CHIRP
チュン…
CRACK
BOOM
YAMAZAKI, YOU!!
WHAT THE HELL ARE YOU HIDING?!!

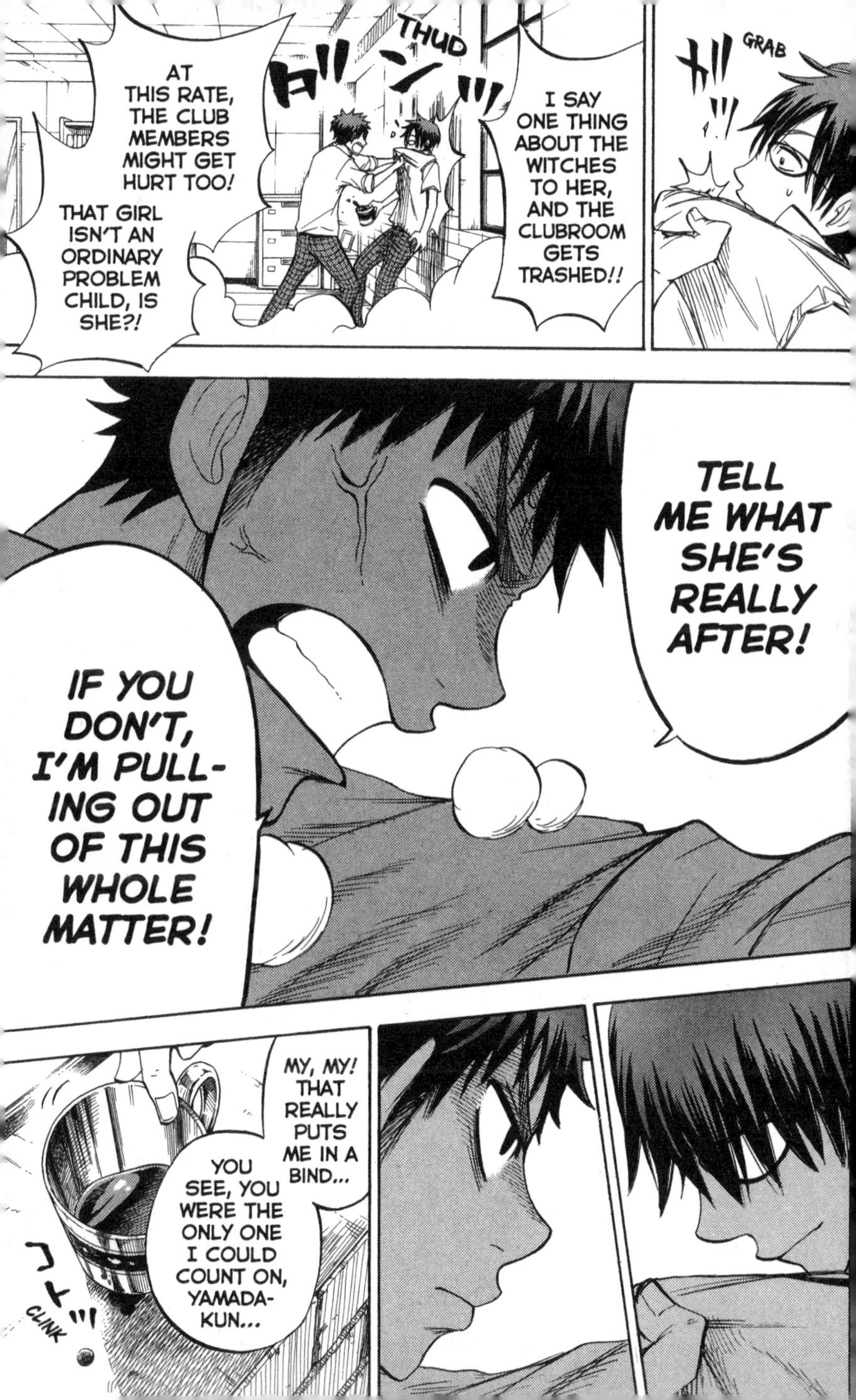
GRAB
I SAY ONE THING ABOUT THE WITCHES TO HER, AND THE CLUBROOM GETS TRASHED!!
THUD
AT THIS RATE, THE CLUB MEMBERS MIGHT GET HURT TOO!
THAT GIRL ISN'T AN ORDINARY PROBLEM CHILD, IS SHE?!
TELL ME WHAT SHE'S REALLY AFTER!
IF YOU DON'T, I'M PULL-ING OUT OF THIS WHOLE MATTER!
MY, MY! THAT REALLY PUTS ME IN A BIND...
YOU SEE, YOU WERE THE ONLY ONE I COULD COUNT ON, YAMADA-KUN...
CLINK

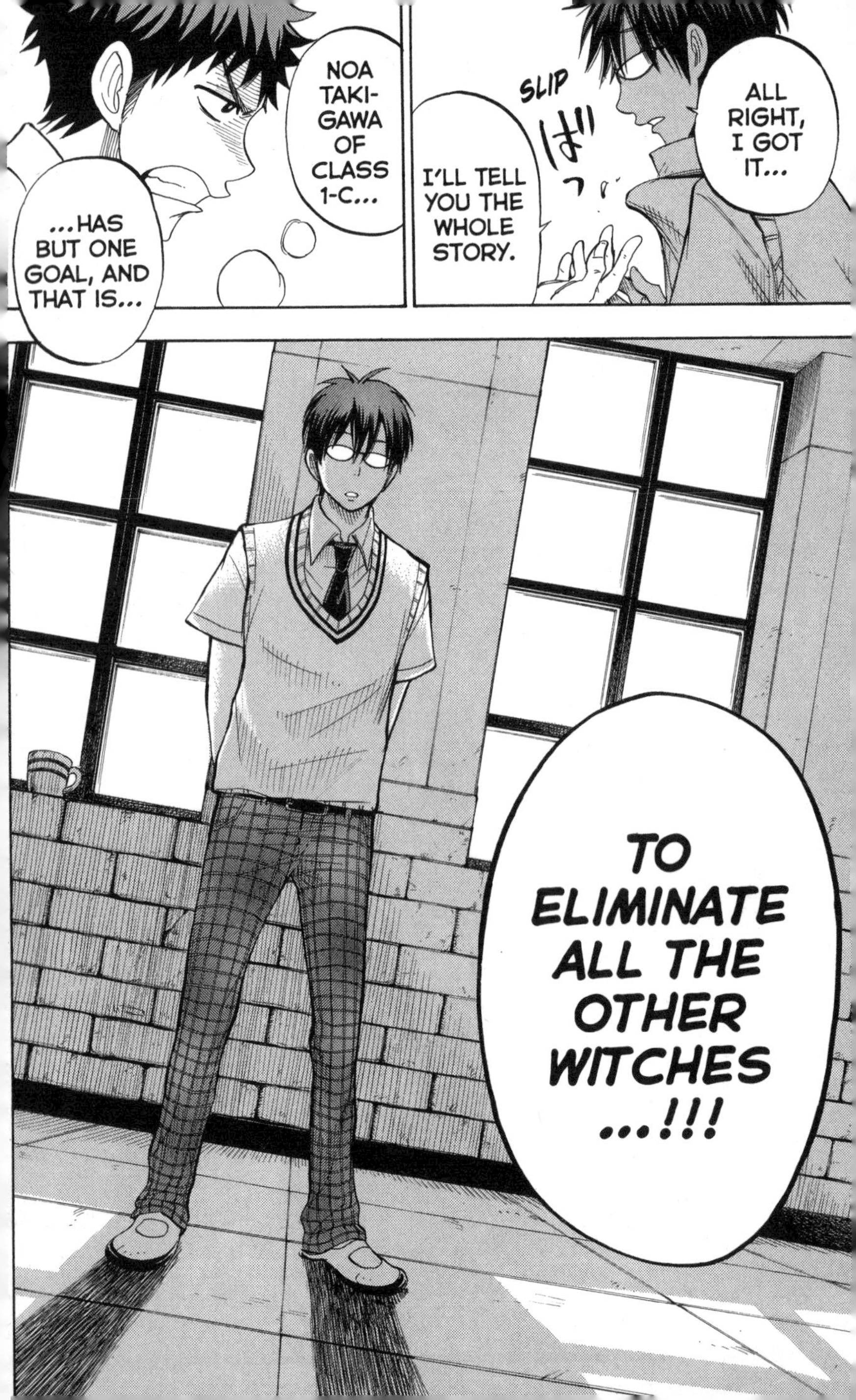
ALL RIGHT, I GOT IT...
SLIP
ぱっ
I'LL TELL YOU THE WHOLE STORY.
NOA TAKI-GAWA OF CLASS 1-C...
...HAS BUT ONE GOAL, AND THAT IS...
TO ELIMINATE ALL THE OTHER WITCHES ...!!!

Chapter 45: Two hotties are here!!

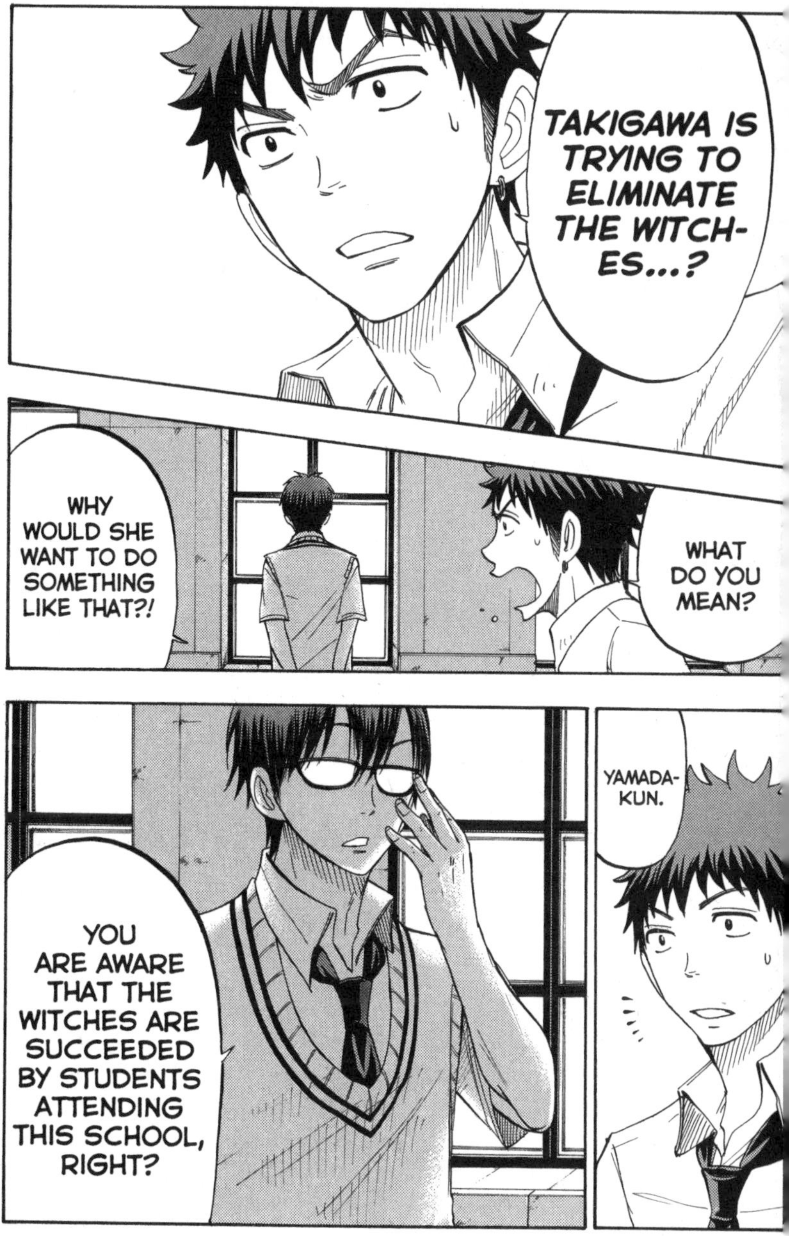
TAKIGAWA IS TRYING TO ELIMINATE THE WITCH-ES...?
WHAT DO YOU MEAN?
WHY WOULD SHE WANT TO DO SOMETHING LIKE THAT?!
YAMADA-KUN.
YOU ARE AWARE THAT THE WITCHES ARE SUCCEEDED BY STUDENTS ATTENDING THIS SCHOOL, RIGHT?

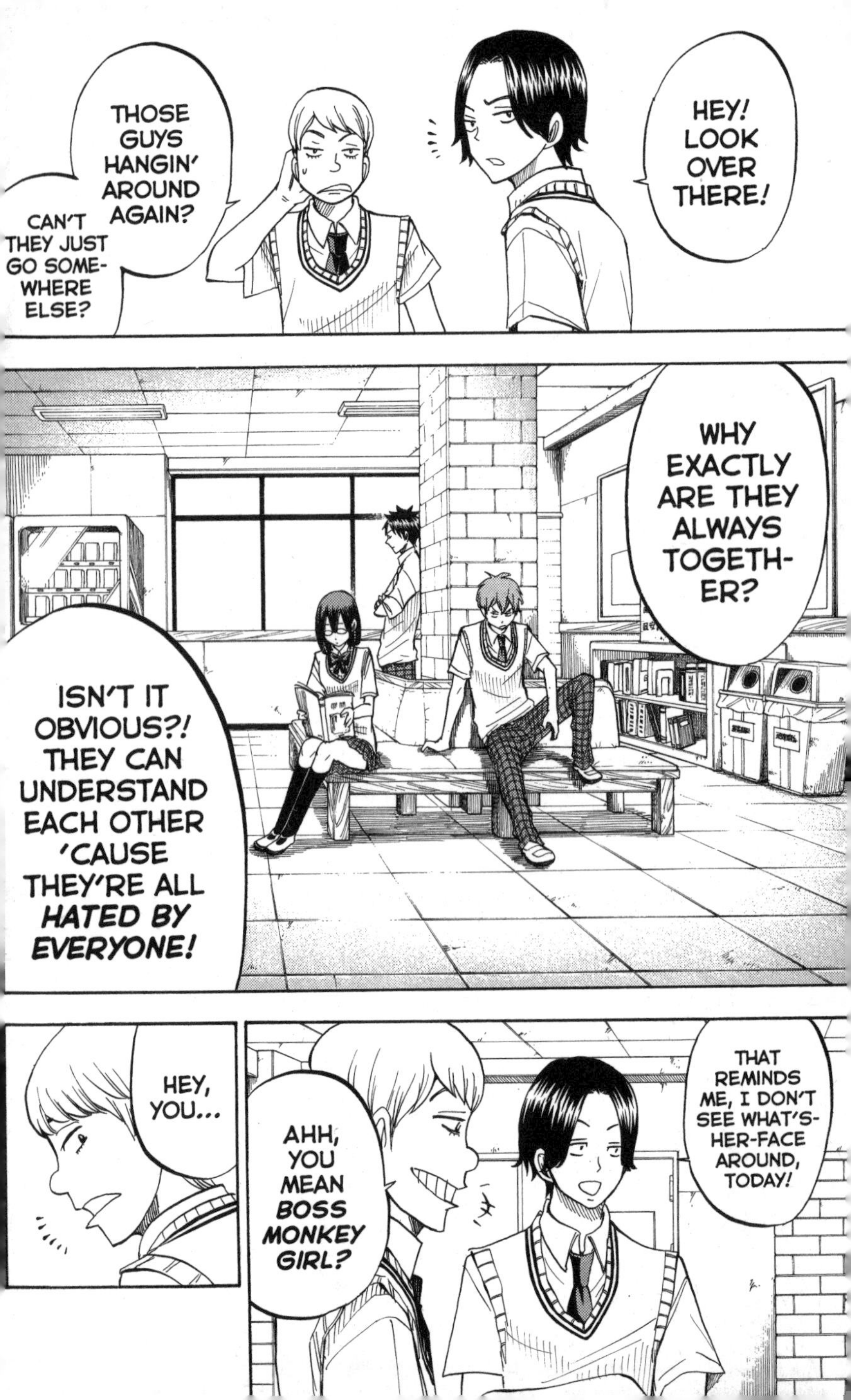
HEY! LOOK OVER THERE!
THOSE GUYS HANGIN' AROUND AGAIN?
CAN'T THEY JUST GO SOMEWHERE ELSE?
WHY EXACTLY ARE THEY ALWAYS TOGETHER?
ISN'T IT OBVIOUS?! THEY CAN UNDERSTAND EACH OTHER 'CAUSE THEY'RE ALL *HATED BY EVERYONE!*
THAT REMINDS ME, I DON'T SEE WHAT'S-HER-FACE AROUND, TODAY!
AHH, YOU MEAN *BOSS MONKEY GIRL?*
HEY, YOU...

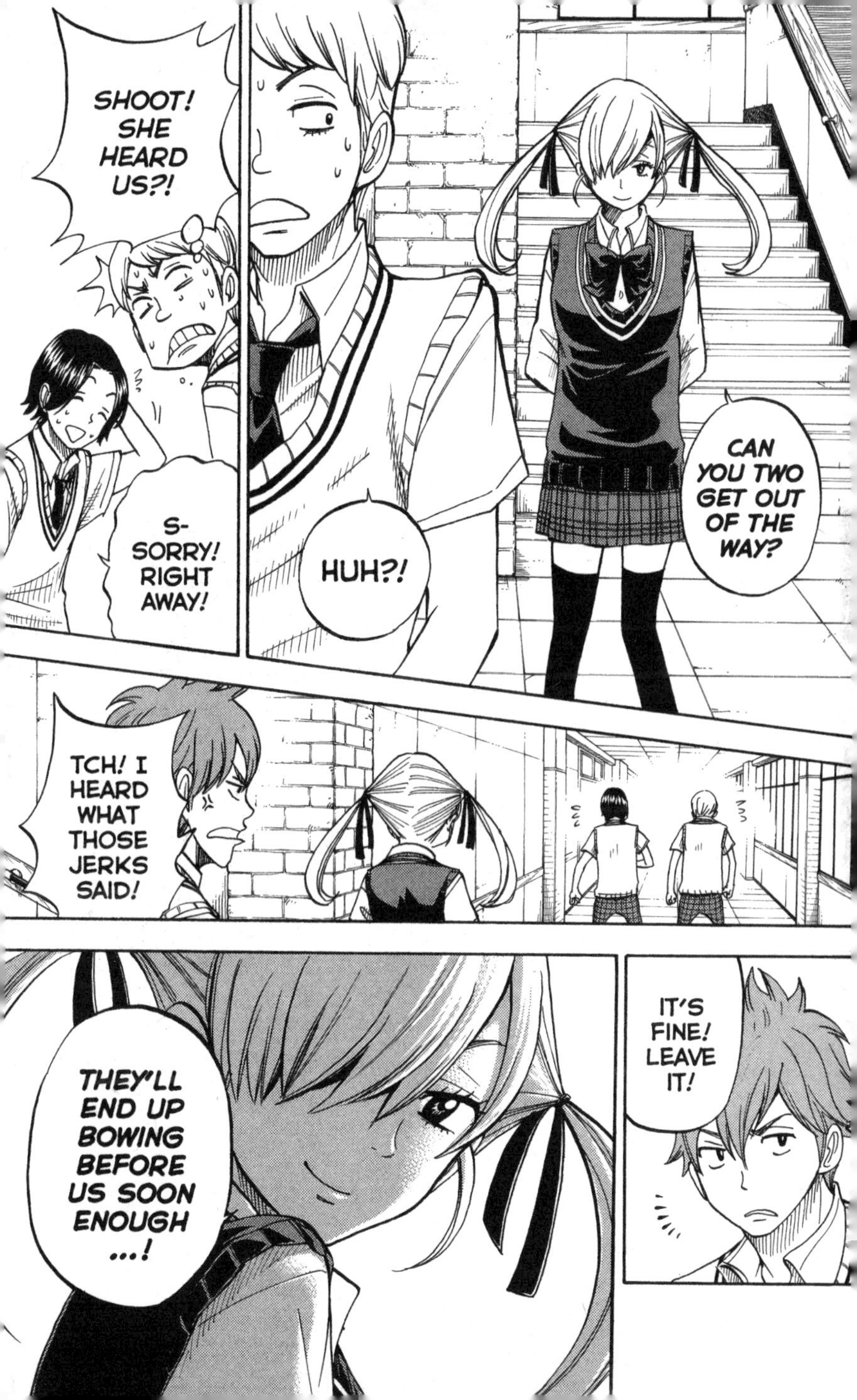
CAN YOU TWO GET OUT OF THE WAY?
HUH?!
SHOOT! SHE HEARD US?!
S-SORRY! RIGHT AWAY!
TCH! I HEARD WHAT THOSE JERKS SAID!
IT'S FINE! LEAVE IT!
THEY'LL END UP BOWING BEFORE US SOON ENOUGH...!

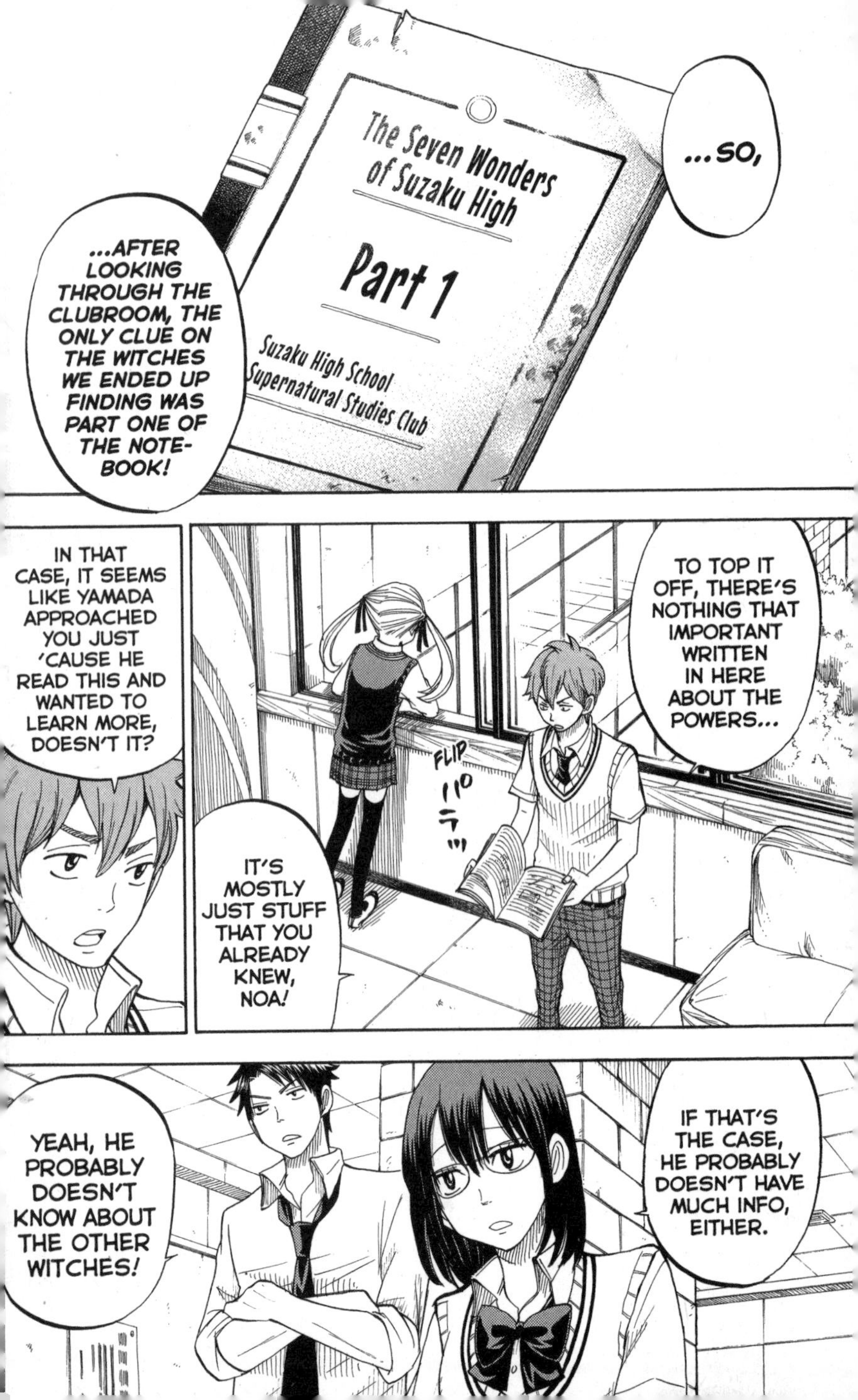
...SO,
The Seven Wonders of Suzaku High
Part 1
Suzaku High School Supernatural Studies Club
...AFTER LOOKING THROUGH THE CLUBROOM, THE ONLY CLUE ON THE WITCHES WE ENDED UP FINDING WAS PART ONE OF THE NOTE-BOOK!
TO TOP IT OFF, THERE'S NOTHING THAT IMPORTANT WRITTEN IN HERE ABOUT THE POWERS...
FLIP
パラッ
IT'S MOSTLY JUST STUFF THAT YOU ALREADY KNEW, NOA!
IN THAT CASE, IT SEEMS LIKE YAMADA APPROACHED YOU JUST 'CAUSE HE READ THIS AND WANTED TO LEARN MORE, DOESN'T IT?
IF THAT'S THE CASE, HE PROBABLY DOESN'T HAVE MUCH INFO, EITHER.
YEAH, HE PROBABLY DOESN'T KNOW ABOUT THE OTHER WITCHES!

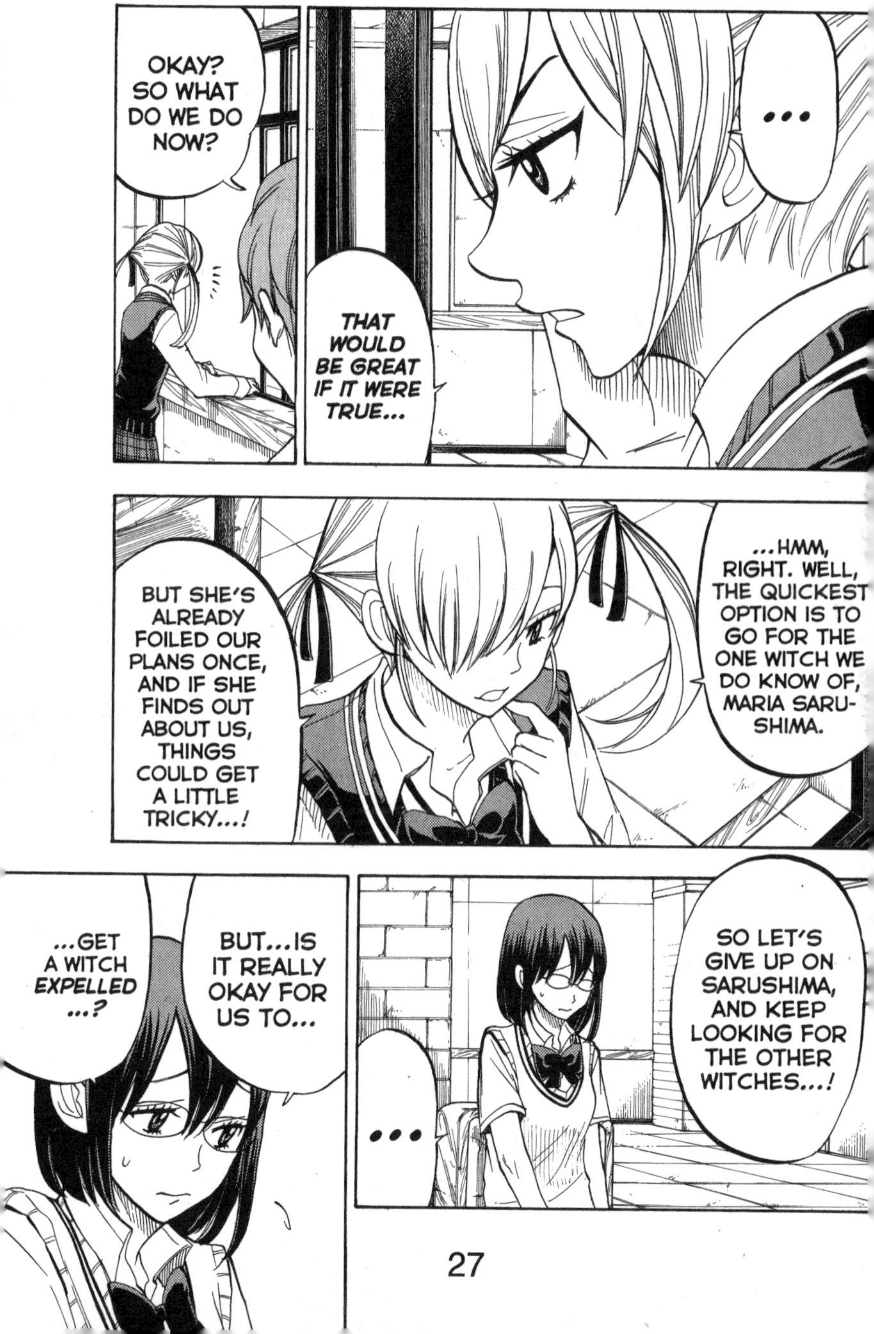
...
THAT WOULD BE GREAT IF IT WERE TRUE...
OKAY? SO WHAT DO WE DO NOW?
...HMM, RIGHT. WELL, THE QUICKEST OPTION IS TO GO FOR THE ONE WITCH WE DO KNOW OF, MARIA SARUSHIMA.
BUT SHE'S ALREADY FOILED OUR PLANS ONCE, AND IF SHE FINDS OUT ABOUT US, THINGS COULD GET A LITTLE TRICKY...!
SO LET'S GIVE UP ON SARUSHIMA, AND KEEP LOOKING FOR THE OTHER WITCHES...!
...
BUT...IS IT REALLY OKAY FOR US TO...
...GET A WITCH EXPELLED...?

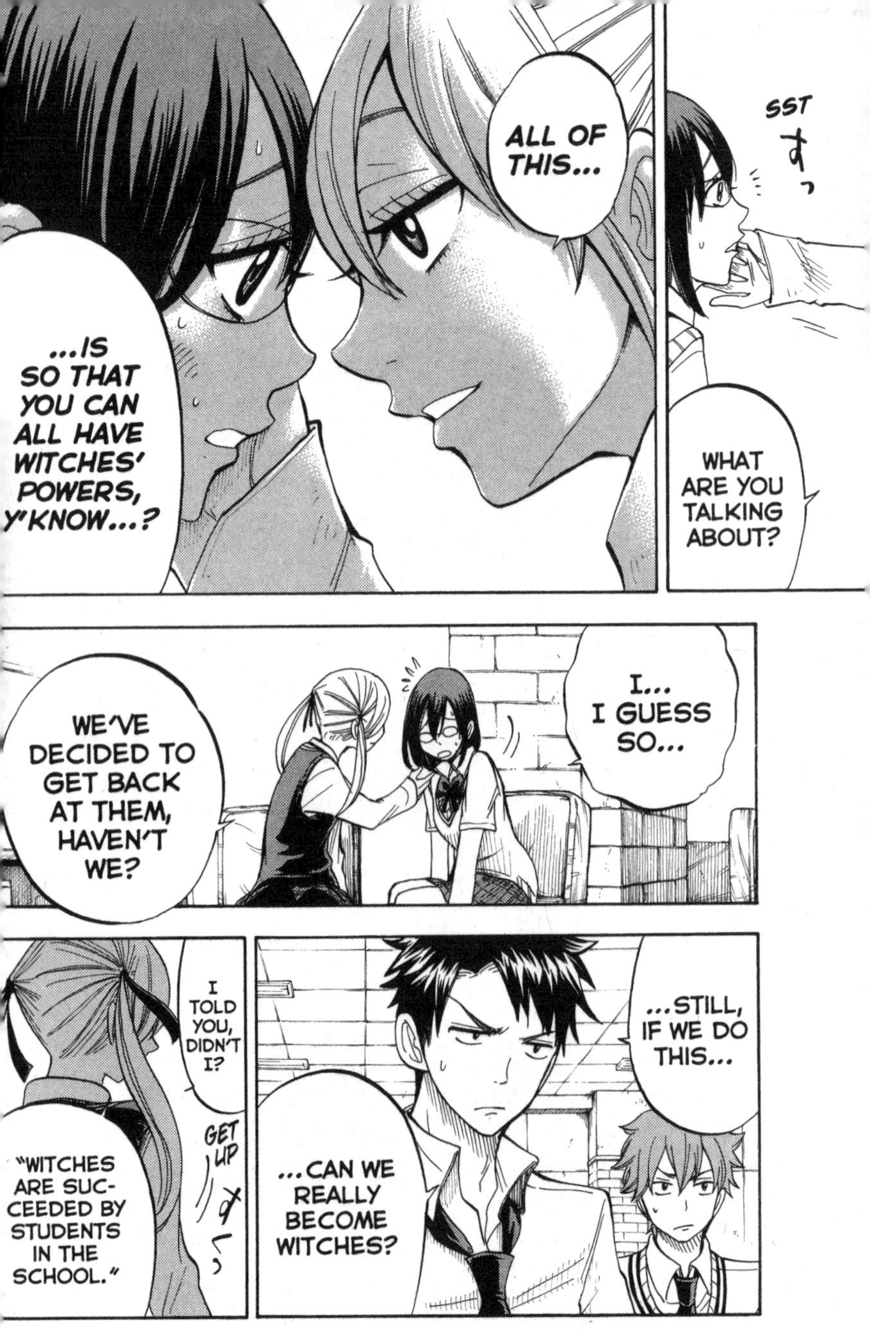
SST
すっ
WHAT ARE YOU TALKING ABOUT?
ALL OF THIS...
...IS SO THAT YOU CAN ALL HAVE WITCHES' POWERS, Y'KNOW...?
I... I GUESS SO...
WE'VE DECIDED TO GET BACK AT THEM, HAVEN'T WE?
...STILL, IF WE DO THIS...
...CAN WE REALLY BECOME WITCHES?
I TOLD YOU, DIDN'T I?
GET UP
"WITCHES ARE SUC-CEEDED BY STUDENTS IN THE SCHOOL."

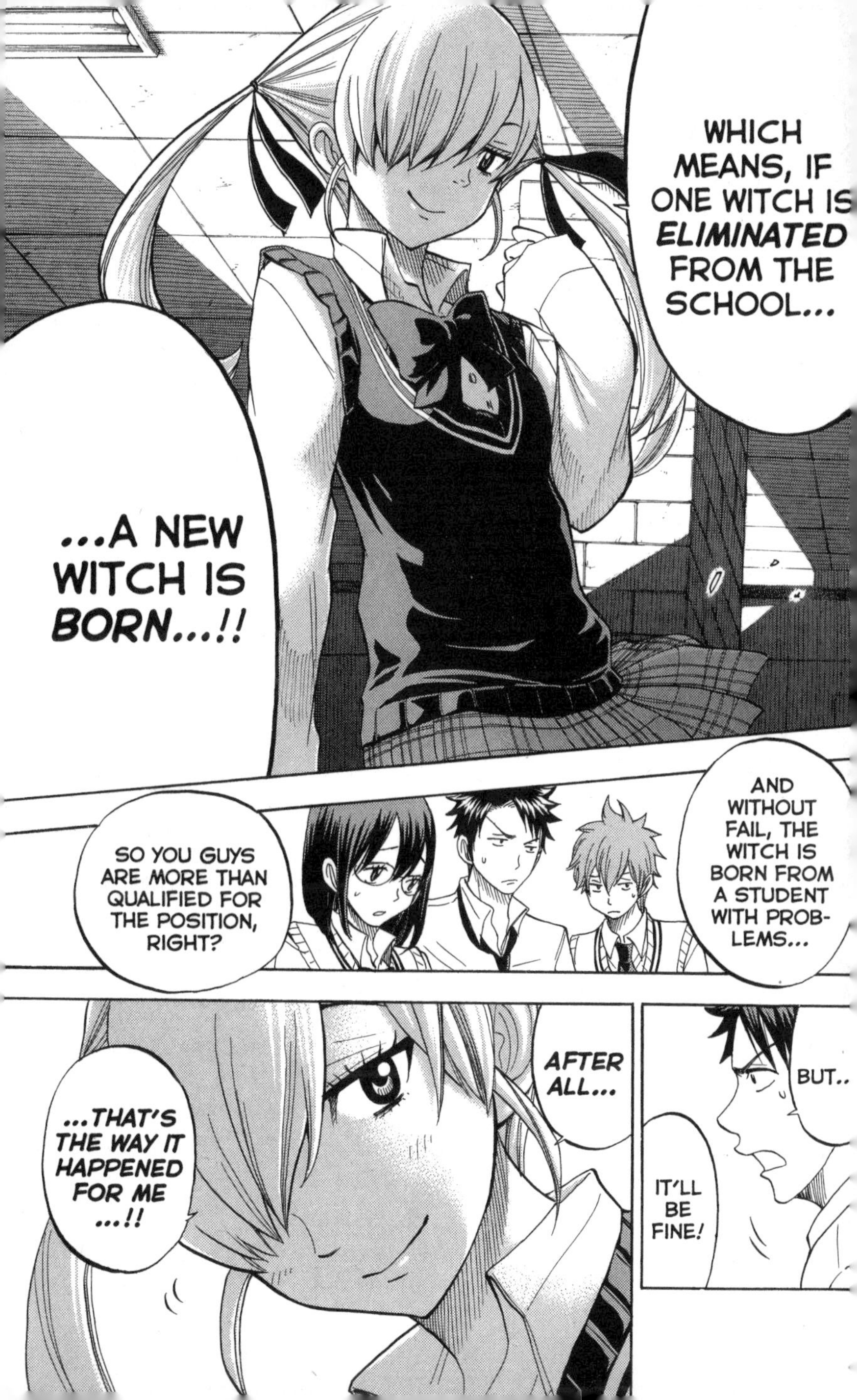
WHICH MEANS, IF ONE WITCH IS ELIMINATED FROM THE SCHOOL...
...A NEW WITCH IS BORN...!!
AND WITHOUT FAIL, THE WITCH IS BORN FROM A STUDENT WITH PROB-LEMS...
SO YOU GUYS ARE MORE THAN QUALIFIED FOR THE POSITION, RIGHT?
BUT..
IT'LL BE FINE!
AFTER ALL...
...THAT'S THE WAY IT HAPPENED FOR ME ...!!

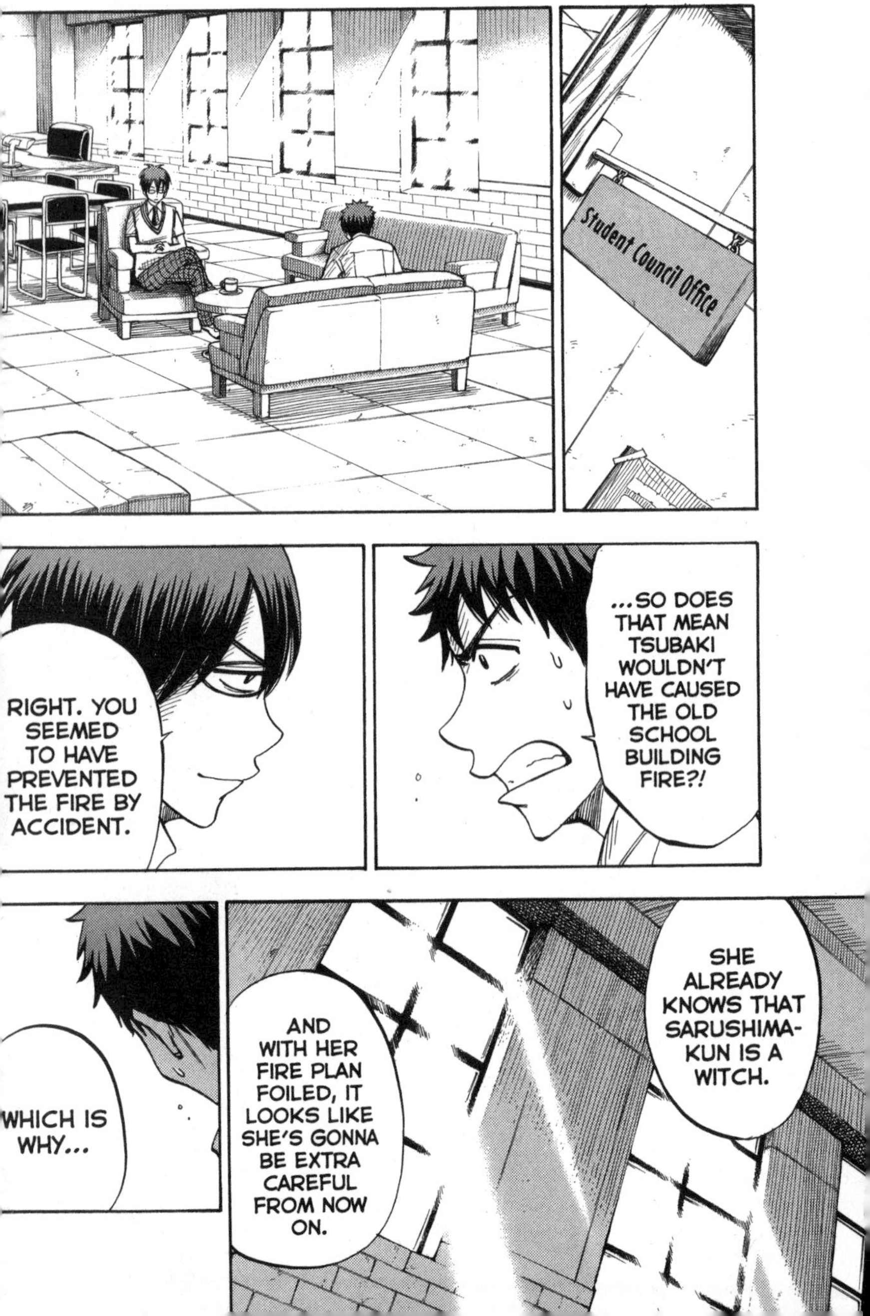
Student Council Office
...SO DOES THAT MEAN TSUBAKI WOULDN'T HAVE CAUSED THE OLD SCHOOL BUILDING FIRE?!
RIGHT. YOU SEEMED TO HAVE PREVENTED THE FIRE BY ACCIDENT.
SHE ALREADY KNOWS THAT SARUSHIMA-KUN IS A WITCH.
AND WITH HER FIRE PLAN FOILED, IT LOOKS LIKE SHE'S GONNA BE EXTRA CAREFUL FROM NOW ON.
WHICH IS WHY...

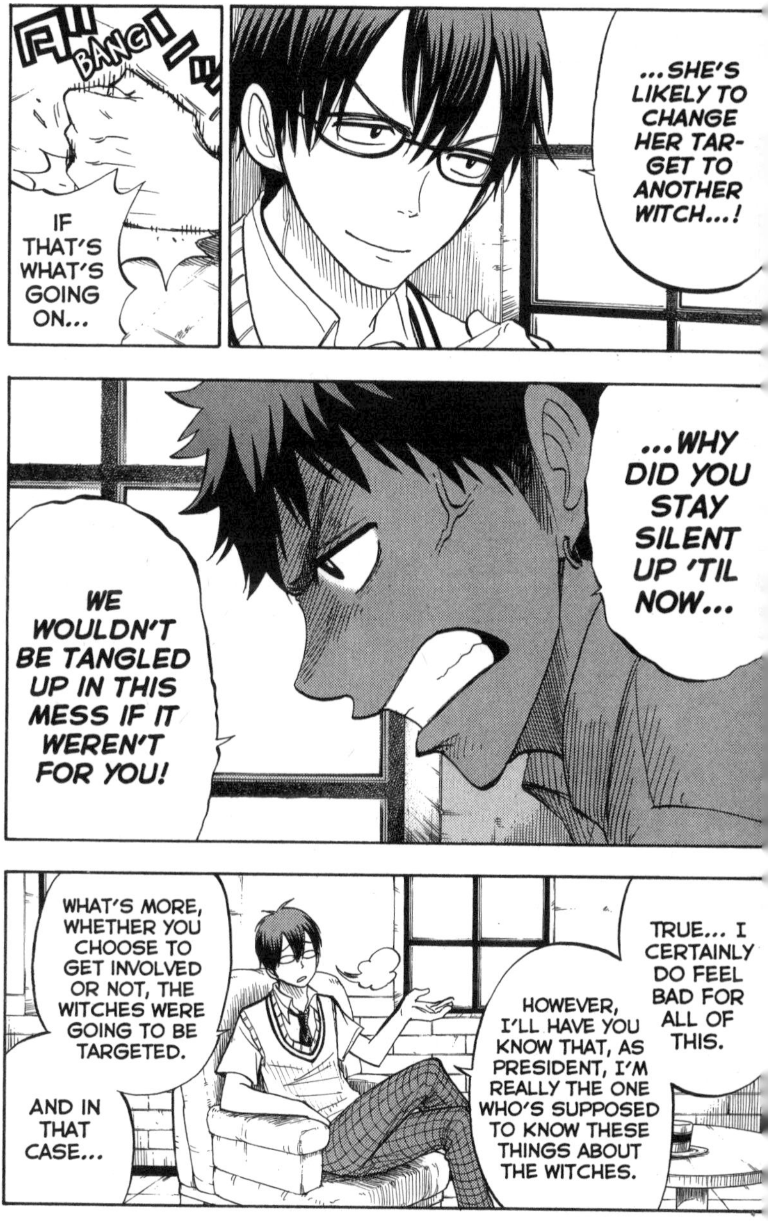
...SHE'S LIKELY TO CHANGE HER TARGET TO ANOTHER WITCH...!
BANG!!
IF THAT'S WHAT'S GOING ON...
...WHY DID YOU STAY SILENT UP 'TIL NOW...
WE WOULDN'T BE TANGLED UP IN THIS MESS IF IT WEREN'T FOR YOU!
TRUE... I CERTAINLY DO FEEL BAD FOR ALL OF THIS.
HOWEVER, I'LL HAVE YOU KNOW THAT, AS PRESIDENT, I'M REALLY THE ONE WHO'S SUPPOSED TO KNOW THESE THINGS ABOUT THE WITCHES.
WHAT'S MORE, WHETHER YOU CHOOSE TO GET INVOLVED OR NOT, THE WITCHES WERE GOING TO BE TARGETED.
AND IN THAT CASE...

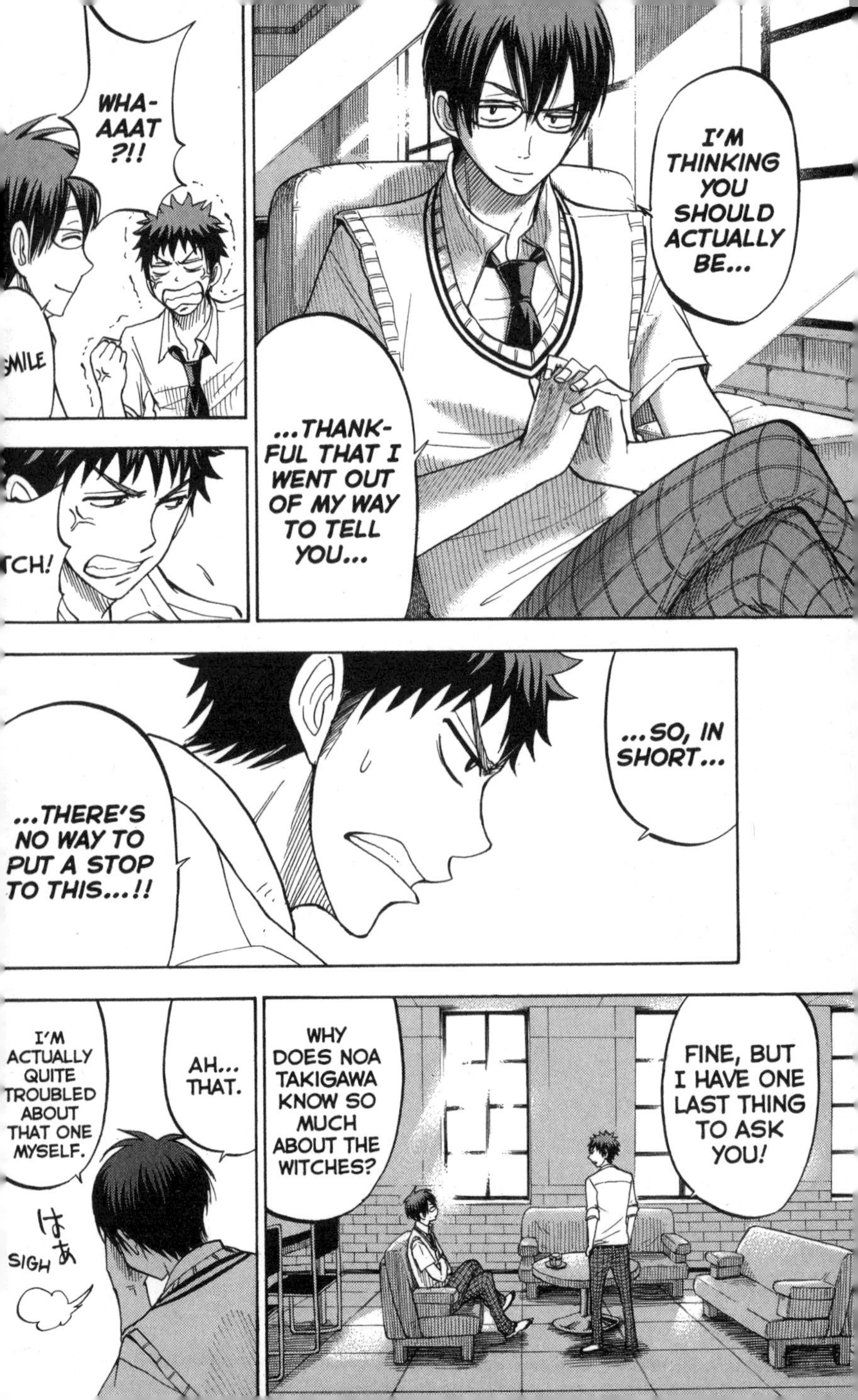
I'M THINKING YOU SHOULD ACTUALLY BE...
...THANK-FUL THAT I WENT OUT OF MY WAY TO TELL YOU...
WHA-AAAT?!!
SMILE
TCH!
...SO, IN SHORT...
...THERE'S NO WAY TO PUT A STOP TO THIS...!!
FINE, BUT I HAVE ONE LAST THING TO ASK YOU!
WHY DOES NOA TAKIGAWA KNOW SO MUCH ABOUT THE WITCHES?
AH... THAT.
I'M ACTUALLY QUITE TROUBLED ABOUT THAT ONE MYSELF.
はあ
SIGH

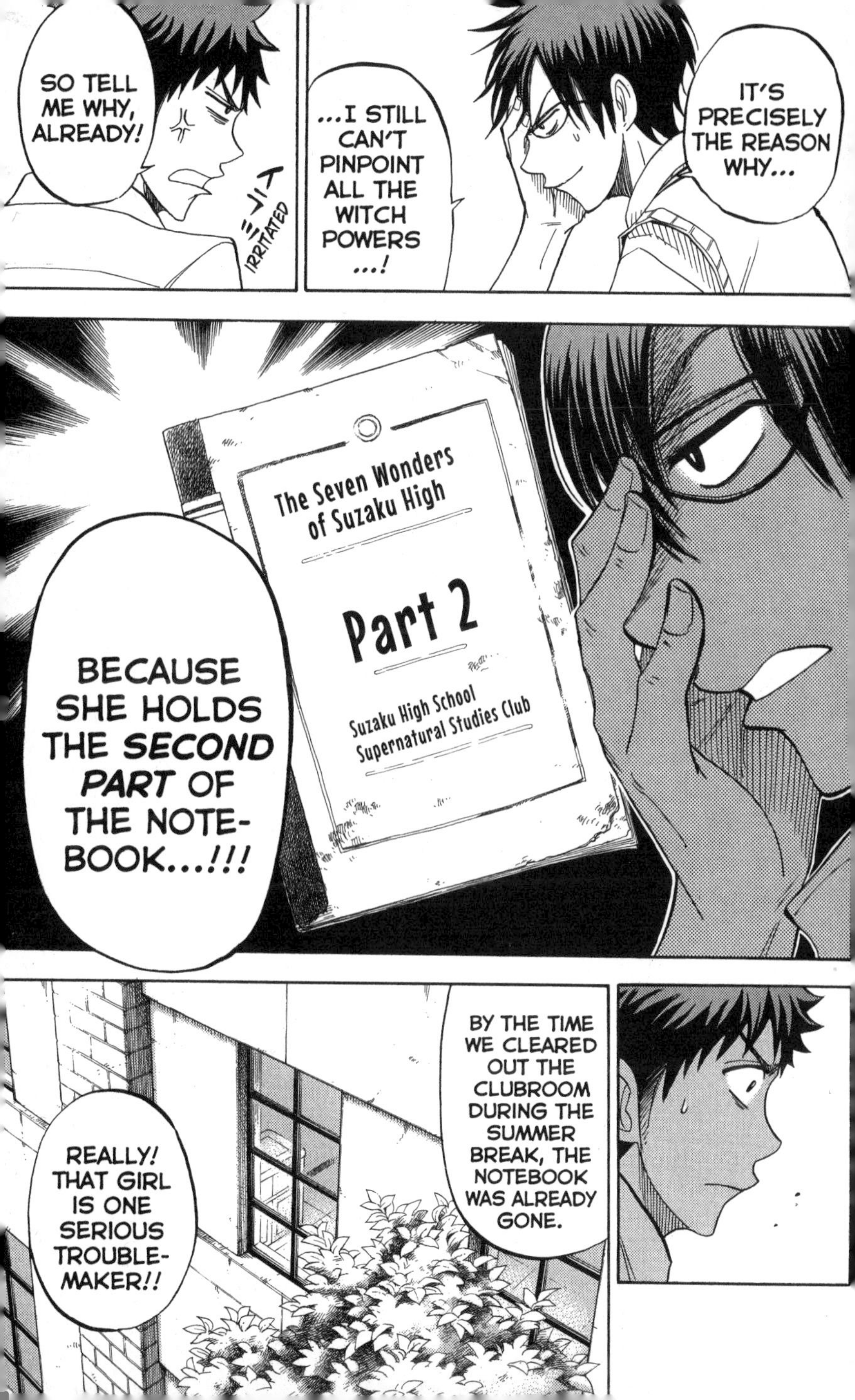
IT'S PRECISELY THE REASON WHY...
...I STILL CAN'T PINPOINT ALL THE WITCH POWERS ...!
SO TELL ME WHY, ALREADY!
IRRITATED
The Seven Wonders of Suzaku High
Part 2
Suzaku High School Supernatural Studies Club
BECAUSE SHE HOLDS THE *SECOND PART* OF THE NOTE-BOOK...!!!
BY THE TIME WE CLEARED OUT THE CLUBROOM DURING THE SUMMER BREAK, THE NOTEBOOK WAS ALREADY GONE.
REALLY! THAT GIRL IS ONE SERIOUS TROUBLE-MAKER!!

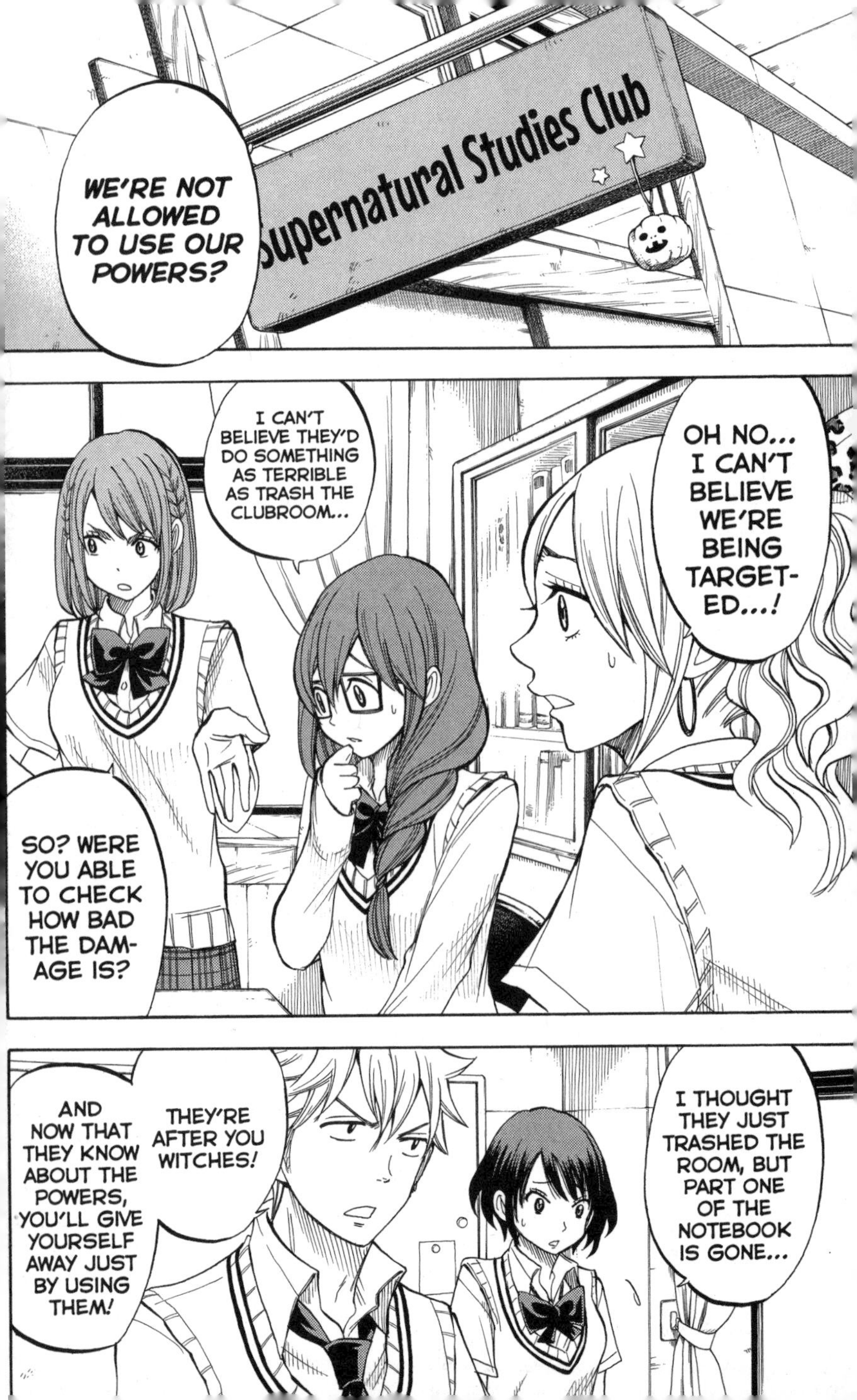
Supernatural Studies Club
WE'RE NOT ALLOWED TO USE OUR POWERS?
OH NO... I CAN'T BELIEVE WE'RE BEING TARGETED...!
I CAN'T BELIEVE THEY'D DO SOMETHING AS TERRIBLE AS TRASH THE CLUBROOM...
SO? WERE YOU ABLE TO CHECK HOW BAD THE DAMAGE IS?
I THOUGHT THEY JUST TRASHED THE ROOM, BUT PART ONE OF THE NOTEBOOK IS GONE...
THEY'RE AFTER YOU WITCHES!
AND NOW THAT THEY KNOW ABOUT THE POWERS, YOU'LL GIVE YOURSELF AWAY JUST BY USING THEM!

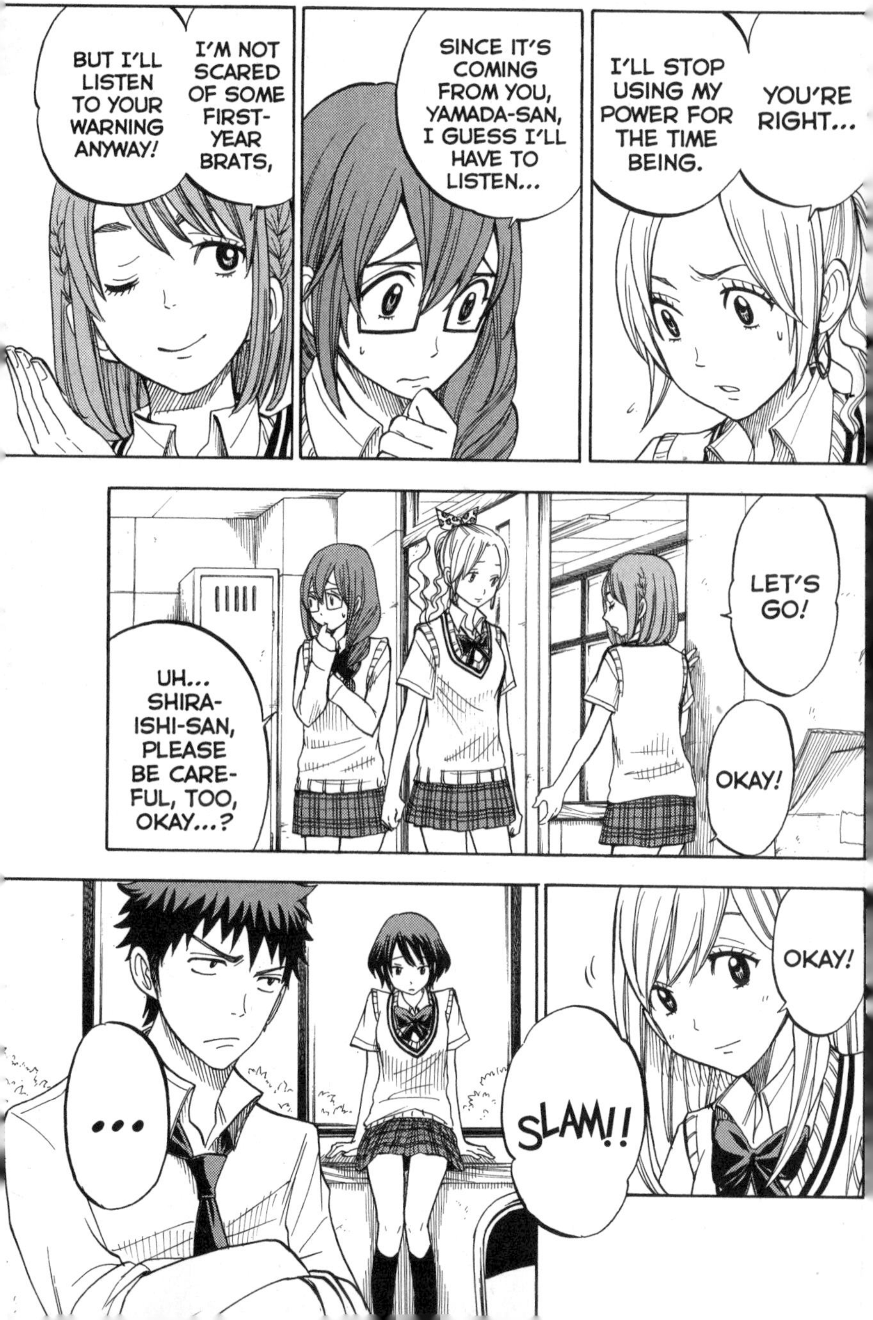
YOU'RE RIGHT...
I'LL STOP USING MY POWER FOR THE TIME BEING.
SINCE IT'S COMING FROM YOU, YAMADA-SAN, I GUESS I'LL HAVE TO LISTEN...
I'M NOT SCARED OF SOME FIRST-YEAR BRATS,
BUT I'LL LISTEN TO YOUR WARNING ANYWAY!
LET'S GO!
OKAY!
UH... SHIRA-ISHI-SAN, PLEASE BE CARE-FUL, TOO, OKAY...?
OKAY!
SLAM!!
...

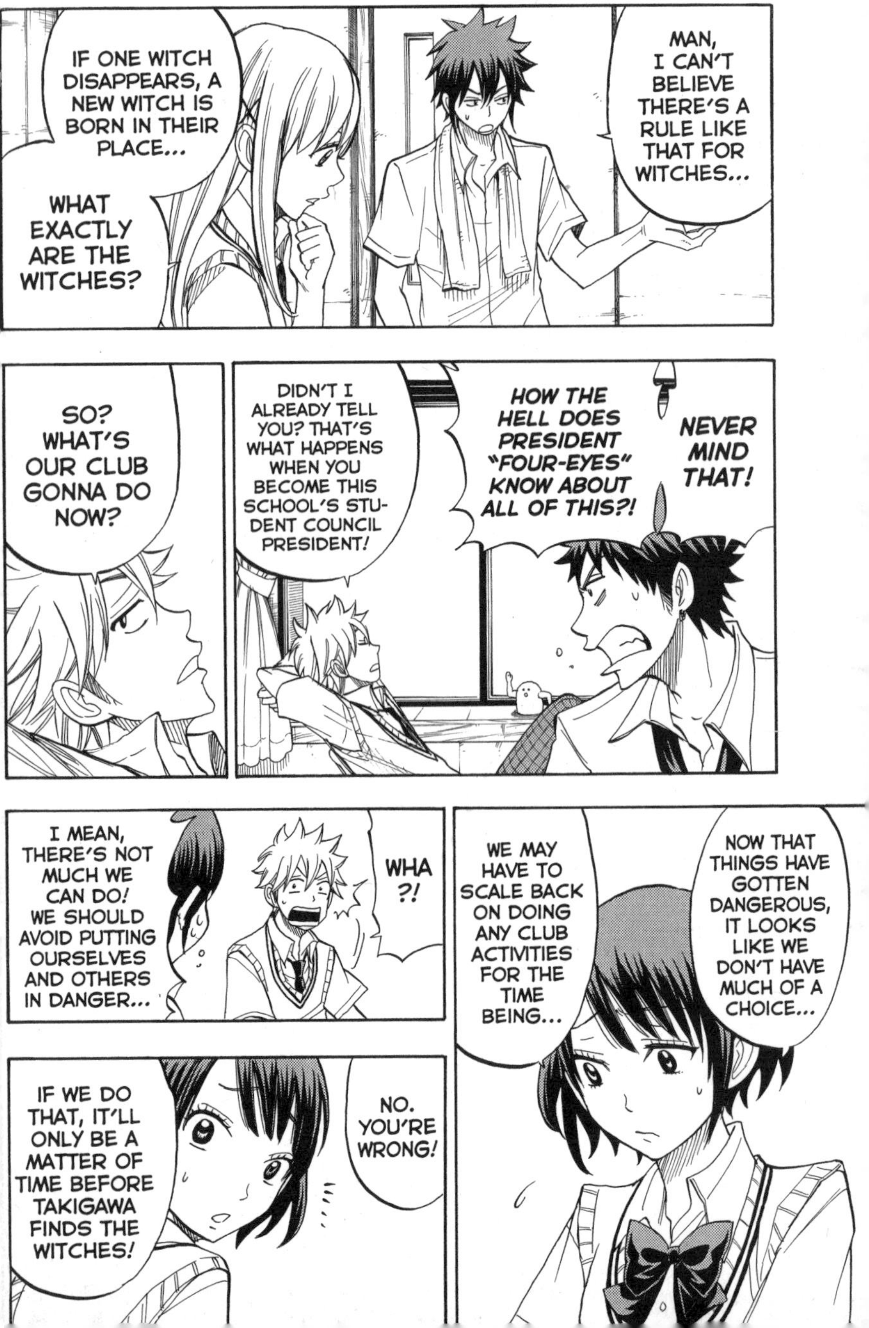
MAN, I CAN'T BELIEVE THERE'S A RULE LIKE THAT FOR WITCHES...
IF ONE WITCH DISAPPEARS, A NEW WITCH IS BORN IN THEIR PLACE...
WHAT EXACTLY ARE THE WITCHES?
NEVER MIND THAT!
HOW THE HELL DOES PRESIDENT "FOUR-EYES" KNOW ABOUT ALL OF THIS?!
DIDN'T I ALREADY TELL YOU? THAT'S WHAT HAPPENS WHEN YOU BECOME THIS SCHOOL'S STUDENT COUNCIL PRESIDENT!
SO? WHAT'S OUR CLUB GONNA DO NOW?
NOW THAT THINGS HAVE GOTTEN DANGEROUS, IT LOOKS LIKE WE DON'T HAVE MUCH OF A CHOICE...
WE MAY HAVE TO SCALE BACK ON DOING ANY CLUB ACTIVITIES FOR THE TIME BEING...
WHA?!
I MEAN, THERE'S NOT MUCH WE CAN DO! WE SHOULD AVOID PUTTING OURSELVES AND OTHERS IN DANGER...
NO. YOU'RE WRONG!
IF WE DO THAT, IT'LL ONLY BE A MATTER OF TIME BEFORE TAKIGAWA FINDS THE WITCHES!

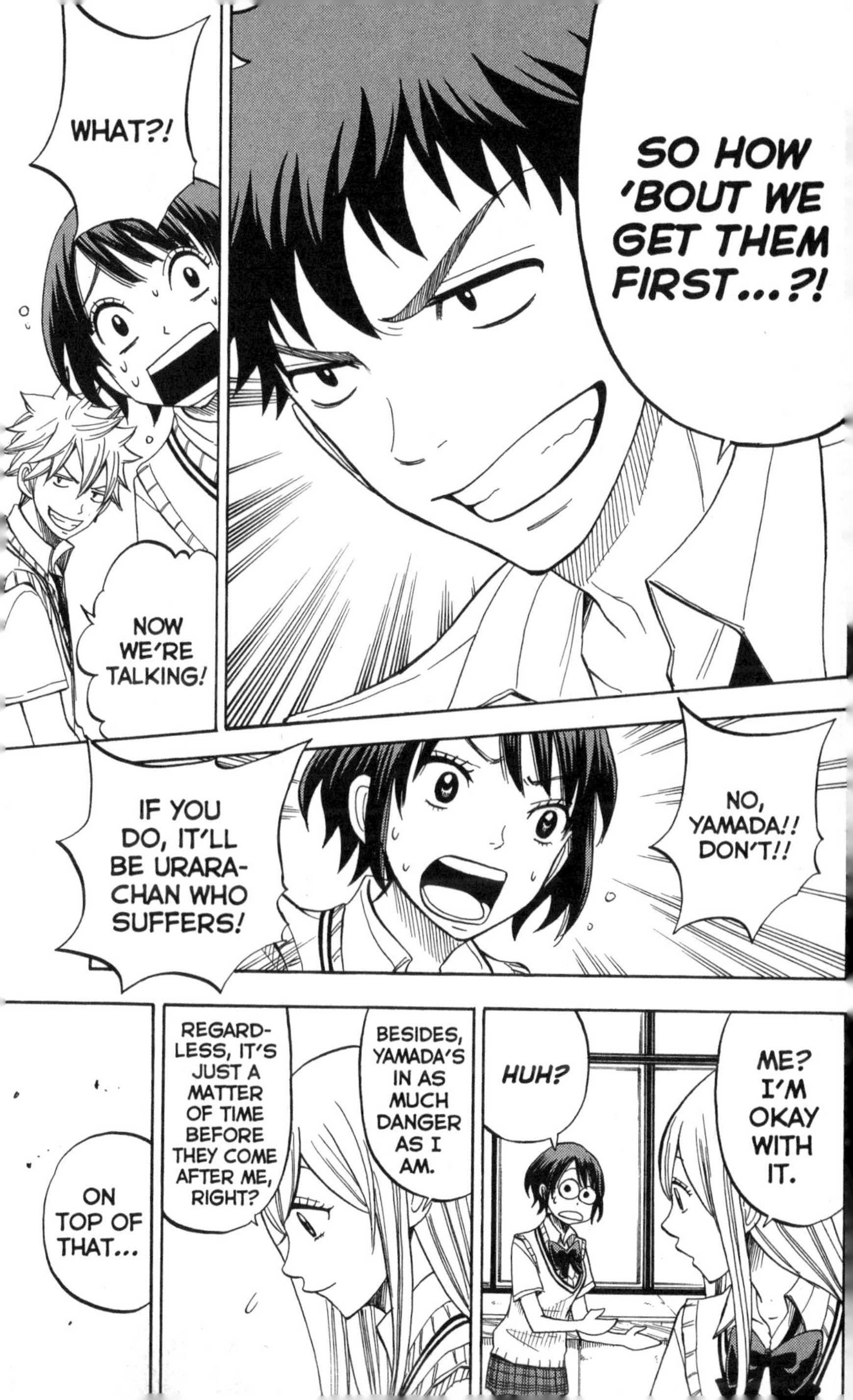
SO HOW 'BOUT WE GET THEM FIRST...?!
WHAT?!
NOW WE'RE TALKING!
NO, YAMADA!! DON'T!!
IF YOU DO, IT'LL BE URARA-CHAN WHO SUFFERS!
ME? I'M OKAY WITH IT.
HUH?
BESIDES, YAMADA'S IN AS MUCH DANGER AS I AM.
REGARDLESS, IT'S JUST A MATTER OF TIME BEFORE THEY COME AFTER ME, RIGHT?
ON TOP OF THAT...

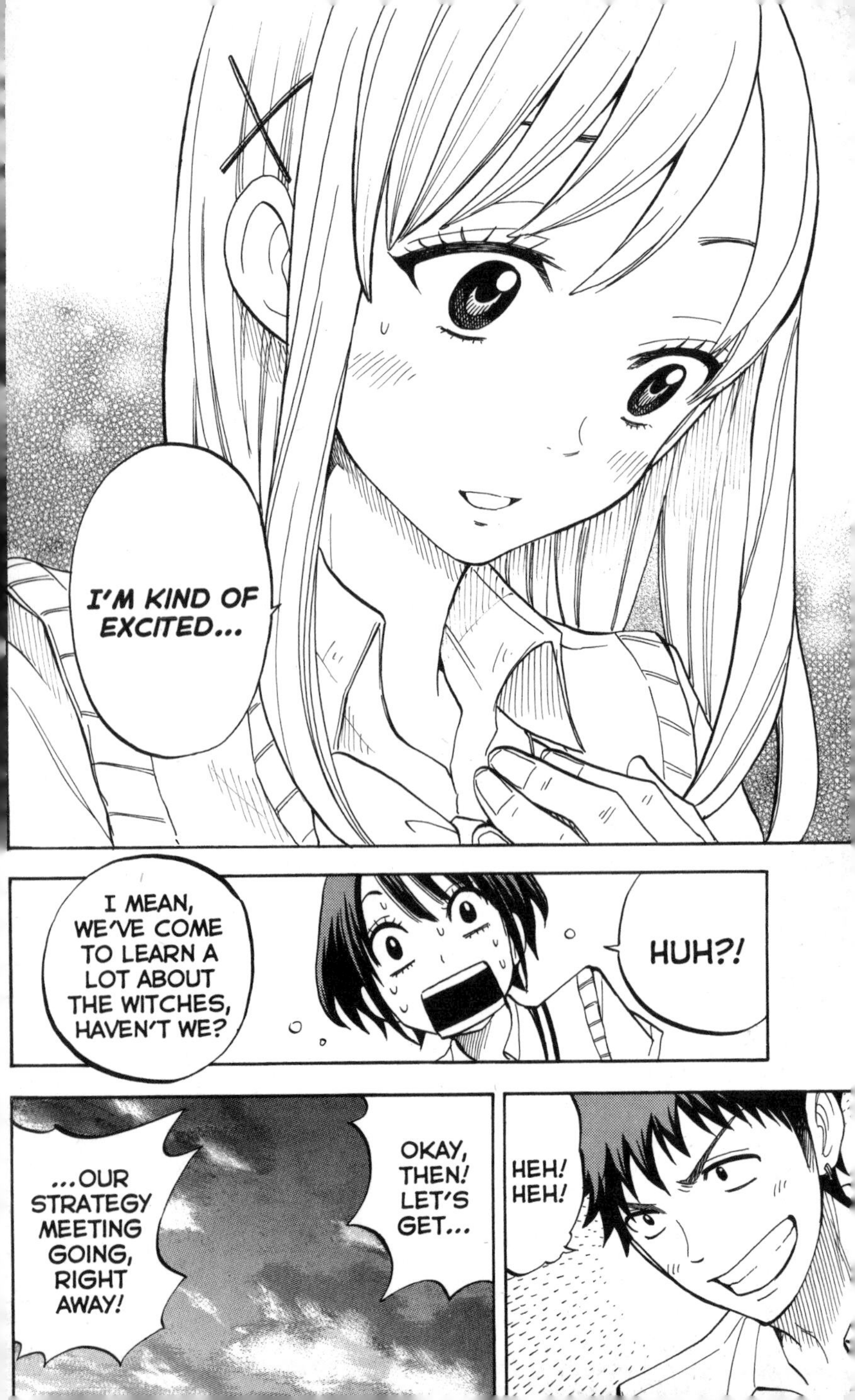
I'M KIND OF EXCITED...
HUH?!
I MEAN, WE'VE COME TO LEARN A LOT ABOUT THE WITCHES, HAVEN'T WE?
HEH! HEH!
OKAY, THEN! LET'S GET...
...OUR STRATEGY MEETING GOING, RIGHT AWAY!

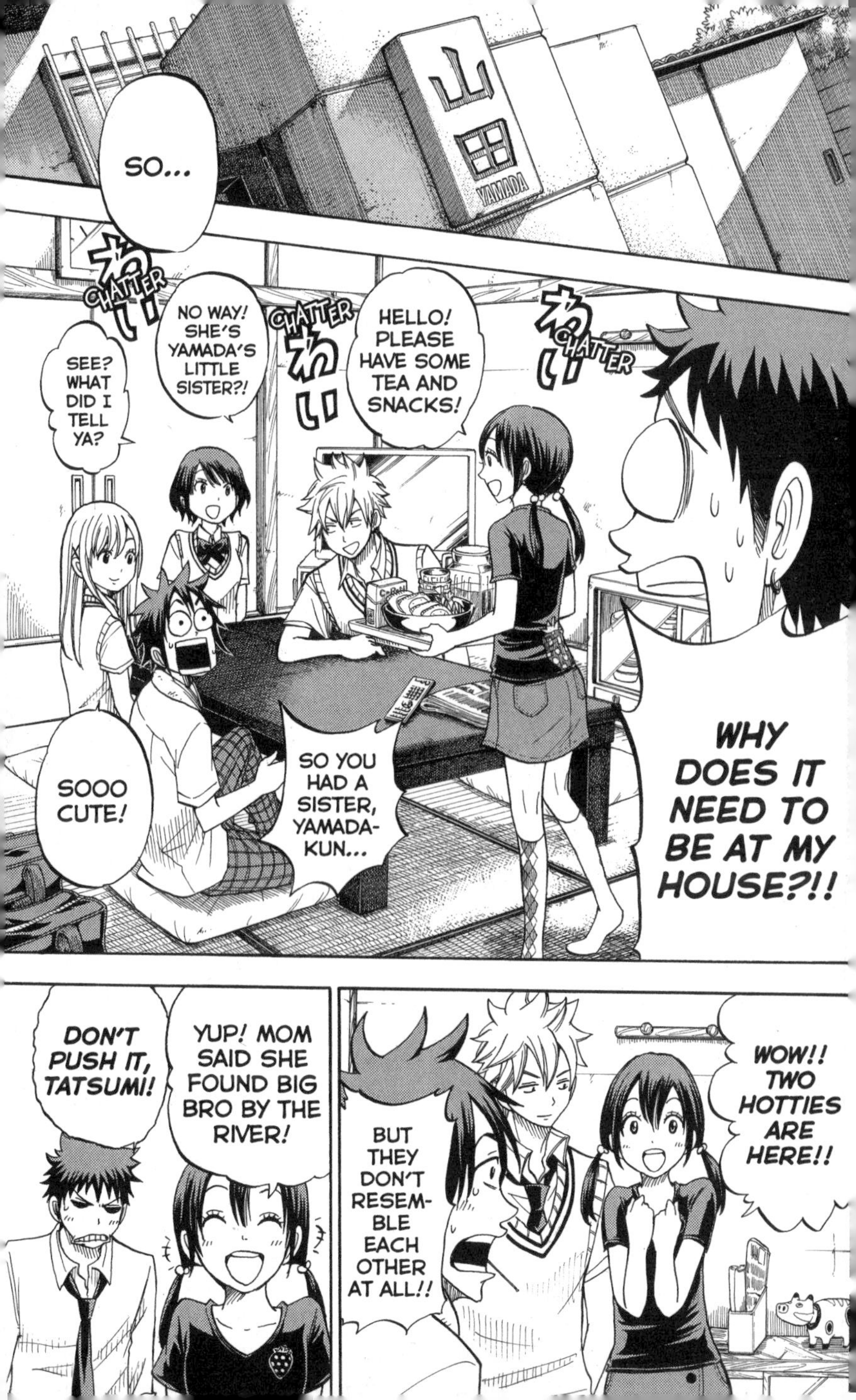
SO...
山田
YAMADA
わい CHATTER
HELLO! PLEASE HAVE SOME TEA AND SNACKS!
わい CHATTER
NO WAY! SHE'S YAMADA'S LITTLE SISTER?!
わい CHATTER
SEE? WHAT DID I TELL YA?
WHY DOES IT NEED TO BE AT MY HOUSE?!!
SO YOU HAD A SISTER, YAMADA-KUN...
SOOO CUTE!
WOW!! TWO HOTTIES ARE HERE!!
BUT THEY DON'T RESEMBLE EACH OTHER AT ALL!!
YUP! MOM SAID SHE FOUND BIG BRO BY THE RIVER!
DON'T PUSH IT, TATSUMI!

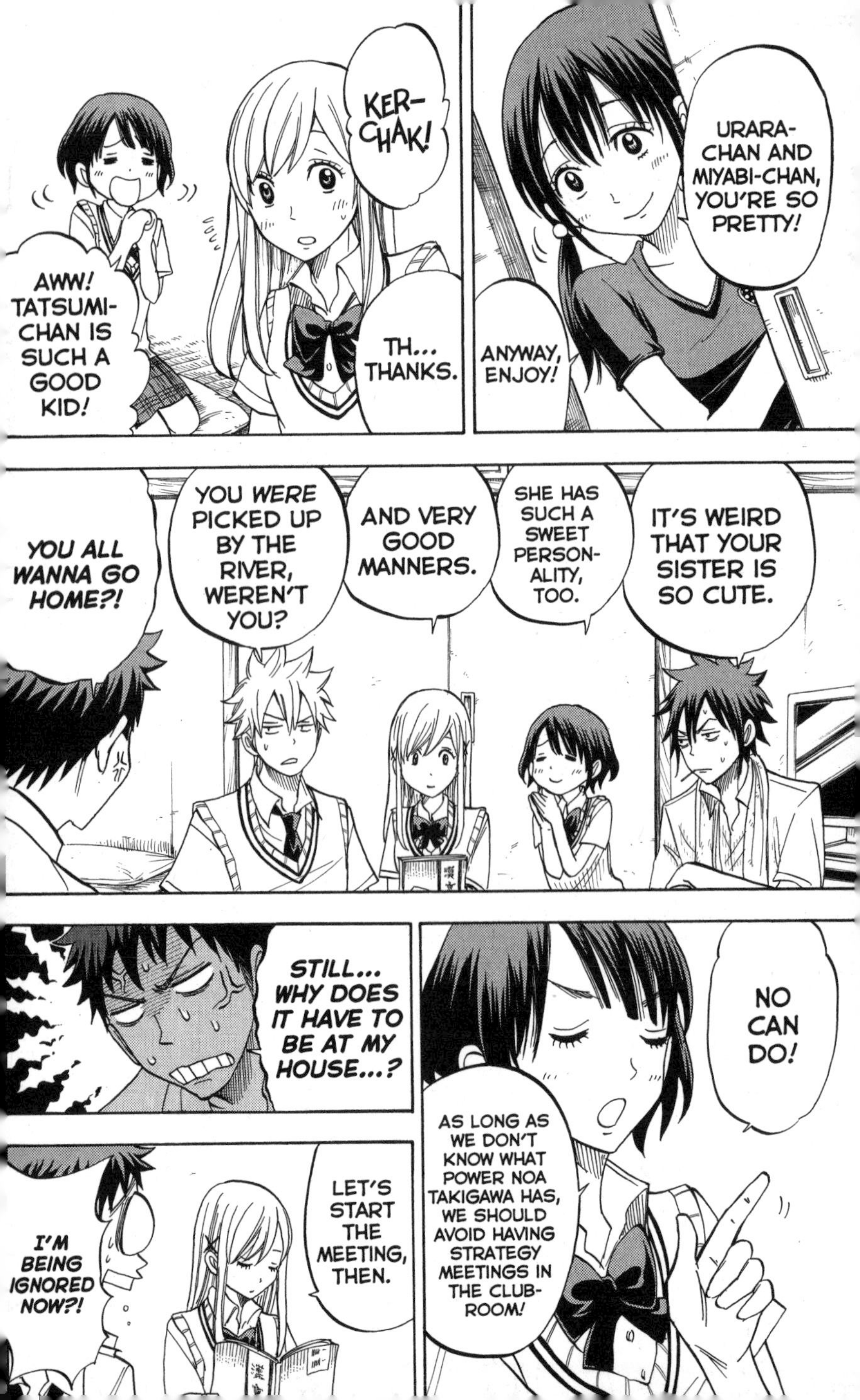
URARA-CHAN AND MIYABI-CHAN, YOU'RE SO PRETTY!
ANYWAY, ENJOY!
KER-CHAK!
TH... THANKS.
AWW! TATSUMI-CHAN IS SUCH A GOOD KID!
IT'S WEIRD THAT YOUR SISTER IS SO CUTE.
SHE HAS SUCH A SWEET PERSON-ALITY, TOO.
AND VERY GOOD MANNERS.
YOU WERE PICKED UP BY THE RIVER, WEREN'T YOU?
YOU ALL WANNA GO HOME?!
NO CAN DO!
AS LONG AS WE DON'T KNOW WHAT POWER NOA TAKIGAWA HAS, WE SHOULD AVOID HAVING STRATEGY MEETINGS IN THE CLUB-ROOM!
STILL... WHY DOES IT HAVE TO BE AT MY HOUSE...?
LET'S START THE MEETING, THEN.
I'M BEING IGNORED NOW?!

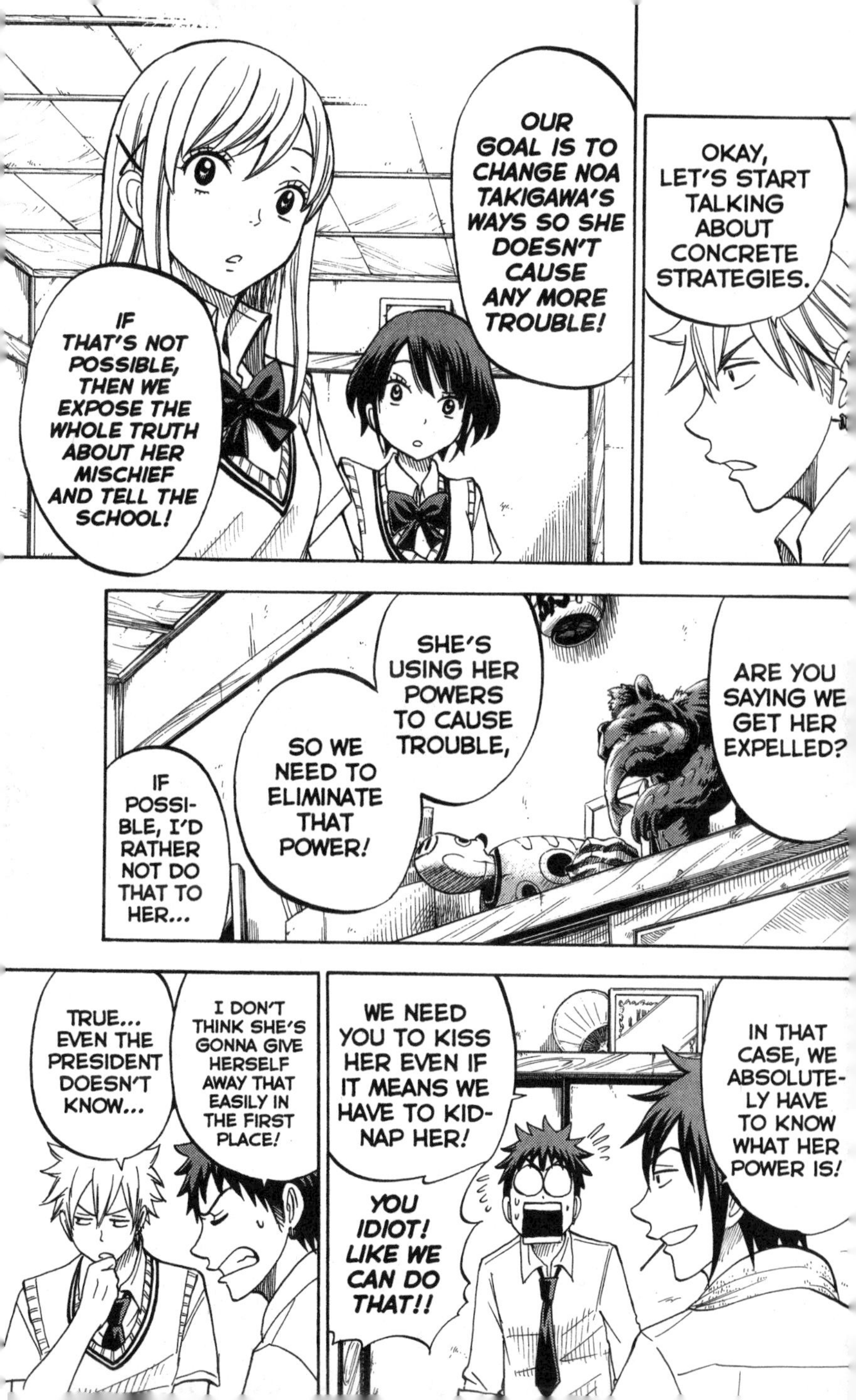
OKAY, LET'S START TALKING ABOUT CONCRETE STRATEGIES.
OUR GOAL IS TO CHANGE NOA TAKIGAWA'S WAYS SO SHE DOESN'T CAUSE ANY MORE TROUBLE!
IF THAT'S NOT POSSIBLE, THEN WE EXPOSE THE WHOLE TRUTH ABOUT HER MISCHIEF AND TELL THE SCHOOL!
ARE YOU SAYING WE GET HER EXPELLED?
SHE'S USING HER POWERS TO CAUSE TROUBLE,
SO WE NEED TO ELIMINATE THAT POWER!
IF POSSIBLE, I'D RATHER NOT DO THAT TO HER...
IN THAT CASE, WE ABSOLUTELY HAVE TO KNOW WHAT HER POWER IS!
WE NEED YOU TO KISS HER EVEN IF IT MEANS WE HAVE TO KIDNAP HER!
YOU IDIOT! LIKE WE CAN DO THAT!!
I DON'T THINK SHE'S GONNA GIVE HERSELF AWAY THAT EASILY IN THE FIRST PLACE!
TRUE... EVEN THE PRESIDENT DOESN'T KNOW...

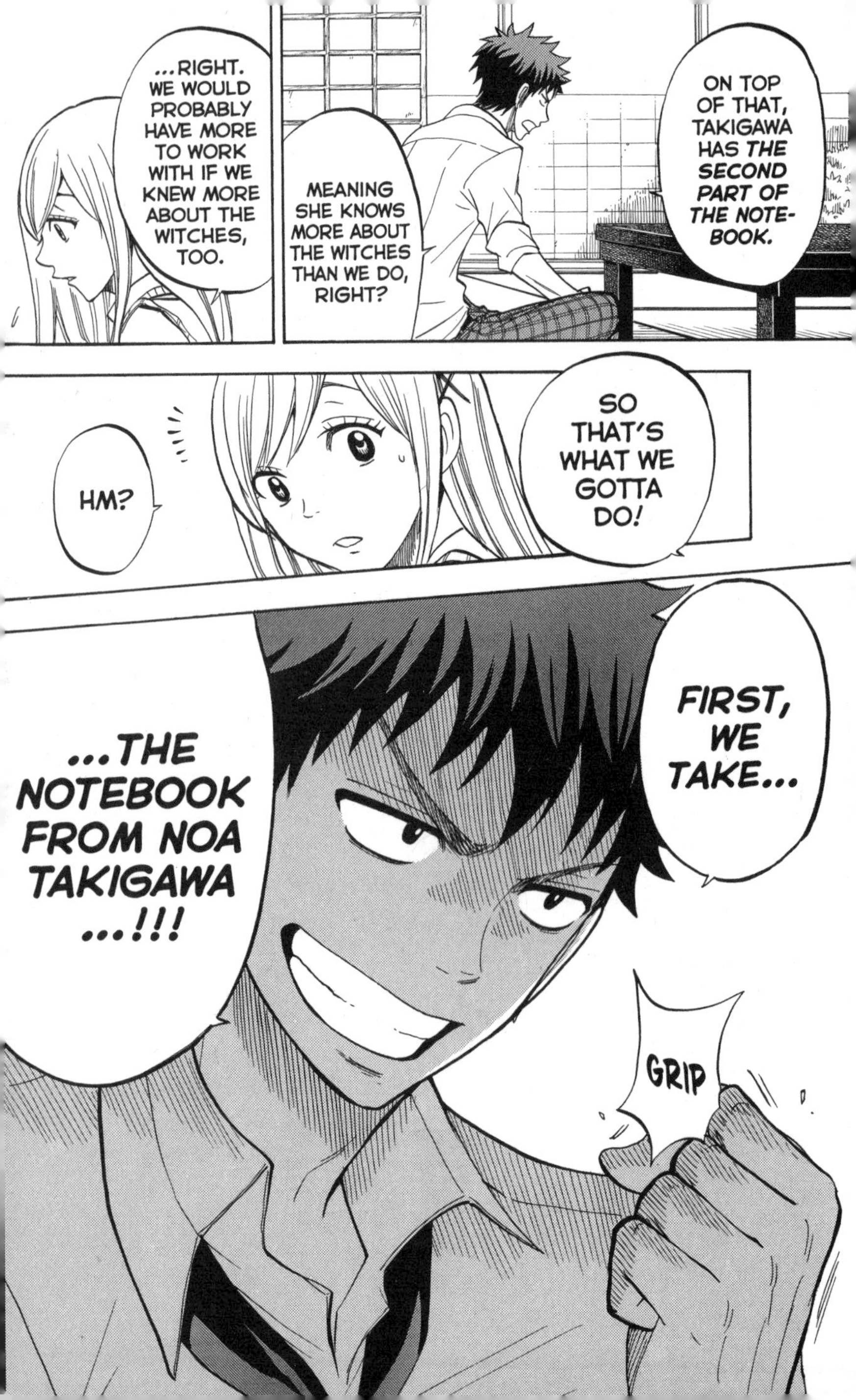
ON TOP OF THAT, TAKIGAWA HAS THE SECOND PART OF THE NOTE-BOOK.
MEANING SHE KNOWS MORE ABOUT THE WITCHES THAN WE DO, RIGHT?
...RIGHT. WE WOULD PROBABLY HAVE MORE TO WORK WITH IF WE KNEW MORE ABOUT THE WITCHES, TOO.
SO THAT'S WHAT WE GOTTA DO!
HM?
FIRST, WE TAKE...
...THE NOTEBOOK FROM NOA TAKIGAWA ...!!!
GRIP

CHAPTER 46: A girl's jealousy is scary!!

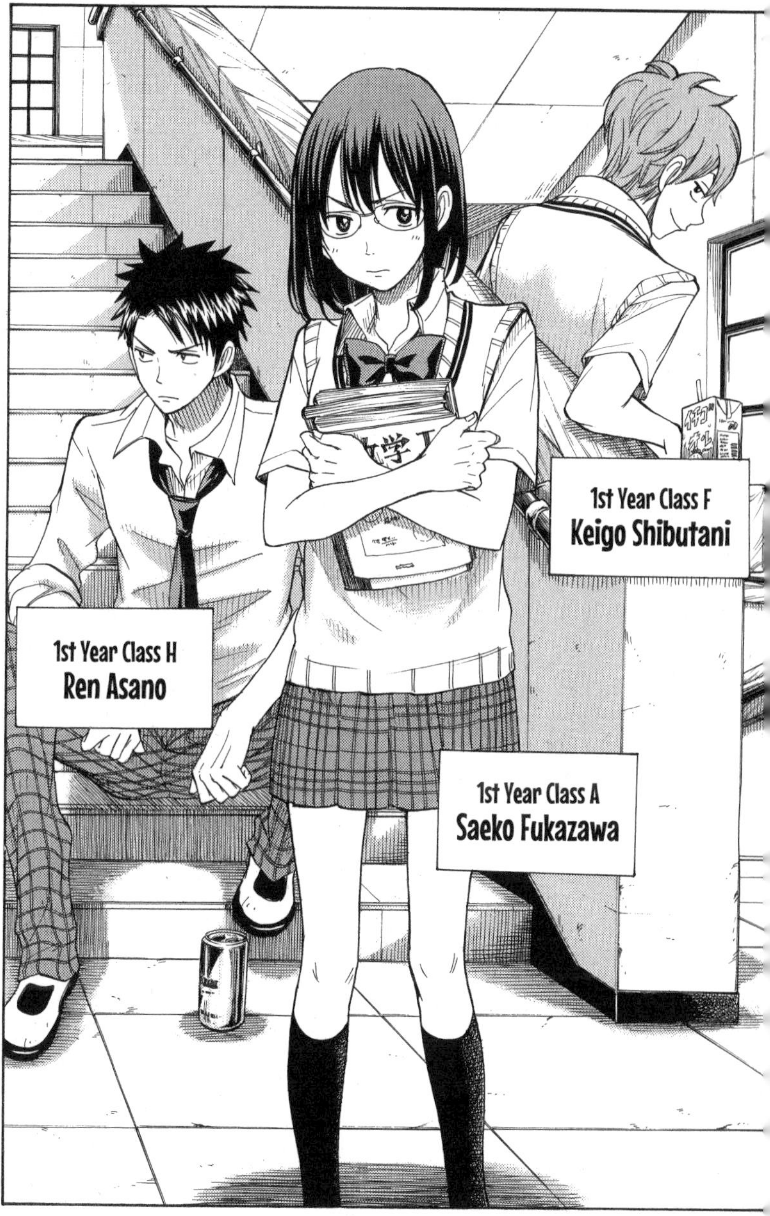
1st Year Class F
Keigo Shibutani
1st Year Class H
Ren Asano
1st Year Class A
Saeko Fukazawa

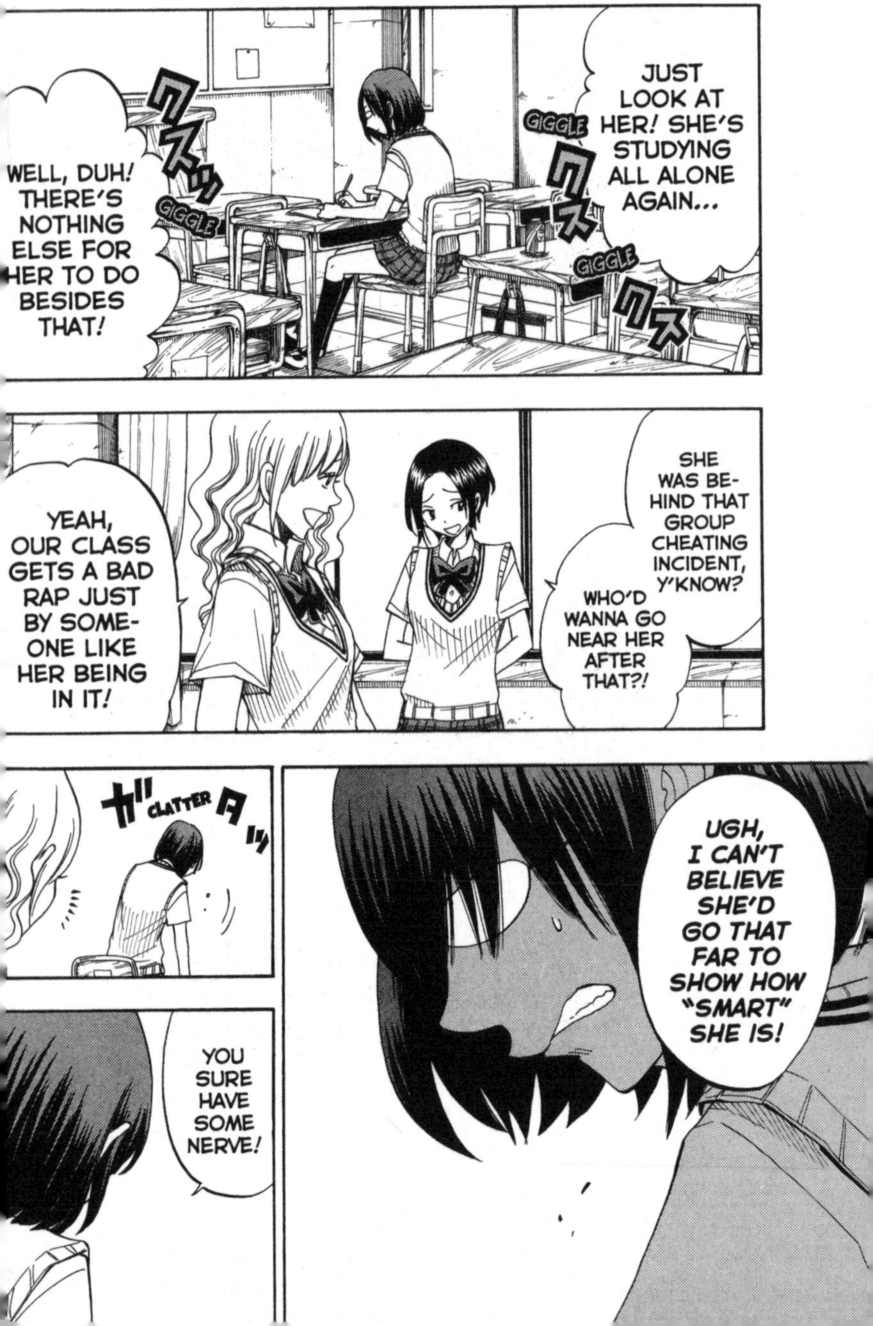
JUST LOOK AT HER! SHE'S STUDYING ALL ALONE AGAIN...
GIGGLE
GIGGLE
GIGGLE
WELL, DUH! THERE'S NOTHING ELSE FOR HER TO DO BESIDES THAT!
SHE WAS BE-HIND THAT GROUP CHEATING INCIDENT, Y'KNOW?
WHO'D WANNA GO NEAR HER AFTER THAT?!
YEAH, OUR CLASS GETS A BAD RAP JUST BY SOME-ONE LIKE HER BEING IN IT!
UGH, I CAN'T BELIEVE SHE'D GO THAT FAR TO SHOW HOW "SMART" SHE IS!
CLATTER
YOU SURE HAVE SOME NERVE!

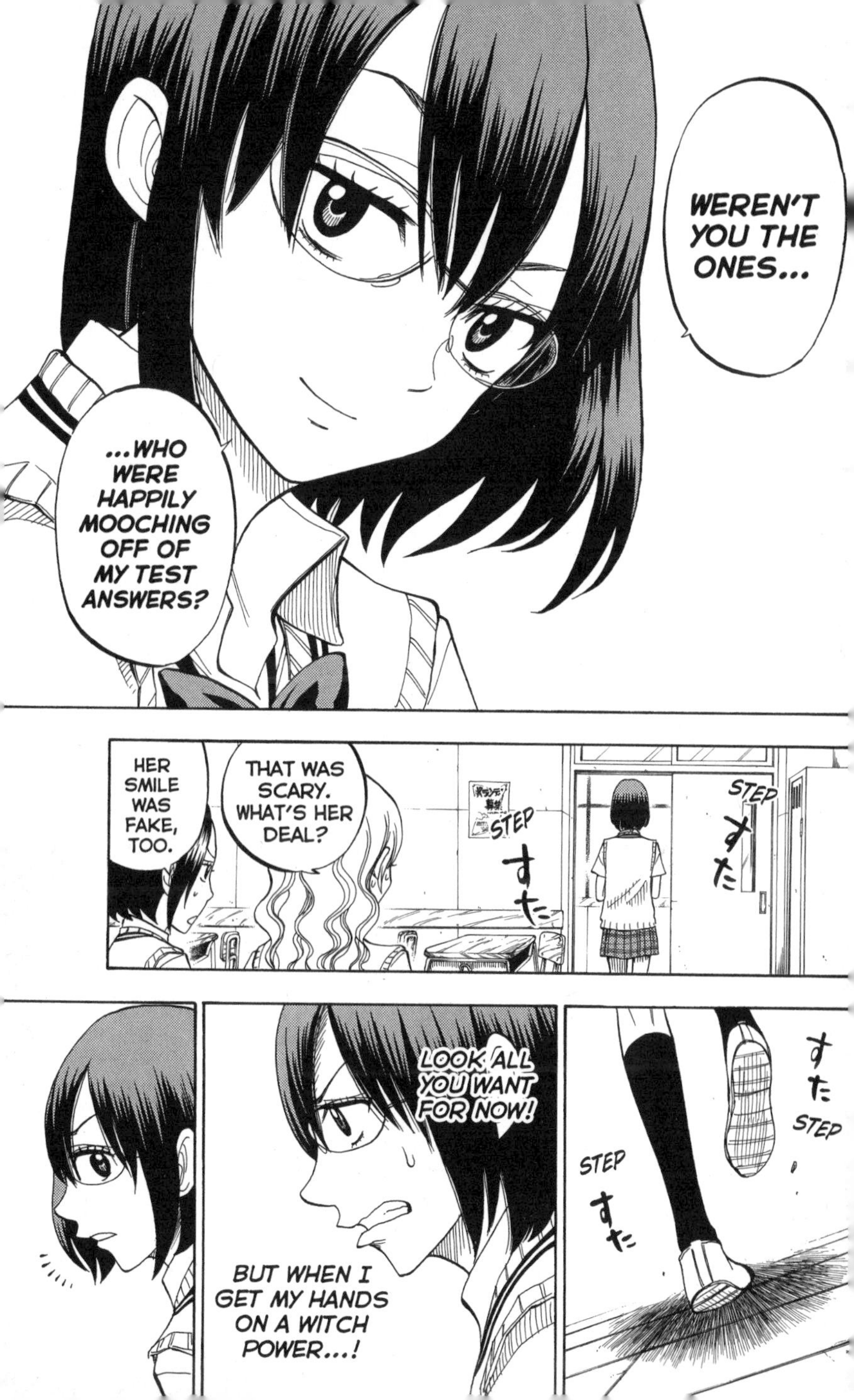
WEREN'T YOU THE ONES...
...WHO WERE HAPPILY MOOCHING OFF OF MY TEST ANSWERS?
STEP
すた
STEP
すた
THAT WAS SCARY. WHAT'S HER DEAL?
HER SMILE WAS FAKE, TOO.
すた
STEP
STEP
すた
LOOK ALL YOU WANT FOR NOW!
BUT WHEN I GET MY HANDS ON A WITCH POWER...!

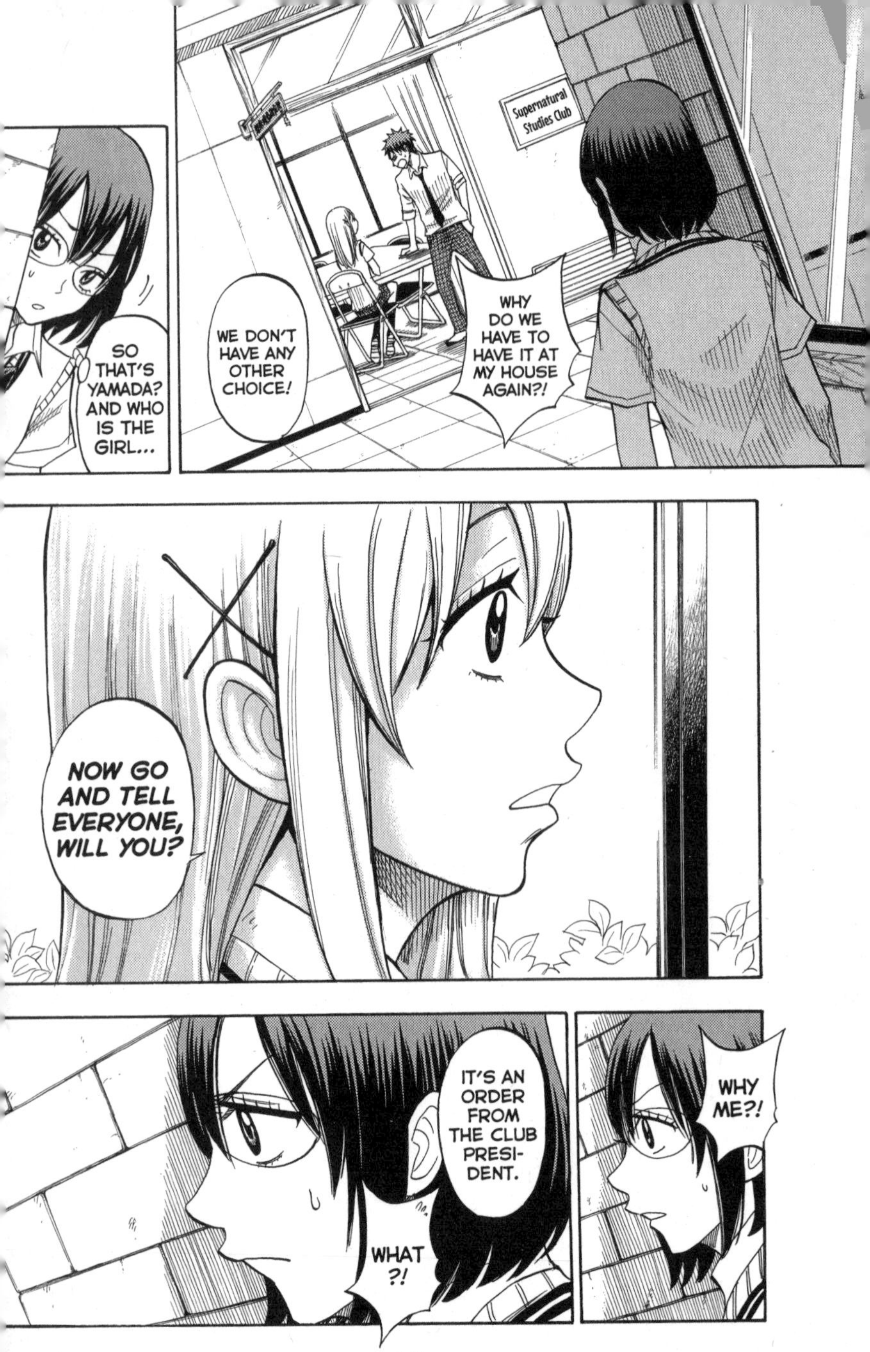
Supernatural Studies Club
WHY DO WE HAVE TO HAVE IT AT MY HOUSE AGAIN?!
WE DON'T HAVE ANY OTHER CHOICE!
SO THAT'S YAMADA? AND WHO IS THE GIRL...
NOW GO AND TELL EVERYONE, WILL YOU?
WHY ME?!
IT'S AN ORDER FROM THE CLUB PRESI-DENT.
WHAT?!

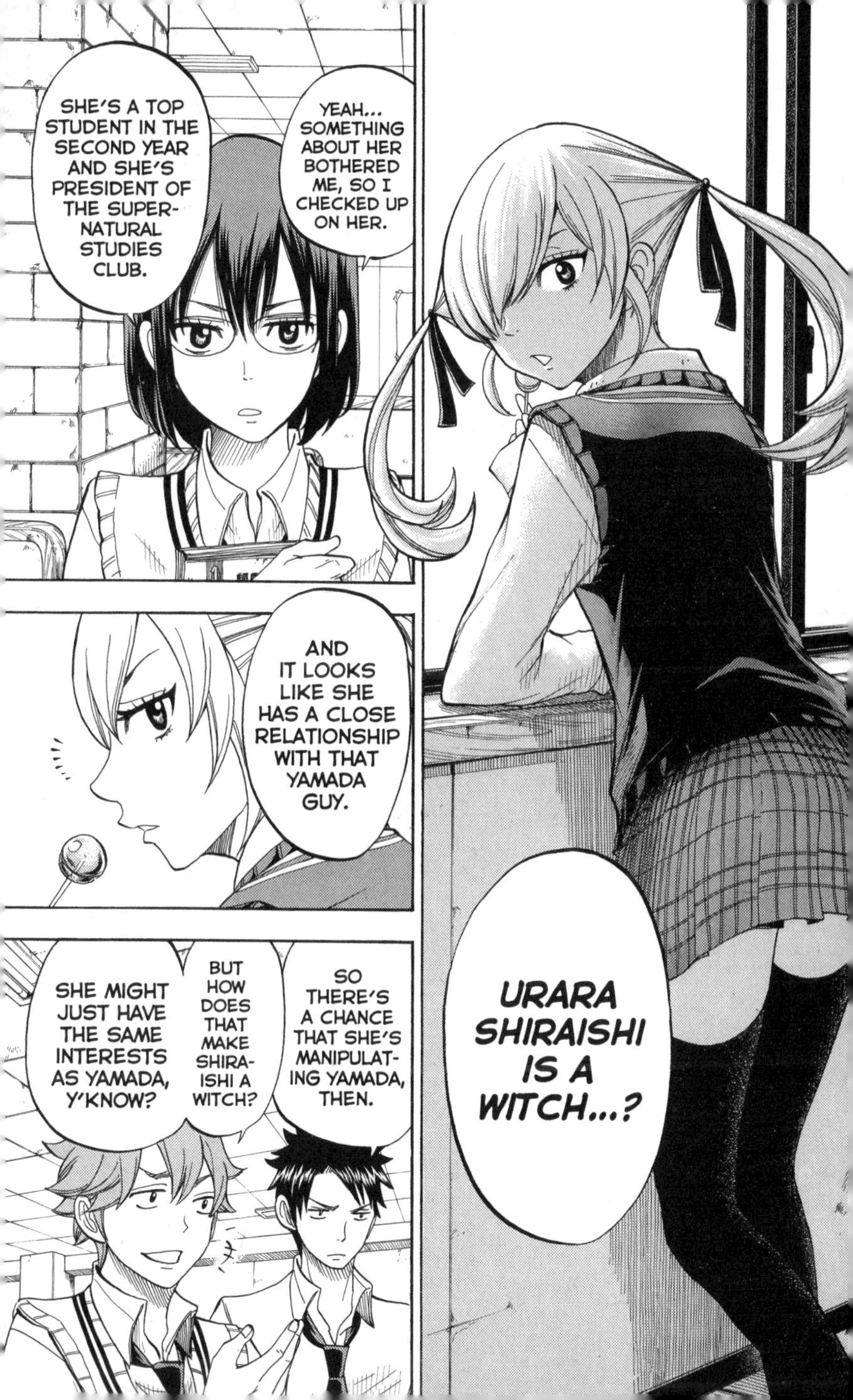
URARA SHIRAISHI IS A WITCH...?
YEAH... SOMETHING ABOUT HER BOTHERED ME, SO I CHECKED UP ON HER.
SHE'S A TOP STUDENT IN THE SECOND YEAR AND SHE'S PRESIDENT OF THE SUPER-NATURAL STUDIES CLUB.
AND IT LOOKS LIKE SHE HAS A CLOSE RELATIONSHIP WITH THAT YAMADA GUY.
SO THERE'S A CHANCE THAT SHE'S MANIPULAT-ING YAMADA, THEN.
BUT HOW DOES THAT MAKE SHIRA-ISHI A WITCH?
SHE MIGHT JUST HAVE THE SAME INTERESTS AS YAMADA, Y'KNOW?

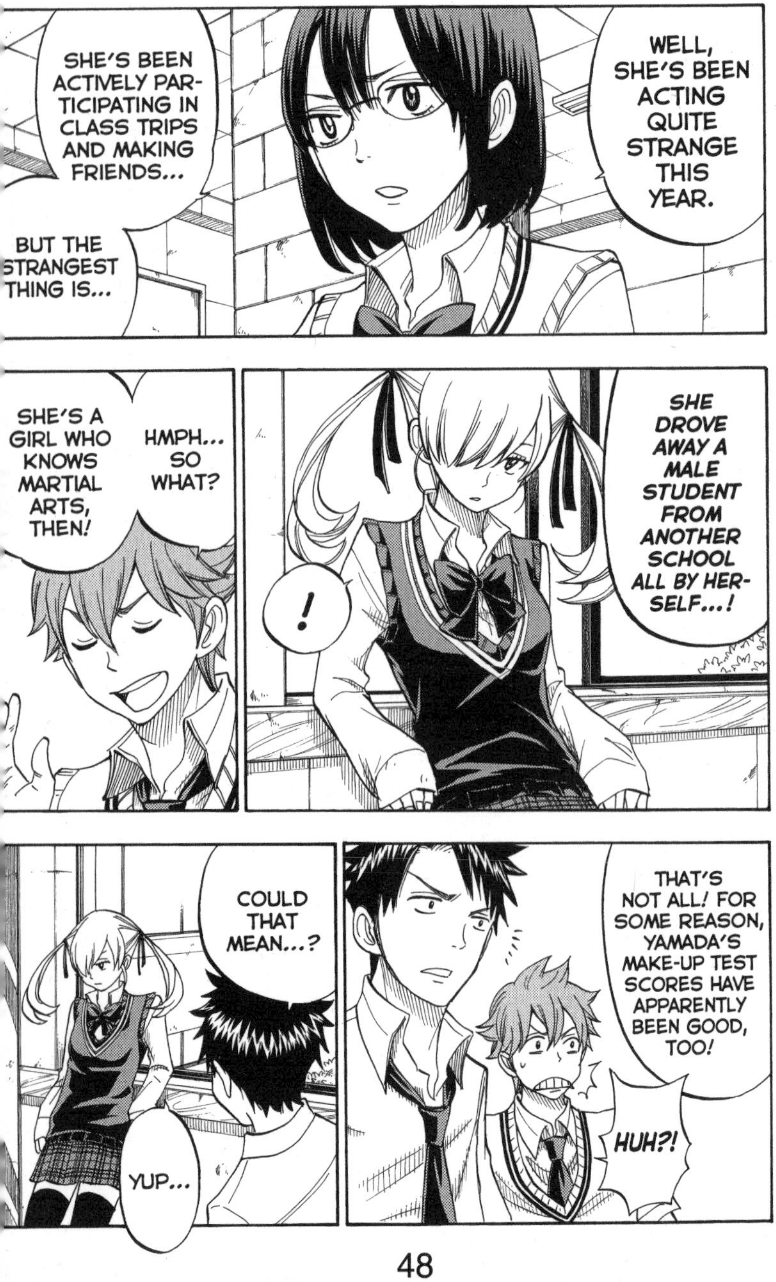
WELL, SHE'S BEEN ACTING QUITE STRANGE THIS YEAR.
SHE'S BEEN ACTIVELY PARTICIPATING IN CLASS TRIPS AND MAKING FRIENDS...
BUT THE STRANGEST THING IS...
SHE DROVE AWAY A MALE STUDENT FROM ANOTHER SCHOOL ALL BY HERSELF...!
!
HMPH... SO WHAT?
SHE'S A GIRL WHO KNOWS MARTIAL ARTS, THEN!
THAT'S NOT ALL! FOR SOME REASON, YAMADA'S MAKE-UP TEST SCORES HAVE APPARENTLY BEEN GOOD, TOO!
HUH?!
COULD THAT MEAN...?
YUP...

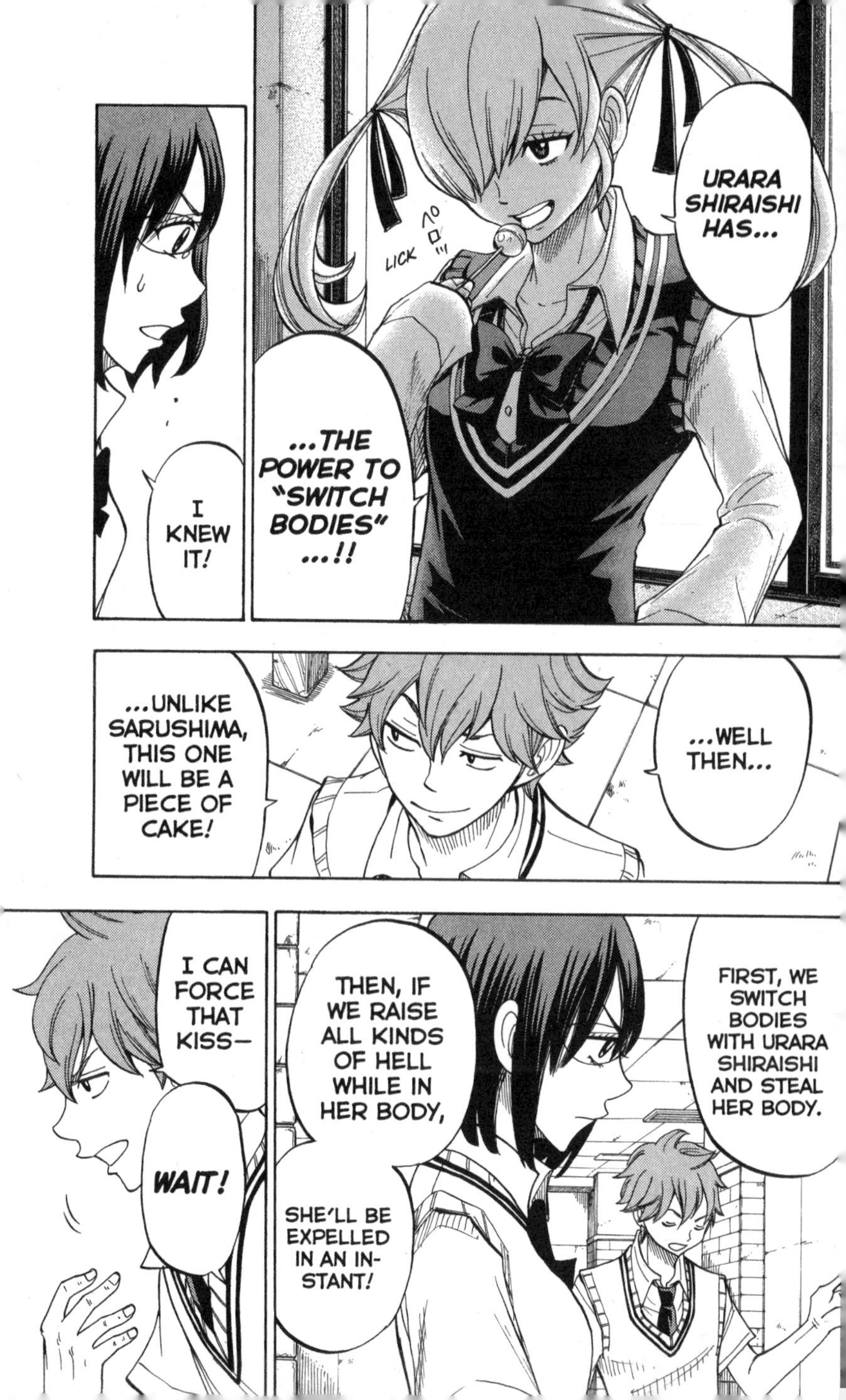
URARA SHIRAISHI HAS...
LICK
...THE POWER TO "SWITCH BODIES" ...!!
I KNEW IT!
...WELL THEN...
...UNLIKE SARUSHIMA, THIS ONE WILL BE A PIECE OF CAKE!
FIRST, WE SWITCH BODIES WITH URARA SHIRAISHI AND STEAL HER BODY.
THEN, IF WE RAISE ALL KINDS OF HELL WHILE IN HER BODY,
SHE'LL BE EXPELLED IN AN IN-STANT!
I CAN FORCE THAT KISS—
WAIT!

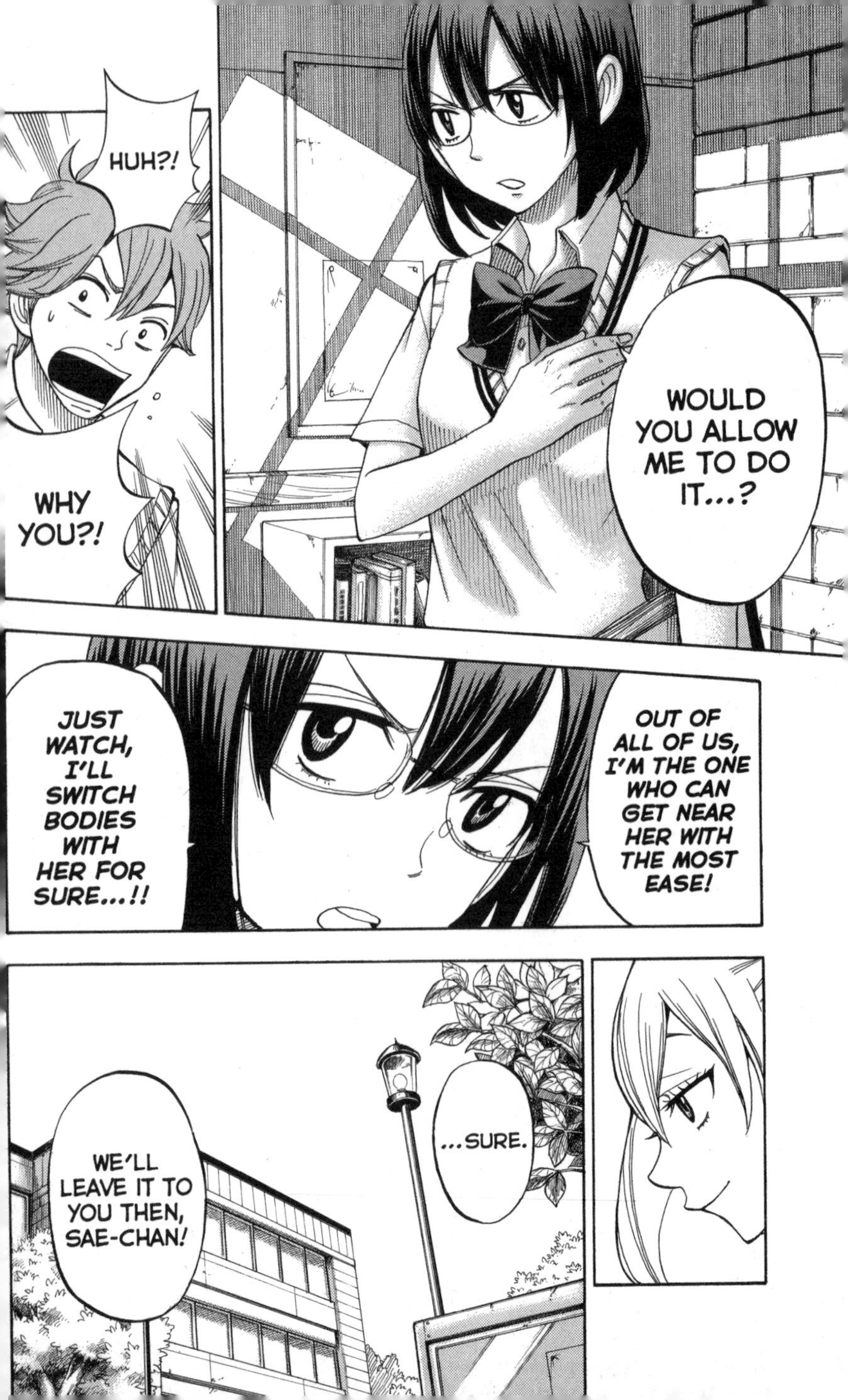
WOULD YOU ALLOW ME TO DO IT...?
HUH?!
WHY YOU?!
OUT OF ALL OF US, I'M THE ONE WHO CAN GET NEAR HER WITH THE MOST EASE!
JUST WATCH, I'LL SWITCH BODIES WITH HER FOR SURE...!!
WE'LL LEAVE IT TO YOU THEN, SAE-CHAN!
...SURE.

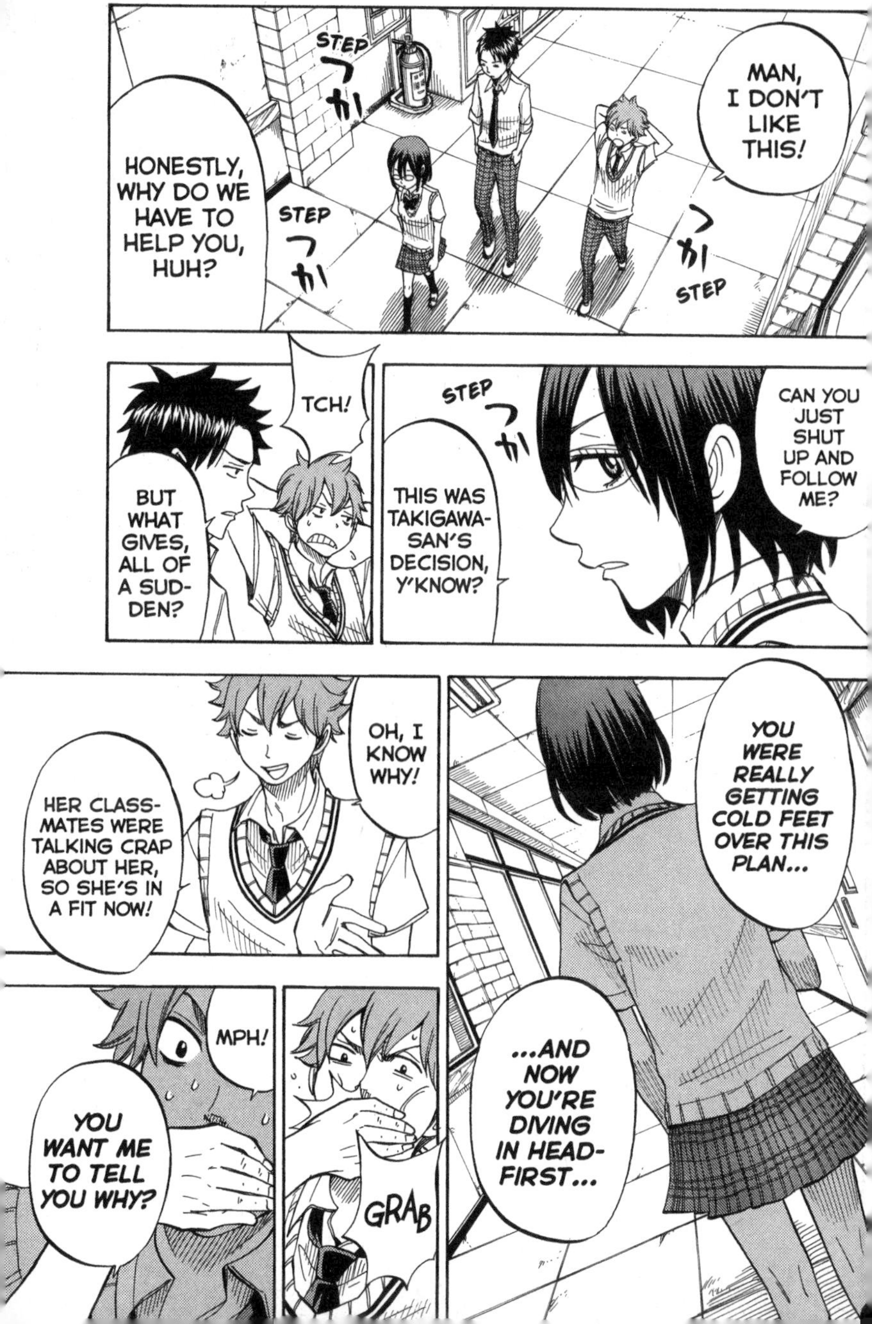
MAN, I DON'T LIKE THIS!
STEP
STEP
STEP
HONESTLY, WHY DO WE HAVE TO HELP YOU, HUH?
CAN YOU JUST SHUT UP AND FOLLOW ME?
STEP
THIS WAS TAKIGAWA-SAN'S DECISION, Y'KNOW?
TCH!
BUT WHAT GIVES, ALL OF A SUD-DEN?
YOU WERE REALLY GETTING COLD FEET OVER THIS PLAN...
...AND NOW YOU'RE DIVING IN HEAD-FIRST...
OH, I KNOW WHY!
HER CLASS-MATES WERE TALKING CRAP ABOUT HER, SO SHE'S IN A FIT NOW!
MPH!
GRAB
YOU WANT ME TO TELL YOU WHY?

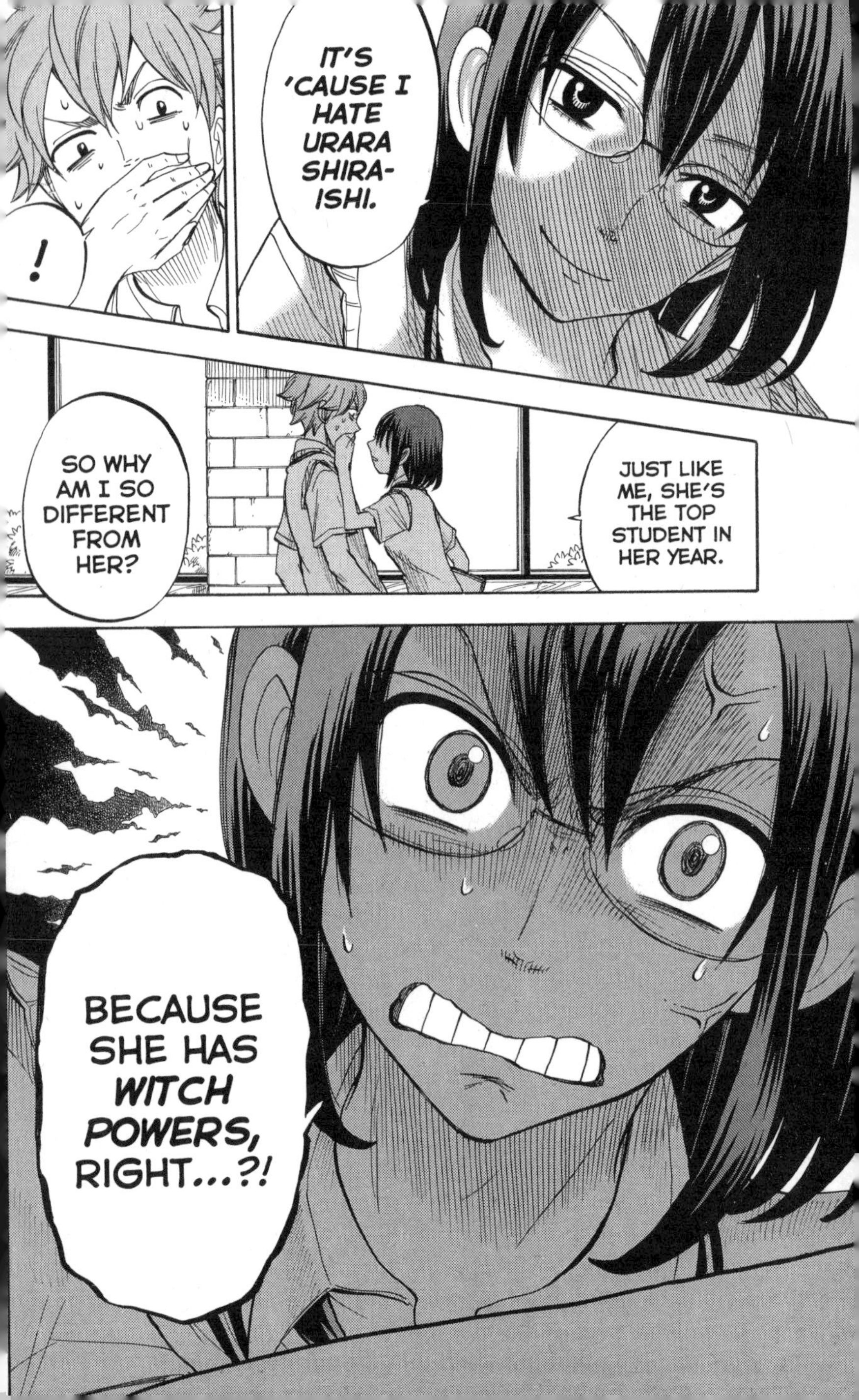
IT'S 'CAUSE I HATE URARA SHIRA-ISHI.
!
JUST LIKE ME, SHE'S THE TOP STUDENT IN HER YEAR.
SO WHY AM I SO DIFFERENT FROM HER?
BECAUSE SHE HAS *WITCH POWERS,* RIGHT...?!

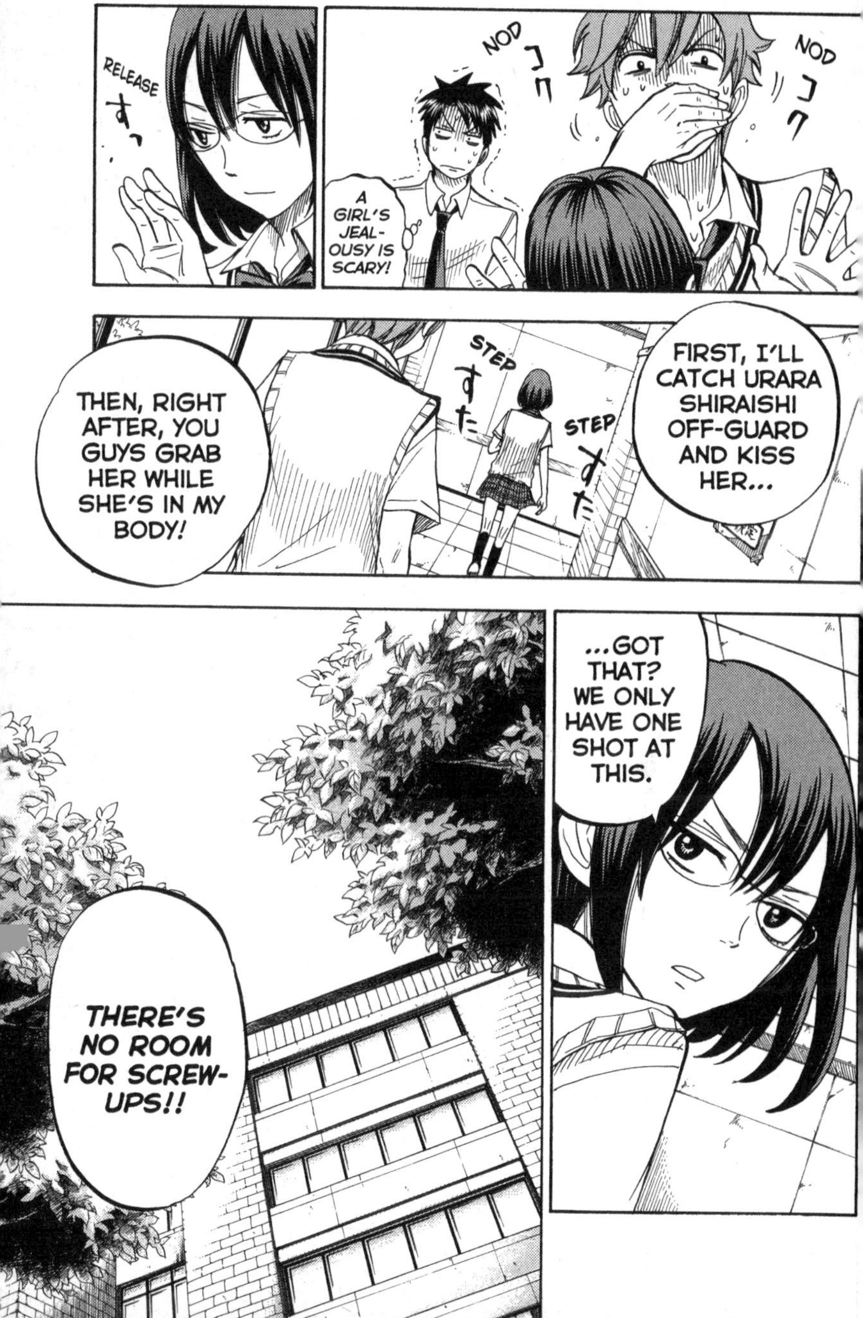
NOD
コク
NOD
コク
A GIRL'S JEAL-OUSY IS SCARY!
RELEASE
す
FIRST, I'LL CATCH URARA SHIRAISHI OFF-GUARD AND KISS HER...
STEP
すた
STEP
すた
THEN, RIGHT AFTER, YOU GUYS GRAB HER WHILE SHE'S IN MY BODY!
...GOT THAT? WE ONLY HAVE ONE SHOT AT THIS.
THERE'S NO ROOM FOR SCREW-UPS!!

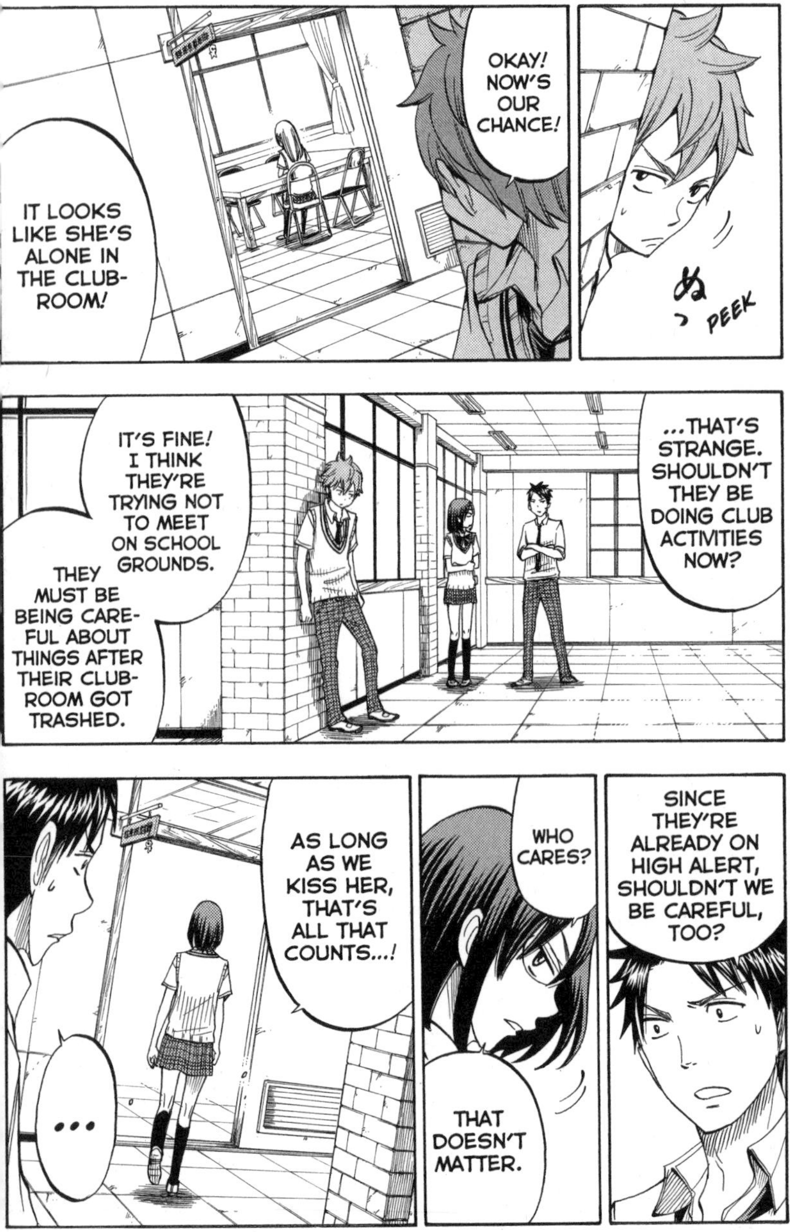
ぬっ
PEEK
OKAY! NOW'S OUR CHANCE!
IT LOOKS LIKE SHE'S ALONE IN THE CLUB-ROOM!
...THAT'S STRANGE. SHOULDN'T THEY BE DOING CLUB ACTIVITIES NOW?
IT'S FINE! I THINK THEY'RE TRYING NOT TO MEET ON SCHOOL GROUNDS.
THEY MUST BE BEING CARE-FUL ABOUT THINGS AFTER THEIR CLUB-ROOM GOT TRASHED.
SINCE THEY'RE ALREADY ON HIGH ALERT, SHOULDN'T WE BE CAREFUL, TOO?
WHO CARES?
THAT DOESN'T MATTER.
AS LONG AS WE KISS HER, THAT'S ALL THAT COUNTS...!
...

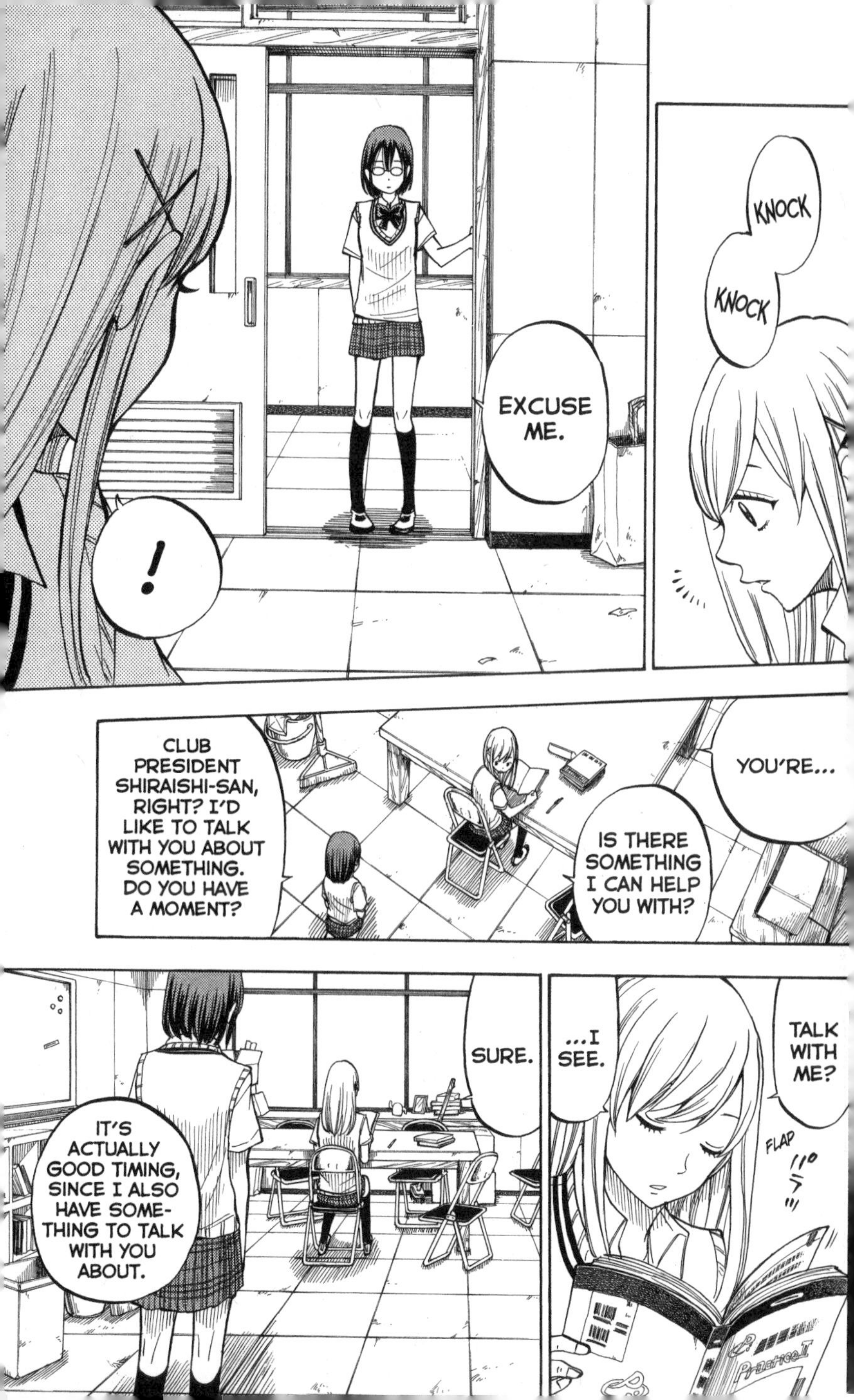
KNOCK
KNOCK
EXCUSE ME.
!
YOU'RE...
IS THERE SOMETHING I CAN HELP YOU WITH?
CLUB PRESIDENT SHIRAISHI-SAN, RIGHT? I'D LIKE TO TALK WITH YOU ABOUT SOMETHING. DO YOU HAVE A MOMENT?
TALK WITH ME?
FLAP
...I SEE.
SURE.
IT'S ACTUALLY GOOD TIMING, SINCE I ALSO HAVE SOME-THING TO TALK WITH YOU ABOUT.

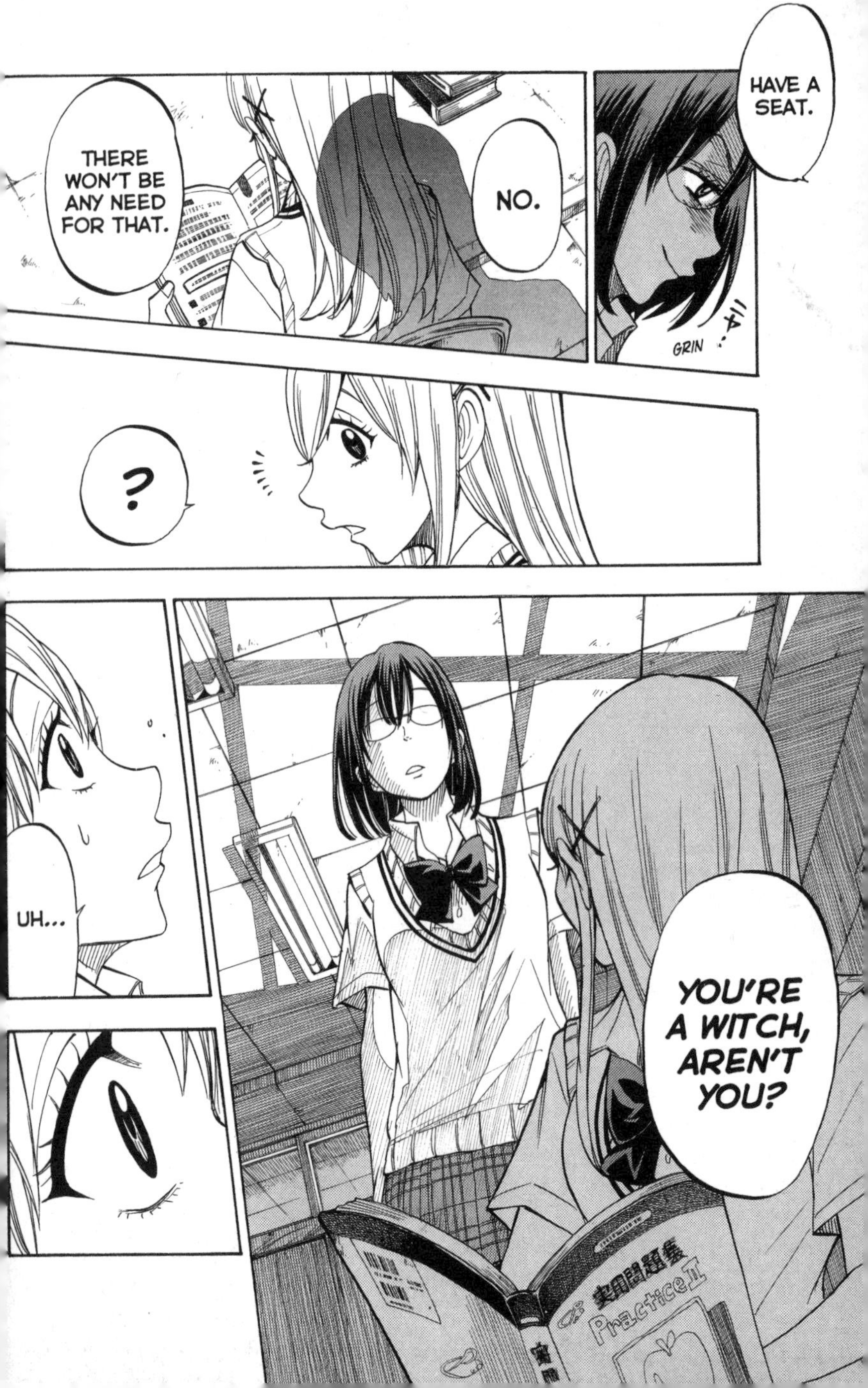
HAVE A SEAT.
GRIN
NO.
THERE WON'T BE ANY NEED FOR THAT.
?
YOU'RE A WITCH, AREN'T YOU?
実用問題集
Practice II
UH...

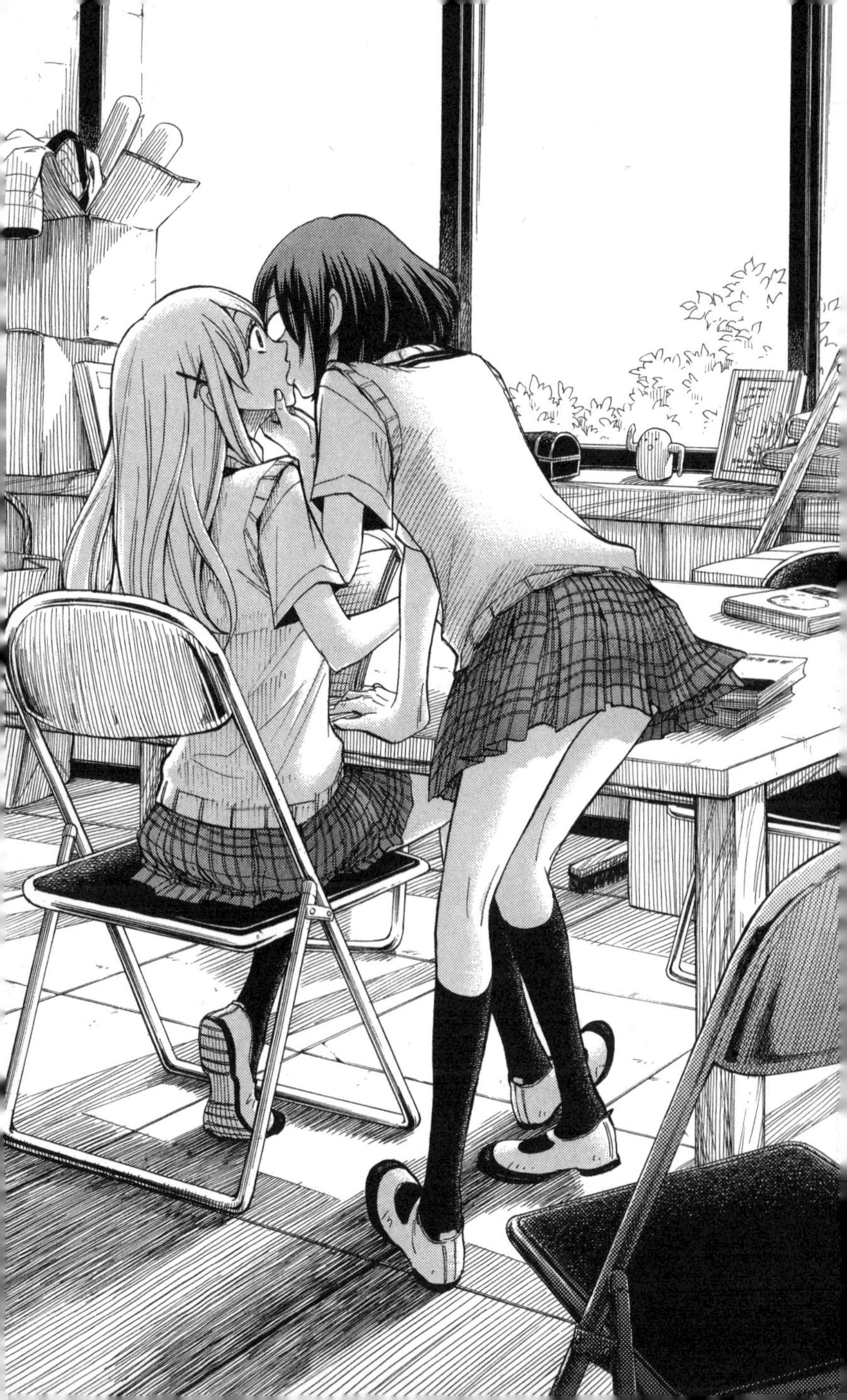

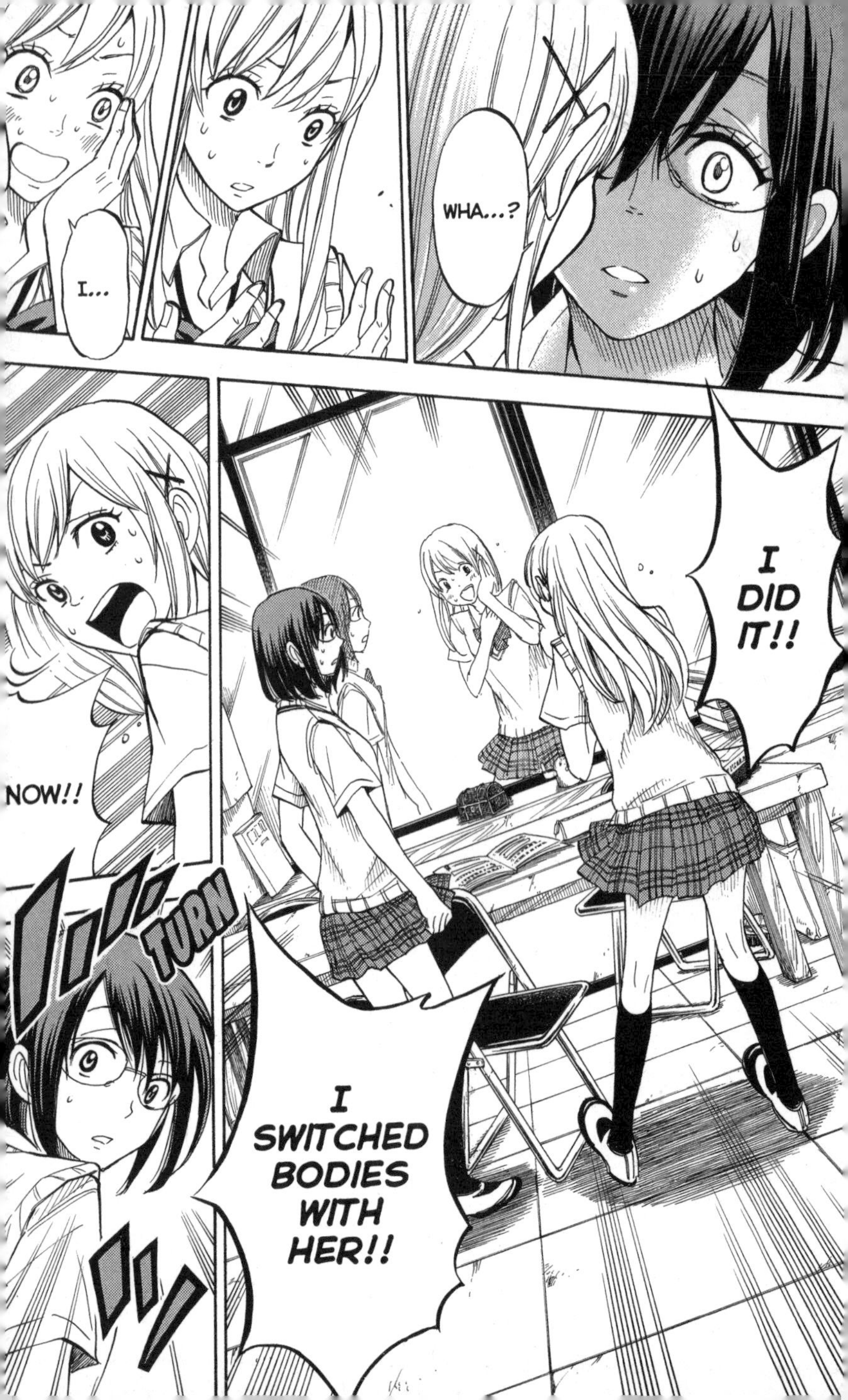
WHA...?
I...
I DID IT!!
I SWITCHED BODIES WITH HER!!
NOW!!
TURN

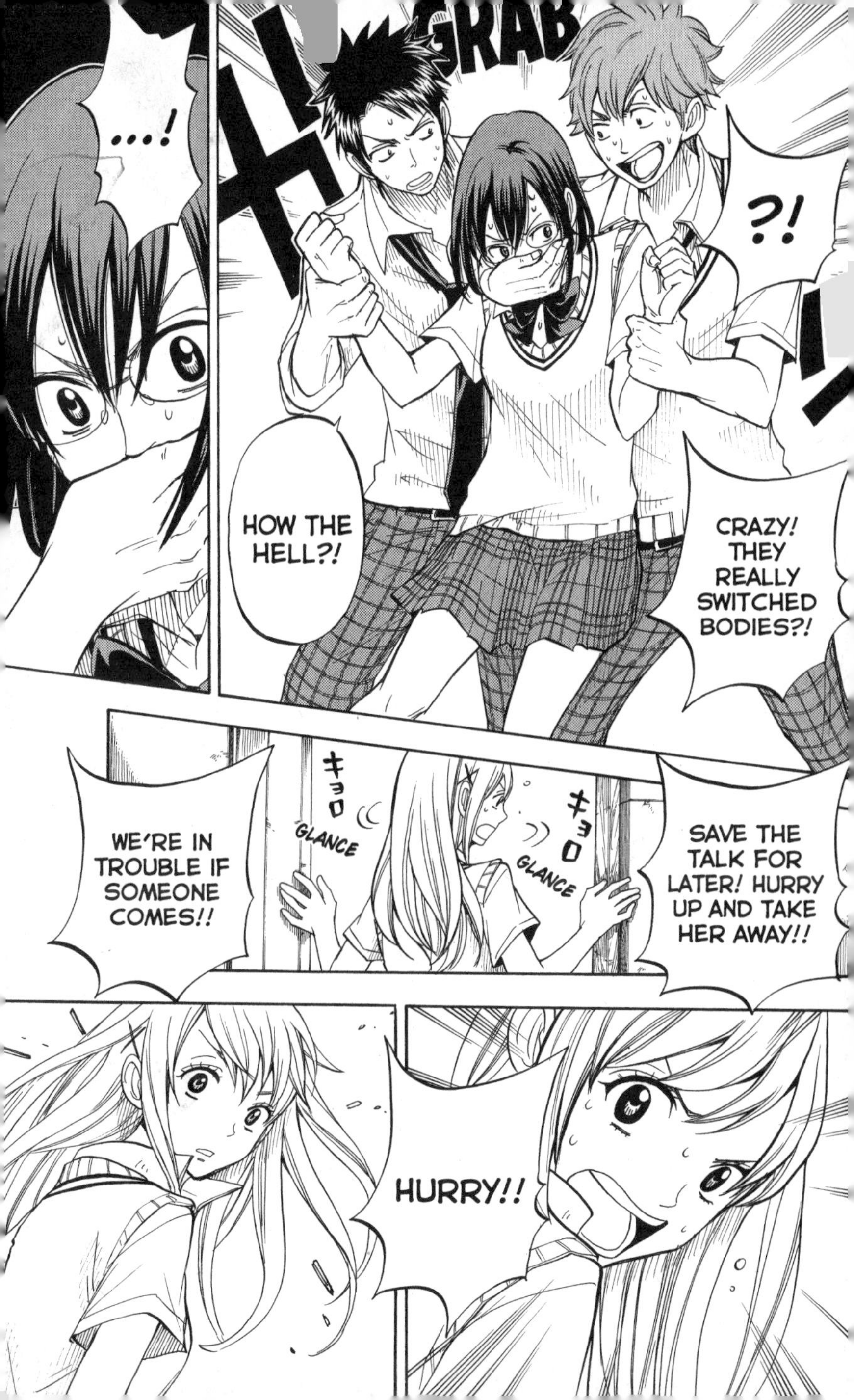
GRAB
?!
CRAZY! THEY REALLY SWITCHED BODIES?!
HOW THE HELL?!
...!
SAVE THE TALK FOR LATER! HURRY UP AND TAKE HER AWAY!!
キョロ
GLANCE
キョロ
GLANCE
WE'RE IN TROUBLE IF SOMEONE COMES!!
HURRY!!

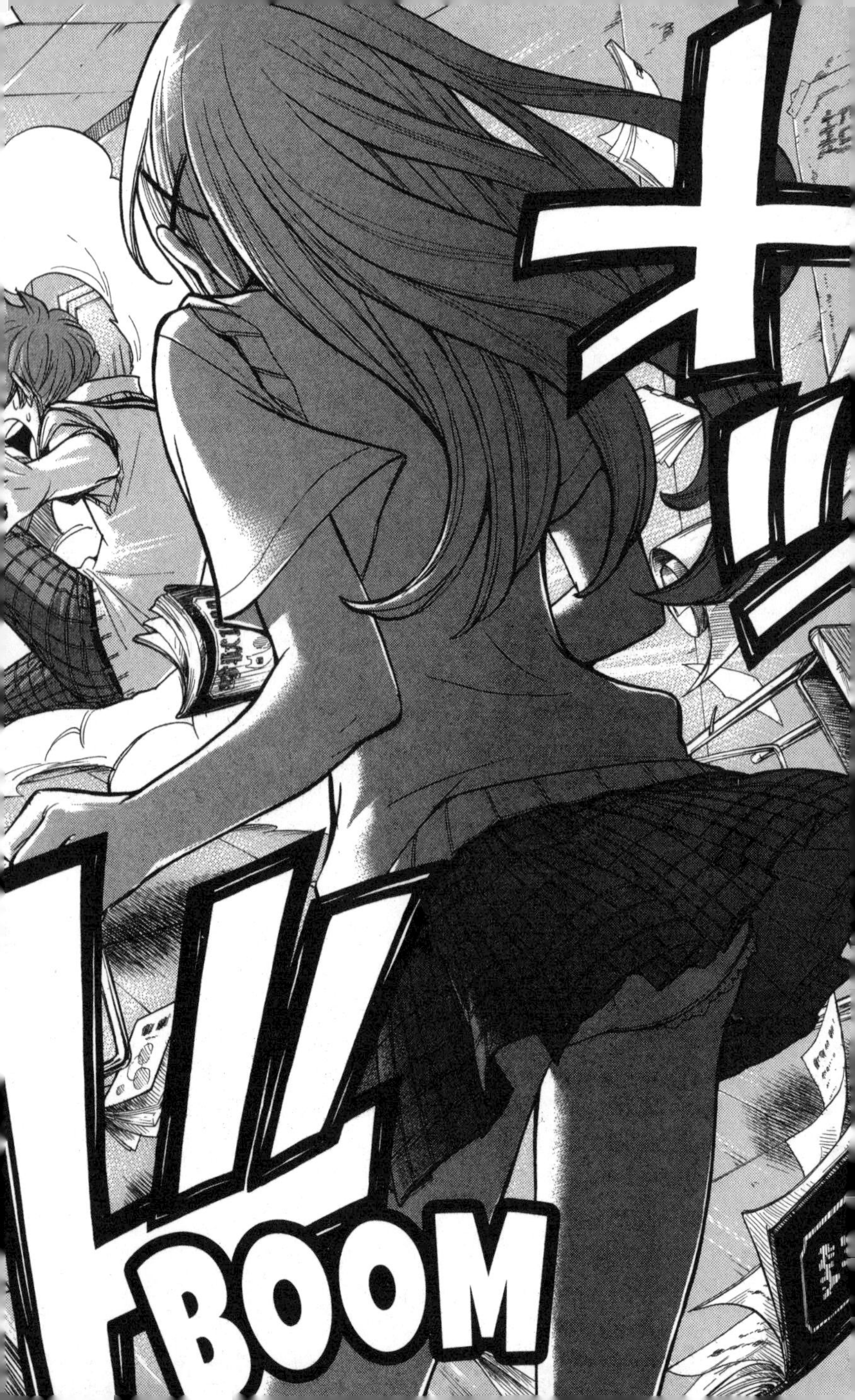
BOOM

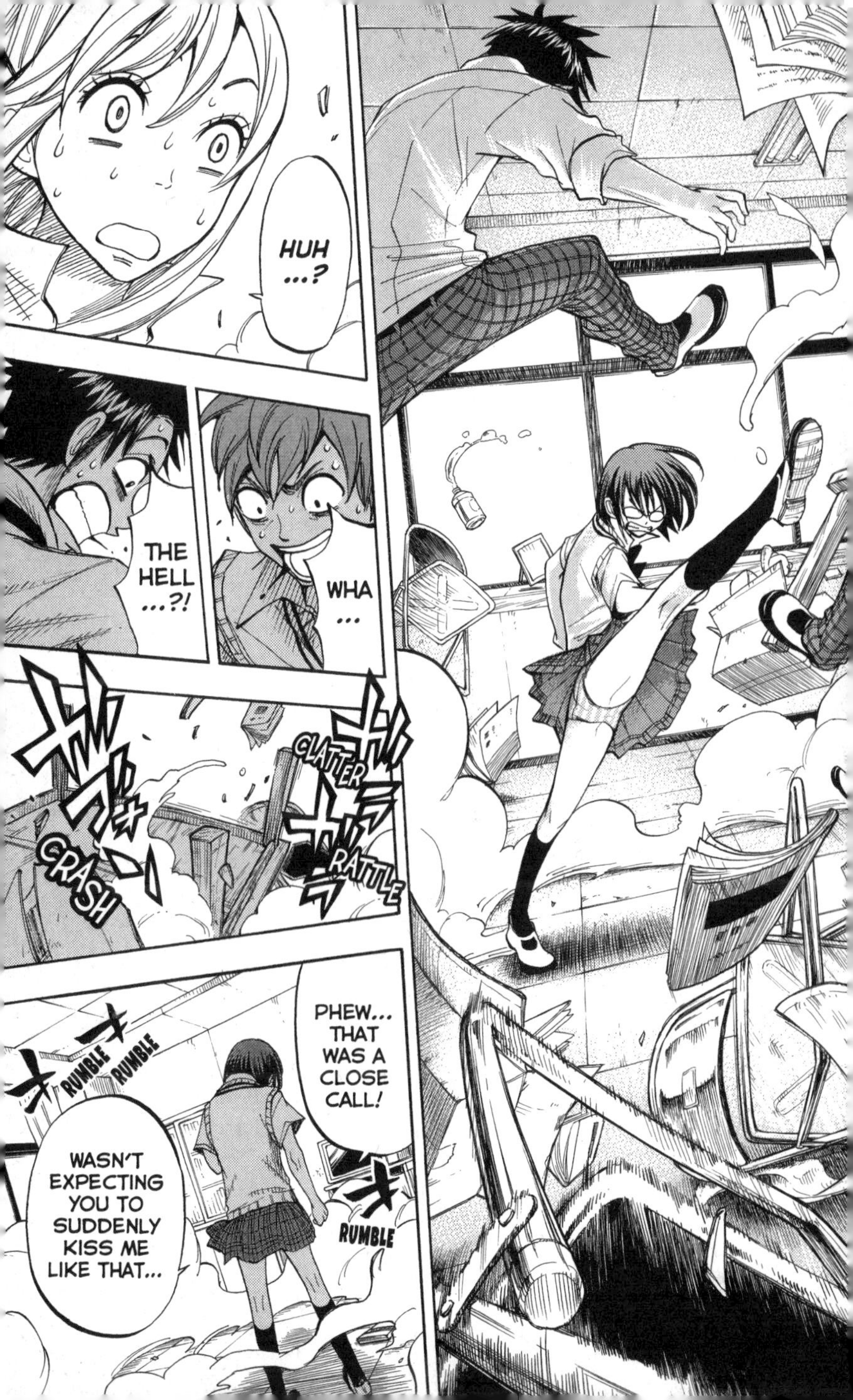
HUH ...?
WHA ...
THE HELL ...?!
CLATTER
RATTLE
CRASH
PHEW... THAT WAS A CLOSE CALL!
RUMBLE RUMBLE
WASN'T EXPECTING YOU TO SUDDENLY KISS ME LIKE THAT...
RUMBLE

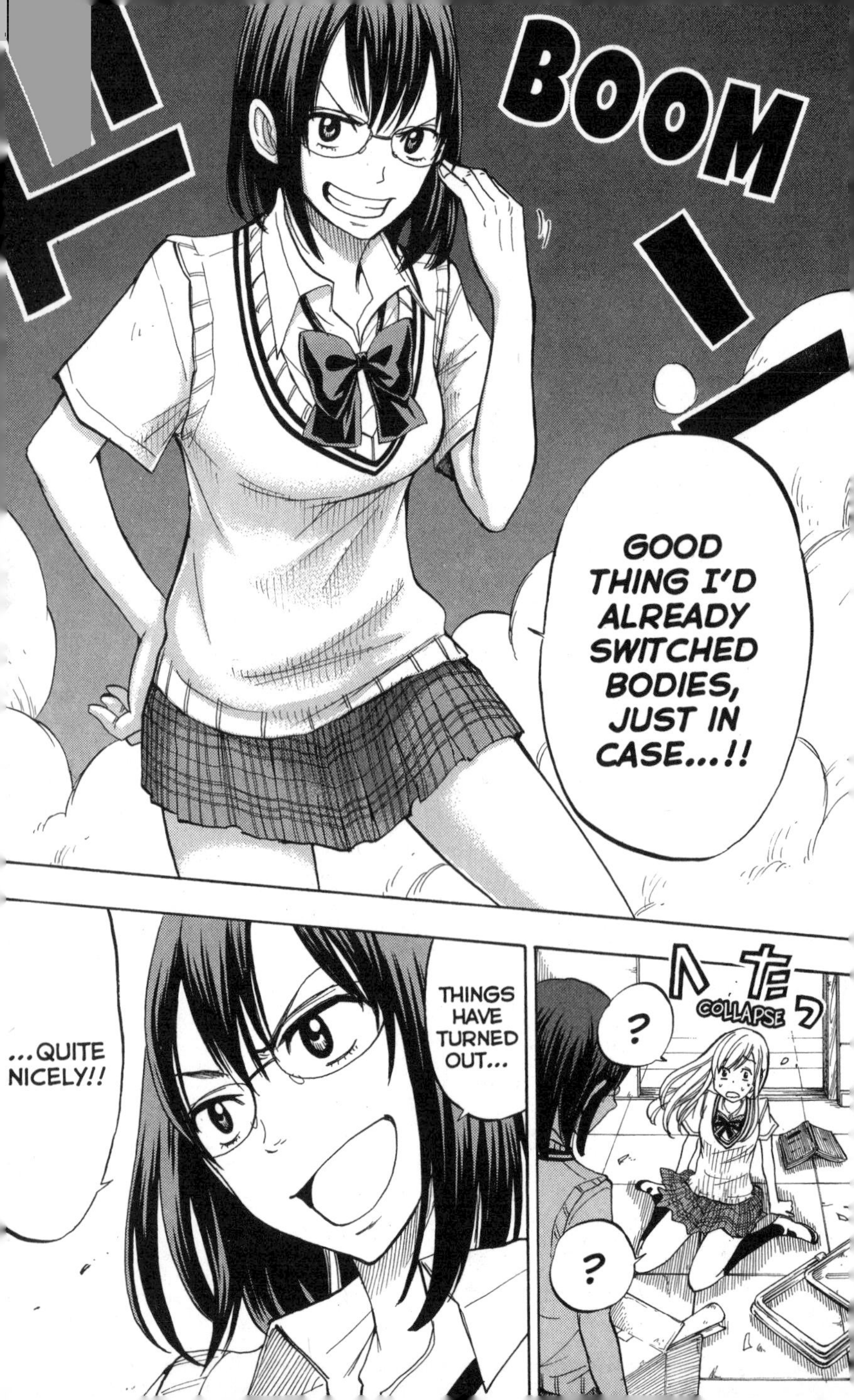
BOOM
GOOD THING I'D ALREADY SWITCHED BODIES, JUST IN CASE...!!
COLLAPSE
?
?
THINGS HAVE TURNED OUT...
...QUITE NICELY!!

CHAPTER 47: Strut...

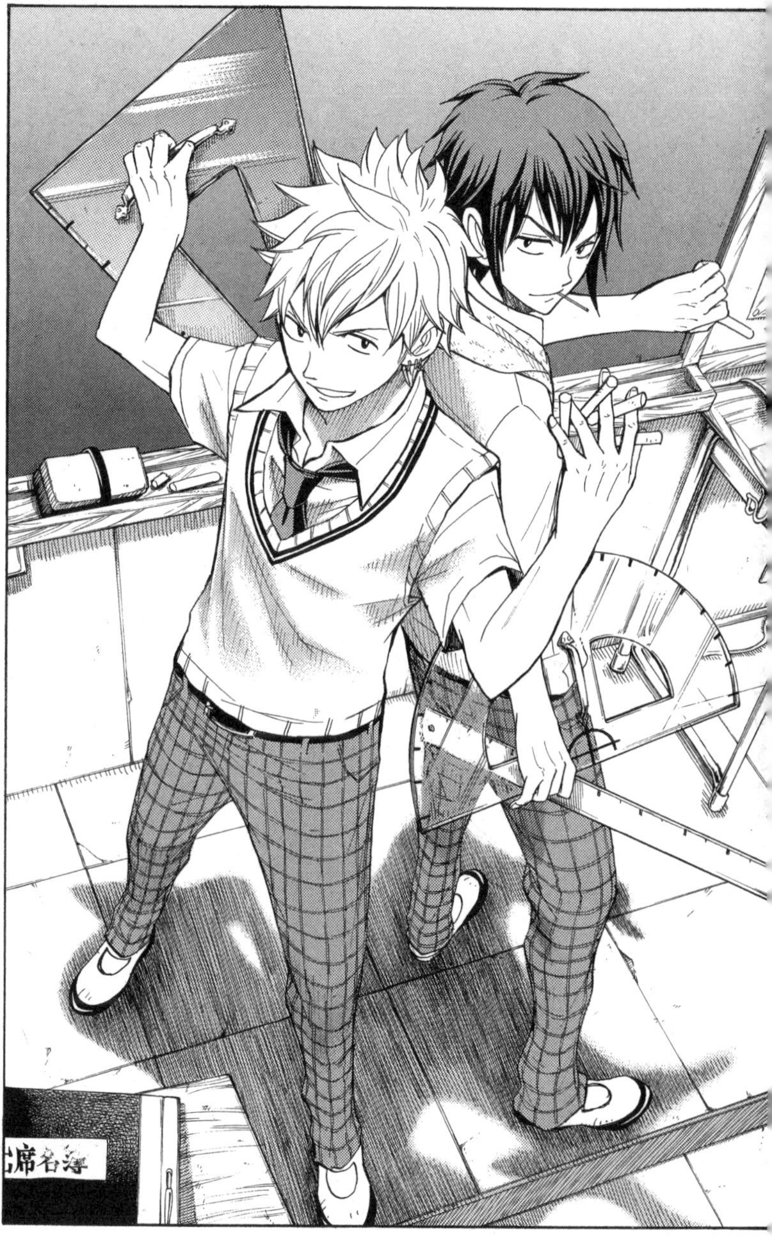

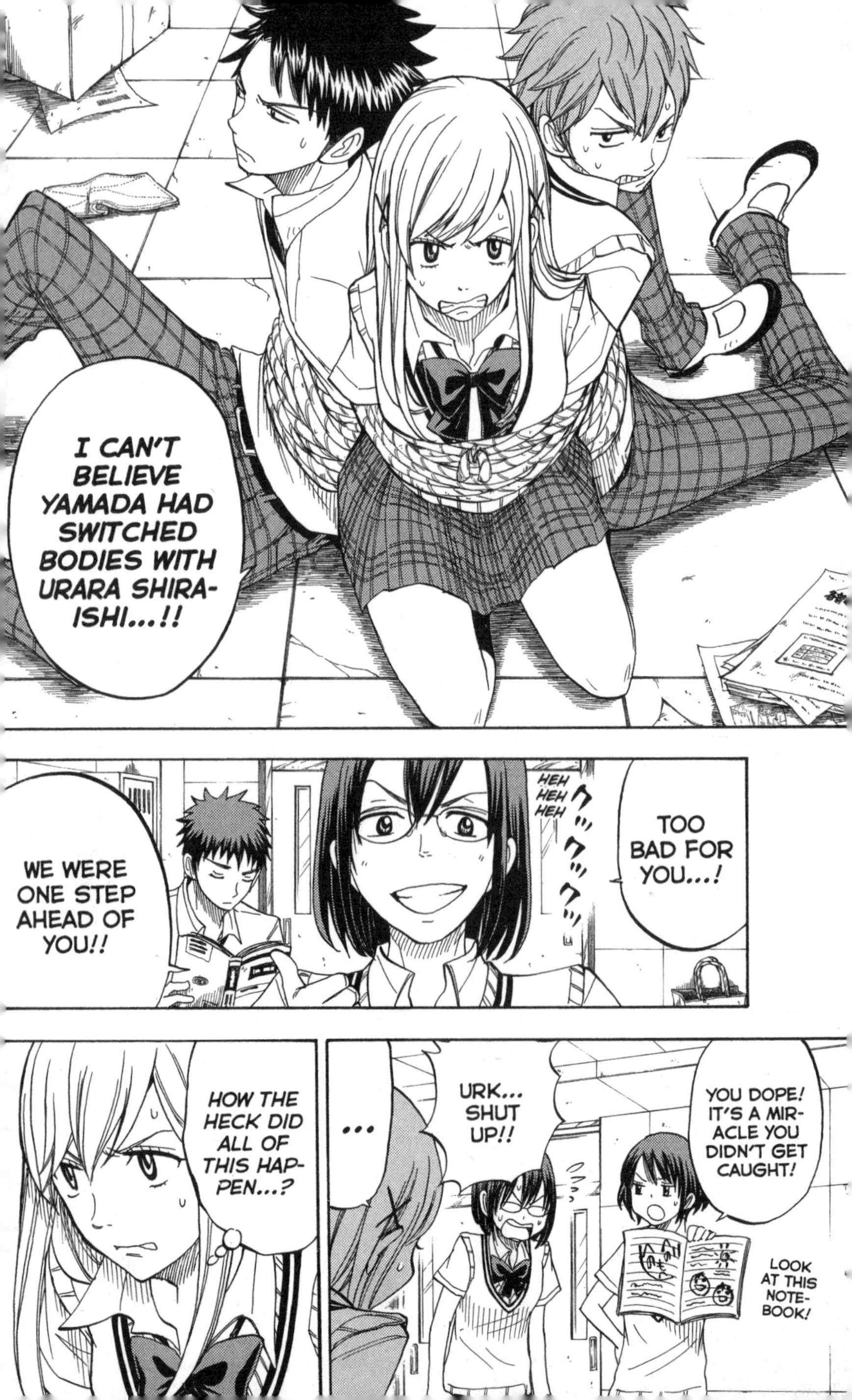
I CAN'T BELIEVE YAMADA HAD SWITCHED BODIES WITH URARA SHIRA-ISHI...!!
TOO BAD FOR YOU...!
HEH HEH HEH
WE WERE ONE STEP AHEAD OF YOU!!
YOU DOPE! IT'S A MIR-ACLE YOU DIDN'T GET CAUGHT!
LOOK AT THIS NOTE-BOOK!
URK... SHUT UP!!
...
HOW THE HECK DID ALL OF THIS HAP-PEN...?

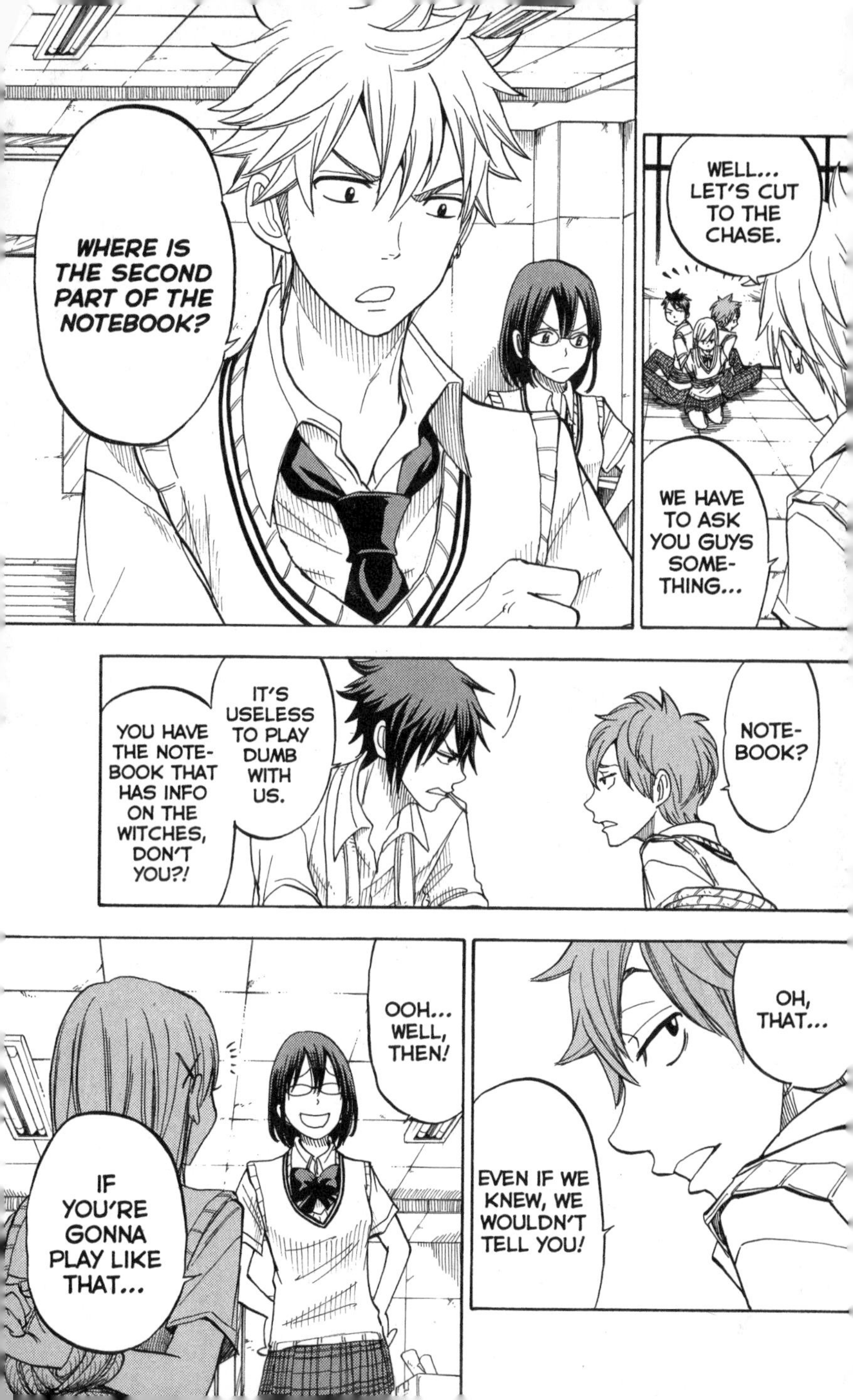
WELL... LET'S CUT TO THE CHASE.
WE HAVE TO ASK YOU GUYS SOMETHING...
WHERE IS THE SECOND PART OF THE NOTEBOOK?
NOTEBOOK?
IT'S USELESS TO PLAY DUMB WITH US.
YOU HAVE THE NOTEBOOK THAT HAS INFO ON THE WITCHES, DON'T YOU?!
OH, THAT...
EVEN IF WE KNEW, WE WOULDN'T TELL YOU!
OOH... WELL, THEN!
IF YOU'RE GONNA PLAY LIKE THAT...

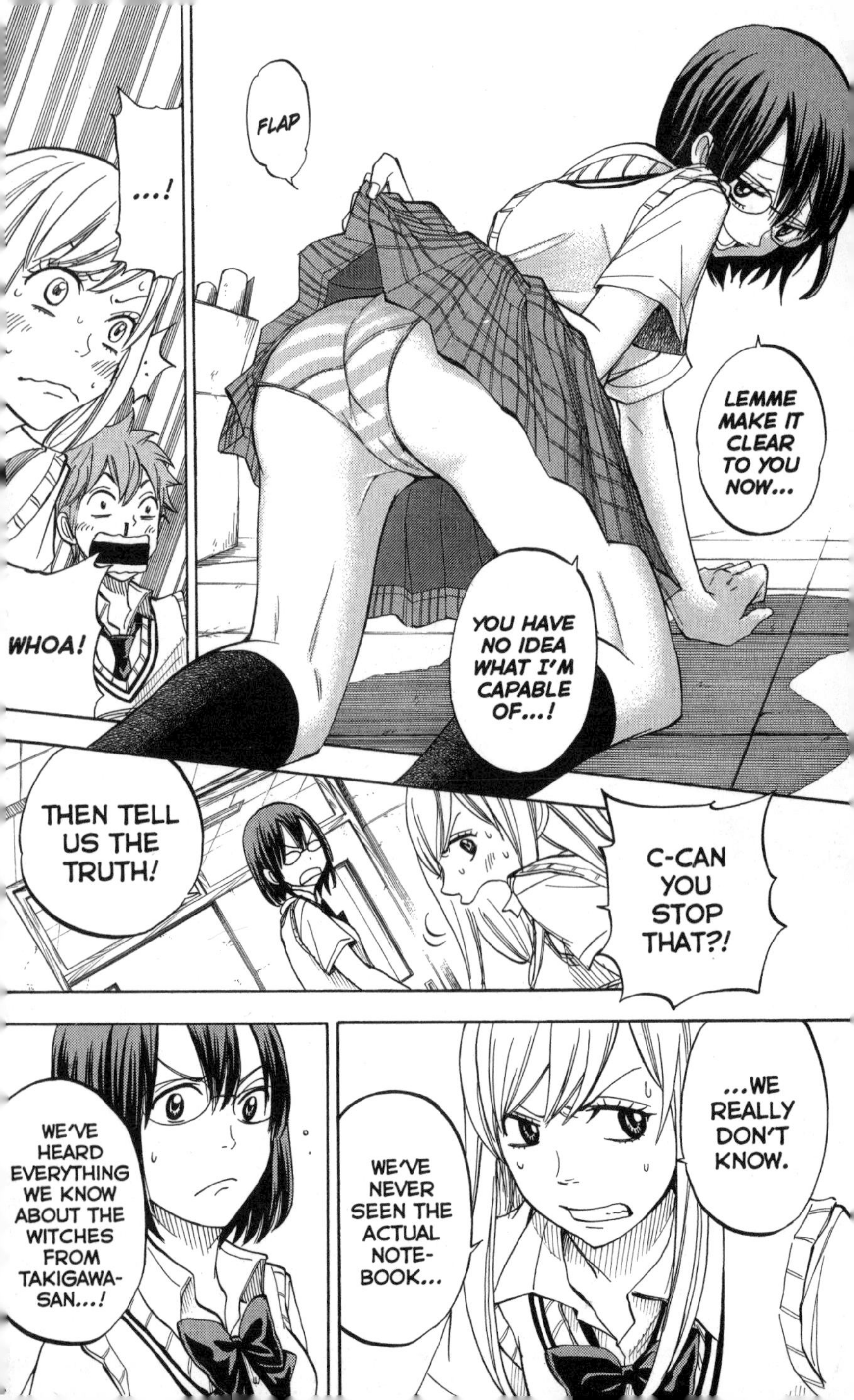
FLAP
LEMME MAKE IT CLEAR TO YOU NOW...
YOU HAVE NO IDEA WHAT I'M CAPABLE OF...!
...!
WHOA!
C-CAN YOU STOP THAT?!
THEN TELL US THE TRUTH!
...WE REALLY DON'T KNOW.
WE'VE NEVER SEEN THE ACTUAL NOTE-BOOK...
WE'VE HEARD EVERYTHING WE KNOW ABOUT THE WITCHES FROM TAKIGAWA-SAN...!

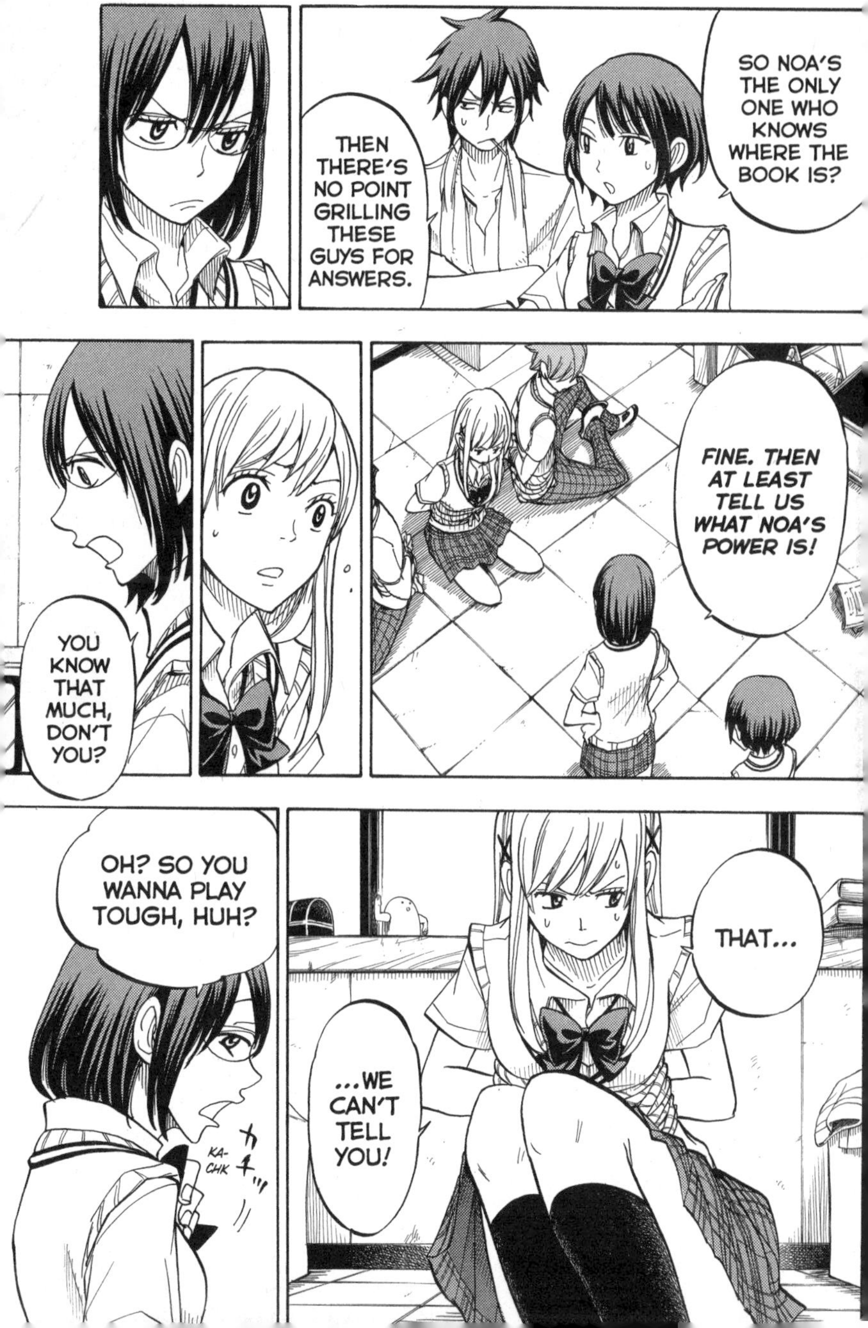
SO NOA'S THE ONLY ONE WHO KNOWS WHERE THE BOOK IS?
THEN THERE'S NO POINT GRILLING THESE GUYS FOR ANSWERS.
FINE. THEN AT LEAST TELL US WHAT NOA'S POWER IS!
YOU KNOW THAT MUCH, DON'T YOU?
THAT...
...WE CAN'T TELL YOU!
OH? SO YOU WANNA PLAY TOUGH, HUH?
KA-CHK

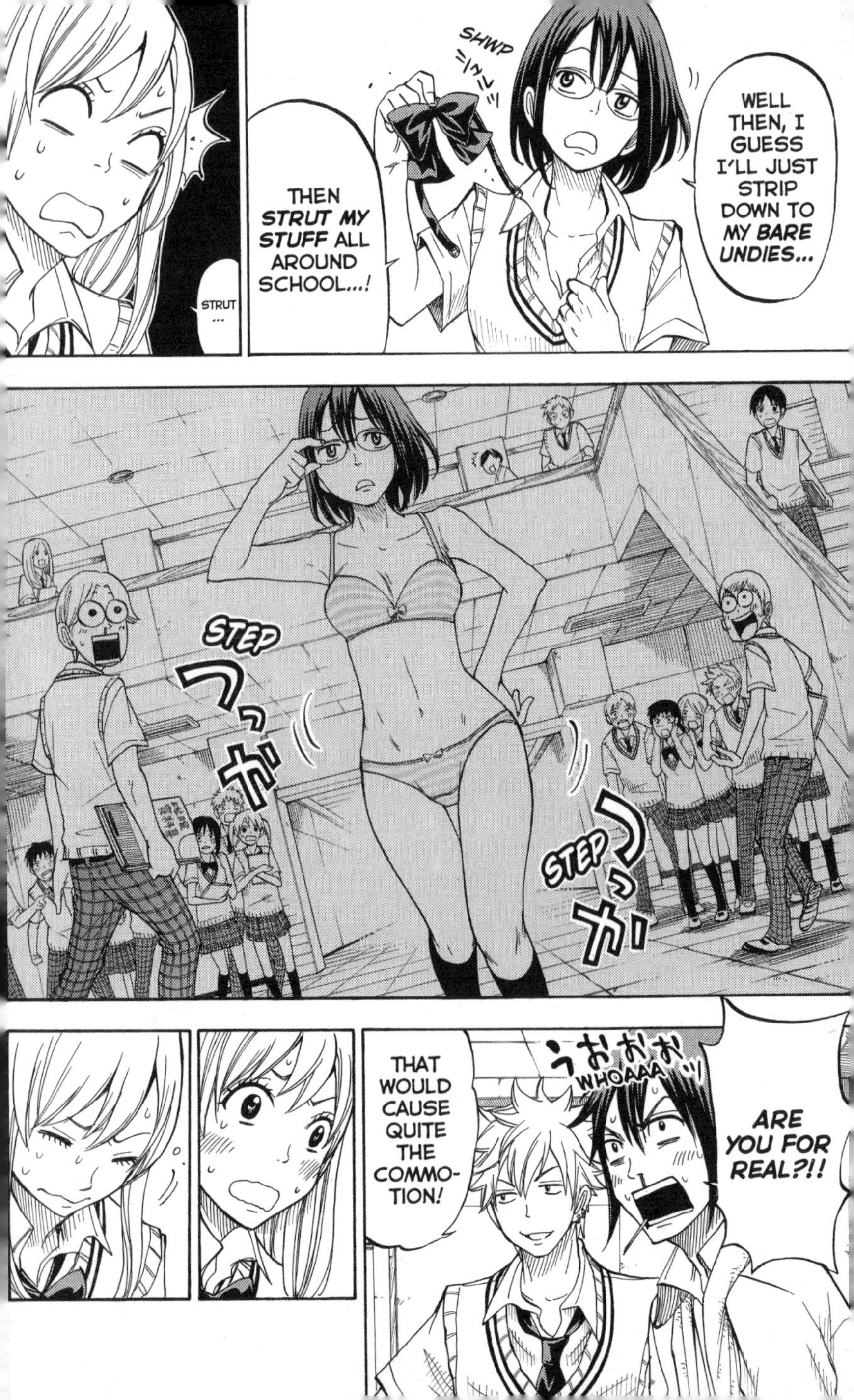
SHWP
WELL THEN, I GUESS I'LL JUST STRIP DOWN TO MY BARE UNDIES...
THEN STRUT MY STUFF ALL AROUND SCHOOL...!
STRUT ...
STEP
STEP
うおおお
WHOAAA
ARE YOU FOR REAL?!!
THAT WOULD CAUSE QUITE THE COMMOTION!

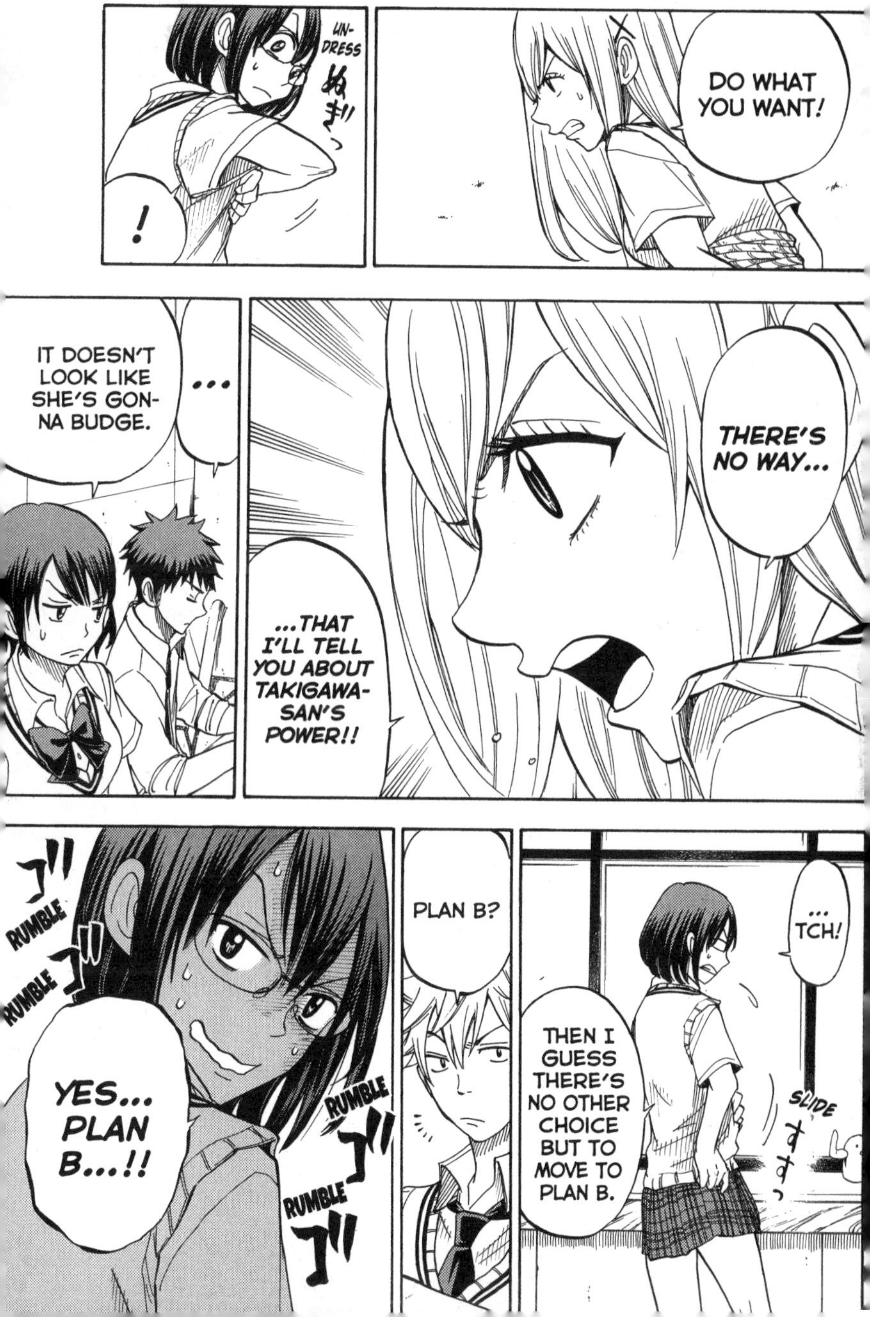
DO WHAT YOU WANT!
UN-DRESS
ぬぎっ
!
THERE'S NO WAY...
...THAT I'LL TELL YOU ABOUT TAKIGAWA-SAN'S POWER!!
...
IT DOESN'T LOOK LIKE SHE'S GON-NA BUDGE.
...TCH!
SLIDE
すすっ
THEN I GUESS THERE'S NO OTHER CHOICE BUT TO MOVE TO PLAN B.
PLAN B?
RUMBLE
ゴゴ
RUMBLE
ゴゴ
YES... PLAN B...!!
RUMBLE
ゴゴ
RUMBLE
ゴゴ

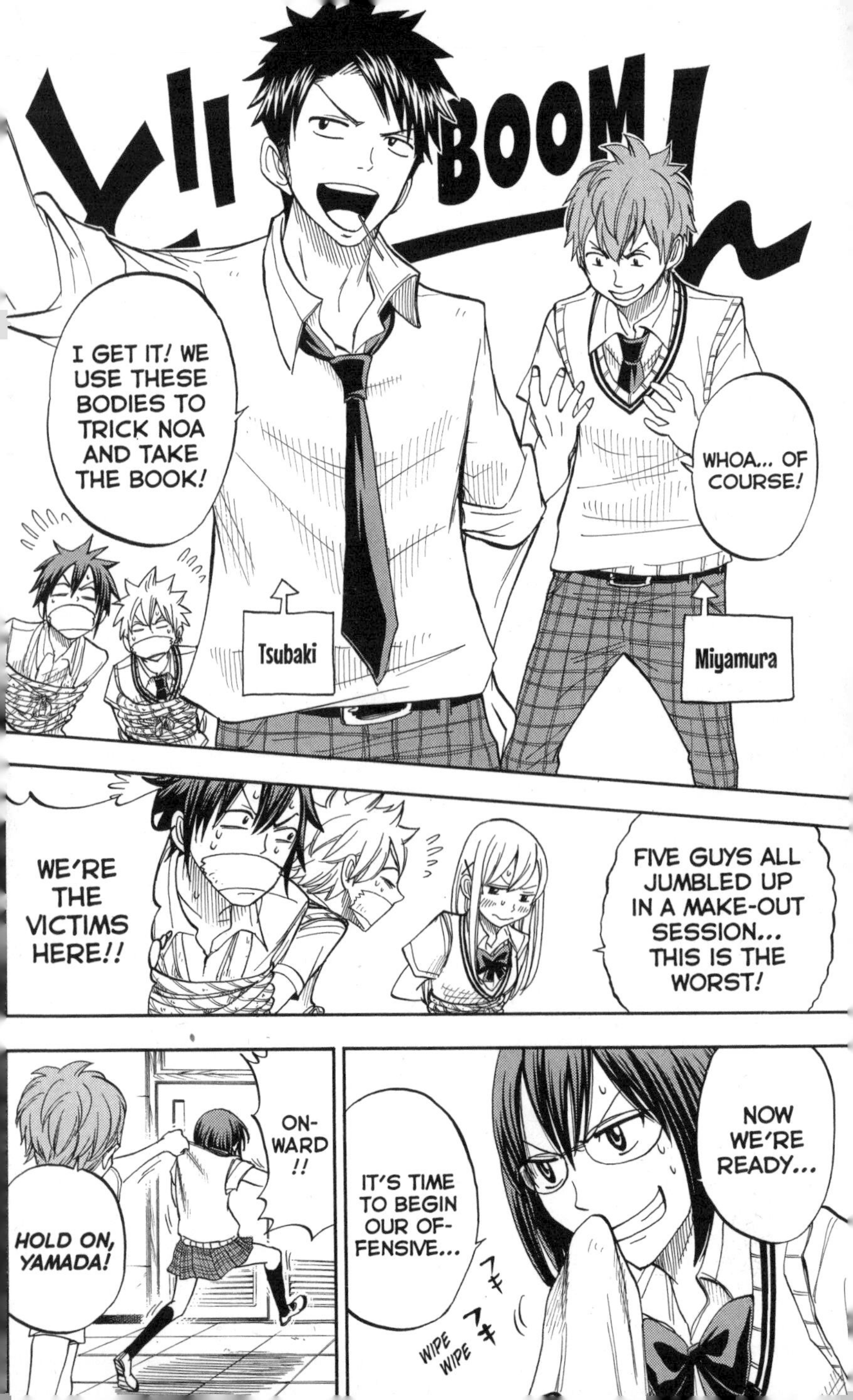
BOOM!
I GET IT! WE USE THESE BODIES TO TRICK NOA AND TAKE THE BOOK!
WHOA... OF COURSE!
Miyamura
Tsubaki
FIVE GUYS ALL JUMBLED UP IN A MAKE-OUT SESSION... THIS IS THE WORST!
WE'RE THE VICTIMS HERE!!
NOW WE'RE READY...
IT'S TIME TO BEGIN OUR OF-FENSIVE...
WIPE WIPE
ON-WARD!!
HOLD ON, YAMADA!

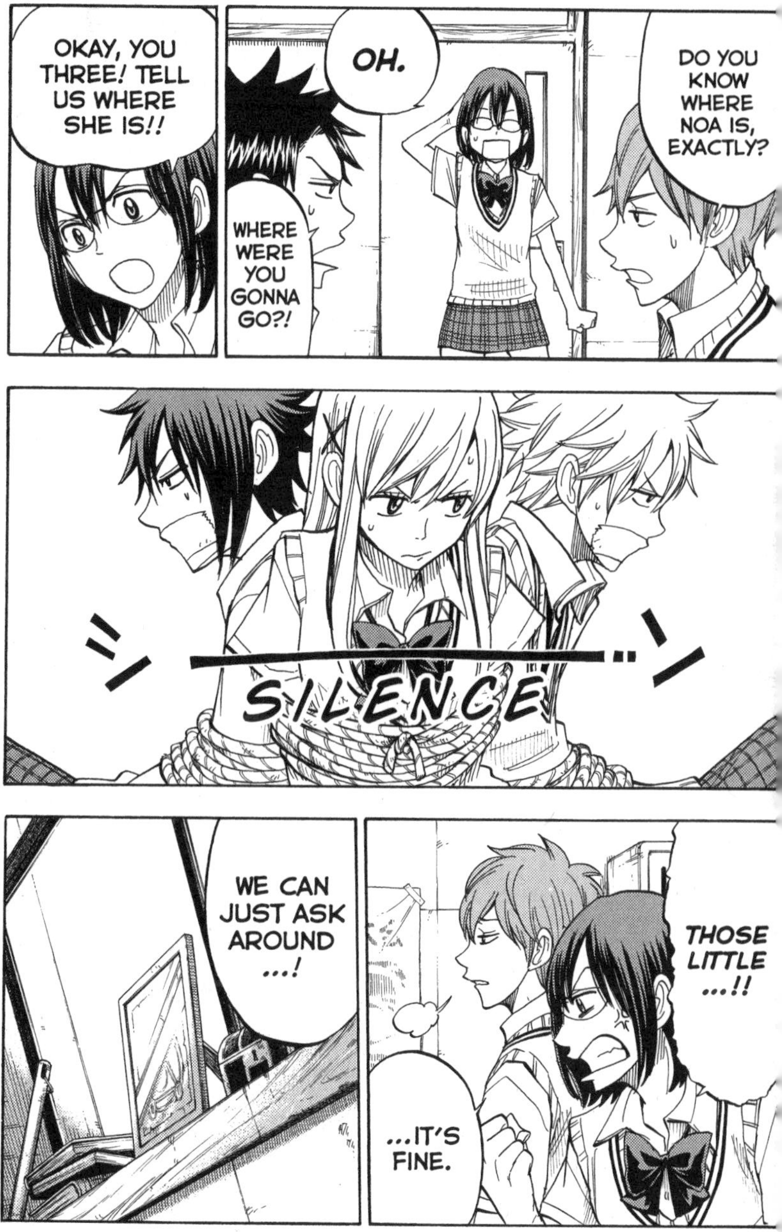
DO YOU KNOW WHERE NOA IS, EXACTLY?
OH.
WHERE WERE YOU GONNA GO?!
OKAY, YOU THREE! TELL US WHERE SHE IS!!
SILENCE
THOSE LITTLE ...!!
...IT'S FINE.
WE CAN JUST ASK AROUND ...!

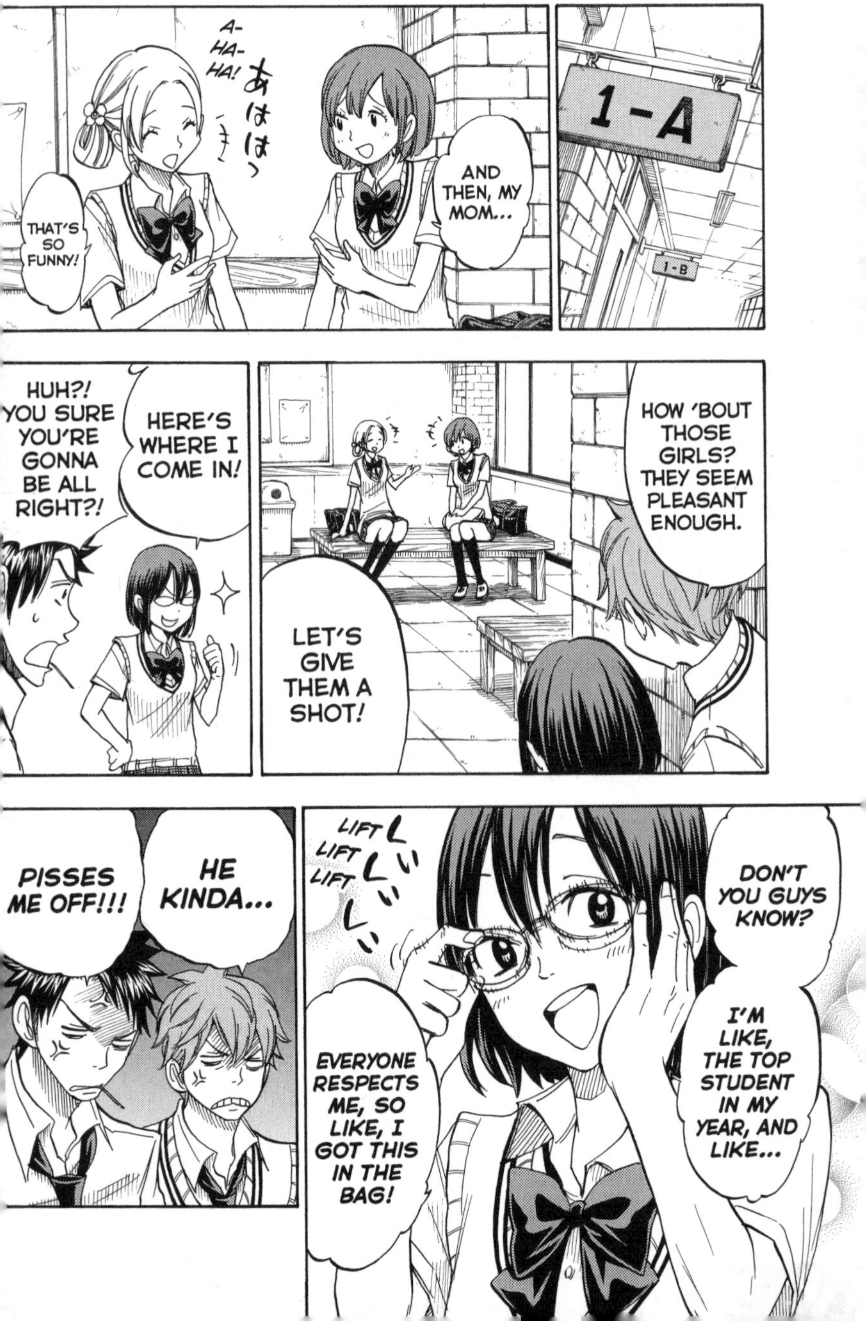
1-A
1-B
AND THEN, MY MOM...
A-HA-HA!
あははっ
THAT'S SO FUNNY!
HOW 'BOUT THOSE GIRLS? THEY SEEM PLEASANT ENOUGH.
LET'S GIVE THEM A SHOT!
HERE'S WHERE I COME IN!
HUH?! YOU SURE YOU'RE GONNA BE ALL RIGHT?!
DON'T YOU GUYS KNOW?
I'M LIKE, THE TOP STUDENT IN MY YEAR, AND LIKE...
LIFT LIFT LIFT
EVERYONE RESPECTS ME, SO LIKE, I GOT THIS IN THE BAG!
HE KINDA...
PISSES ME OFF!!!

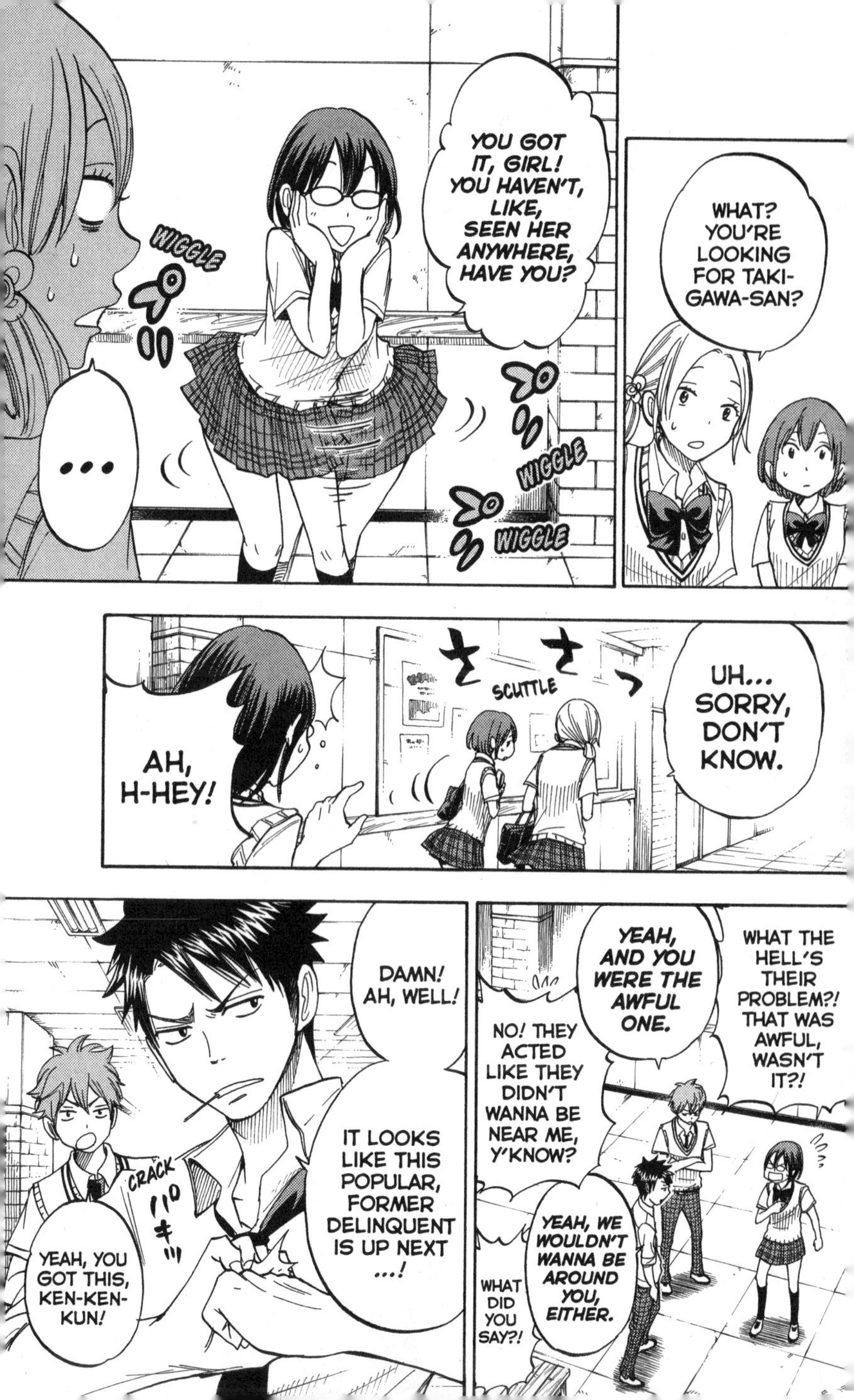

WHAT? YOU'RE LOOKING FOR TAKI-GAWA-SAN?
YOU GOT IT, GIRL! YOU HAVEN'T, LIKE, SEEN HER ANYWHERE, HAVE YOU?
WIGGLE
WIGGLE
WIGGLE
...
UH... SORRY, DON'T KNOW.
SCUTTLE
AH, H-HEY!
WHAT THE HELL'S THEIR PROBLEM?! THAT WAS AWFUL, WASN'T IT?!
YEAH, AND YOU WERE THE AWFUL ONE.
NO! THEY ACTED LIKE THEY DIDN'T WANNA BE NEAR ME, Y'KNOW?
YEAH, WE WOULDN'T WANNA BE AROUND YOU, EITHER.
WHAT DID YOU SAY?!
DAMN! AH, WELL!
IT LOOKS LIKE THIS POPULAR, FORMER DELINQUENT IS UP NEXT ...!
CRACK
YEAH, YOU GOT THIS, KEN-KEN-KUN!

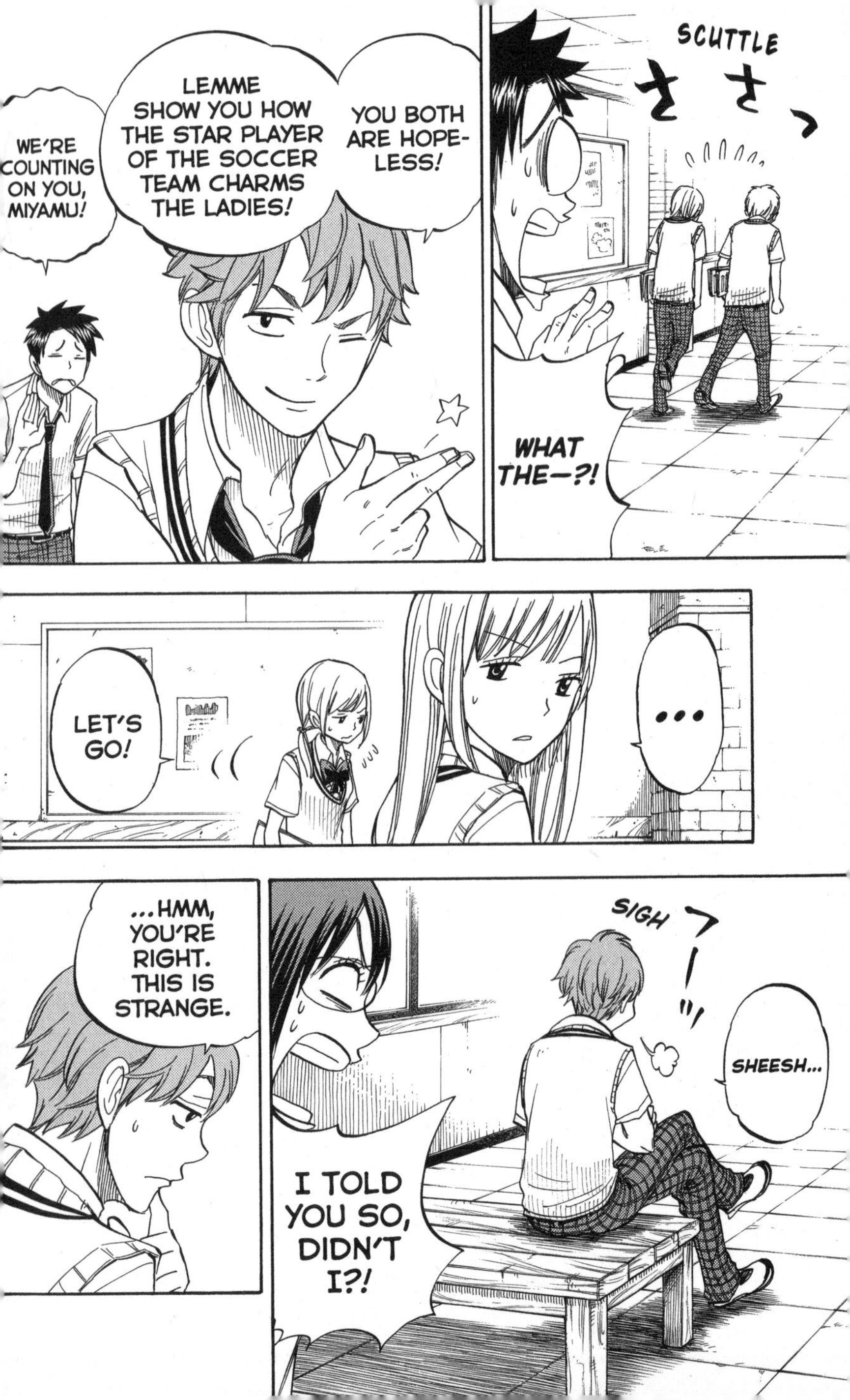
SCUTTLE
さ さっ
WHAT THE—?!
YOU BOTH ARE HOPELESS!
LEMME SHOW YOU HOW THE STAR PLAYER OF THE SOCCER TEAM CHARMS THE LADIES!
WE'RE COUNTING ON YOU, MIYAMU!
...
LET'S GO!
SIGH
SHEESH...
I TOLD YOU SO, DIDN'T I?!
...HMM, YOU'RE RIGHT. THIS IS STRANGE.

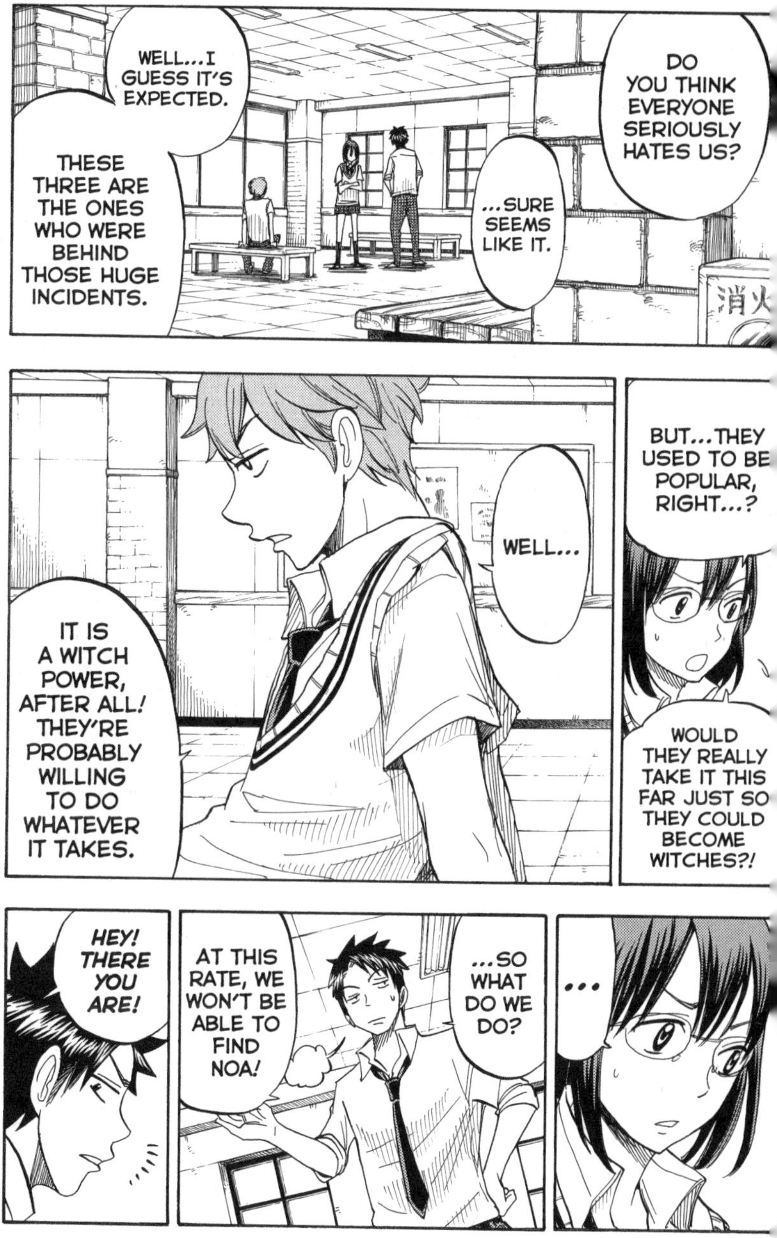
DO YOU THINK EVERYONE SERIOUSLY HATES US?
...SURE SEEMS LIKE IT.
WELL...I GUESS IT'S EXPECTED.
THESE THREE ARE THE ONES WHO WERE BEHIND THOSE HUGE INCIDENTS.
BUT...THEY USED TO BE POPULAR, RIGHT...?
WOULD THEY REALLY TAKE IT THIS FAR JUST SO THEY COULD BECOME WITCHES?!
WELL...
IT IS A WITCH POWER, AFTER ALL! THEY'RE PROBABLY WILLING TO DO WHATEVER IT TAKES.
...
...SO WHAT DO WE DO?
AT THIS RATE, WE WON'T BE ABLE TO FIND NOA!
HEY! THERE YOU ARE!

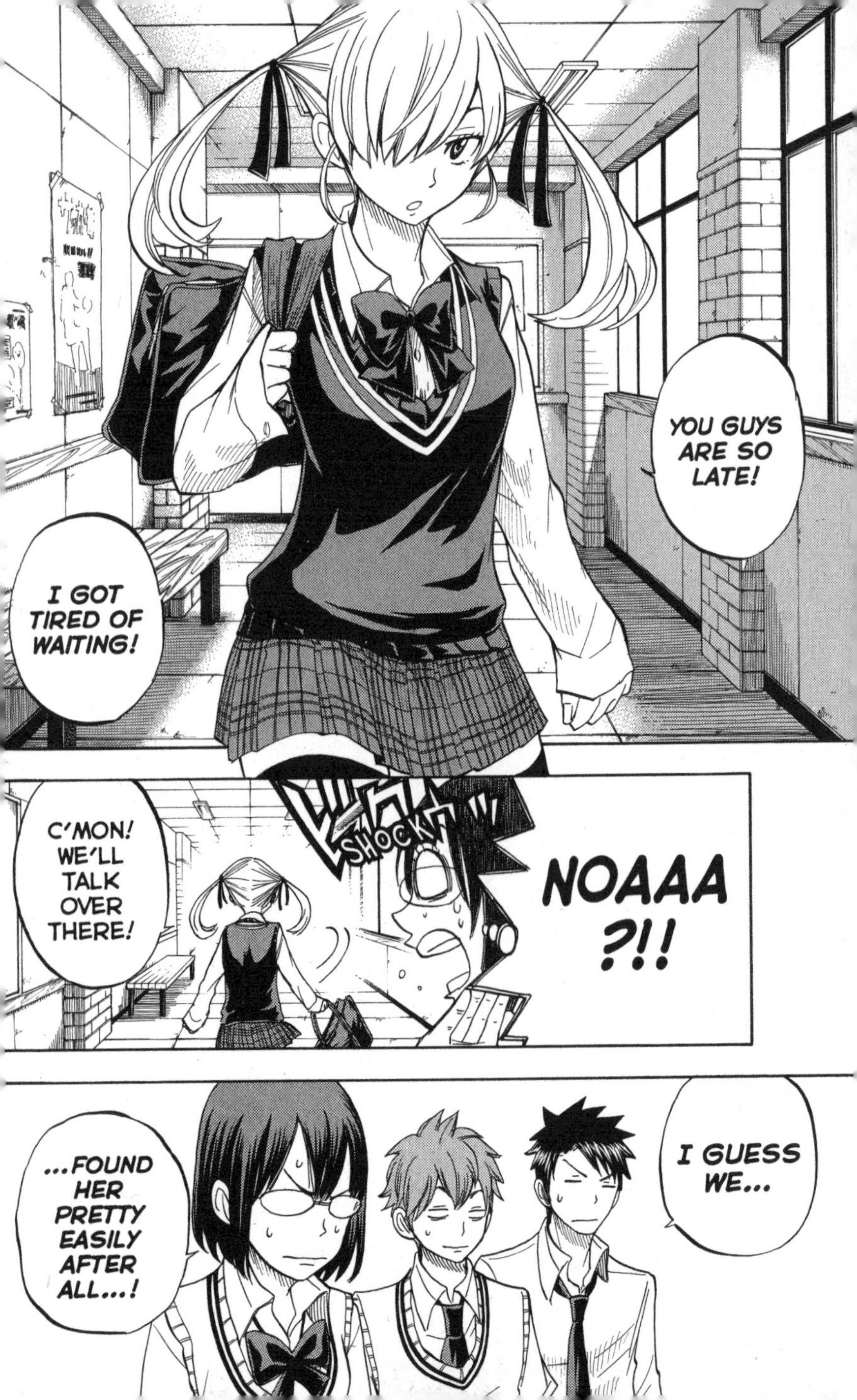
YOU GUYS ARE SO LATE!
I GOT TIRED OF WAITING!
SHOCK
NOAAA ?!!
C'MON! WE'LL TALK OVER THERE!
I GUESS WE...
...FOUND HER PRETTY EASILY AFTER ALL...!

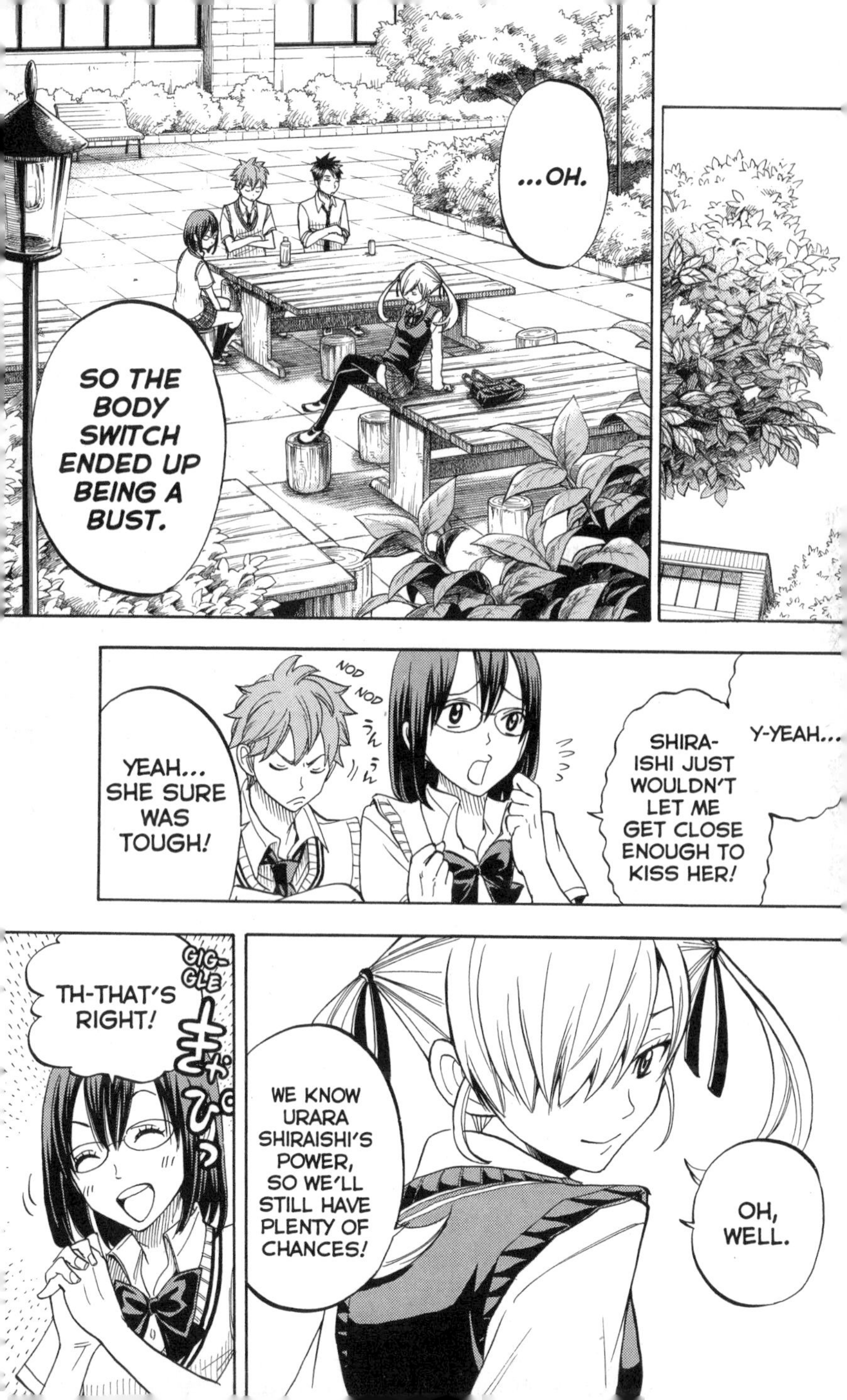
...OH.
SO THE BODY SWITCH ENDED UP BEING A BUST.
Y-YEAH...
SHIRA-ISHI JUST WOULDN'T LET ME GET CLOSE ENOUGH TO KISS HER!
NOD NOD
うんうん
YEAH... SHE SURE WAS TOUGH!
OH, WELL.
WE KNOW URARA SHIRAISHI'S POWER, SO WE'LL STILL HAVE PLENTY OF CHANCES!
GIG-GLE
きゃぴっ
TH-THAT'S RIGHT!

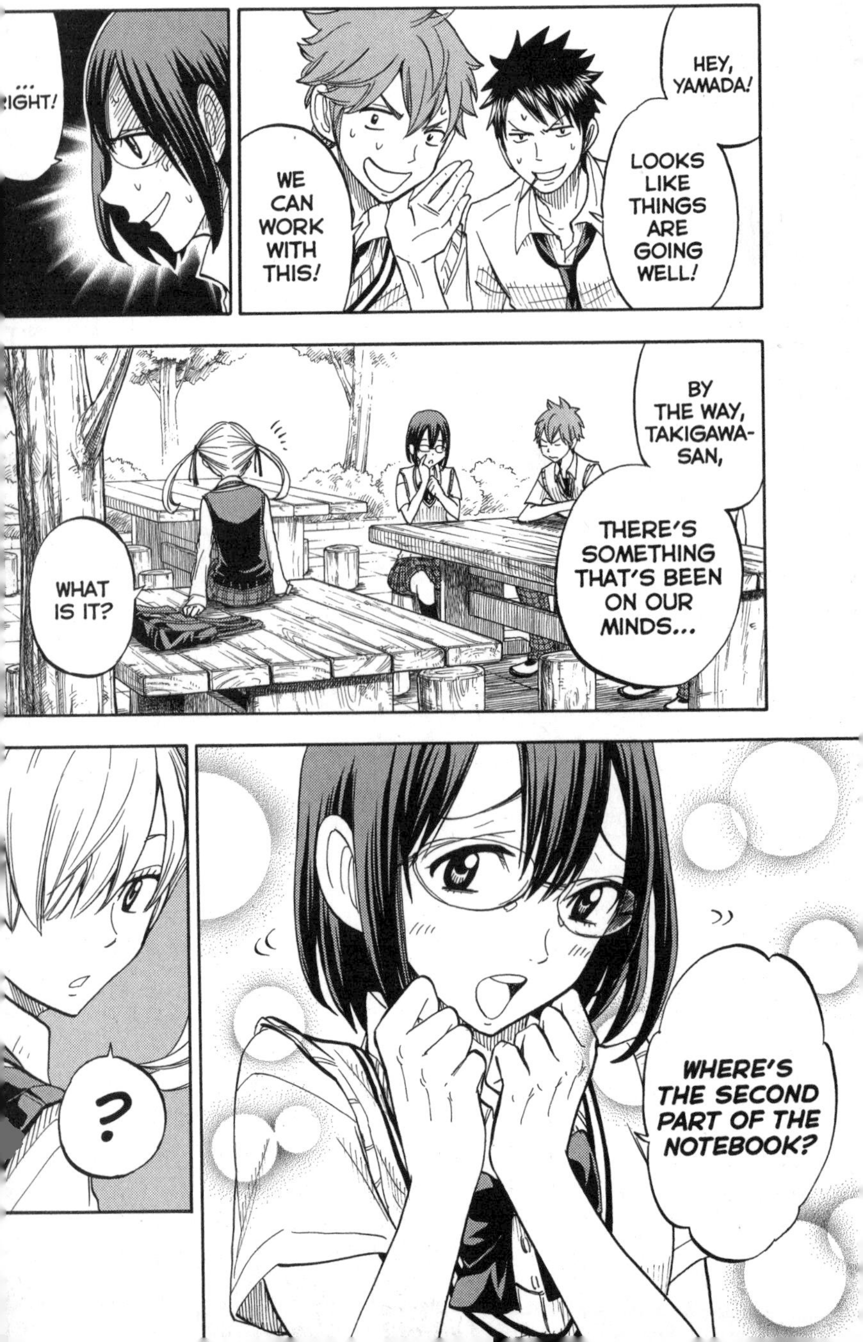
HEY, YAMADA!
LOOKS LIKE THINGS ARE GOING WELL!
WE CAN WORK WITH THIS!
...RIGHT!
BY THE WAY, TAKIGAWA-SAN,
THERE'S SOMETHING THAT'S BEEN ON OUR MINDS...
WHAT IS IT?
WHERE'S THE SECOND PART OF THE NOTEBOOK?
?

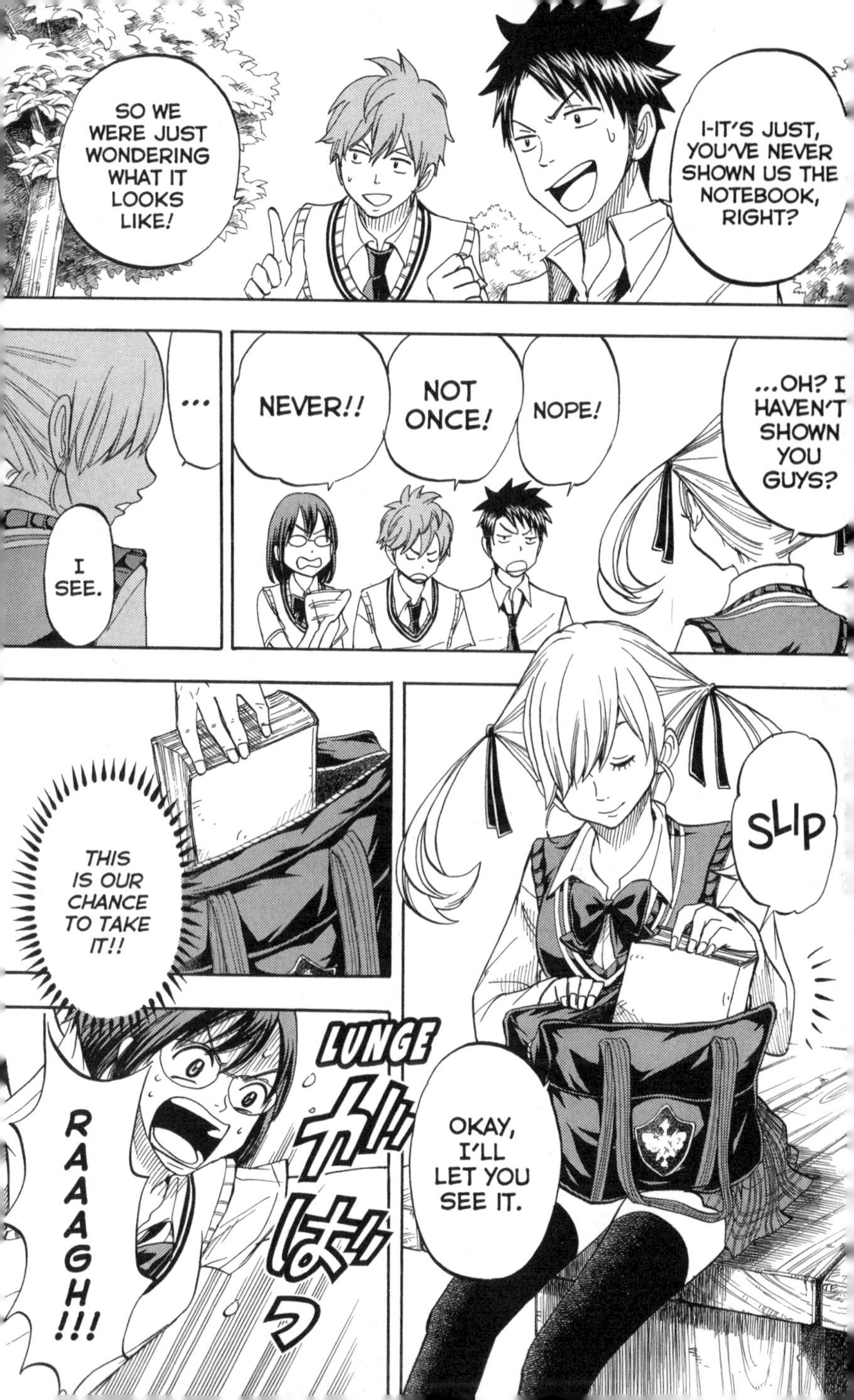
I-IT'S JUST, YOU'VE NEVER SHOWN US THE NOTEBOOK, RIGHT?
SO WE WERE JUST WONDERING WHAT IT LOOKS LIKE!
...OH? I HAVEN'T SHOWN YOU GUYS?
NOPE!
NOT ONCE!
NEVER!!
...
I SEE.
SLIP
OKAY, I'LL LET YOU SEE IT.
THIS IS OUR CHANCE TO TAKE IT!!
LUNGE
RAAAGH!!!

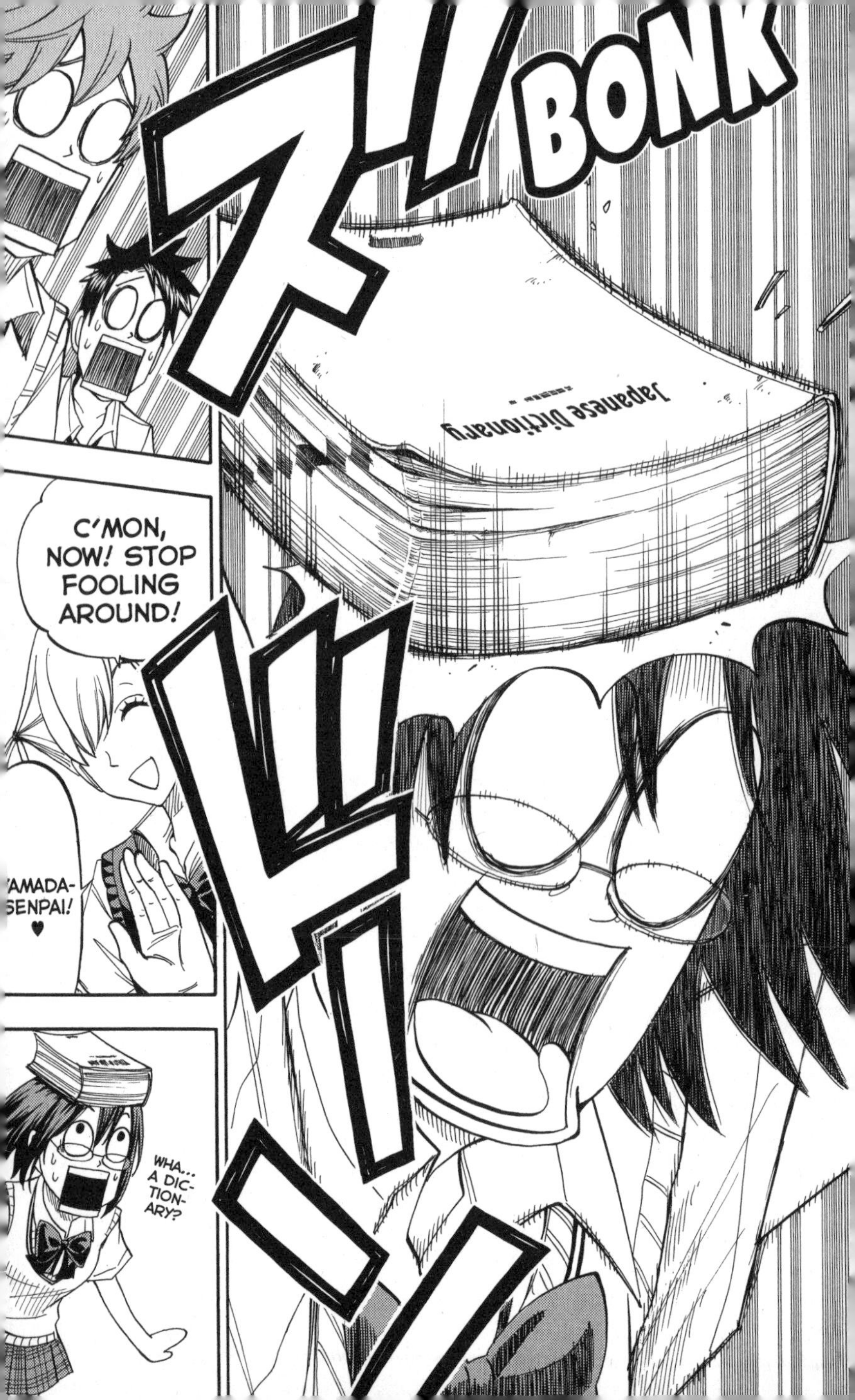
BONK
Japanese Dictionary
C'MON, NOW! STOP FOOLING AROUND!
YAMADA-SENPAI! ♥
WHA... A DICTIONARY?

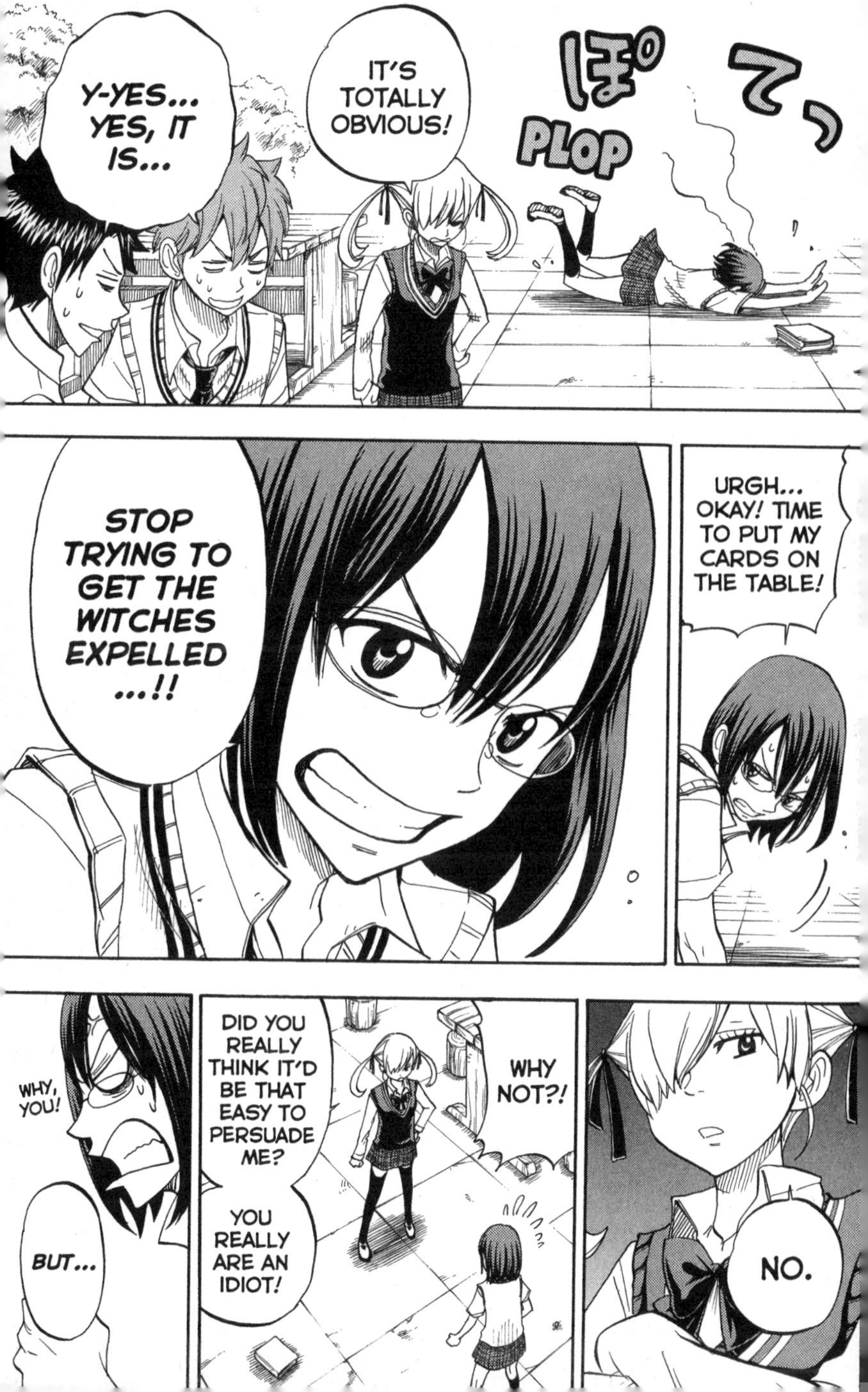
ぽてっ
PLOP
IT'S TOTALLY OBVIOUS!
Y-YES... YES, IT IS...
URGH... OKAY! TIME TO PUT MY CARDS ON THE TABLE!
STOP TRYING TO GET THE WITCHES EXPELLED ...!!
NO.
WHY NOT?!
DID YOU REALLY THINK IT'D BE THAT EASY TO PERSUADE ME?
YOU REALLY ARE AN IDIOT!
WHY, YOU!
BUT...

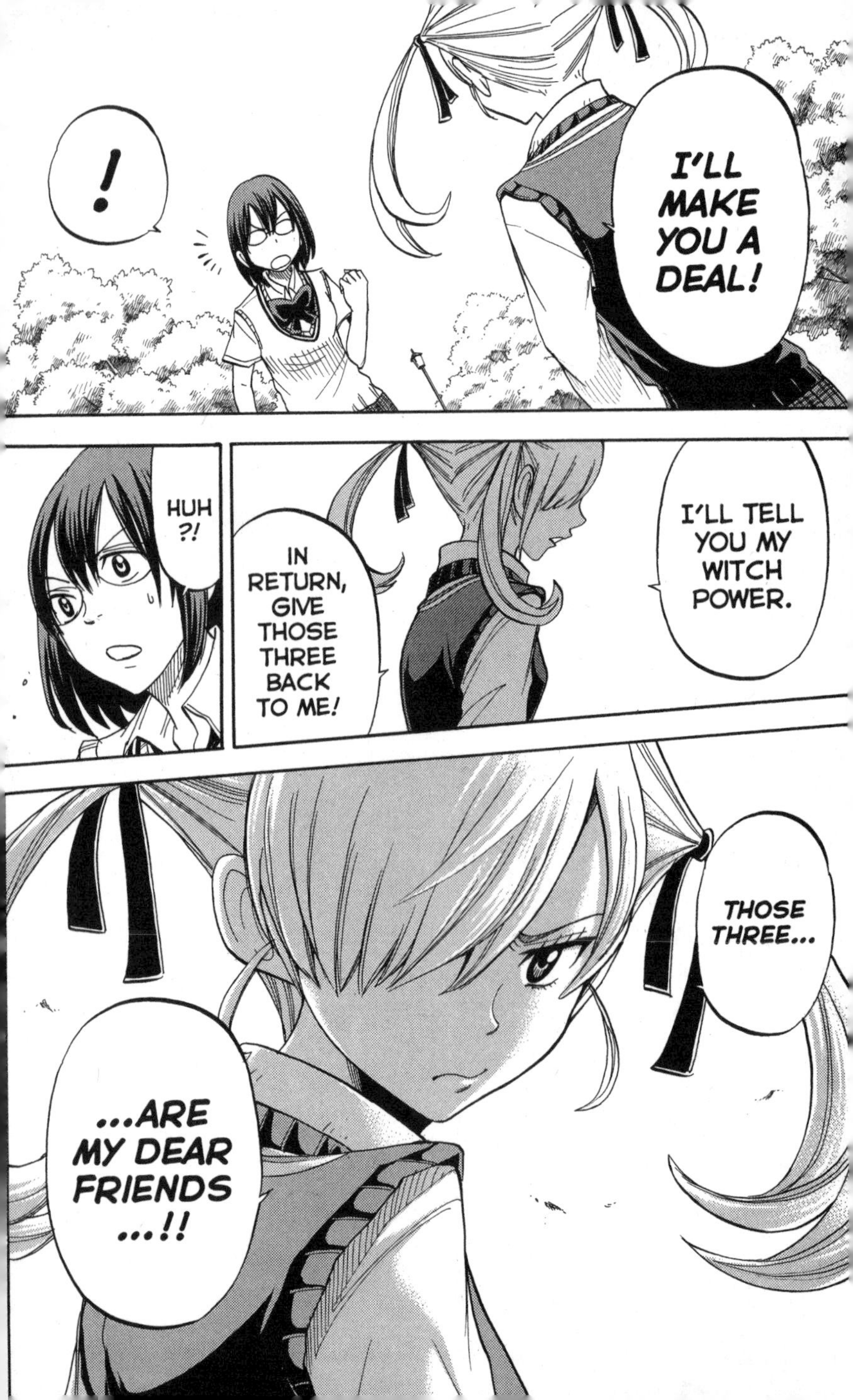
I'LL MAKE YOU A DEAL!
!
I'LL TELL YOU MY WITCH POWER.
IN RETURN, GIVE THOSE THREE BACK TO ME!
HUH ?!
THOSE THREE...
...ARE MY DEAR FRIENDS ...!!

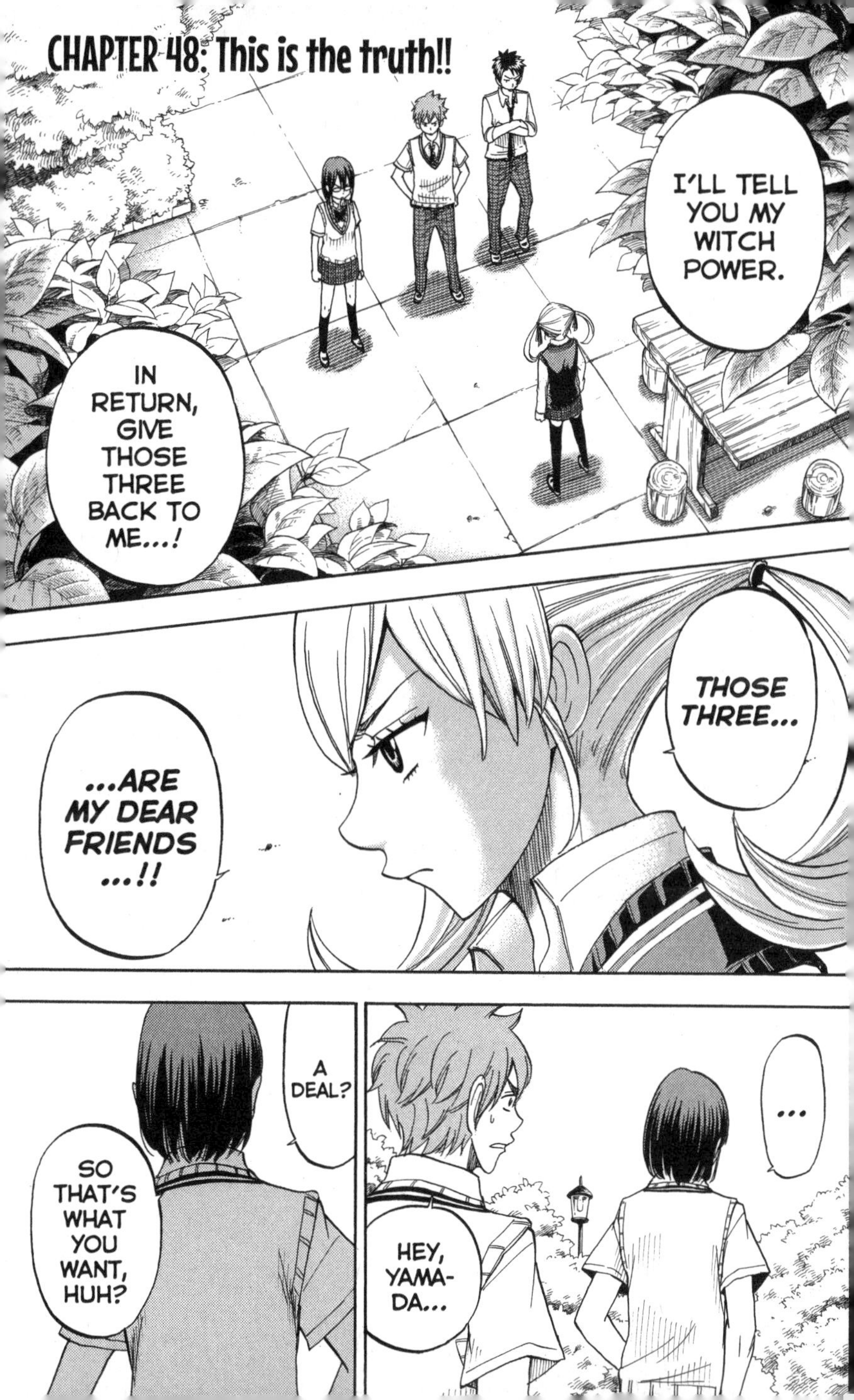
CHAPTER 48: This is the truth!!
I'LL TELL YOU MY WITCH POWER.
IN RETURN, GIVE THOSE THREE BACK TO ME...!
THOSE THREE...
...ARE MY DEAR FRIENDS...!!
...
HEY, YAMADA...
A DEAL?
SO THAT'S WHAT YOU WANT, HUH?

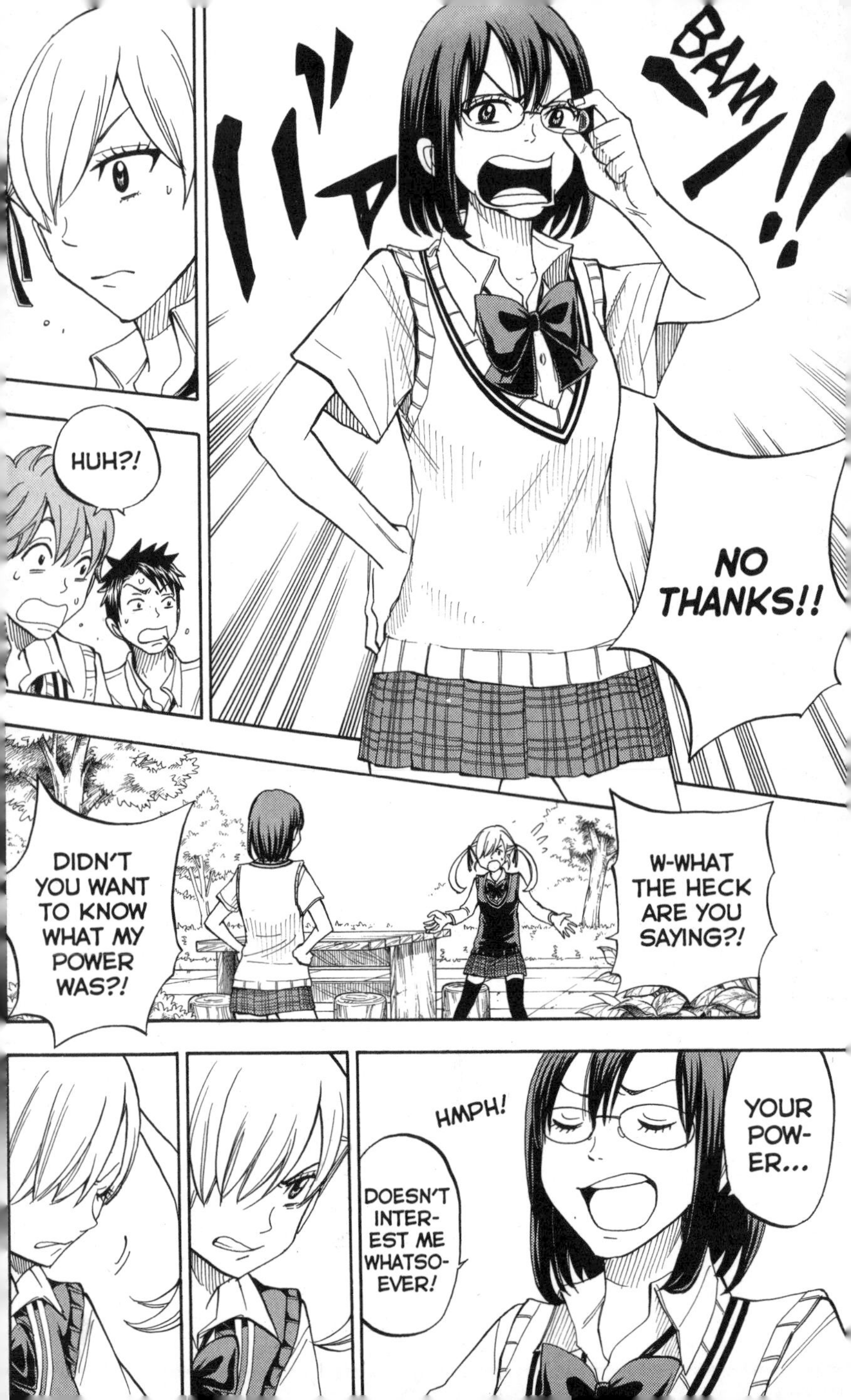
BAM!!
NO THANKS!!
HUH?!
W-WHAT THE HECK ARE YOU SAYING?!
DIDN'T YOU WANT TO KNOW WHAT MY POWER WAS?!
YOUR POWER...
HMPH!
DOESN'T INTEREST ME WHATSOEVER!

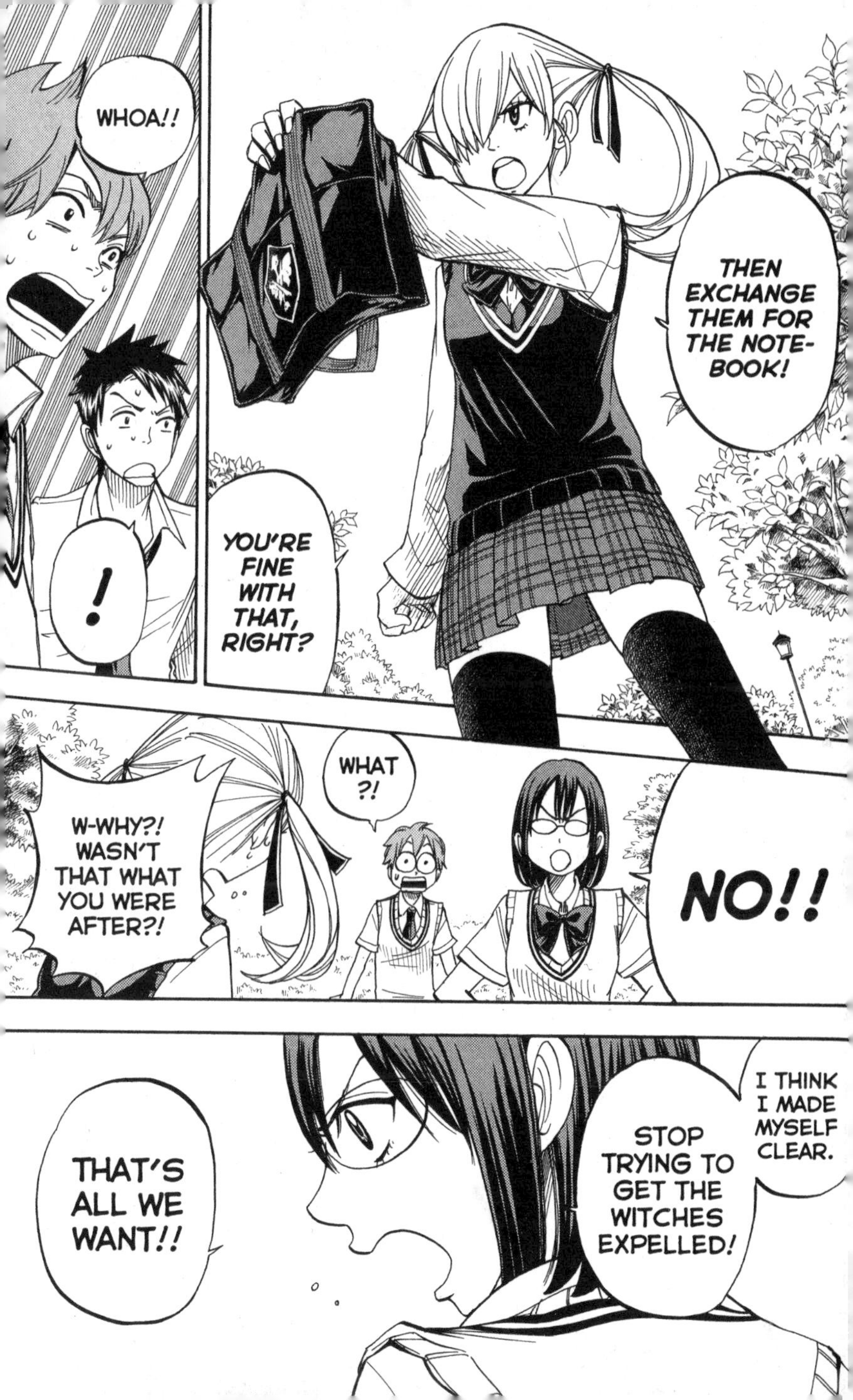
THEN EXCHANGE THEM FOR THE NOTE-BOOK!
YOU'RE FINE WITH THAT, RIGHT?
WHOA!!
!
NO!!
WHAT ?!
W-WHY?! WASN'T THAT WHAT YOU WERE AFTER?!
I THINK I MADE MYSELF CLEAR.
STOP TRYING TO GET THE WITCHES EXPELLED!
THAT'S ALL WE WANT!!

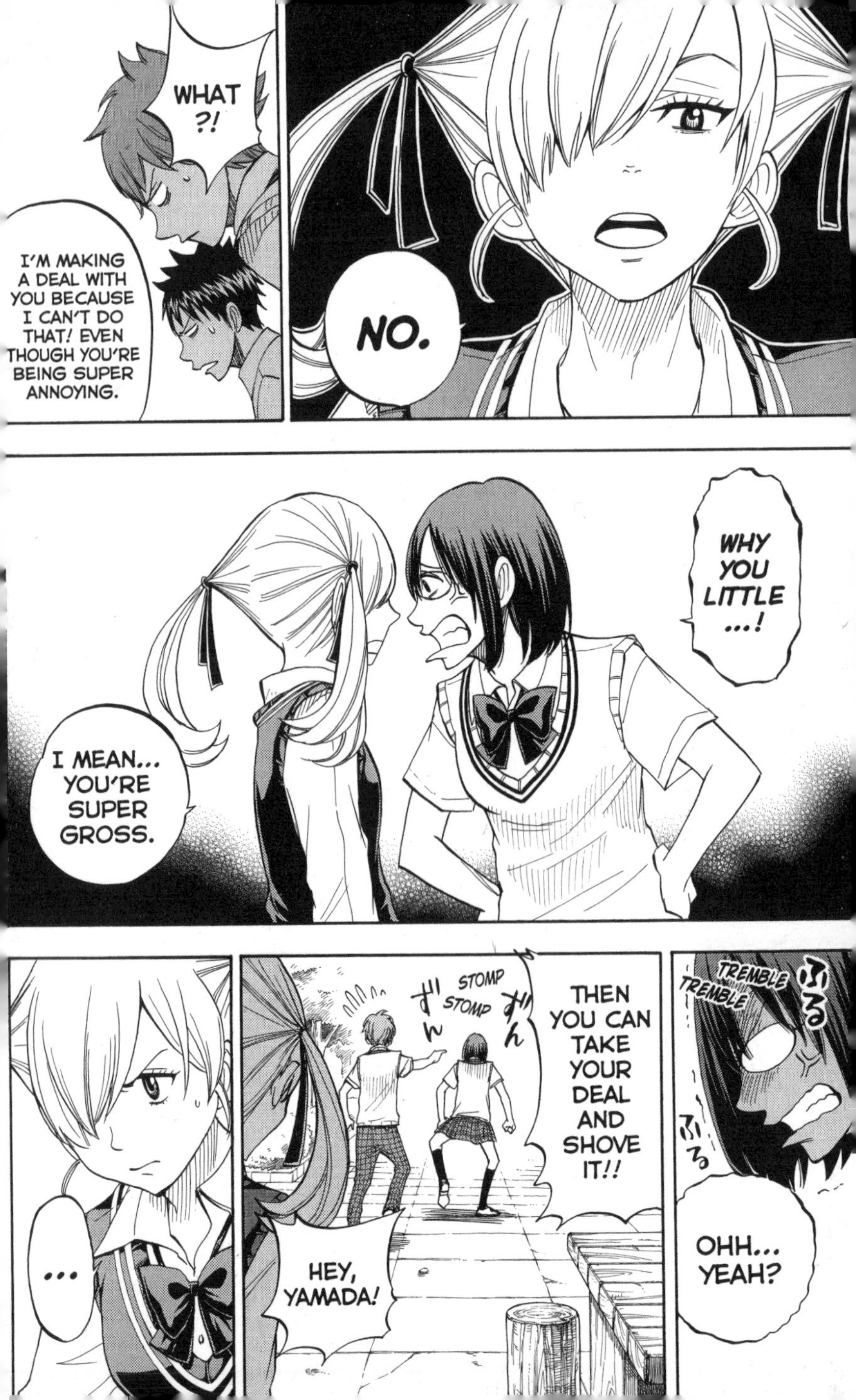
NO.
WHAT ?!
I'M MAKING A DEAL WITH YOU BECAUSE I CAN'T DO THAT! EVEN THOUGH YOU'RE BEING SUPER ANNOYING.
WHY YOU LITTLE ...!
I MEAN... YOU'RE SUPER GROSS.
ふる
TREMBLE TREMBLE
ふる
OHH... YEAH?
ずん
ずん
STOMP STOMP
THEN YOU CAN TAKE YOUR DEAL AND SHOVE IT!!
HEY, YAMADA!
...

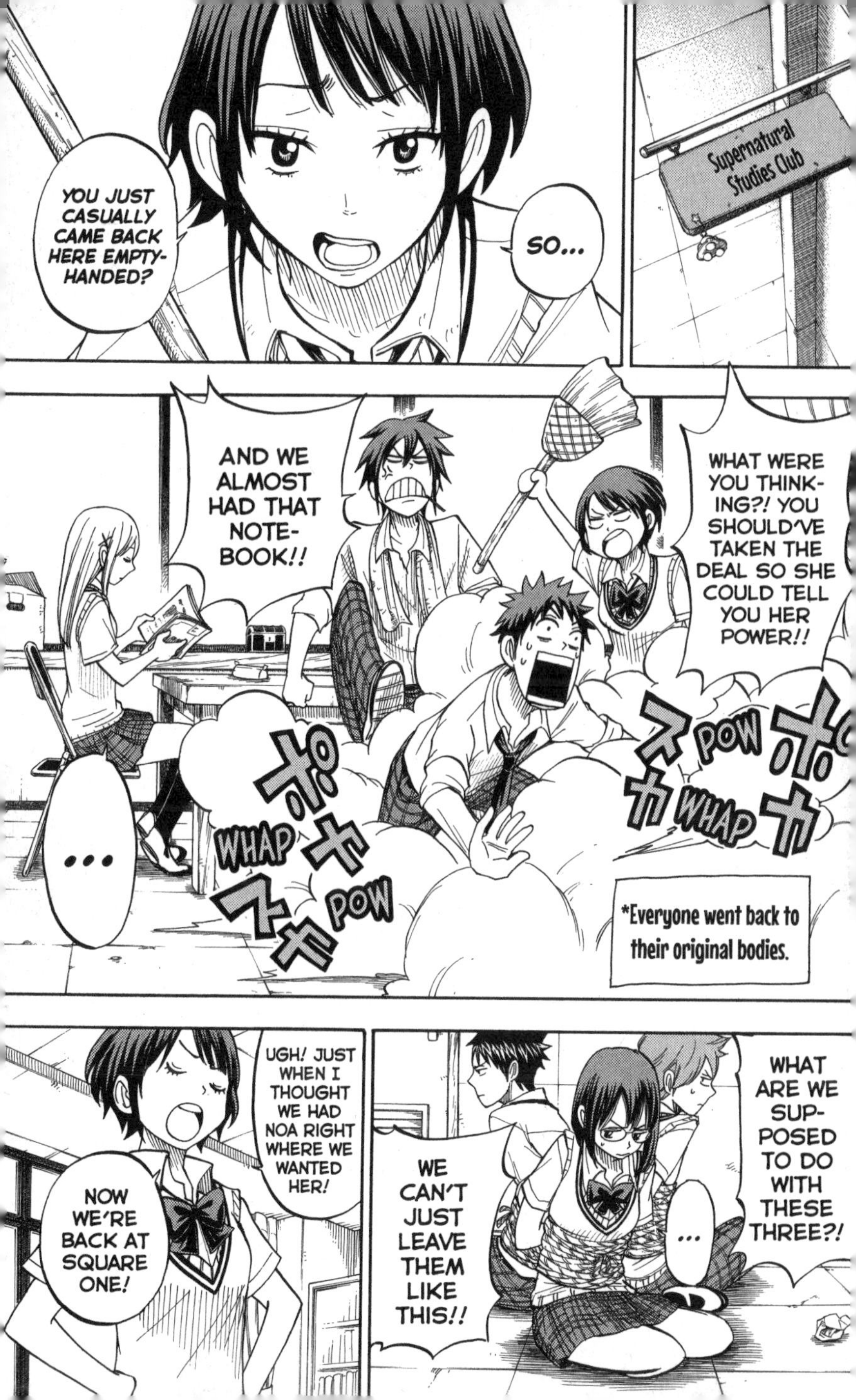
Supernatural Studies Club
SO...
YOU JUST CASUALLY CAME BACK HERE EMPTY-HANDED?
WHAT WERE YOU THINKING?! YOU SHOULD'VE TAKEN THE DEAL SO SHE COULD TELL YOU HER POWER!!
AND WE ALMOST HAD THAT NOTEBOOK!!
ポカ POW
ポカ WHAP
ポカ WHAP
ポカ POW
*Everyone went back to their original bodies.
...
WHAT ARE WE SUPPOSED TO DO WITH THESE THREE?!
...
WE CAN'T JUST LEAVE THEM LIKE THIS!!
UGH! JUST WHEN I THOUGHT WE HAD NOA RIGHT WHERE WE WANTED HER!
NOW WE'RE BACK AT SQUARE ONE!

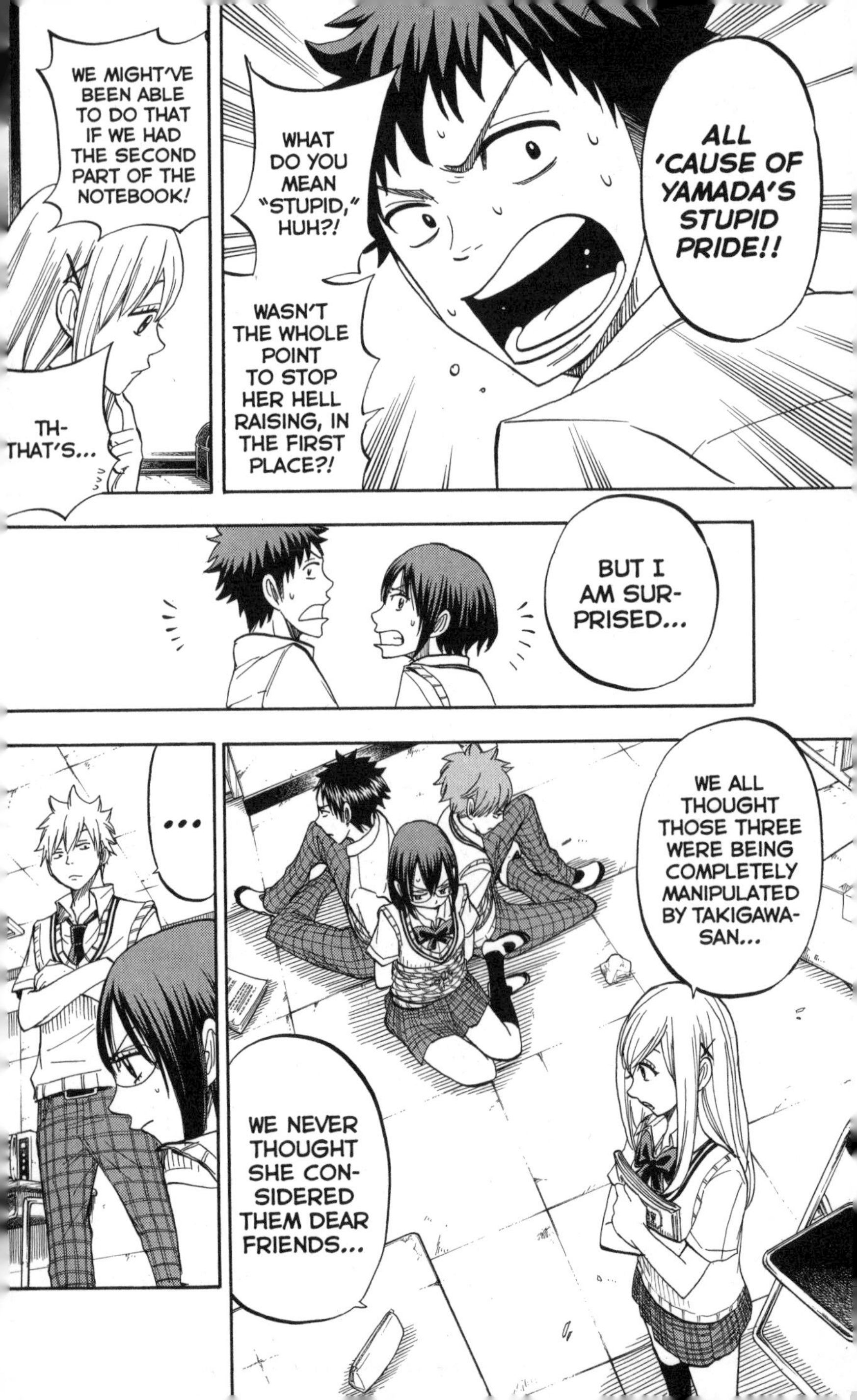
ALL 'CAUSE OF YAMADA'S STUPID PRIDE!!
WHAT DO YOU MEAN "STUPID," HUH?!
WASN'T THE WHOLE POINT TO STOP HER HELL RAISING, IN THE FIRST PLACE?!
WE MIGHT'VE BEEN ABLE TO DO THAT IF WE HAD THE SECOND PART OF THE NOTEBOOK!
TH- THAT'S...
BUT I AM SUR- PRISED...
WE ALL THOUGHT THOSE THREE WERE BEING COMPLETELY MANIPULATED BY TAKIGAWA-SAN...
WE NEVER THOUGHT SHE CON- SIDERED THEM DEAR FRIENDS...
...

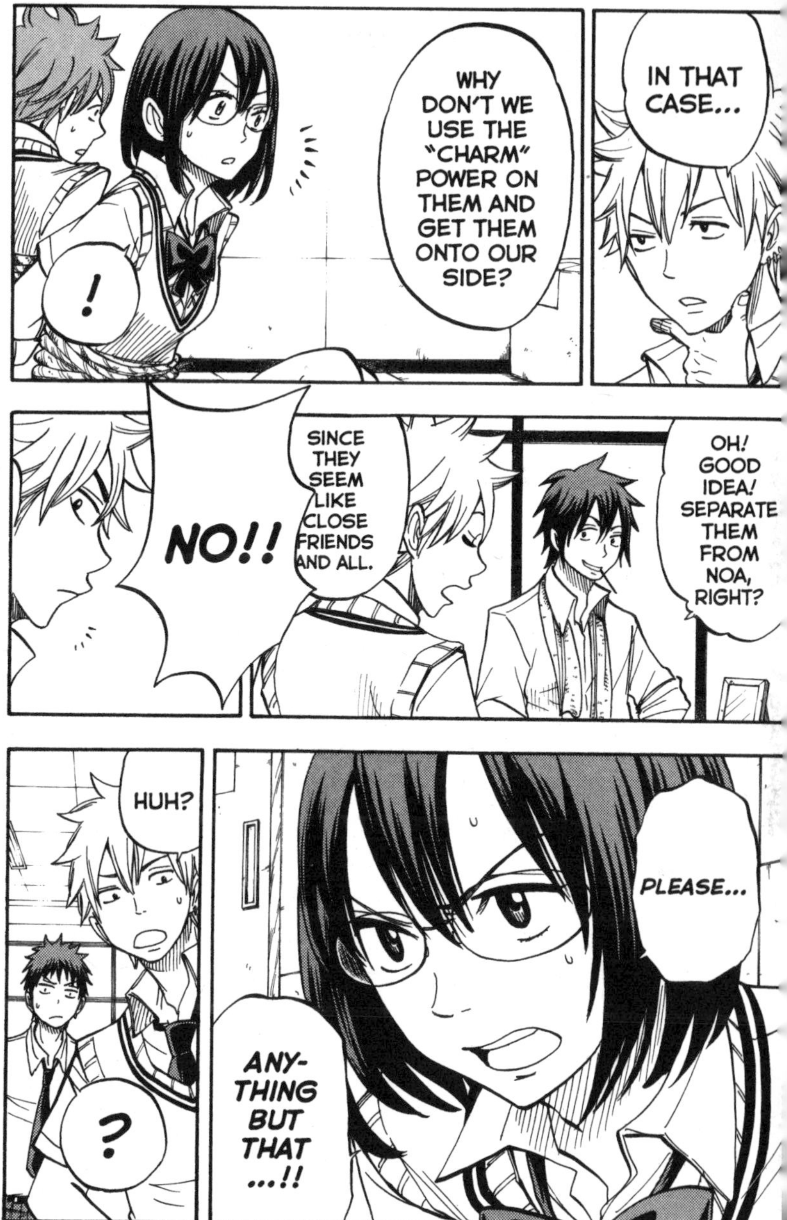
IN THAT CASE...
WHY DON'T WE USE THE "CHARM" POWER ON THEM AND GET THEM ONTO OUR SIDE?
!
OH! GOOD IDEA! SEPARATE THEM FROM NOA, RIGHT?
SINCE THEY SEEM LIKE CLOSE FRIENDS AND ALL.
NO!!
PLEASE...
ANY-THING BUT THAT ...!!
HUH?
?

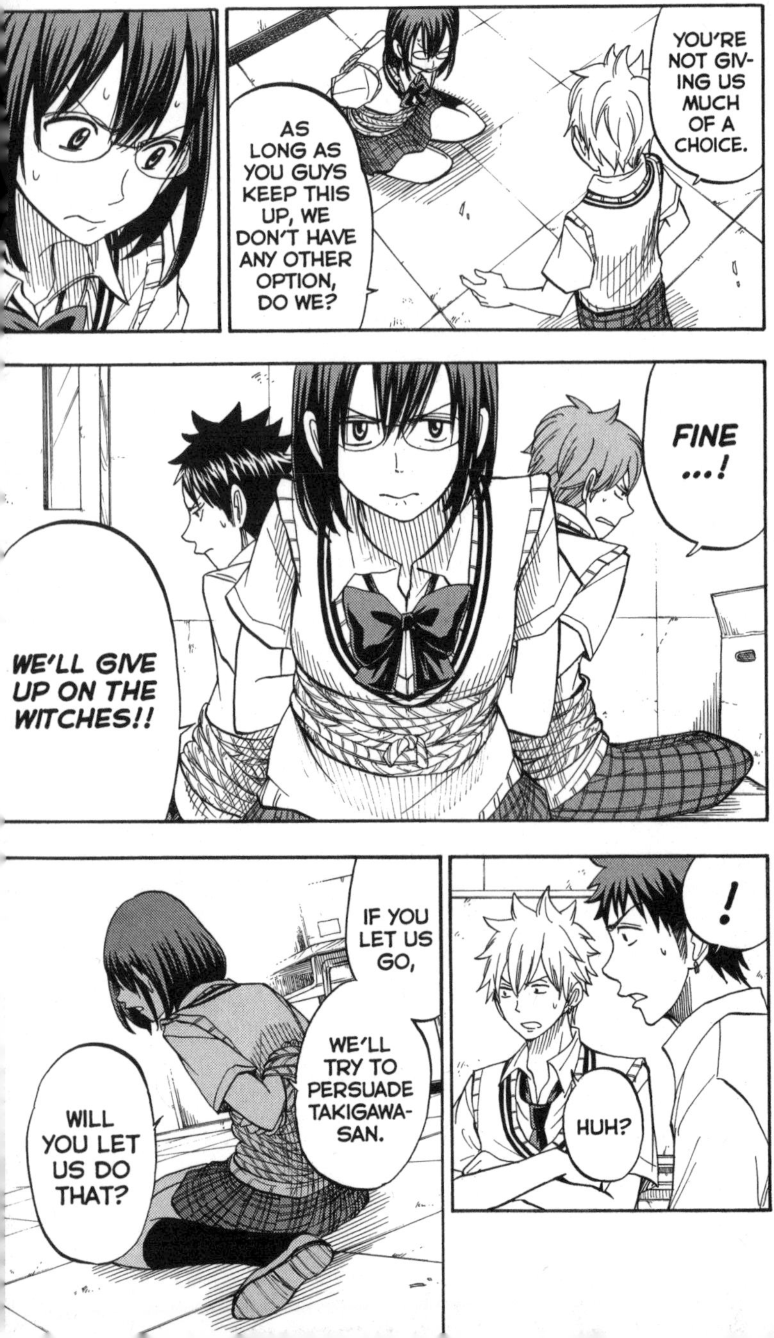
YOU'RE NOT GIVING US MUCH OF A CHOICE.
AS LONG AS YOU GUYS KEEP THIS UP, WE DON'T HAVE ANY OTHER OPTION, DO WE?
FINE ...!
WE'LL GIVE UP ON THE WITCHES!!
!
HUH?
IF YOU LET US GO,
WE'LL TRY TO PERSUADE TAKIGAWA-SAN.
WILL YOU LET US DO THAT?

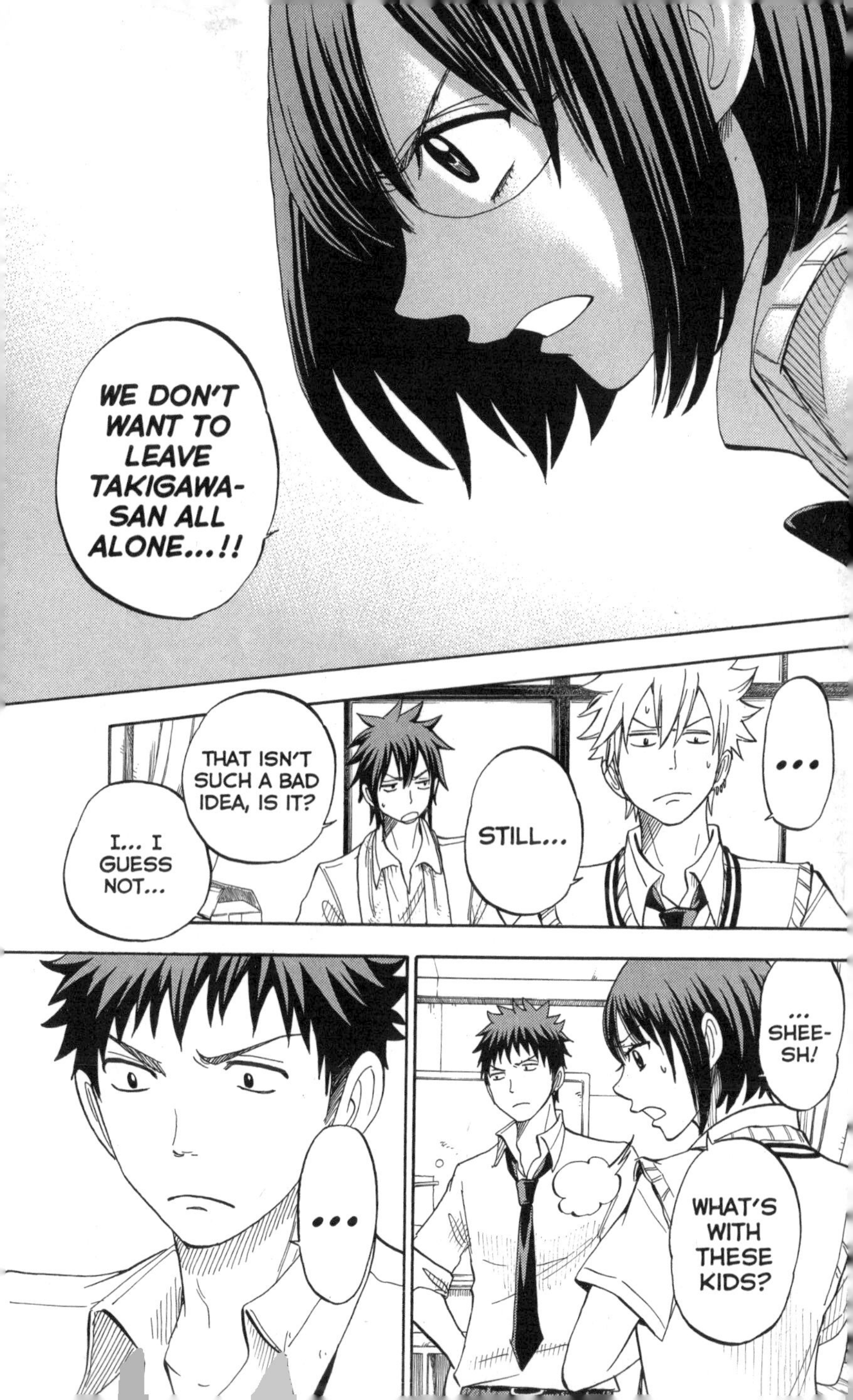
WE DON'T WANT TO LEAVE TAKIGAWA-SAN ALL ALONE...!!
...
STILL...
THAT ISN'T SUCH A BAD IDEA, IS IT?
I... I GUESS NOT...
...SHEE-SH!
WHAT'S WITH THESE KIDS?
...

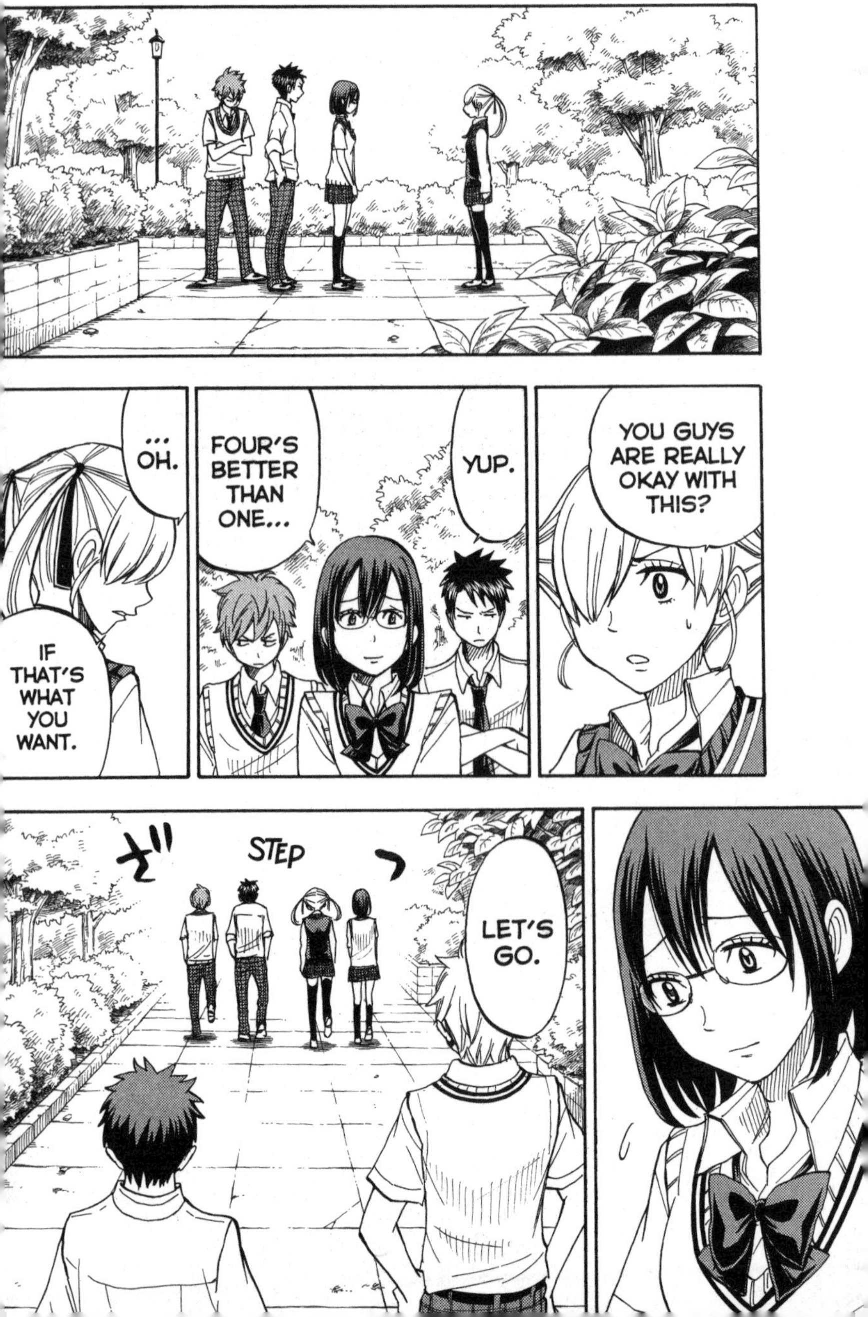
YOU GUYS ARE REALLY OKAY WITH THIS?
YUP.
FOUR'S BETTER THAN ONE...
... OH.
IF THAT'S WHAT YOU WANT.
LET'S GO.
STEP
ざ

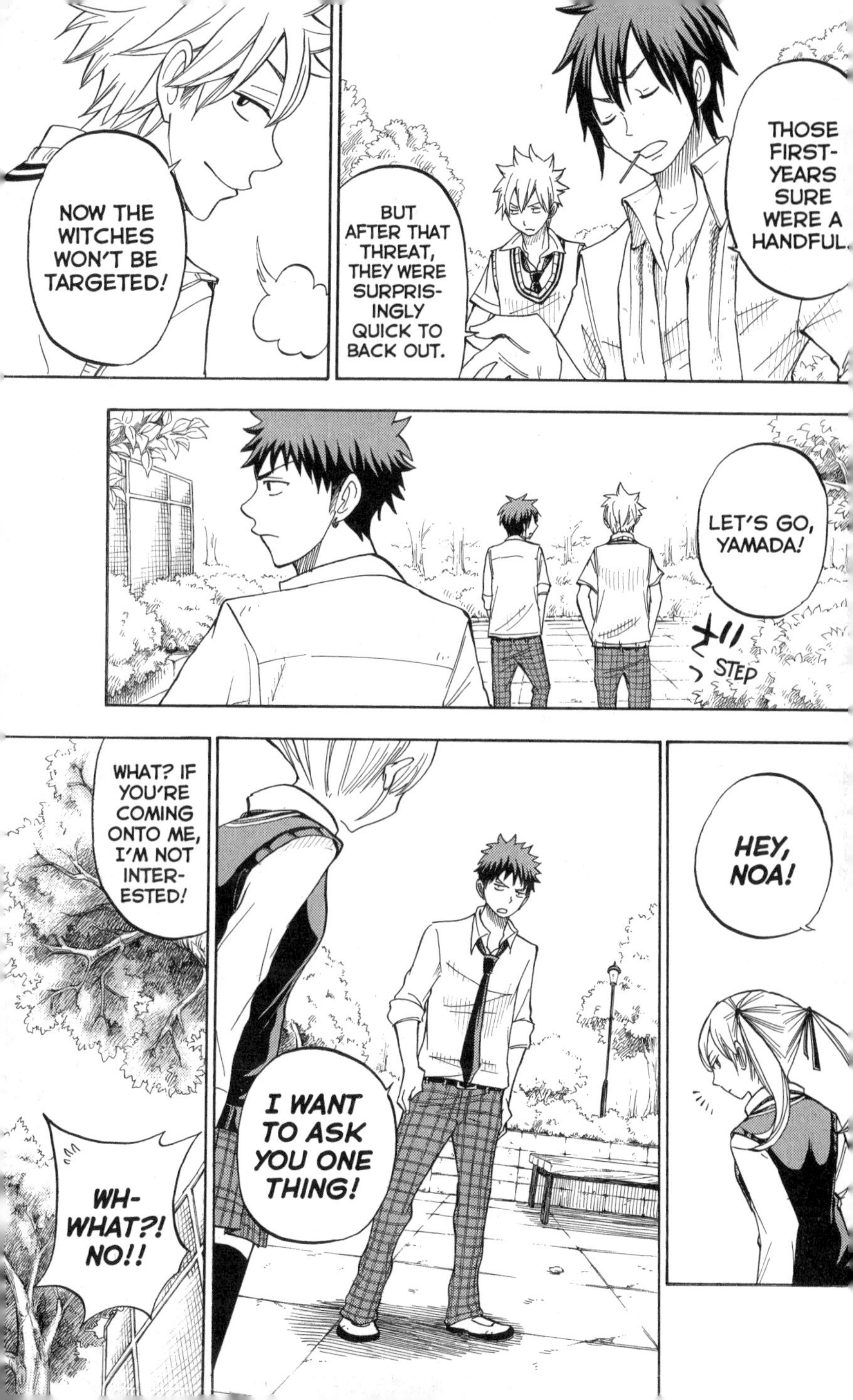
THOSE FIRST-YEARS SURE WERE A HANDFUL.
BUT AFTER THAT THREAT, THEY WERE SURPRISINGLY QUICK TO BACK OUT.
NOW THE WITCHES WON'T BE TARGETED!
LET'S GO, YAMADA!
STEP
HEY, NOA!
I WANT TO ASK YOU ONE THING!
WHAT? IF YOU'RE COMING ONTO ME, I'M NOT INTERESTED!
WH-WHAT?! NO!!

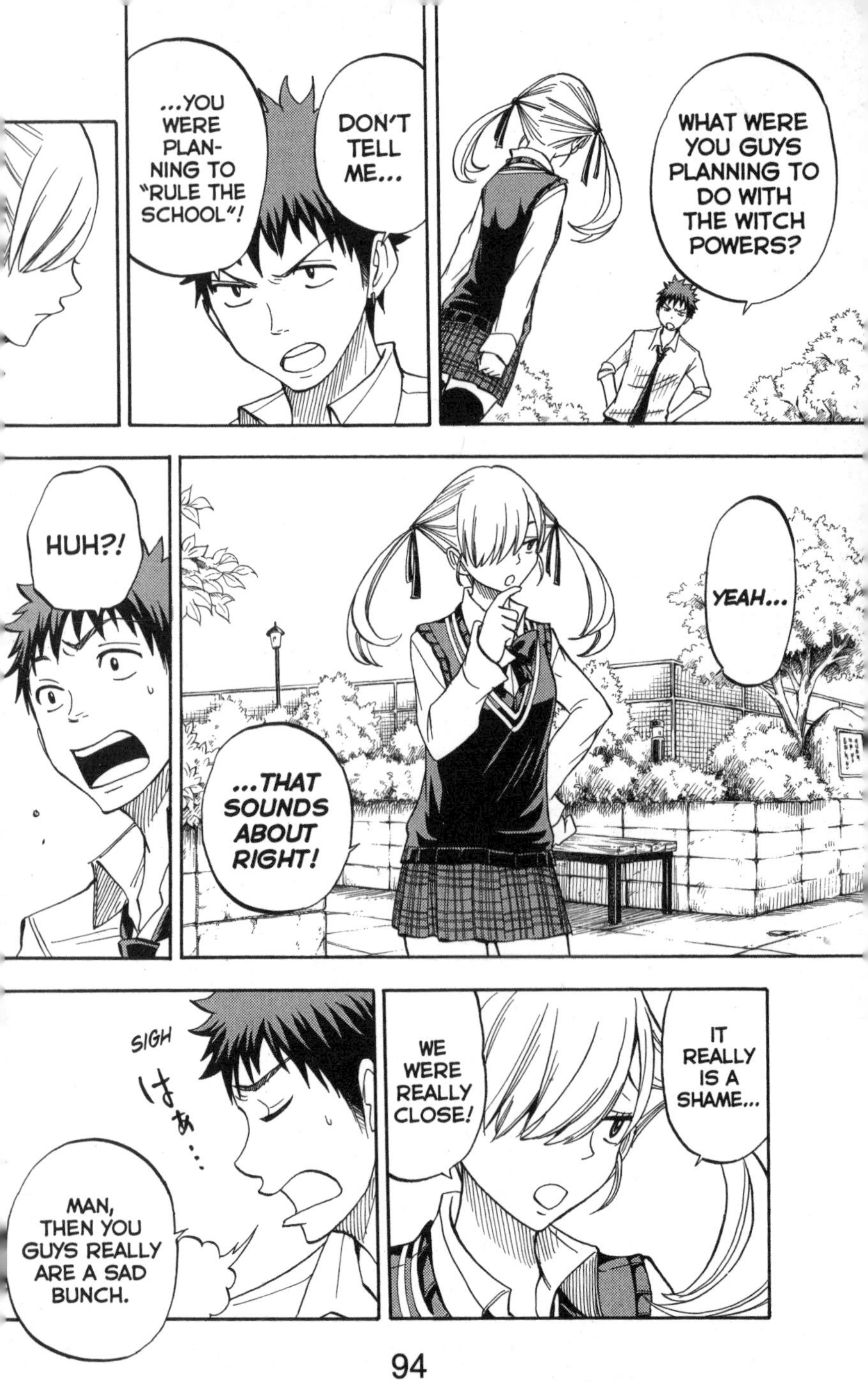
WHAT WERE YOU GUYS PLANNING TO DO WITH THE WITCH POWERS?
DON'T TELL ME...
...YOU WERE PLAN-NING TO "RULE THE SCHOOL"!
YEAH...
...THAT SOUNDS ABOUT RIGHT!
HUH?!
IT REALLY IS A SHAME...
WE WERE REALLY CLOSE!
SIGH
はぁ...
MAN, THEN YOU GUYS REALLY ARE A SAD BUNCH.

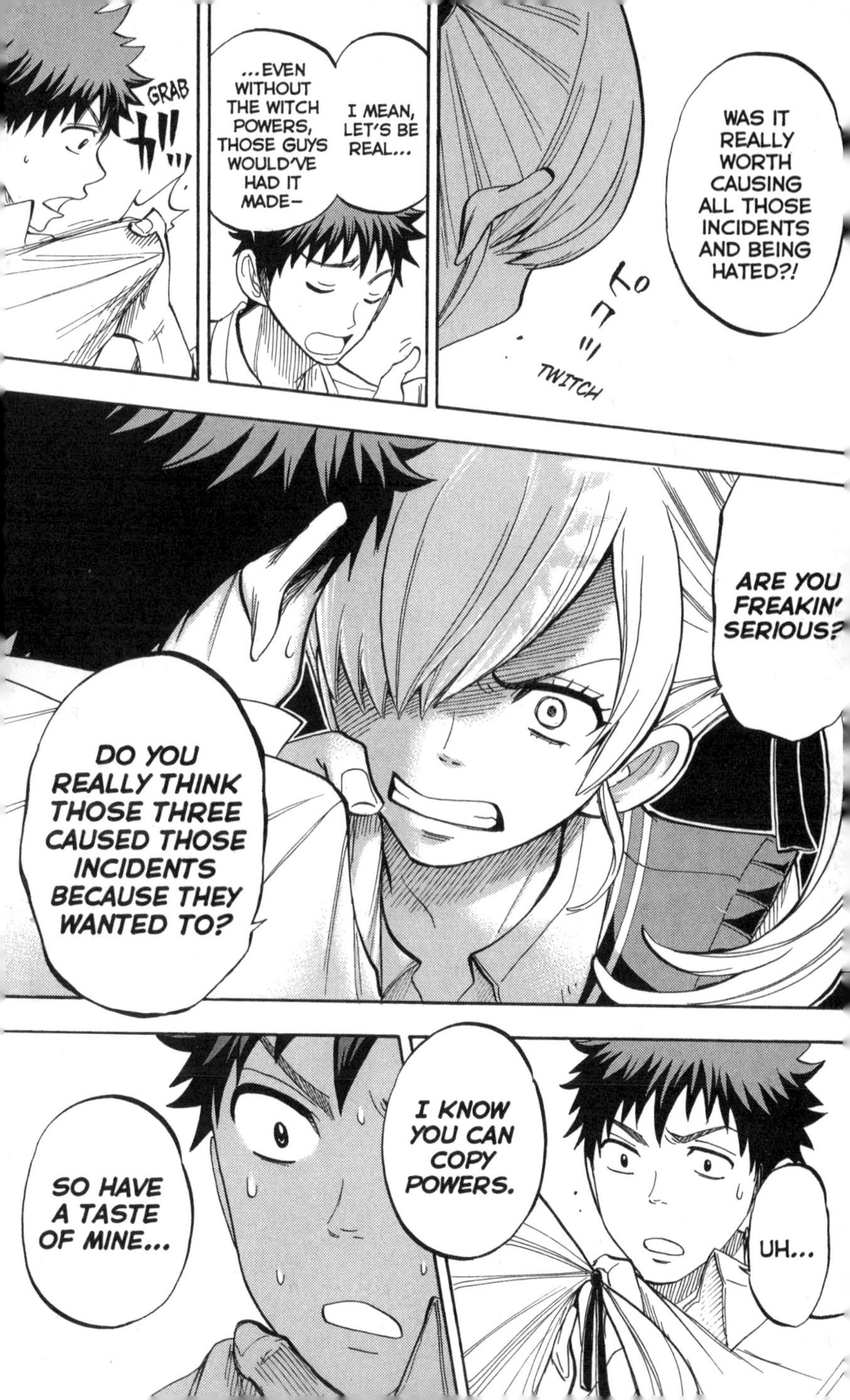
WAS IT REALLY WORTH CAUSING ALL THOSE INCIDENTS AND BEING HATED?!
ピクッ
TWITCH
I MEAN, LET'S BE REAL...
...EVEN WITHOUT THE WITCH POWERS, THOSE GUYS WOULD'VE HAD IT MADE–
ガッ
GRAB
ARE YOU FREAKIN' SERIOUS?
DO YOU REALLY THINK THOSE THREE CAUSED THOSE INCIDENTS BECAUSE THEY WANTED TO?
UH...
I KNOW YOU CAN COPY POWERS.
SO HAVE A TASTE OF MINE...

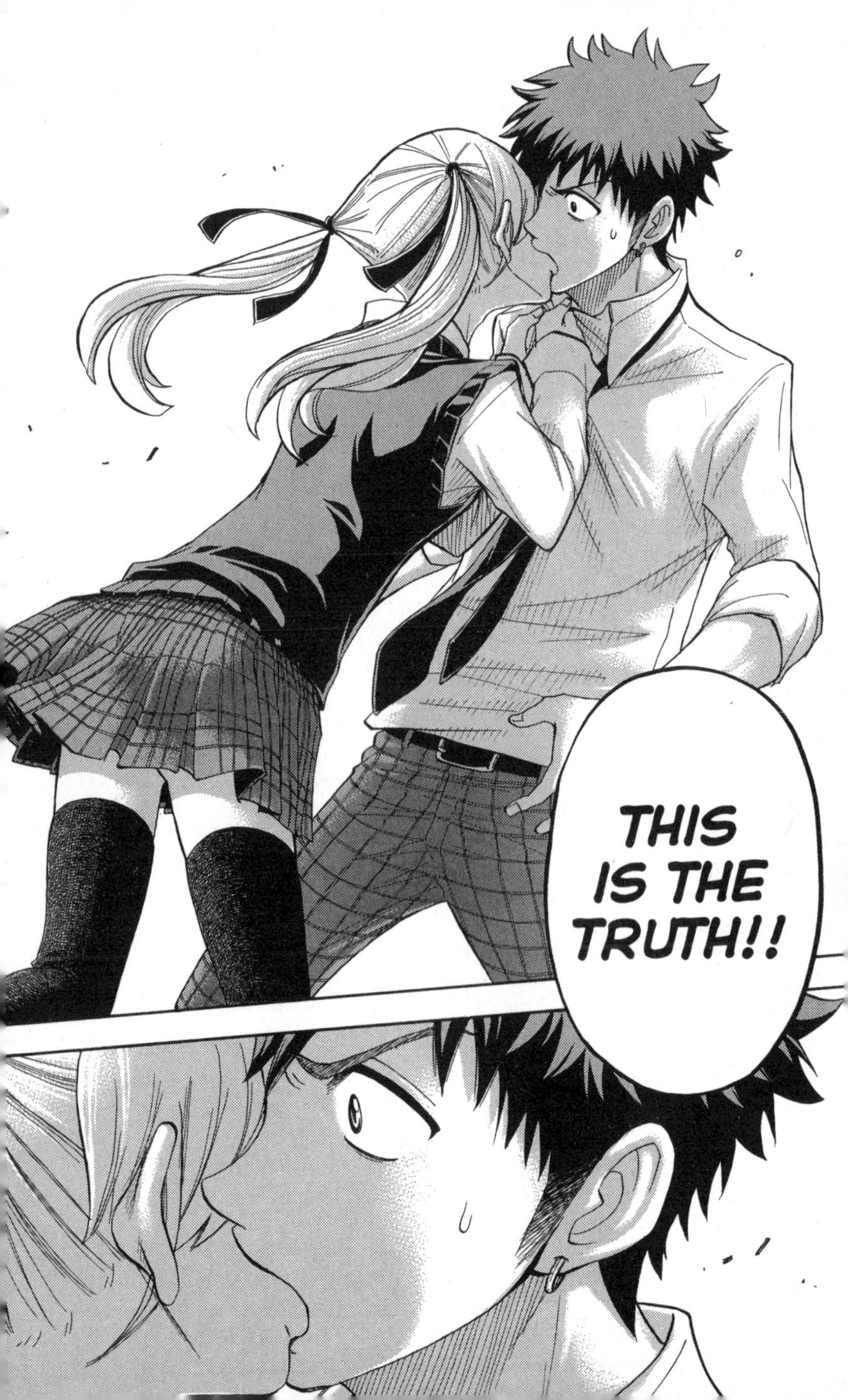
THIS IS THE TRUTH!!

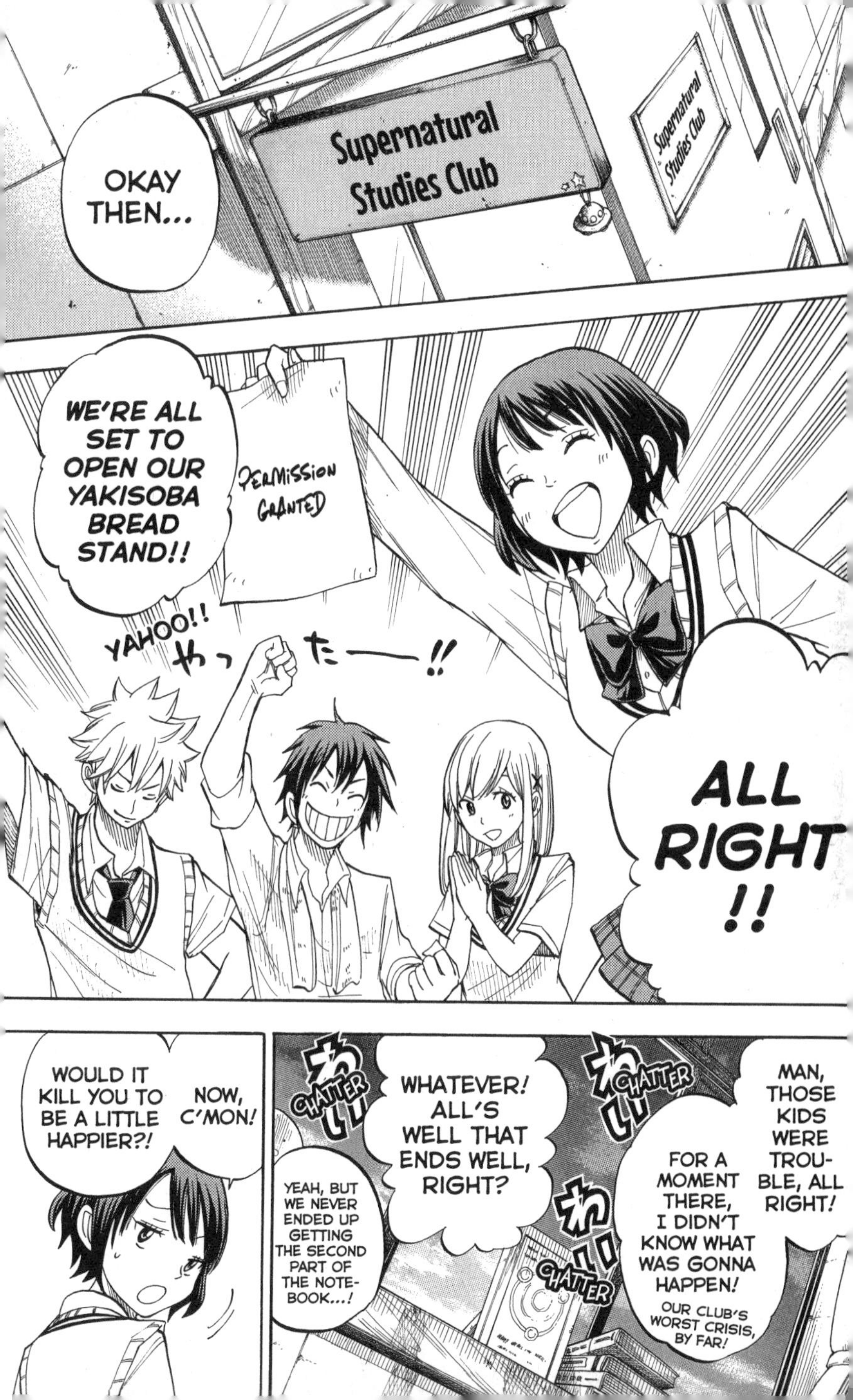
Supernatural Studies Club
Supernatural Studies Club
OKAY THEN...
WE'RE ALL SET TO OPEN OUR YAKISOBA BREAD STAND!!
PERMISSION GRANTED
YAHOO!!
やったーー!!
ALL RIGHT!!
MAN, THOSE KIDS WERE TROUBLE, ALL RIGHT!
CHATTER
FOR A MOMENT THERE, I DIDN'T KNOW WHAT WAS GONNA HAPPEN!
OUR CLUB'S WORST CRISIS, BY FAR!
CHATTER
WHATEVER! ALL'S WELL THAT ENDS WELL, RIGHT?
CHATTER
YEAH, BUT WE NEVER ENDED UP GETTING THE SECOND PART OF THE NOTE-BOOK...!
NOW, C'MON!
WOULD IT KILL YOU TO BE A LITTLE HAPPIER?!

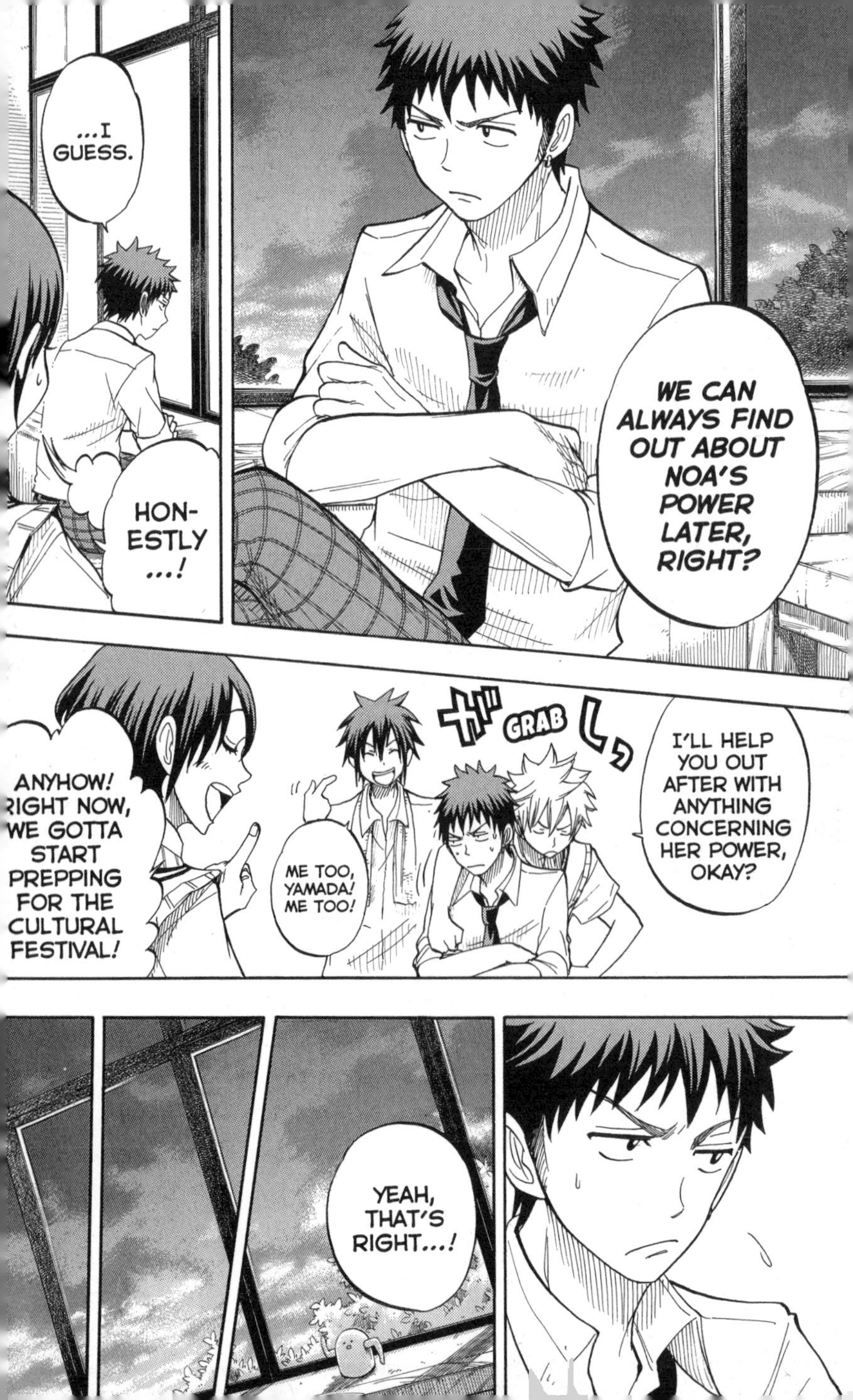
WE CAN ALWAYS FIND OUT ABOUT NOA'S POWER LATER, RIGHT?
...I GUESS.
HON-ESTLY ...!
I'LL HELP YOU OUT AFTER WITH ANYTHING CONCERNING HER POWER, OKAY?
GRAB
ME TOO, YAMADA! ME TOO!
ANYHOW! RIGHT NOW, WE GOTTA START PREPPING FOR THE CULTURAL FESTIVAL!
YEAH, THAT'S RIGHT...!

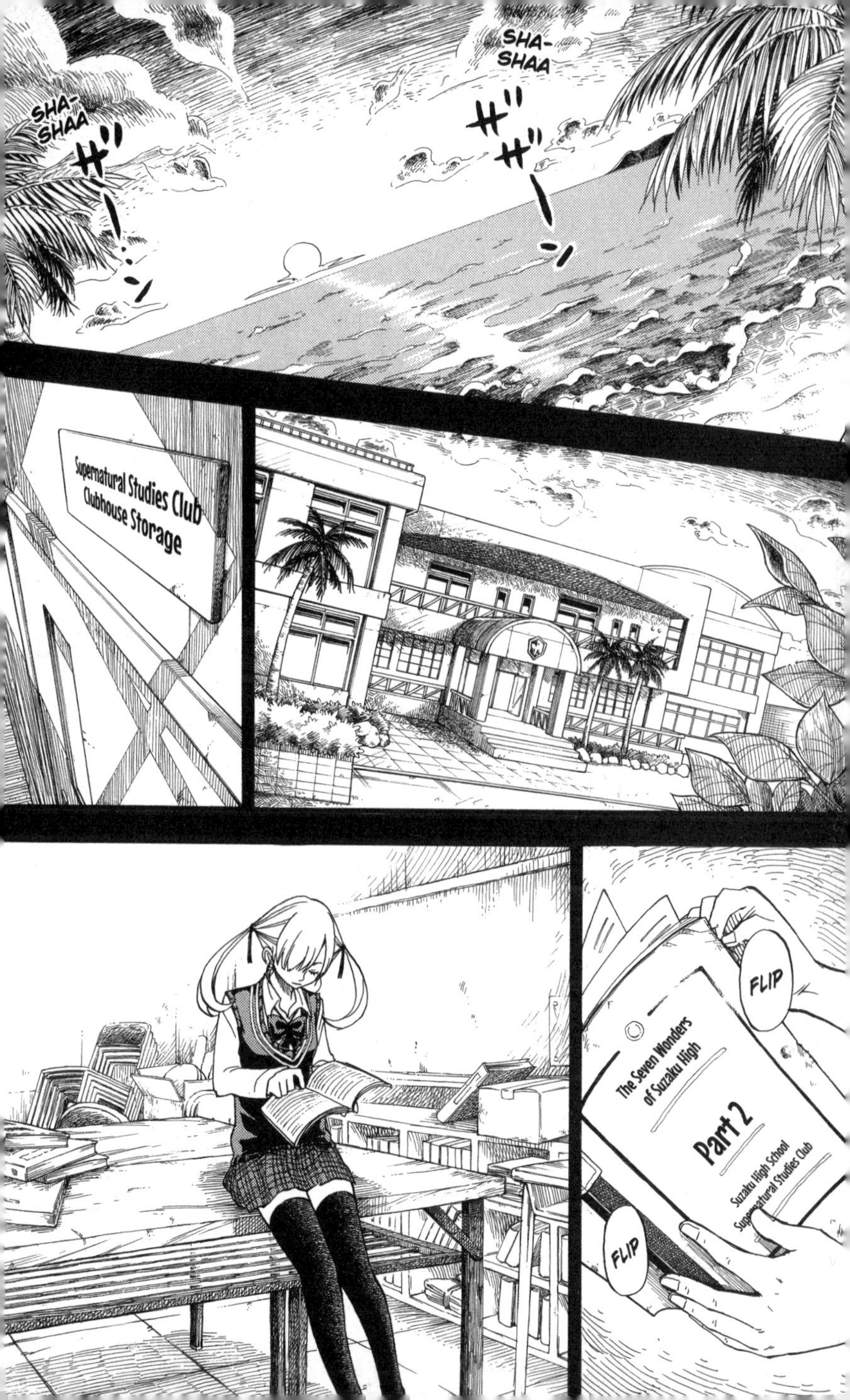
SHA-SHAA
SHA-SHAA
Supernatural Studies Club Clubhouse Storage
FLIP
The Seven Wonders of Suzaku High
Part 2
Suzaku High School Supernatural Studies Club
FLIP

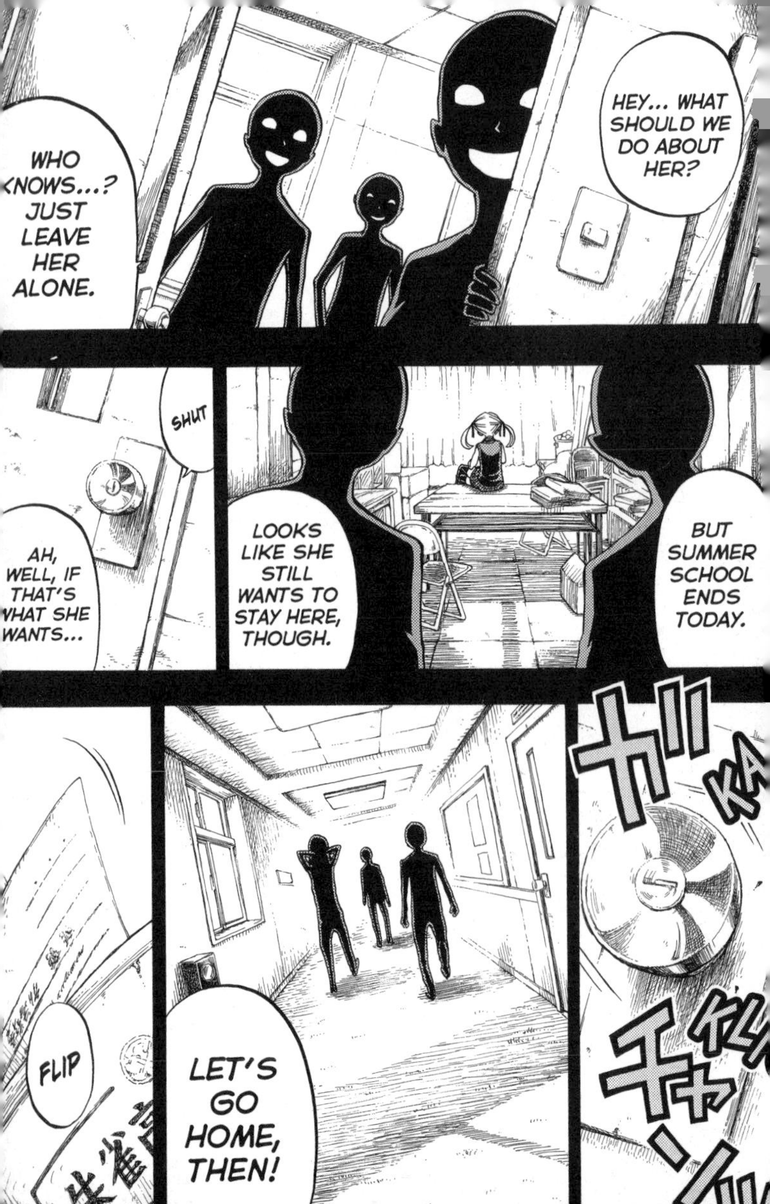
HEY... WHAT SHOULD WE DO ABOUT HER?
WHO KNOWS...? JUST LEAVE HER ALONE.
BUT SUMMER SCHOOL ENDS TODAY.
LOOKS LIKE SHE STILL WANTS TO STAY HERE, THOUGH.
SHUT
AH, WELL, IF THAT'S WHAT SHE WANTS...
KA
LET'S GO HOME, THEN!
FLIP

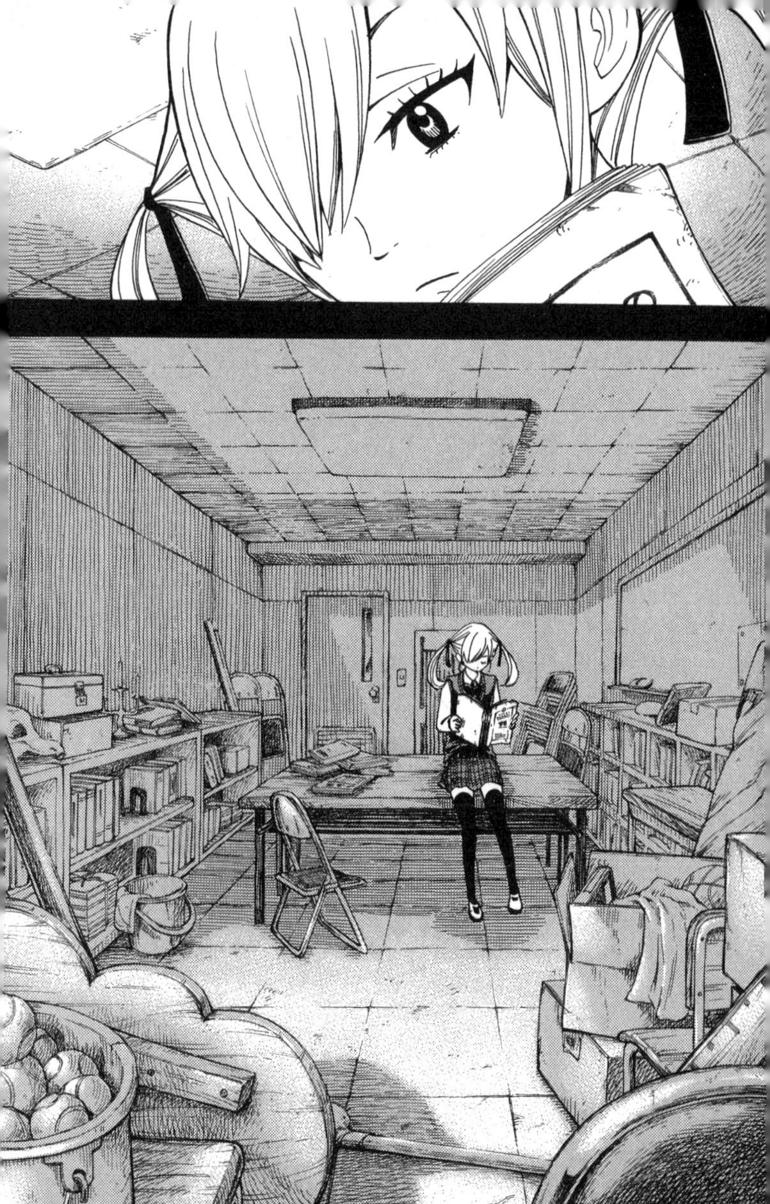

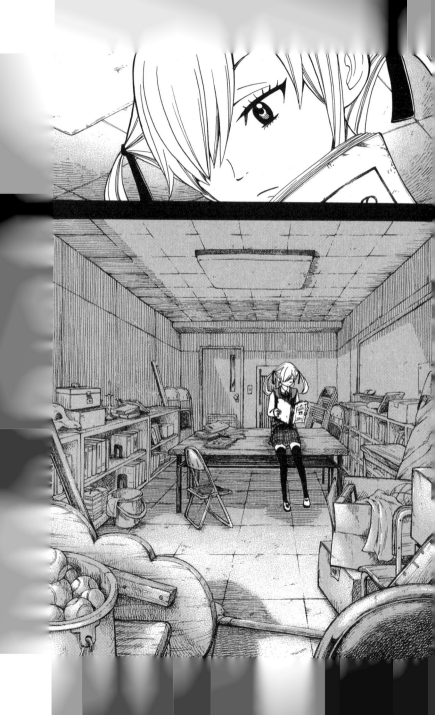

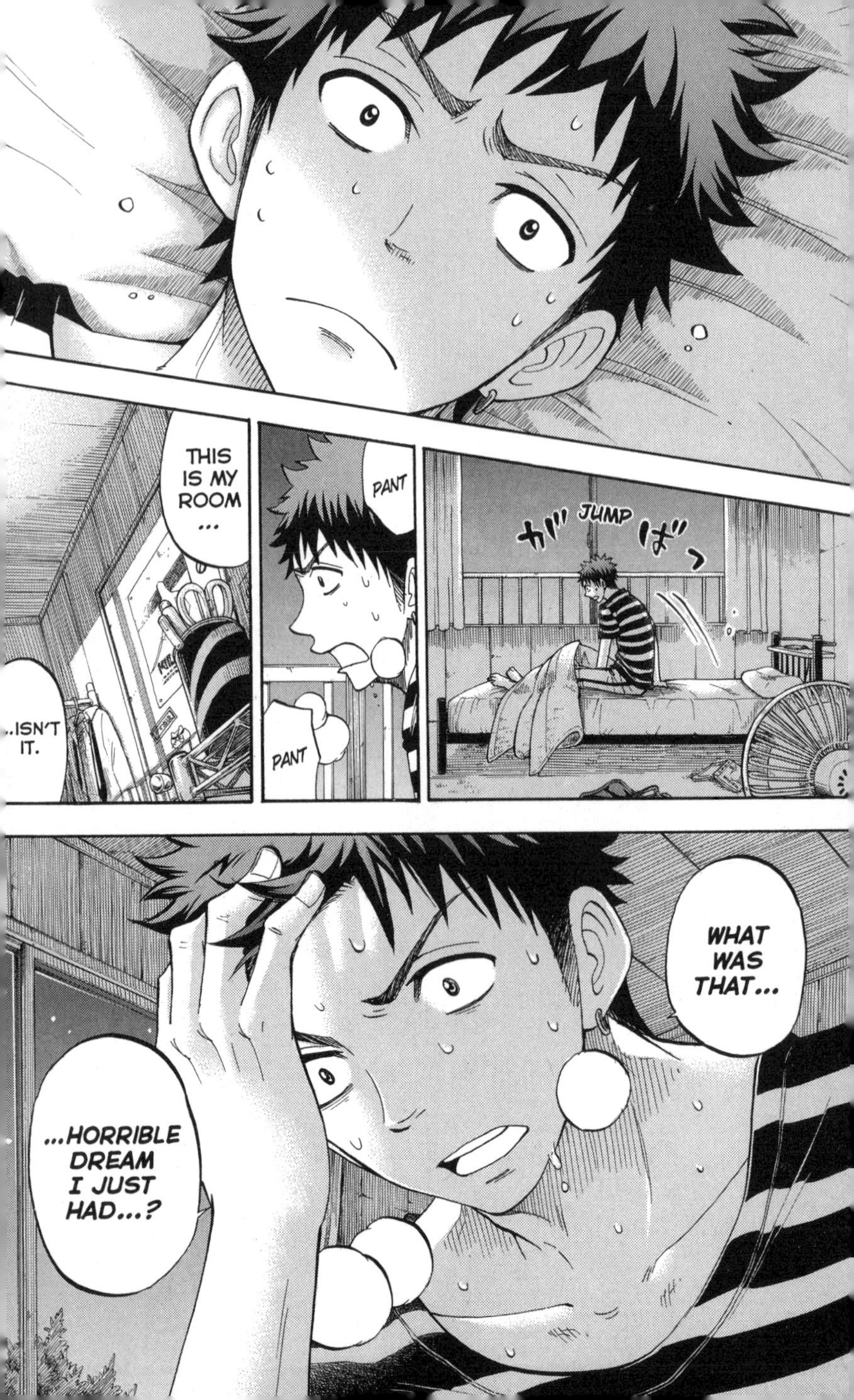
JUMP
PANT
PANT
THIS IS MY ROOM ...
...ISN'T IT.
WHAT WAS THAT...
...HORRIBLE DREAM I JUST HAD...?

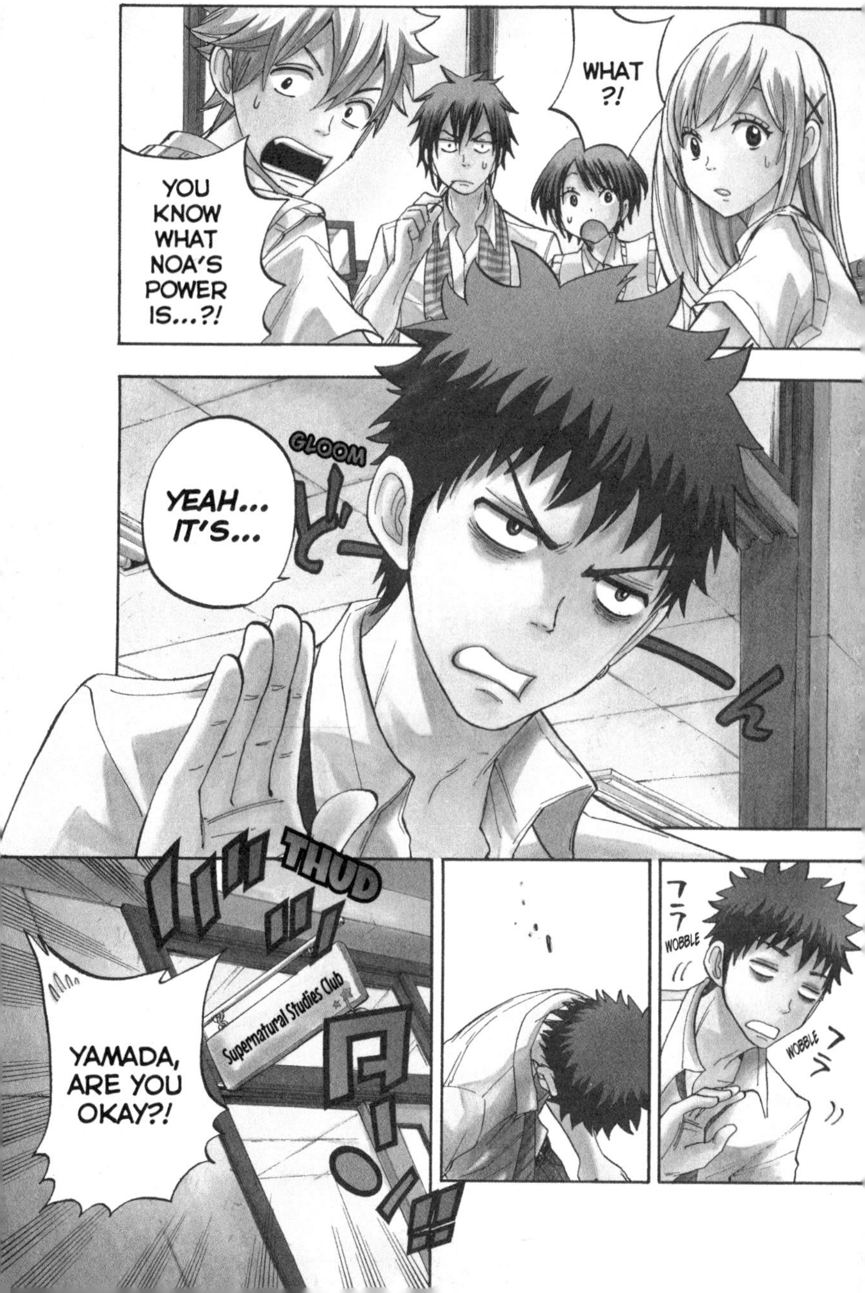
YOU KNOW WHAT NOA'S POWER IS...?!
WHAT ?!
GLOOM
YEAH... IT'S...
フラ
WOBBLE
WOBBLE
THUD
Supernatural Studies Club
YAMADA, ARE YOU OKAY?!

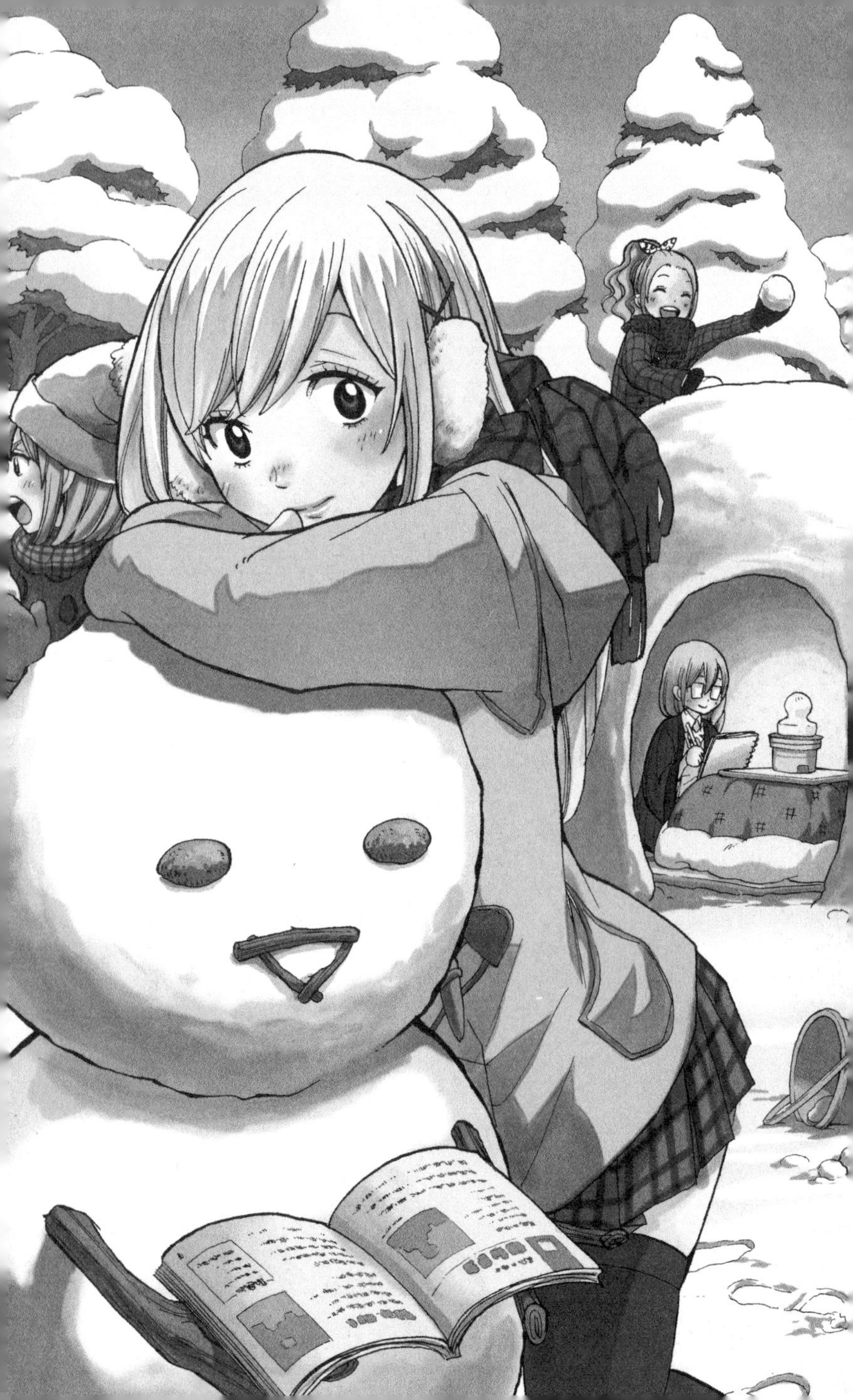

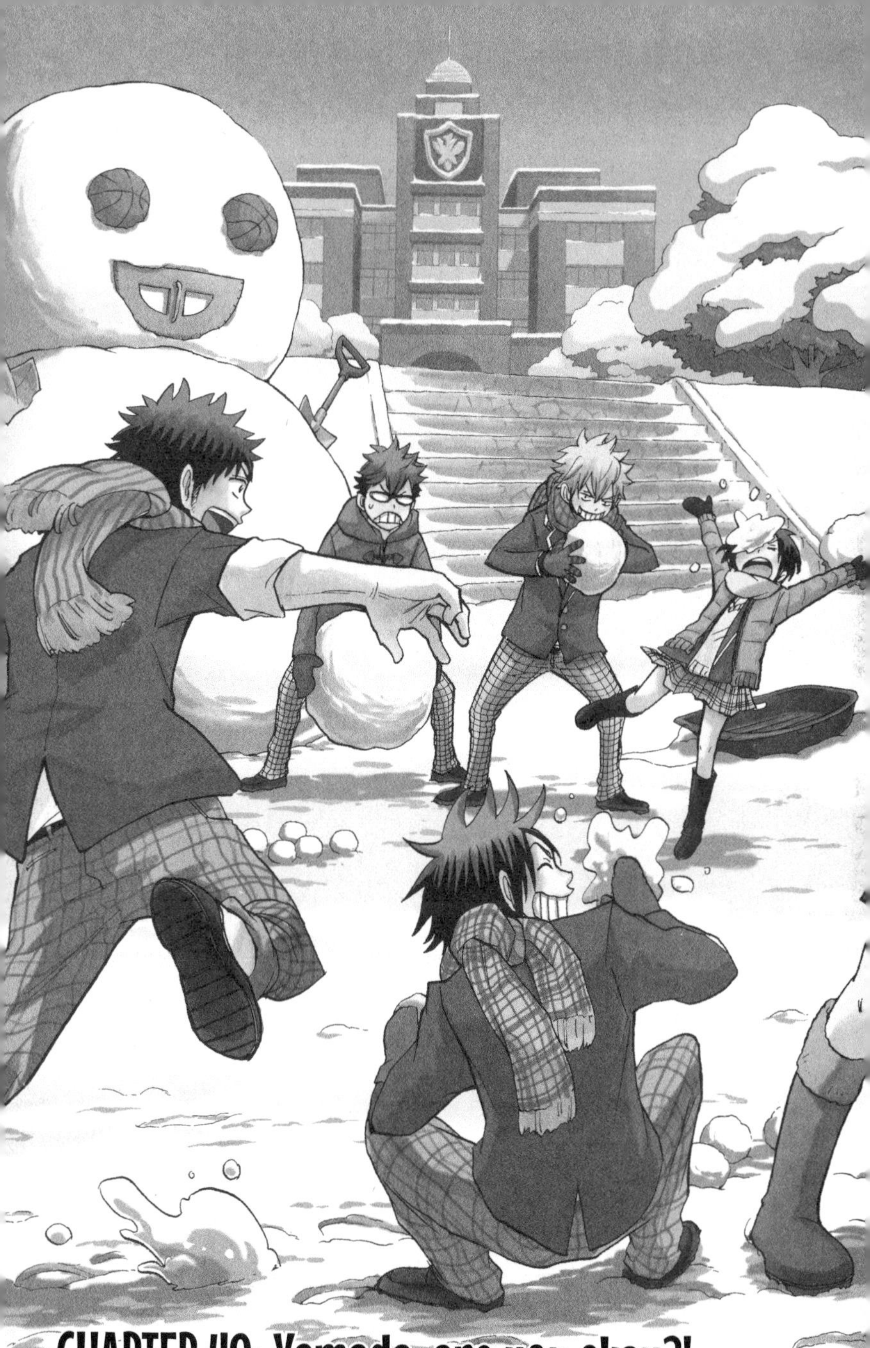

CHAPTER 49: Yamada, are you okay?!

Yamada-kun
AND THE
Seven Witches

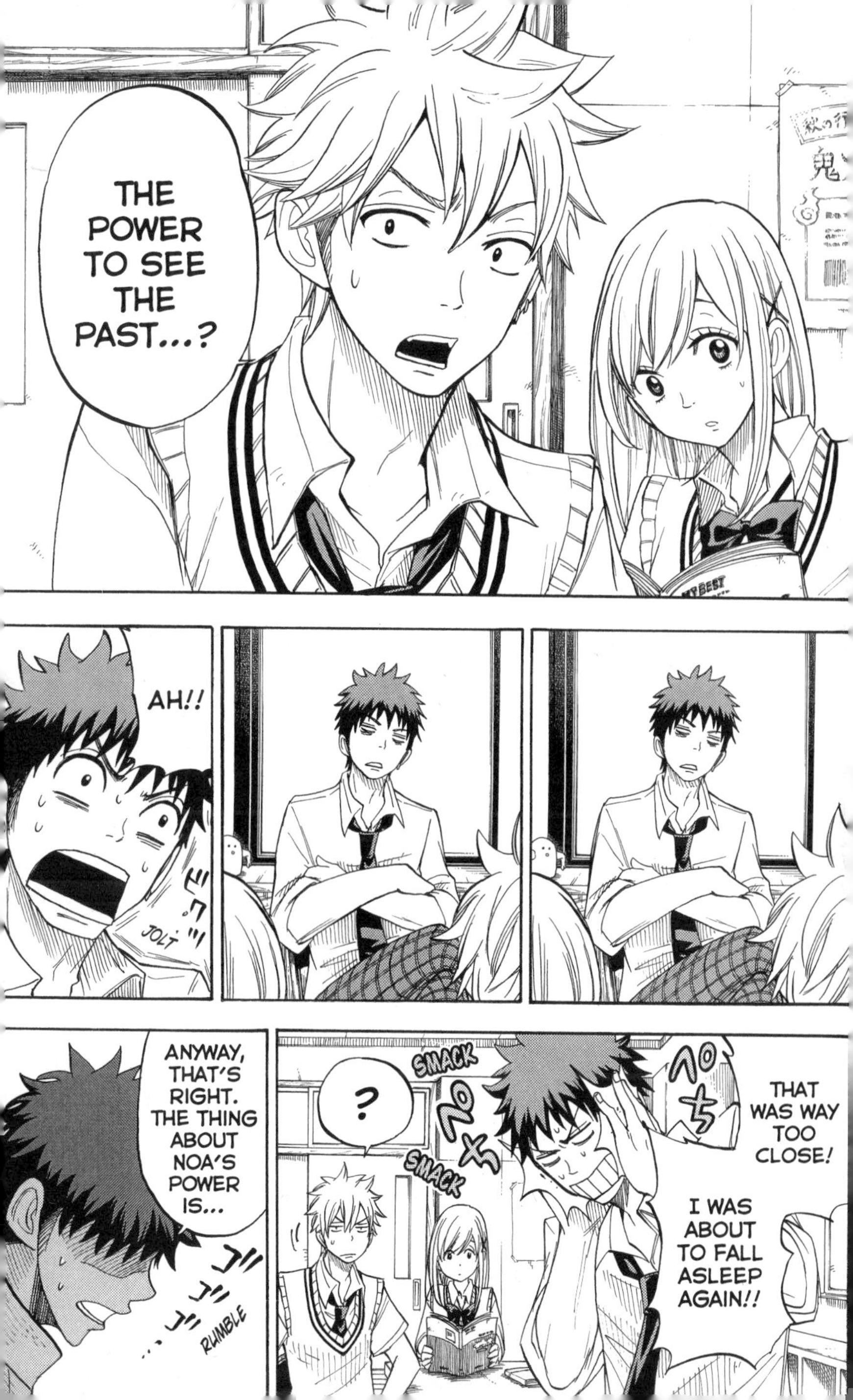
THE POWER TO SEE THE PAST...?
AH!!
JOLT
THAT WAS WAY TOO CLOSE!
SMACK
?
SMACK
I WAS ABOUT TO FALL ASLEEP AGAIN!!
ANYWAY, THAT'S RIGHT. THE THING ABOUT NOA'S POWER IS...
RUMBLE

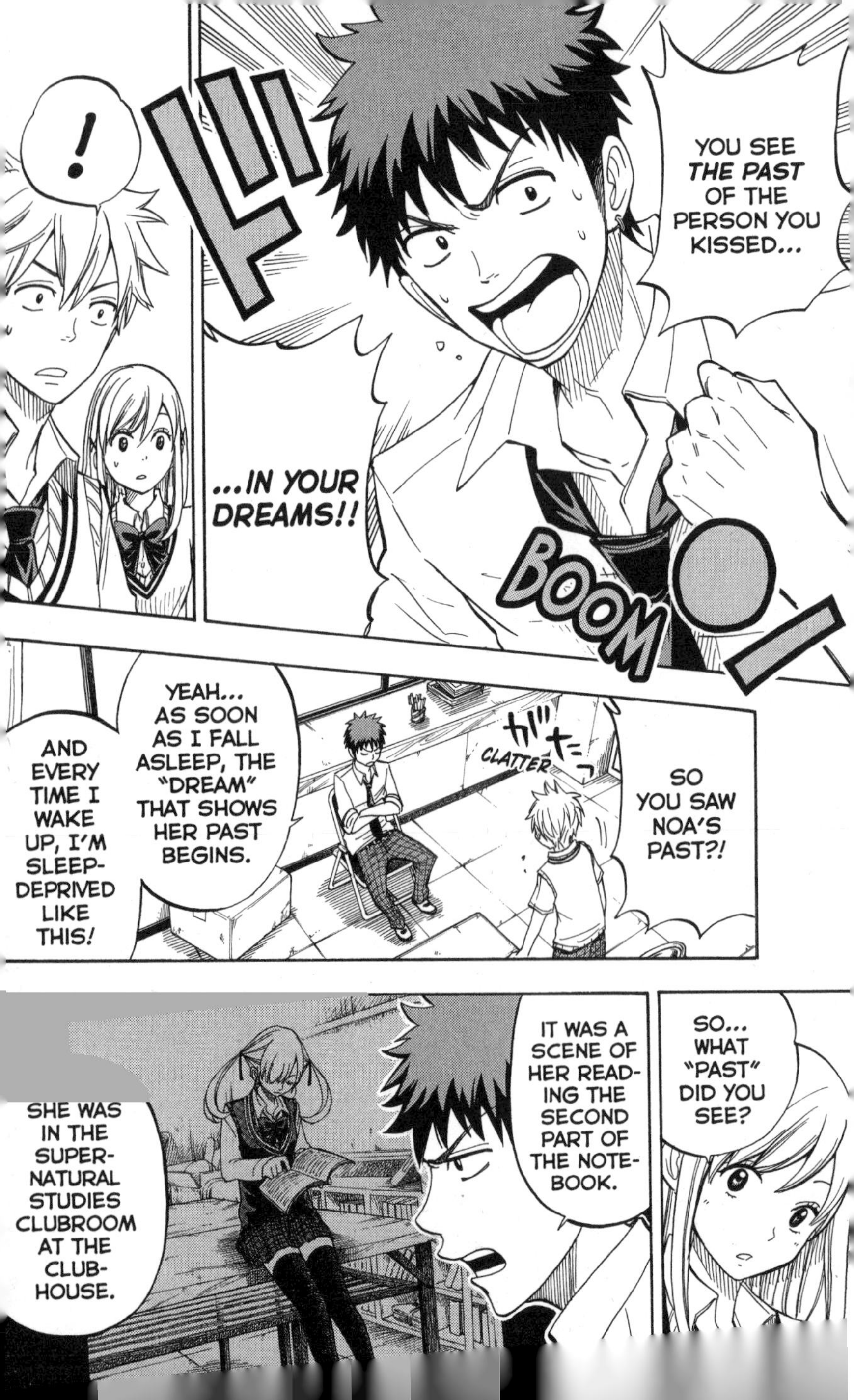
YOU SEE THE PAST OF THE PERSON YOU KISSED...
...IN YOUR DREAMS!!
BOOM
!
SO YOU SAW NOA'S PAST?!
CLATTER
YEAH... AS SOON AS I FALL ASLEEP, THE "DREAM" THAT SHOWS HER PAST BEGINS.
AND EVERY TIME I WAKE UP, I'M SLEEP-DEPRIVED LIKE THIS!
SO... WHAT "PAST" DID YOU SEE?
IT WAS A SCENE OF HER READ-ING THE SECOND PART OF THE NOTE-BOOK.
SHE WAS IN THE SUPER-NATURAL STUDIES CLUBROOM AT THE CLUB-HOUSE.

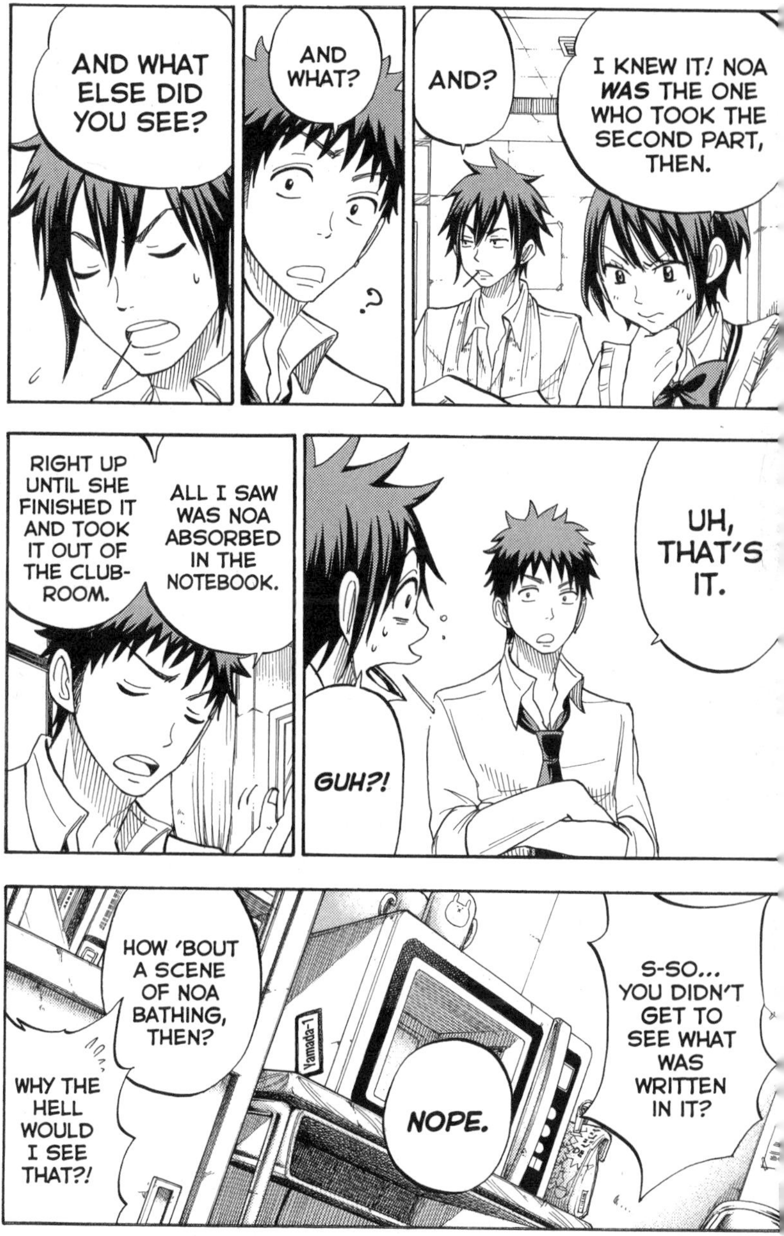
I KNEW IT! NOA *WAS* THE ONE WHO TOOK THE SECOND PART, THEN.
AND?
AND WHAT?
AND WHAT ELSE DID YOU SEE?
UH, THAT'S IT.
GUH?!
ALL I SAW WAS NOA ABSORBED IN THE NOTEBOOK.
RIGHT UP UNTIL SHE FINISHED IT AND TOOK IT OUT OF THE CLUB-ROOM.
S-SO... YOU DIDN'T GET TO SEE WHAT WAS WRITTEN IN IT?
NOPE.
Yamada-1
HOW 'BOUT A SCENE OF NOA BATHING, THEN?
WHY THE HELL WOULD I SEE THAT?!

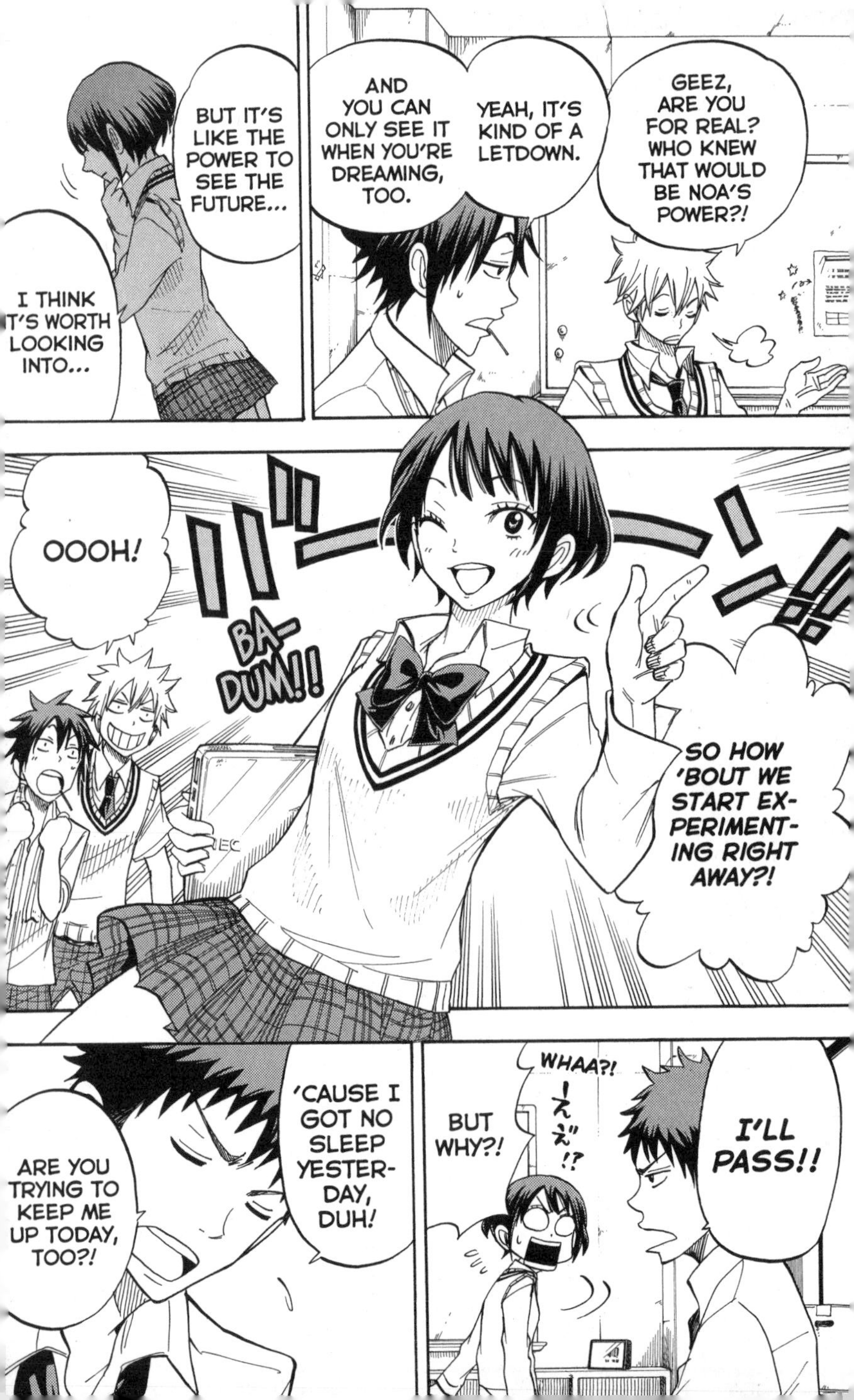
GEEZ, ARE YOU FOR REAL? WHO KNEW THAT WOULD BE NOA'S POWER?!
YEAH, IT'S KIND OF A LETDOWN.
AND YOU CAN ONLY SEE IT WHEN YOU'RE DREAMING, TOO.
BUT IT'S LIKE THE POWER TO SEE THE FUTURE...
I THINK IT'S WORTH LOOKING INTO...
SO HOW 'BOUT WE START EXPERIMENTING RIGHT AWAY?!
BA-DUM!!
OOOH!
I'LL PASS!!
WHAA?!
ええ!?
BUT WHY?!
'CAUSE I GOT NO SLEEP YESTERDAY, DUH!
ARE YOU TRYING TO KEEP ME UP TODAY, TOO?!

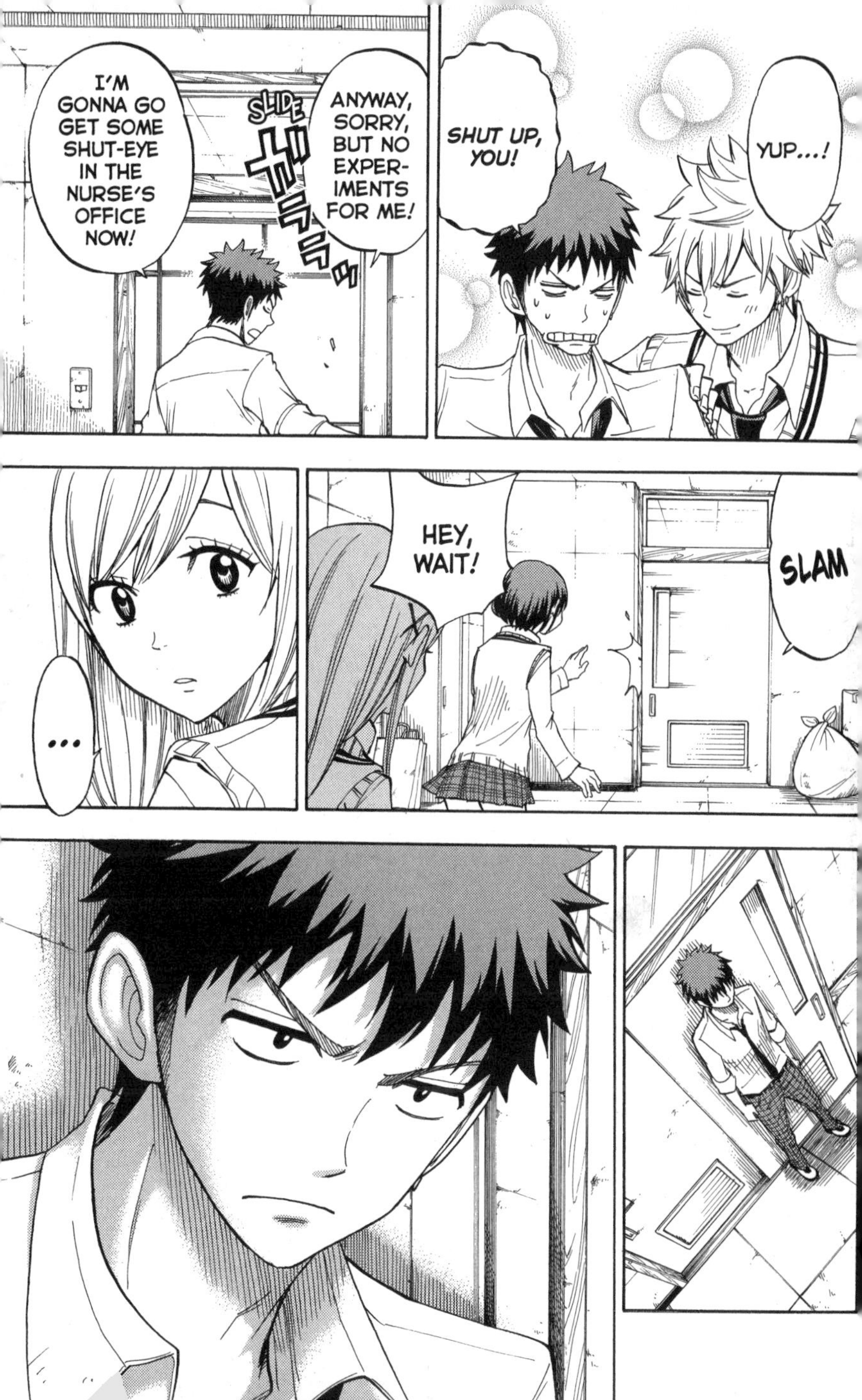
YUP...!
SHUT UP, YOU!
ANYWAY, SORRY, BUT NO EXPER-IMENTS FOR ME!
SLIDE
I'M GONNA GO GET SOME SHUT-EYE IN THE NURSE'S OFFICE NOW!
SLAM
HEY, WAIT!
...

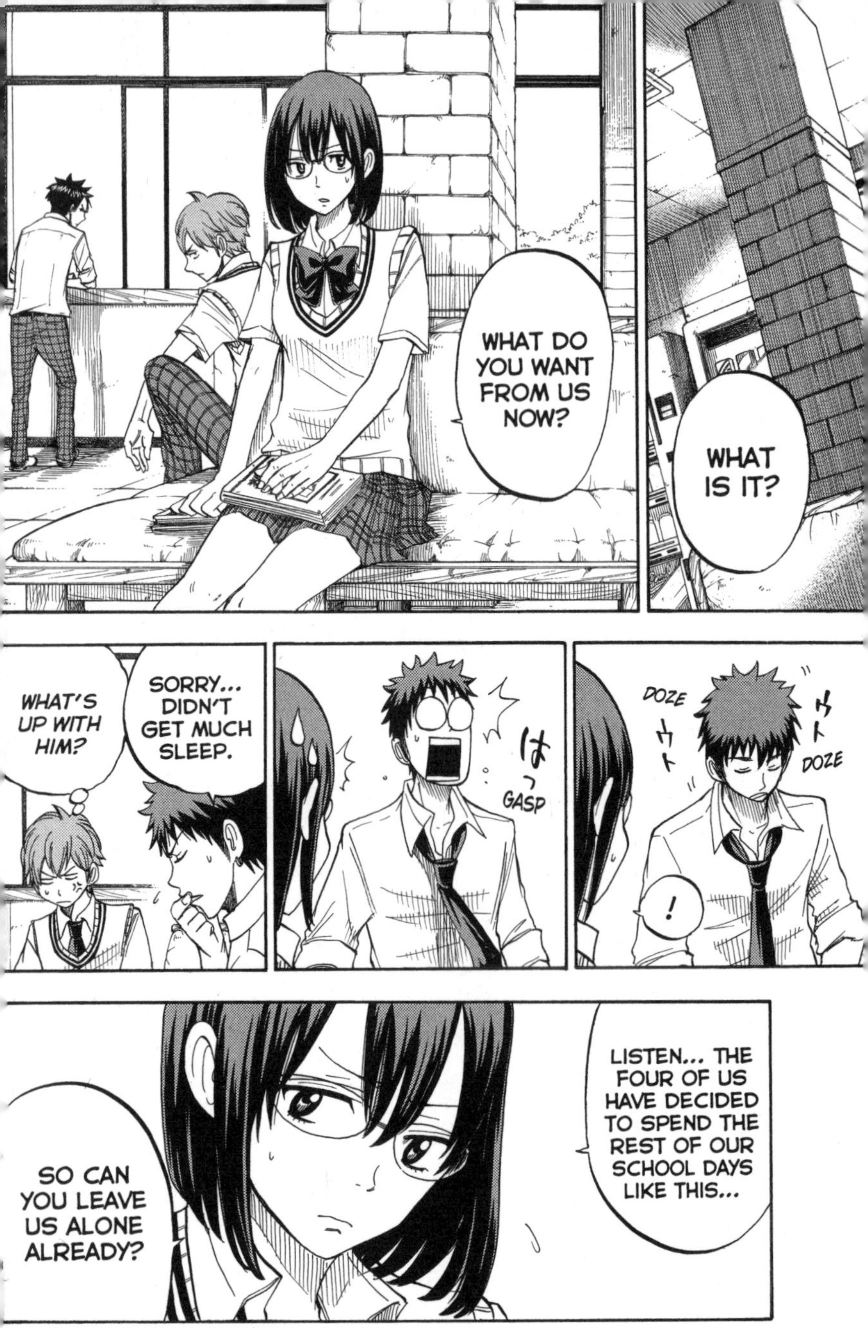
WHAT IS IT?
WHAT DO YOU WANT FROM US NOW?
DOZE
ウト
ウト
DOZE
!
はっ
GASP
SORRY... DIDN'T GET MUCH SLEEP.
WHAT'S UP WITH HIM?
LISTEN... THE FOUR OF US HAVE DECIDED TO SPEND THE REST OF OUR SCHOOL DAYS LIKE THIS...
SO CAN YOU LEAVE US ALONE ALREADY?

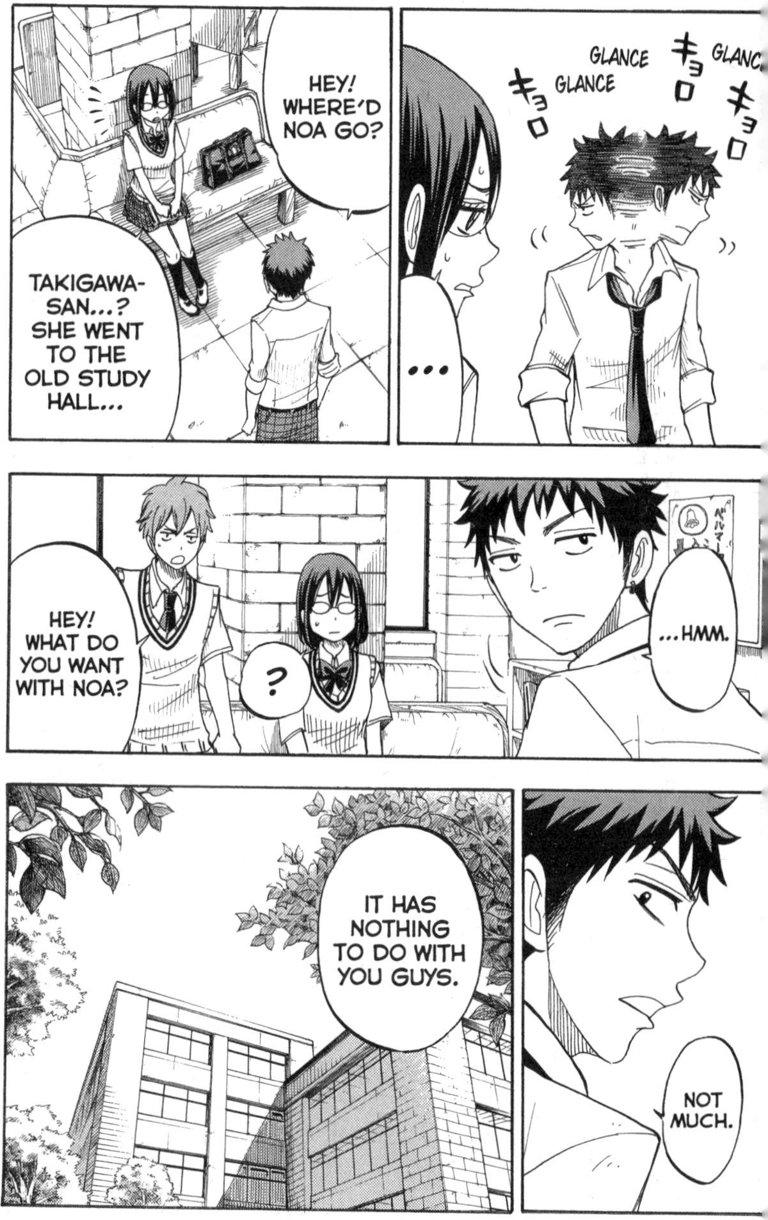
GLANCE
キョロ
GLANCE
キョロ
GLANC
キョロ
...
HEY! WHERE'D NOA GO?
TAKIGAWA-SAN...? SHE WENT TO THE OLD STUDY HALL...
...HMM.
HEY! WHAT DO YOU WANT WITH NOA?
?
NOT MUCH.
IT HAS NOTHING TO DO WITH YOU GUYS.

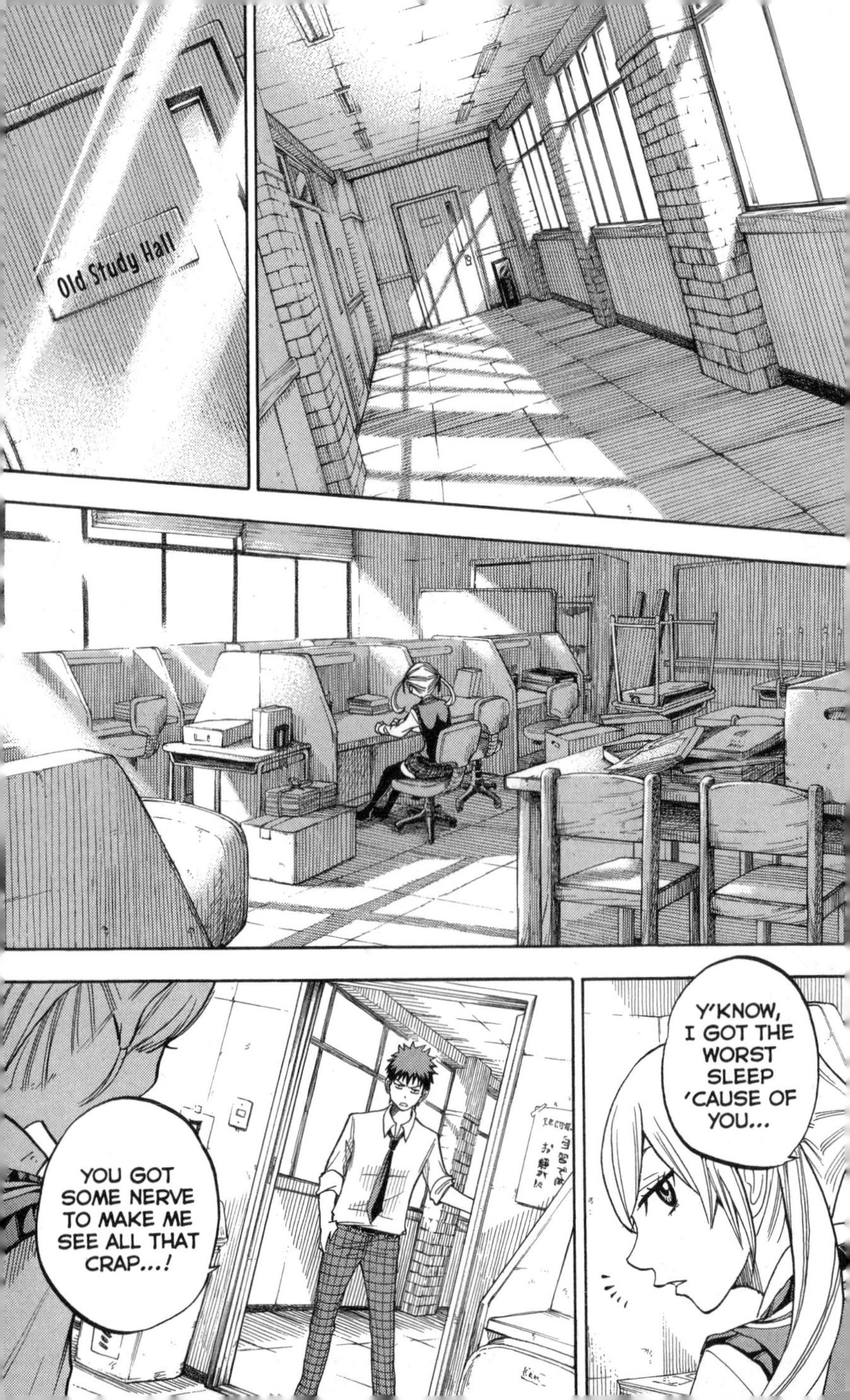
Old Study Hall
Y'KNOW, I GOT THE WORST SLEEP 'CAUSE OF YOU...
YOU GOT SOME NERVE TO MAKE ME SEE ALL THAT CRAP...!

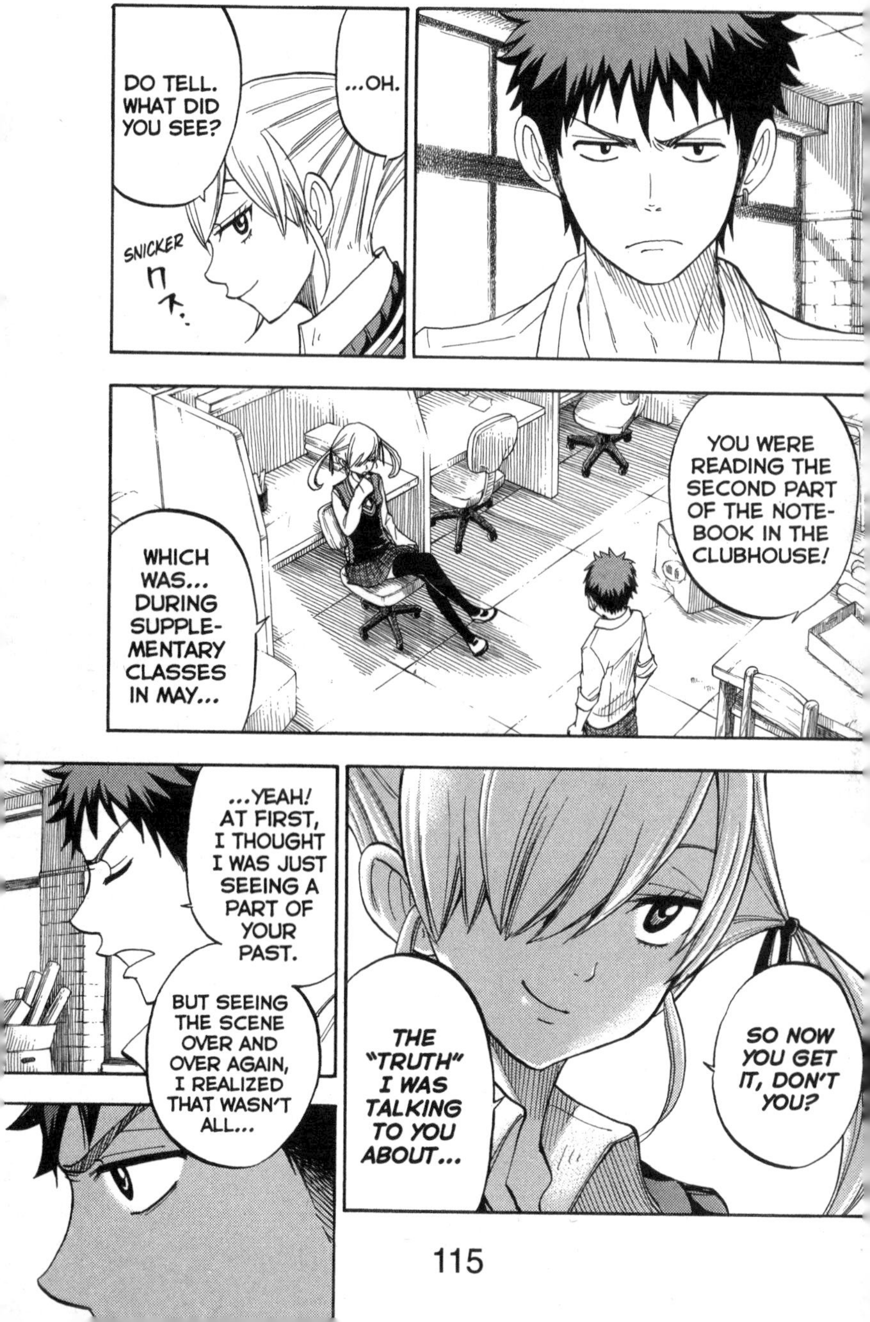
...OH.
DO TELL. WHAT DID YOU SEE?
SNICKER
YOU WERE READING THE SECOND PART OF THE NOTE-BOOK IN THE CLUBHOUSE!
WHICH WAS... DURING SUPPLE-MENTARY CLASSES IN MAY...
SO NOW YOU GET IT, DON'T YOU?
THE "TRUTH" I WAS TALKING TO YOU ABOUT...
...YEAH! AT FIRST, I THOUGHT I WAS JUST SEEING A PART OF YOUR PAST.
BUT SEEING THE SCENE OVER AND OVER AGAIN, I REALIZED THAT WASN'T ALL...

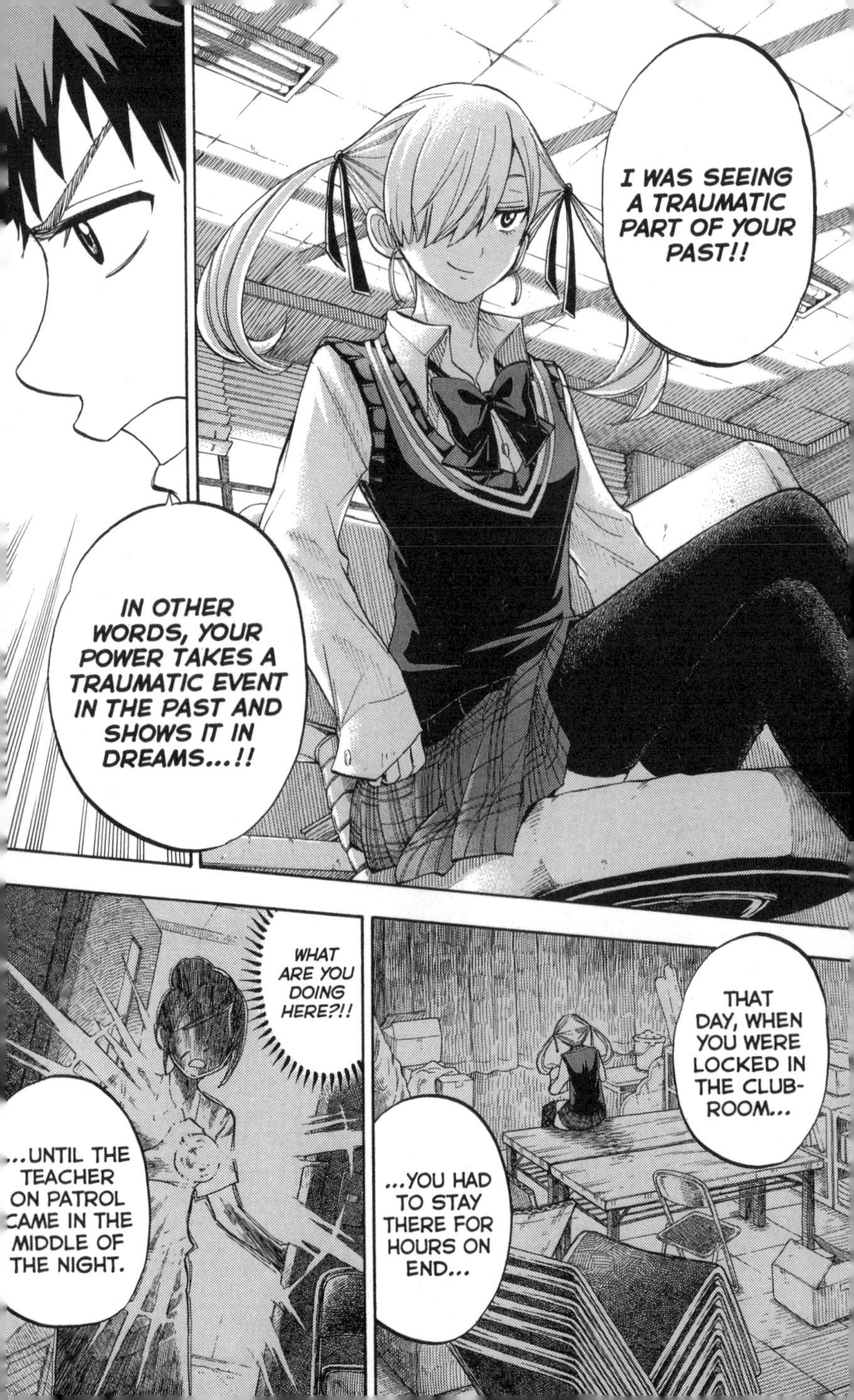
I WAS SEEING A TRAUMATIC PART OF YOUR PAST!!
IN OTHER WORDS, YOUR POWER TAKES A TRAUMATIC EVENT IN THE PAST AND SHOWS IT IN DREAMS...!!
THAT DAY, WHEN YOU WERE LOCKED IN THE CLUB-ROOM...
...YOU HAD TO STAY THERE FOR HOURS ON END...
WHAT ARE YOU DOING HERE?!!
...UNTIL THE TEACHER ON PATROL CAME IN THE MIDDLE OF THE NIGHT.

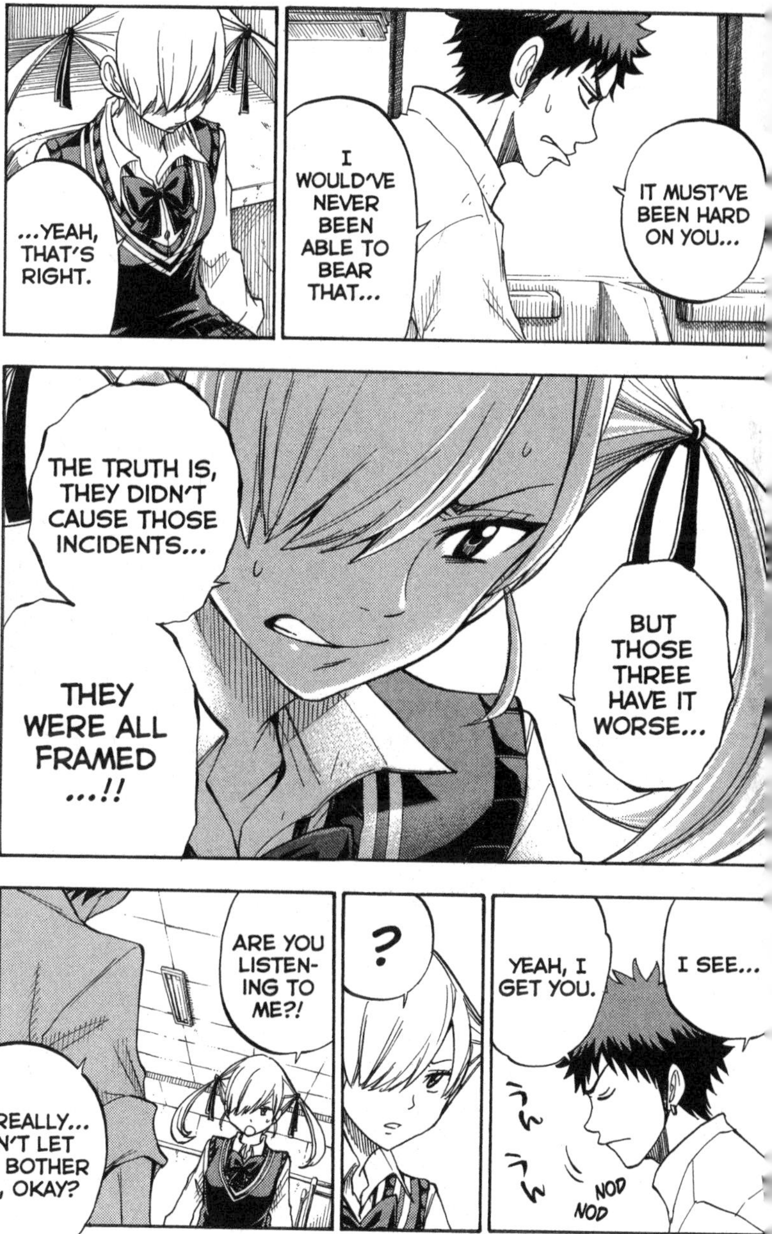
IT MUST'VE BEEN HARD ON YOU...
I WOULD'VE NEVER BEEN ABLE TO BEAR THAT...
...YEAH, THAT'S RIGHT.
BUT THOSE THREE HAVE IT WORSE...
THE TRUTH IS, THEY DIDN'T CAUSE THOSE INCIDENTS...
THEY WERE ALL FRAMED ...!!
I SEE...
YEAH, I GET YOU.
NOD NOD
?
ARE YOU LISTEN-ING TO ME?!
BUT REALLY... DON'T LET THAT BOTHER YOU, OKAY?

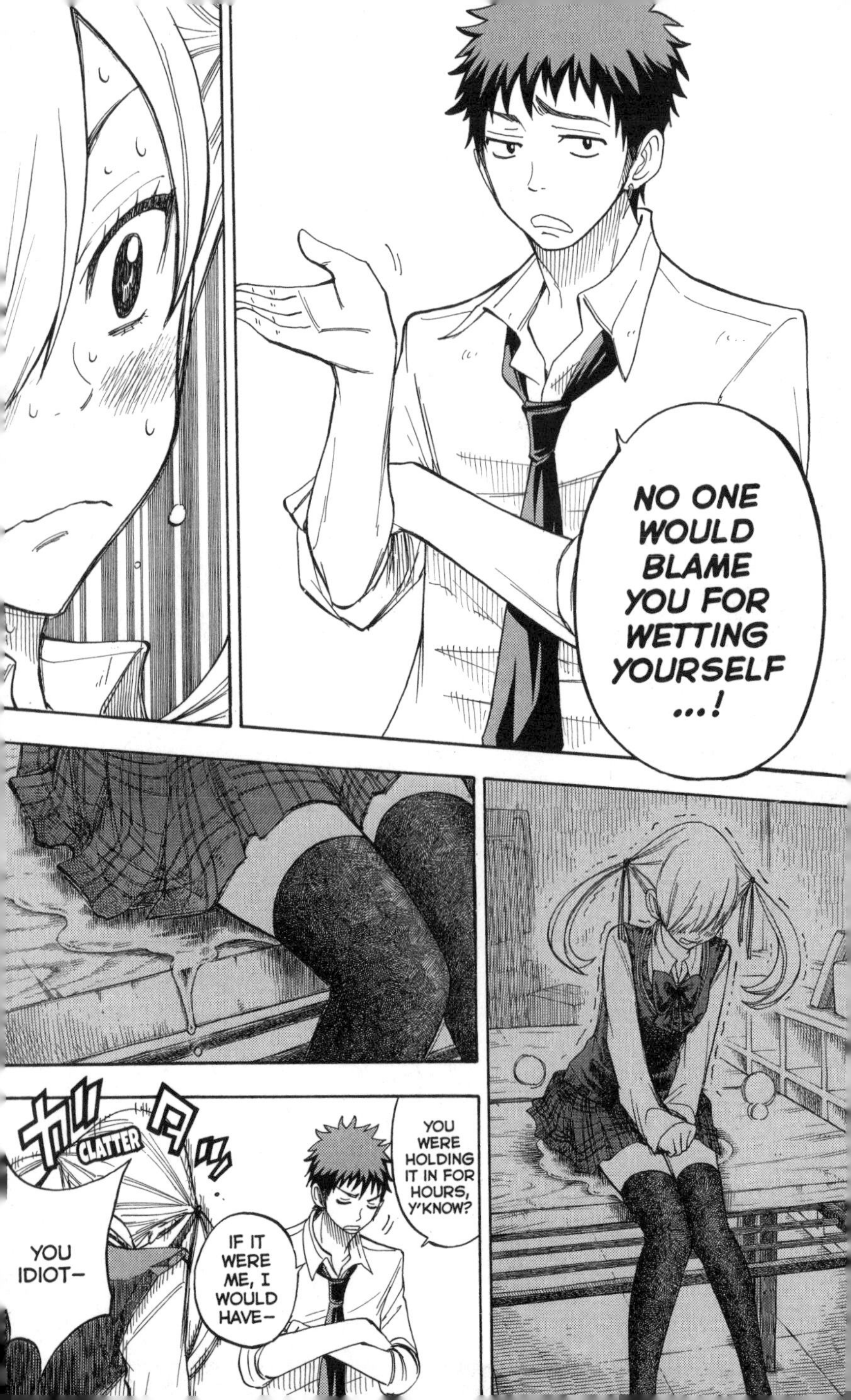
NO ONE WOULD BLAME YOU FOR WETTING YOURSELF ...!
YOU WERE HOLDING IT IN FOR HOURS, Y'KNOW?
IF IT WERE ME, I WOULD HAVE—
CLATTER
YOU IDIOT—

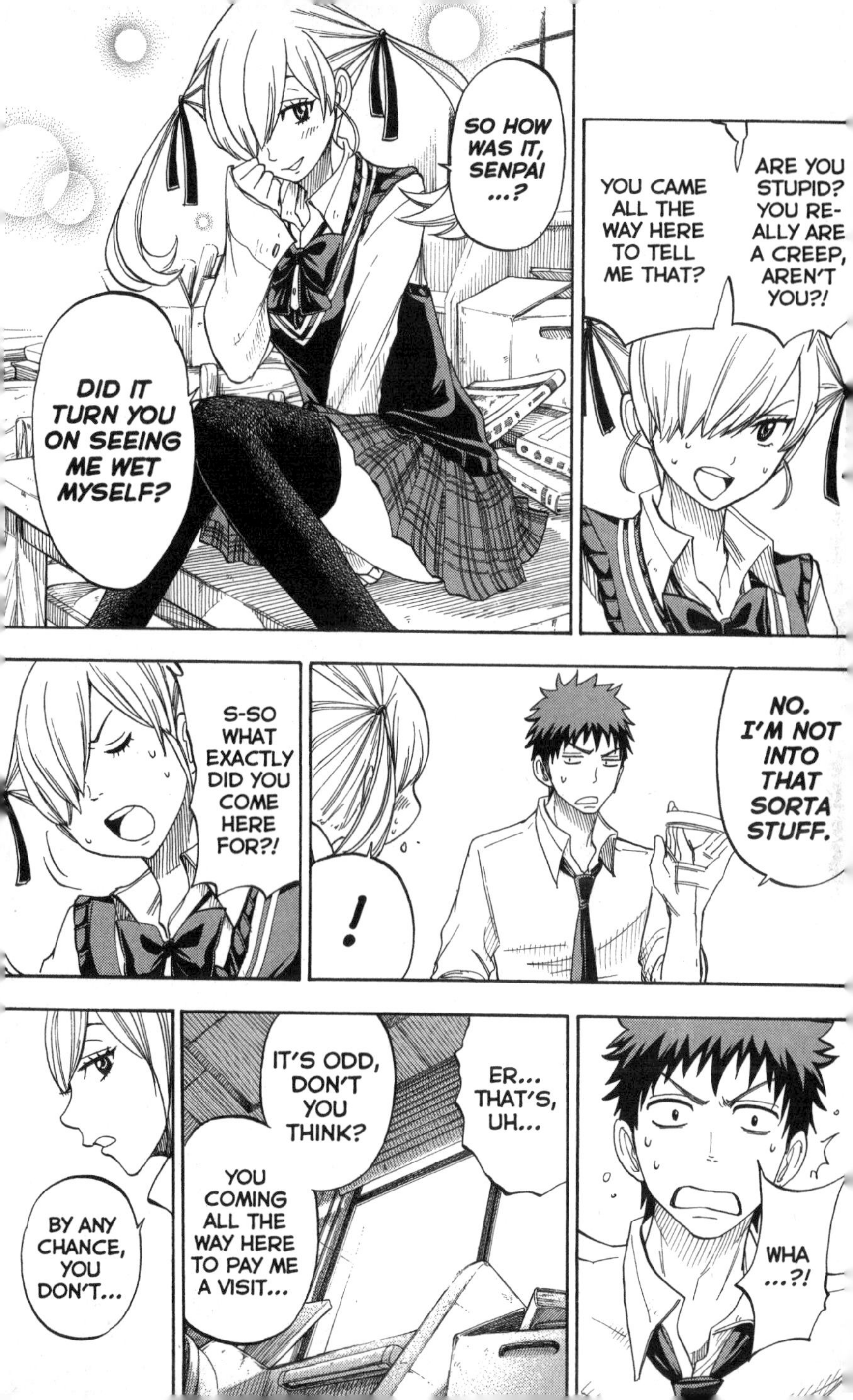
ARE YOU STUPID? YOU RE-ALLY ARE A CREEP, AREN'T YOU?!
YOU CAME ALL THE WAY HERE TO TELL ME THAT?
SO HOW WAS IT, SENPAI ...?
DID IT TURN YOU ON SEEING ME WET MYSELF?
NO. I'M NOT INTO THAT SORTA STUFF.
!
S-SO WHAT EXACTLY DID YOU COME HERE FOR?!
WHA ...?!
ER... THAT'S, UH...
IT'S ODD, DON'T YOU THINK?
YOU COMING ALL THE WAY HERE TO PAY ME A VISIT...
BY ANY CHANCE, YOU DON'T...

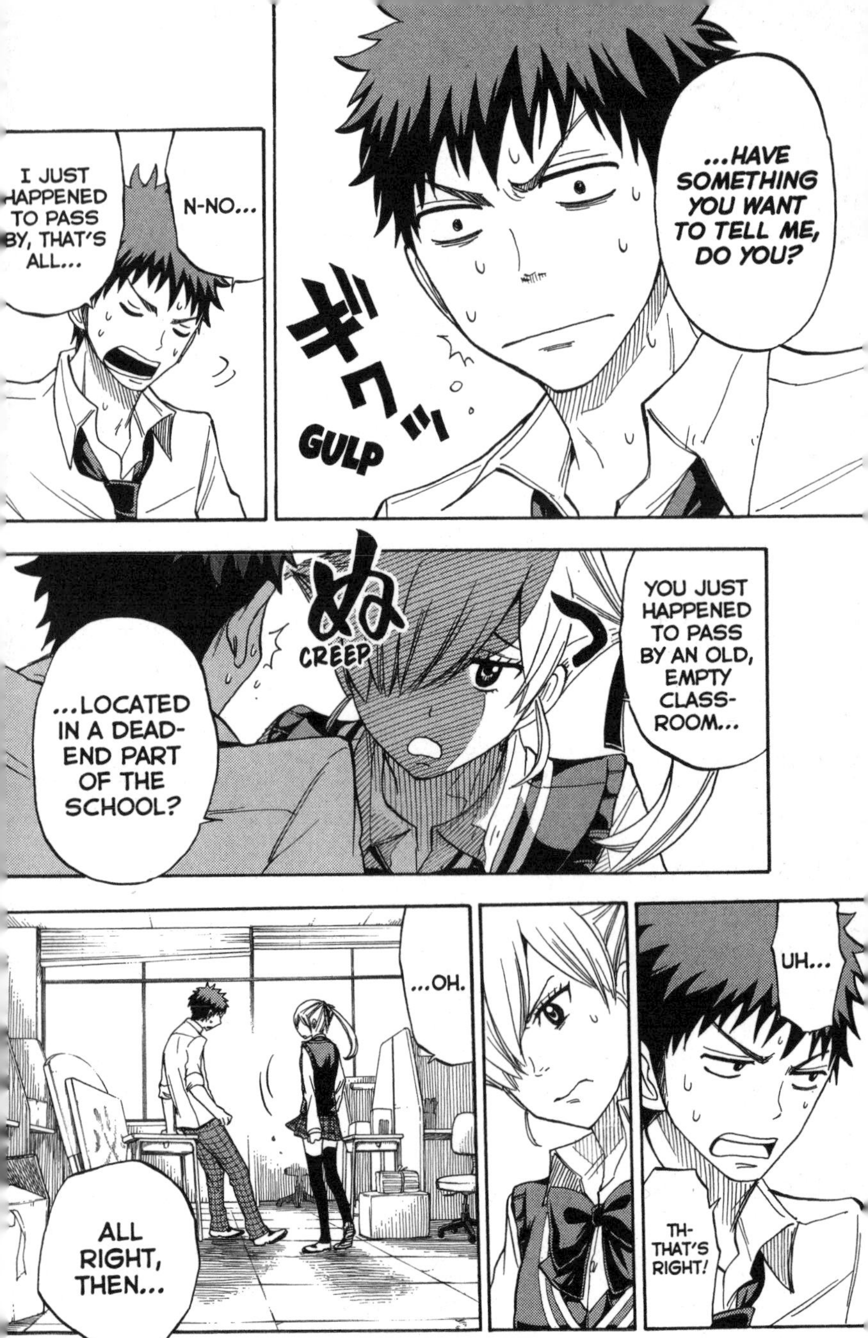
...HAVE SOMETHING YOU WANT TO TELL ME, DO YOU?
ギクッ
GULP
N-NO...
I JUST HAPPENED TO PASS BY, THAT'S ALL...
YOU JUST HAPPENED TO PASS BY AN OLD, EMPTY CLASS-ROOM...
ぬっ
CREEP
...LOCATED IN A DEAD-END PART OF THE SCHOOL?
UH...
TH-THAT'S RIGHT!
...OH.
ALL RIGHT, THEN...

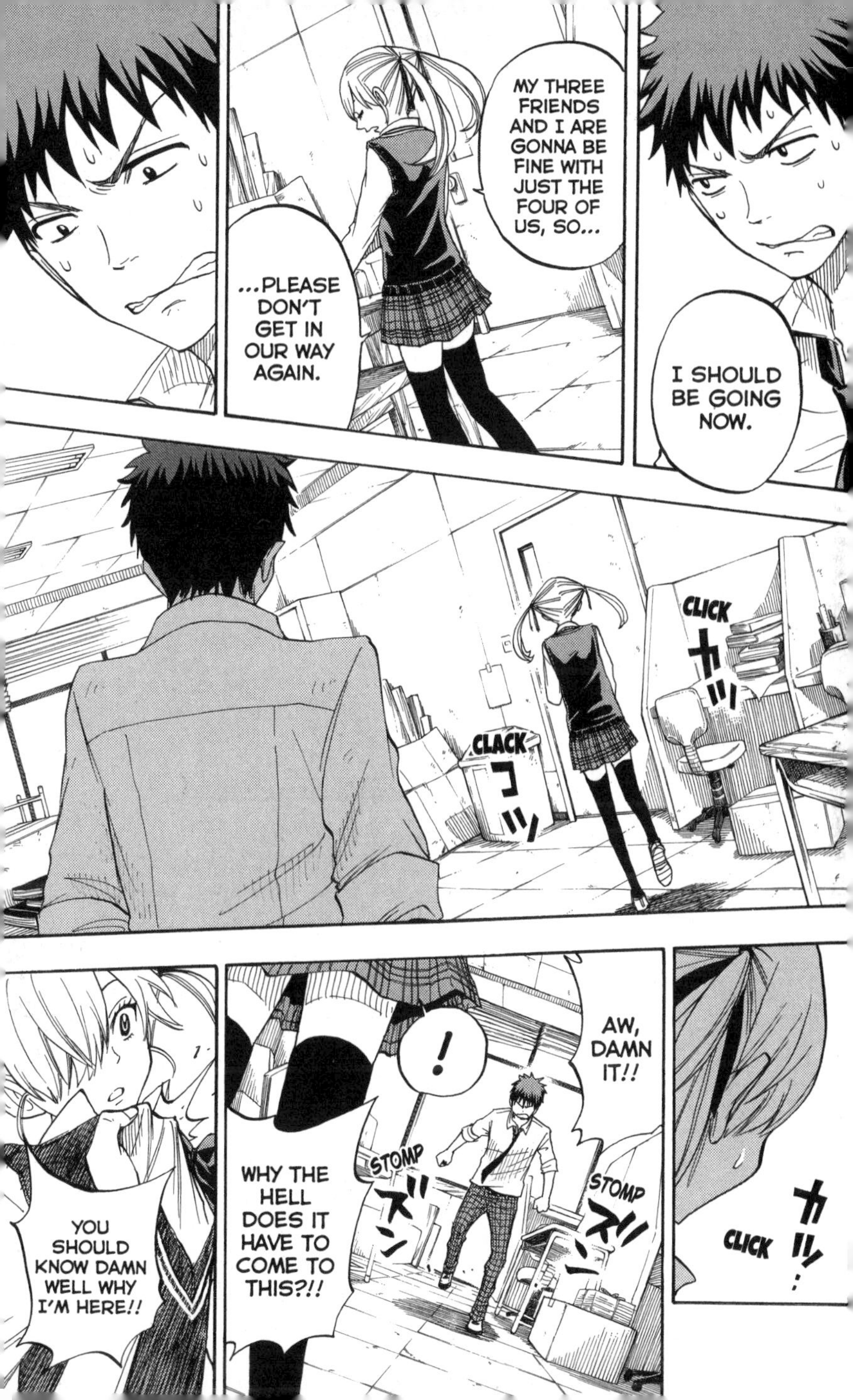
I SHOULD BE GOING NOW.
MY THREE FRIENDS AND I ARE GONNA BE FINE WITH JUST THE FOUR OF US, SO...
...PLEASE DON'T GET IN OUR WAY AGAIN.
CLICK
カッ
CLACK
コッ
カッ
CLICK
AW, DAMN IT!!
!
STOMP
ズン
WHY THE HELL DOES IT HAVE TO COME TO THIS?!!
STOMP
ズン
YOU SHOULD KNOW DAMN WELL WHY I'M HERE!!

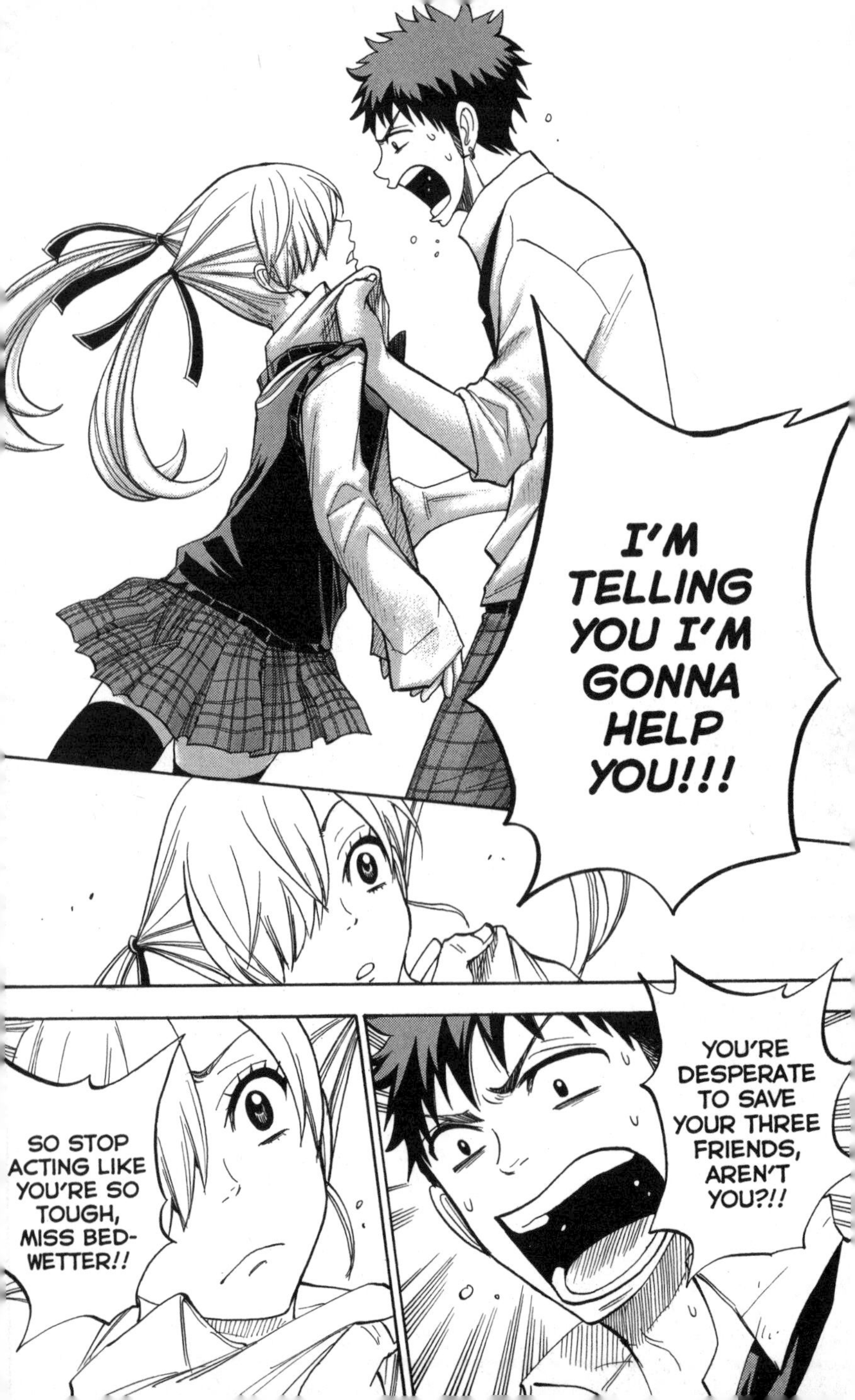
I'M TELLING YOU I'M GONNA HELP YOU!!!
YOU'RE DESPERATE TO SAVE YOUR THREE FRIENDS, AREN'T YOU?!!
SO STOP ACTING LIKE YOU'RE SO TOUGH, MISS BED-WETTER!!

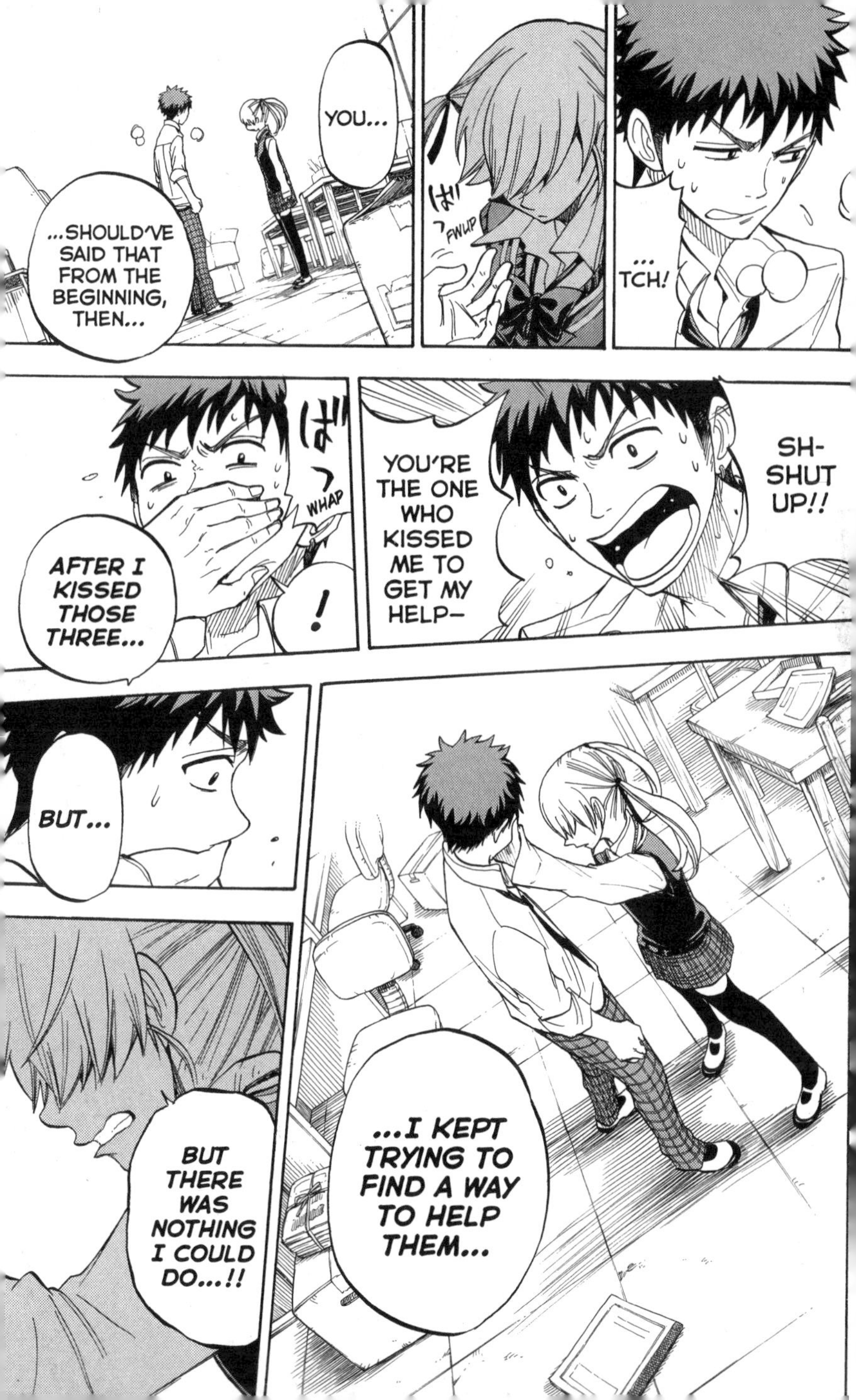
...TCH!
ぱっ
FWUP
YOU...
...SHOULD'VE SAID THAT FROM THE BEGINNING, THEN...
SH- SHUT UP!!
YOU'RE THE ONE WHO KISSED ME TO GET MY HELP—
ばっ
WHAP
!
AFTER I KISSED THOSE THREE...
...I KEPT TRYING TO FIND A WAY TO HELP THEM...
BUT...
BUT THERE WAS NOTHING I COULD DO...!!

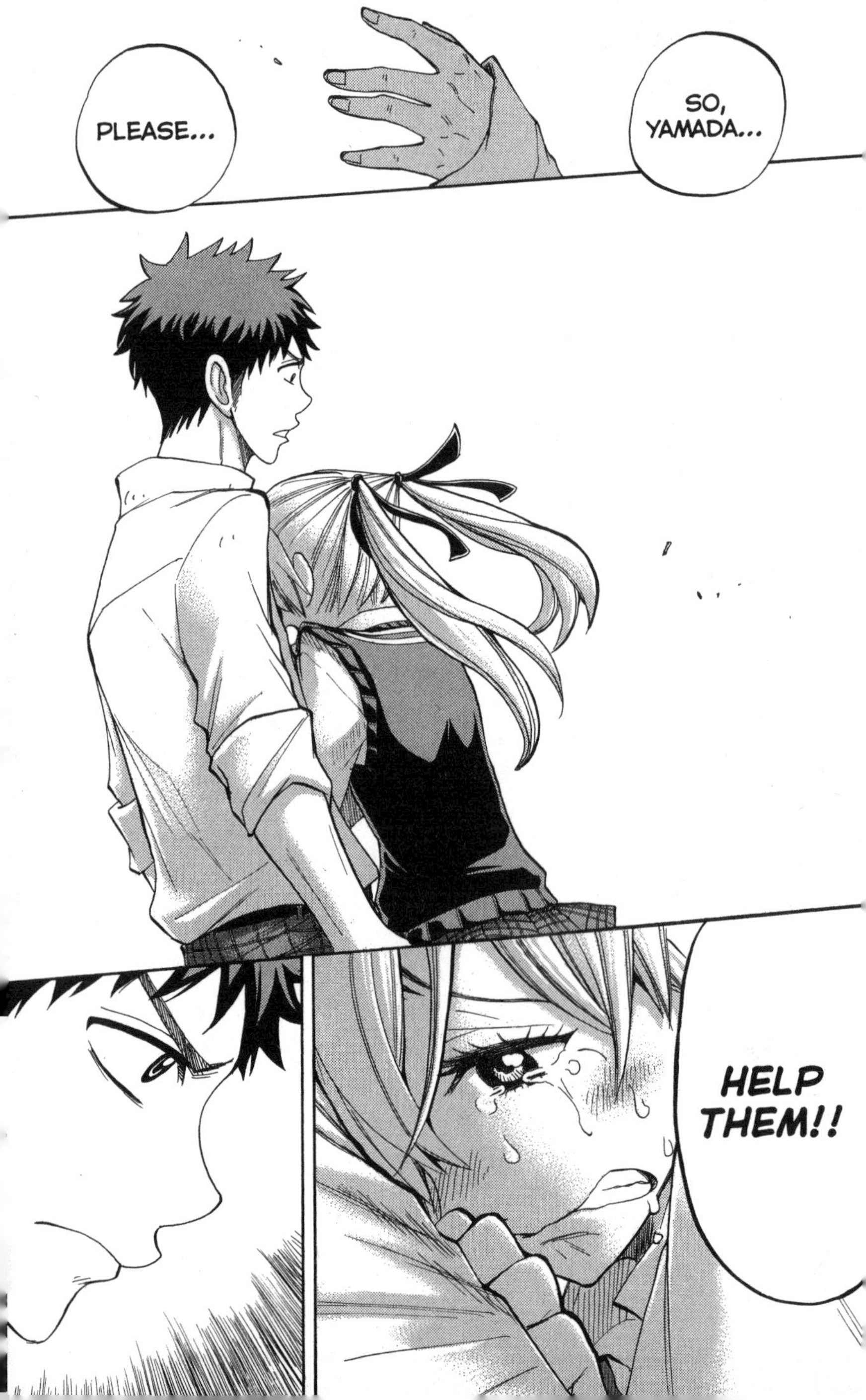
SO, YAMADA...
PLEASE...
HELP THEM!!

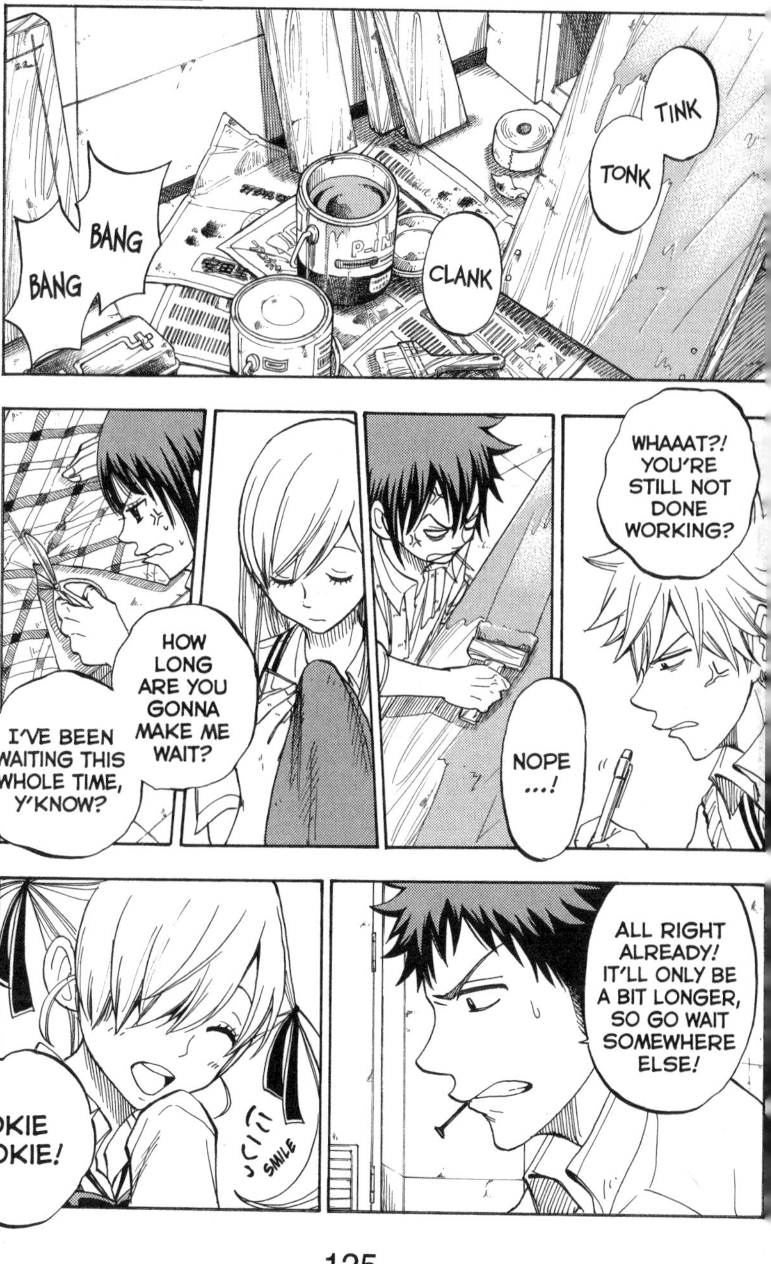
TINK
TONK
CLANK
BANG
BANG
WHAAAT?! YOU'RE STILL NOT DONE WORKING?
NOPE ...!
HOW LONG ARE YOU GONNA MAKE ME WAIT?
I'VE BEEN WAITING THIS WHOLE TIME, Y'KNOW?
ALL RIGHT ALREADY! IT'LL ONLY BE A BIT LONGER, SO GO WAIT SOMEWHERE ELSE!
SMILE
OKIE DOKIE!

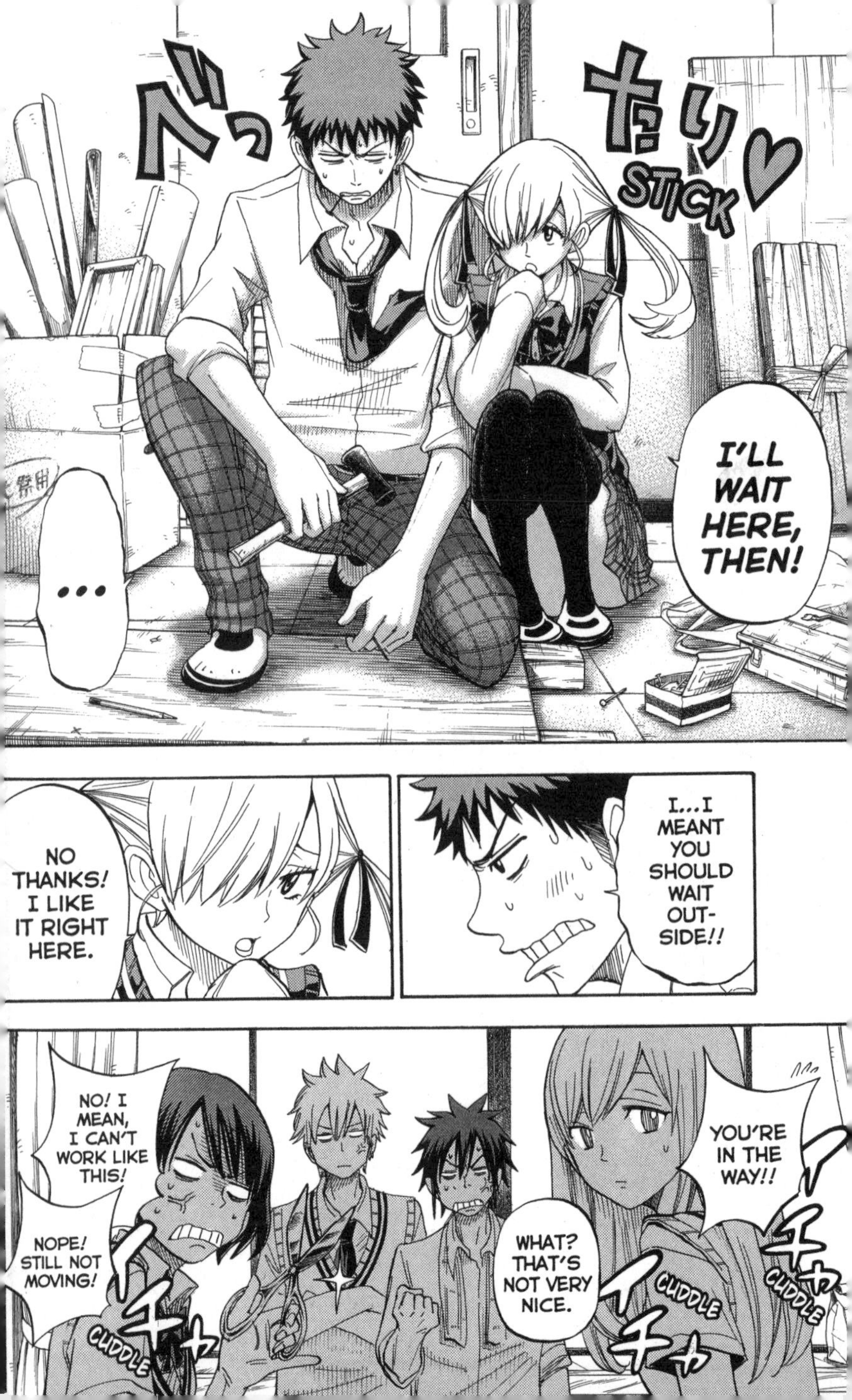
べったり
STICK
I'LL WAIT HERE, THEN!
...
I...I MEANT YOU SHOULD WAIT OUT-SIDE!!
NO THANKS! I LIKE IT RIGHT HERE.
YOU'RE IN THE WAY!!
イチャ
CUDDLE
WHAT? THAT'S NOT VERY NICE.
イチャ
CUDDLE
NO! I MEAN, I CAN'T WORK LIKE THIS!
NOPE! STILL NOT MOVING!
イチャ
CUDDLE

CHAPTER 50: Well, you did say that.

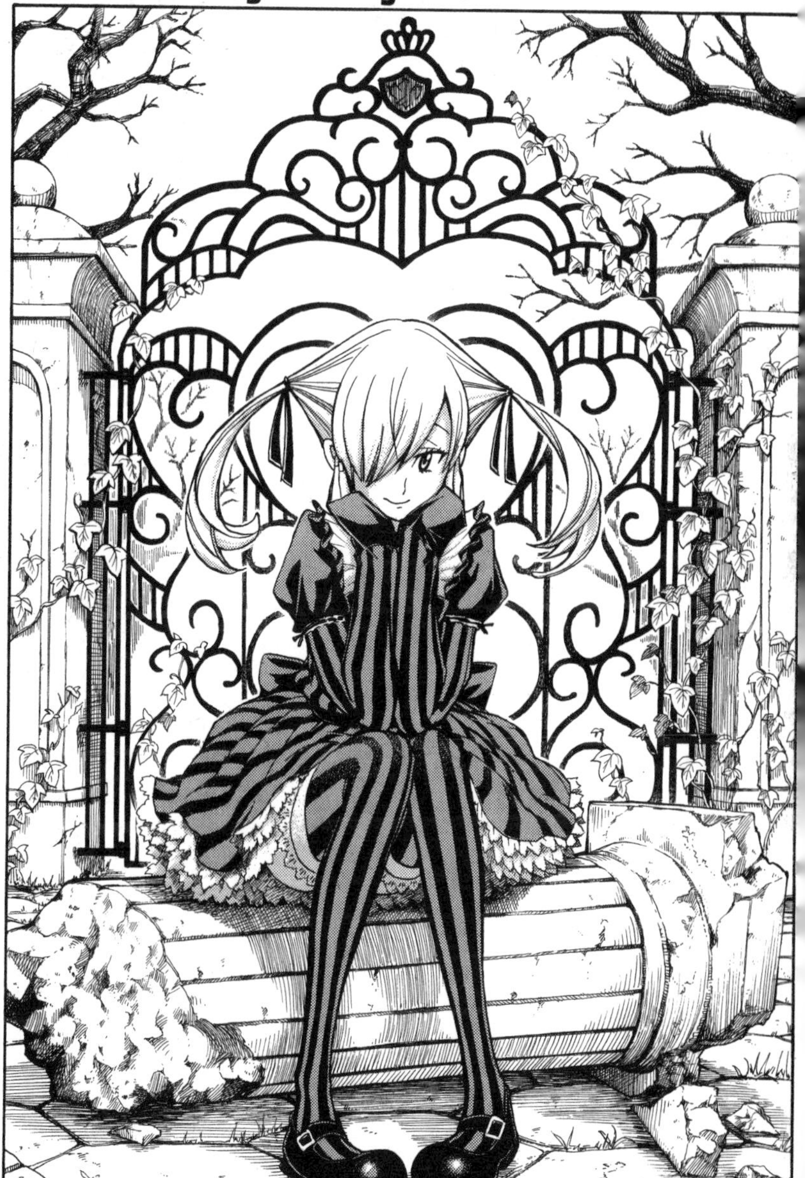

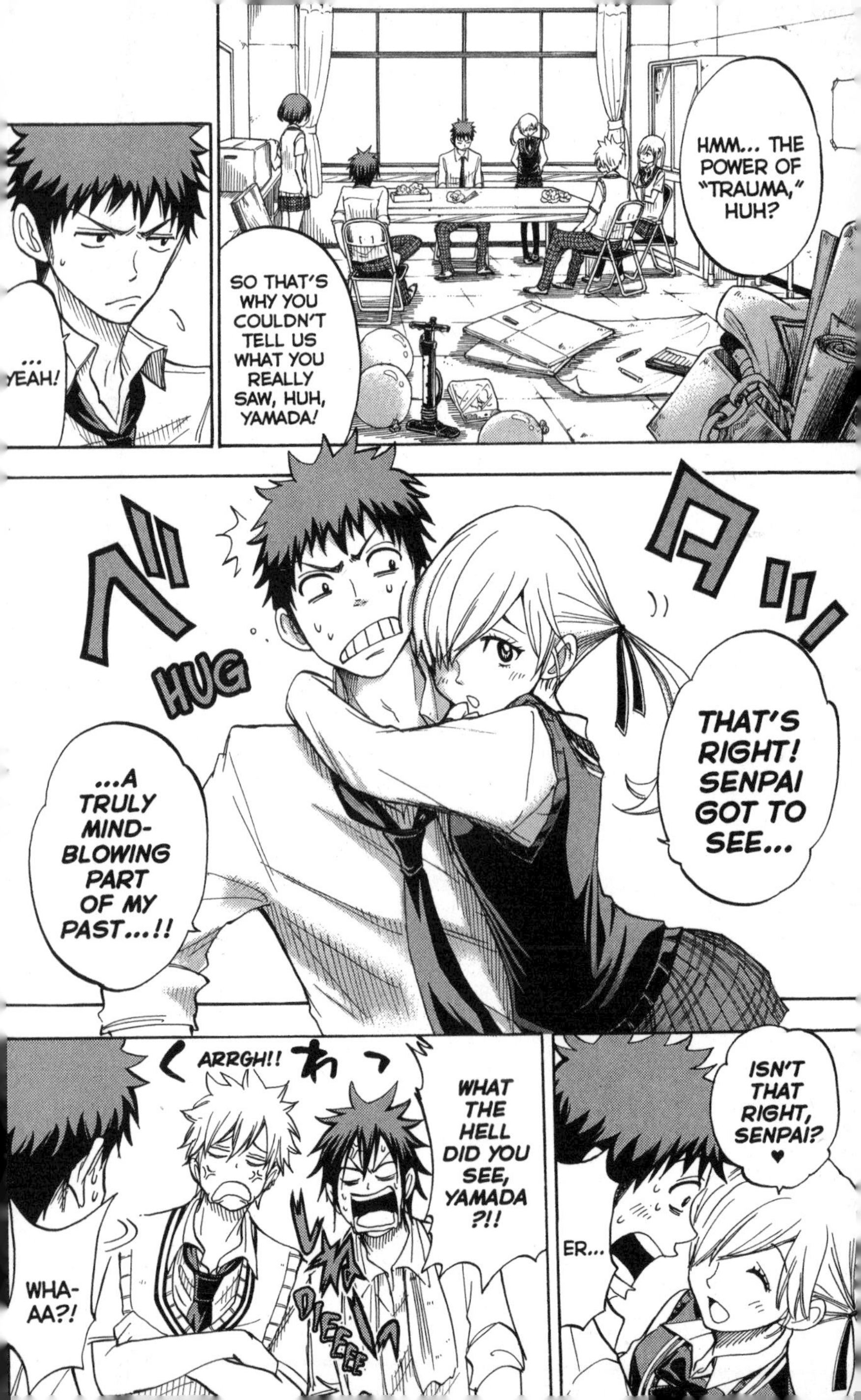
HMM... THE POWER OF "TRAUMA," HUH?
SO THAT'S WHY YOU COULDN'T TELL US WHAT YOU REALLY SAW, HUH, YAMADA!
...YEAH!
THAT'S RIGHT! SENPAI GOT TO SEE...
HUG
...A TRULY MIND-BLOWING PART OF MY PAST...!!
ISN'T THAT RIGHT, SENPAI? ♥
ER...
ARRGH!!
WHAT THE HELL DID YOU SEE, YAMADA?!!
DIEEEE
WHA-AA?!

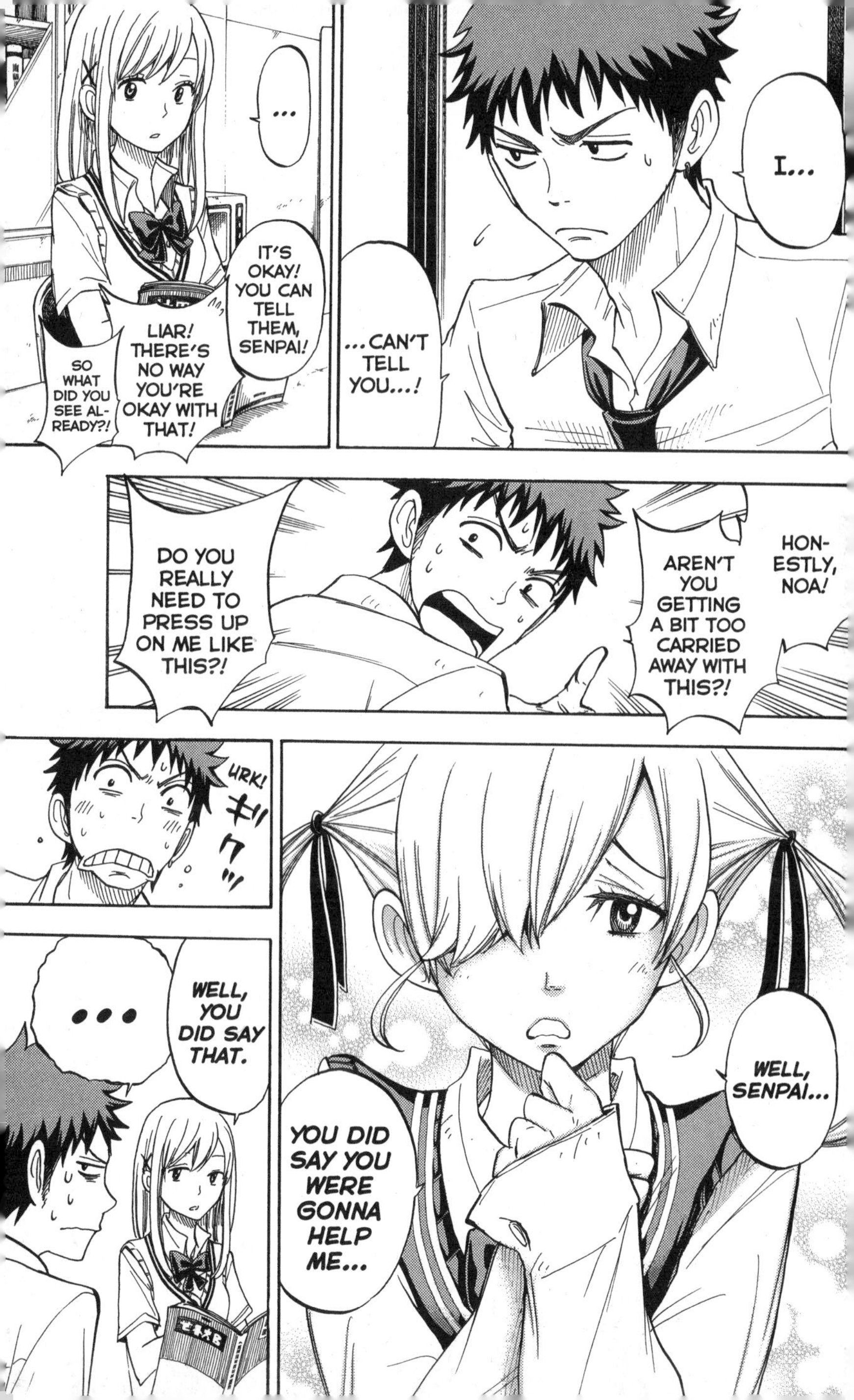
I...
...CAN'T TELL YOU...!
...
IT'S OKAY! YOU CAN TELL THEM, SENPAI!
LIAR! THERE'S NO WAY YOU'RE OKAY WITH THAT!
SO WHAT DID YOU SEE AL-READY?!
HON-ESTLY, NOA!
AREN'T YOU GETTING A BIT TOO CARRIED AWAY WITH THIS?!
DO YOU REALLY NEED TO PRESS UP ON ME LIKE THIS?!
WELL, SENPAI...
YOU DID SAY YOU WERE GONNA HELP ME...
URK!
ギクッ
WELL, YOU DID SAY THAT.
•••

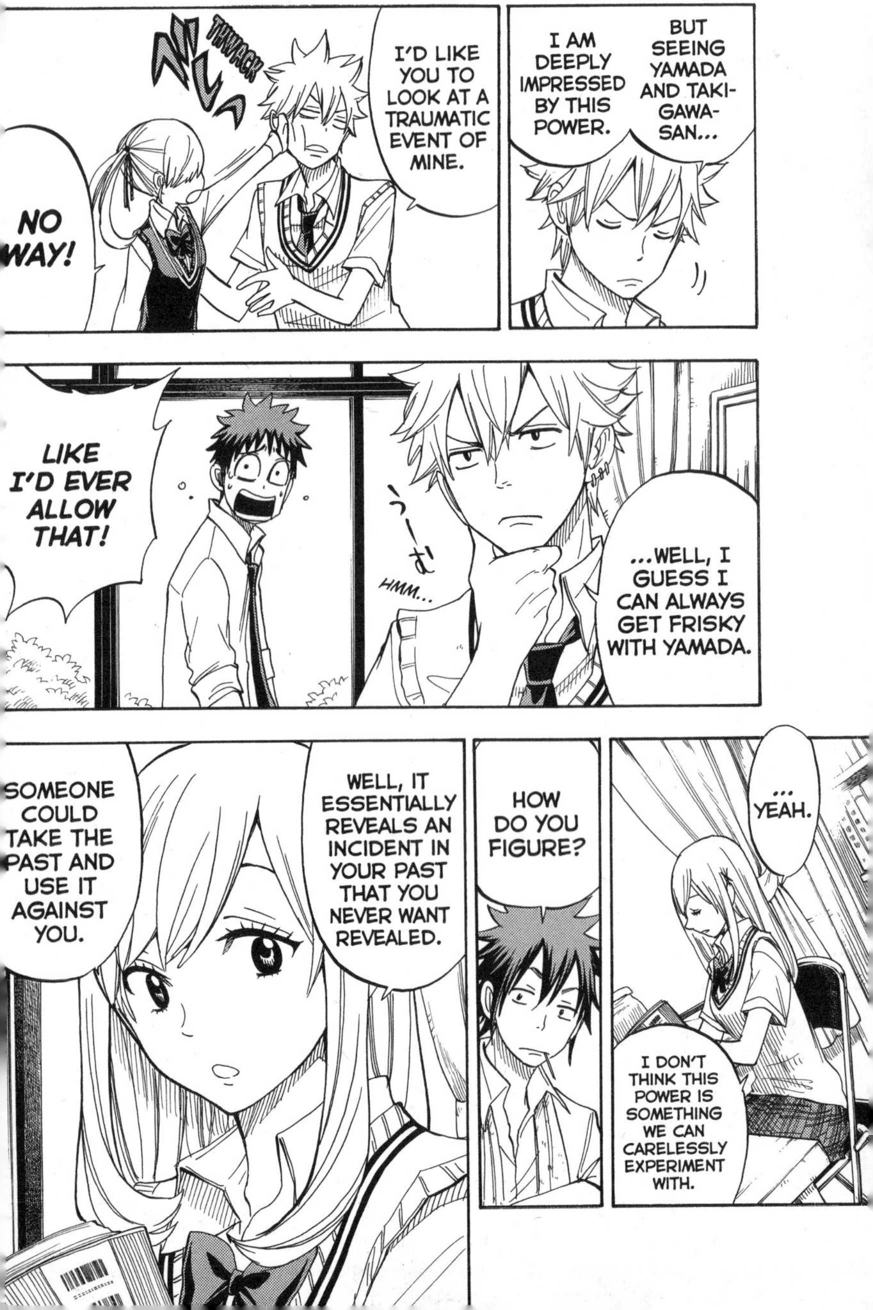
BUT SEEING YAMADA AND TAKI-GAWA-SAN...
I AM DEEPLY IMPRESSED BY THIS POWER.
I'D LIKE YOU TO LOOK AT A TRAUMATIC EVENT OF MINE.
THWACK
NO WAY!
...WELL, I GUESS I CAN ALWAYS GET FRISKY WITH YAMADA.
HMM...
LIKE I'D EVER ALLOW THAT!
...YEAH.
I DON'T THINK THIS POWER IS SOMETHING WE CAN CARELESSLY EXPERIMENT WITH.
HOW DO YOU FIGURE?
WELL, IT ESSENTIALLY REVEALS AN INCIDENT IN YOUR PAST THAT YOU NEVER WANT REVEALED.
SOMEONE COULD TAKE THE PAST AND USE IT AGAINST YOU.

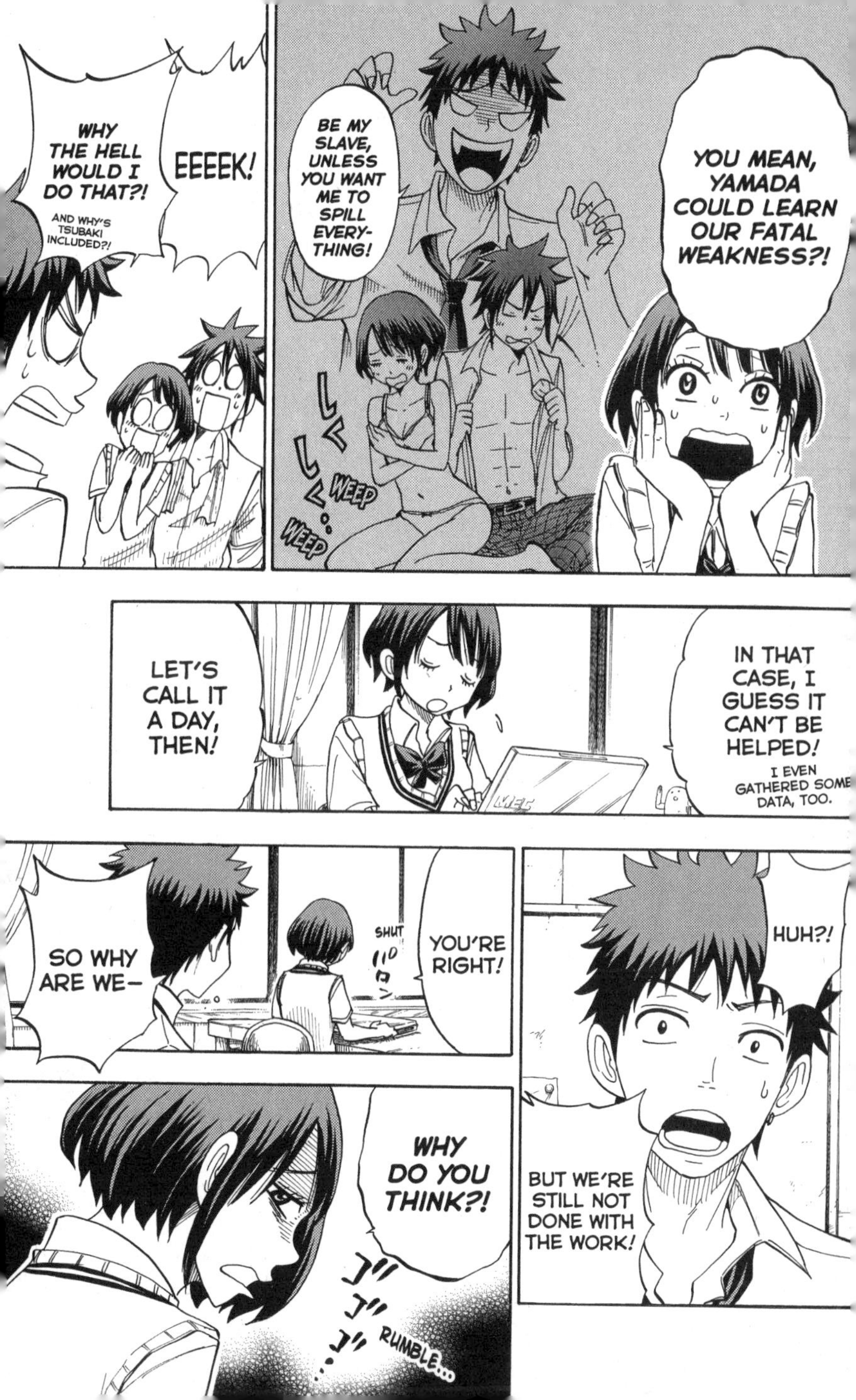
YOU MEAN, YAMADA COULD LEARN OUR FATAL WEAKNESS?!
BE MY SLAVE, UNLESS YOU WANT ME TO SPILL EVERY-THING!
WEEP
WEEP
EEEEK!
WHY THE HELL WOULD I DO THAT?!
AND WHY'S TSUBAKI INCLUDED?!
IN THAT CASE, I GUESS IT CAN'T BE HELPED!
I EVEN GATHERED SOME DATA, TOO.
LET'S CALL IT A DAY, THEN!
HUH?!
BUT WE'RE STILL NOT DONE WITH THE WORK!
YOU'RE RIGHT!
SHUT
SO WHY ARE WE—
WHY DO YOU THINK?!
RUMBLE...

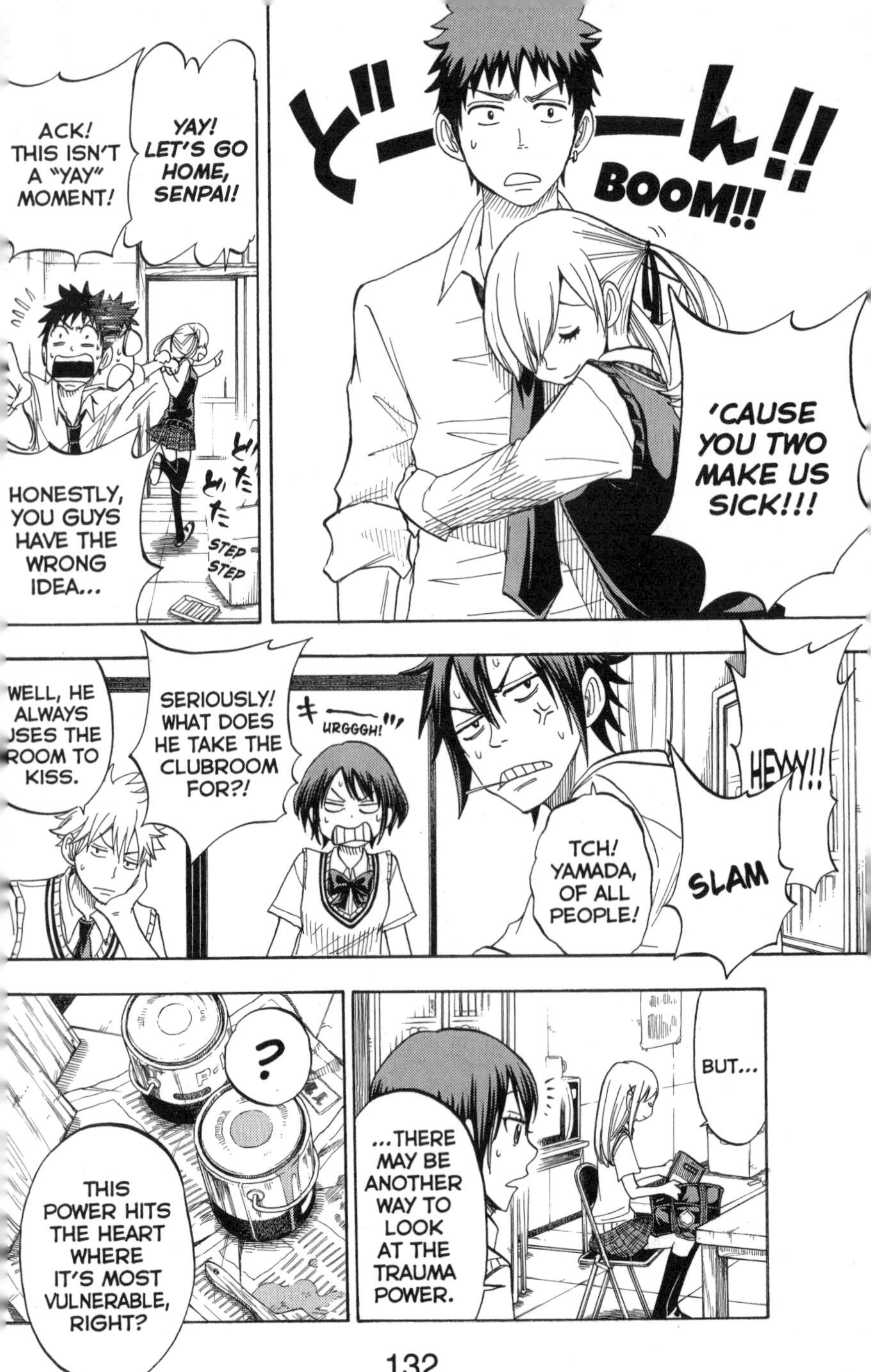
どーーん!!
BOOM!!
'CAUSE YOU TWO MAKE US SICK!!!
YAY! LET'S GO HOME, SENPAI!
ACK! THIS ISN'T A "YAY" MOMENT!
どた どた
STEP STEP
HONESTLY, YOU GUYS HAVE THE WRONG IDEA...
HEYYY!!
SLAM
TCH! YAMADA, OF ALL PEOPLE!
キー URGGGH!
SERIOUSLY! WHAT DOES HE TAKE THE CLUBROOM FOR?!
WELL, HE ALWAYS USES THE ROOM TO KISS.
BUT...
...THERE MAY BE ANOTHER WAY TO LOOK AT THE TRAUMA POWER.
?
THIS POWER HITS THE HEART WHERE IT'S MOST VULNERABLE, RIGHT?

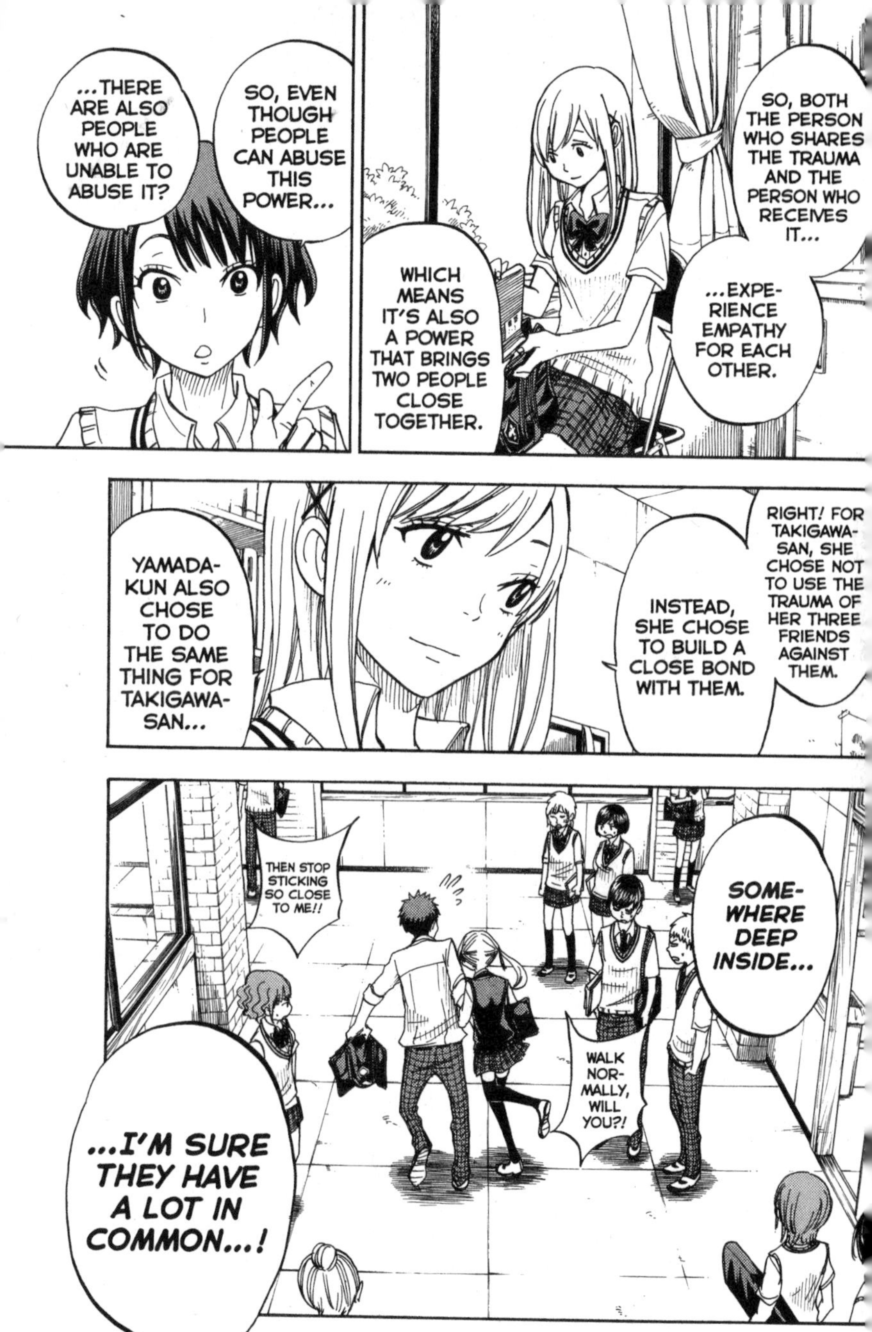
SO, BOTH THE PERSON WHO SHARES THE TRAUMA AND THE PERSON WHO RECEIVES IT...
...EXPE-RIENCE EMPATHY FOR EACH OTHER.
WHICH MEANS IT'S ALSO A POWER THAT BRINGS TWO PEOPLE CLOSE TOGETHER.
SO, EVEN THOUGH PEOPLE CAN ABUSE THIS POWER...
...THERE ARE ALSO PEOPLE WHO ARE UNABLE TO ABUSE IT?
RIGHT! FOR TAKIGAWA-SAN, SHE CHOSE NOT TO USE THE TRAUMA OF HER THREE FRIENDS AGAINST THEM.
INSTEAD, SHE CHOSE TO BUILD A CLOSE BOND WITH THEM.
YAMADA-KUN ALSO CHOSE TO DO THE SAME THING FOR TAKIGAWA-SAN...
SOME-WHERE DEEP INSIDE...
WALK NOR-MALLY, WILL YOU?!
THEN STOP STICKING SO CLOSE TO ME!!
...I'M SURE THEY HAVE A LOT IN COMMON...!

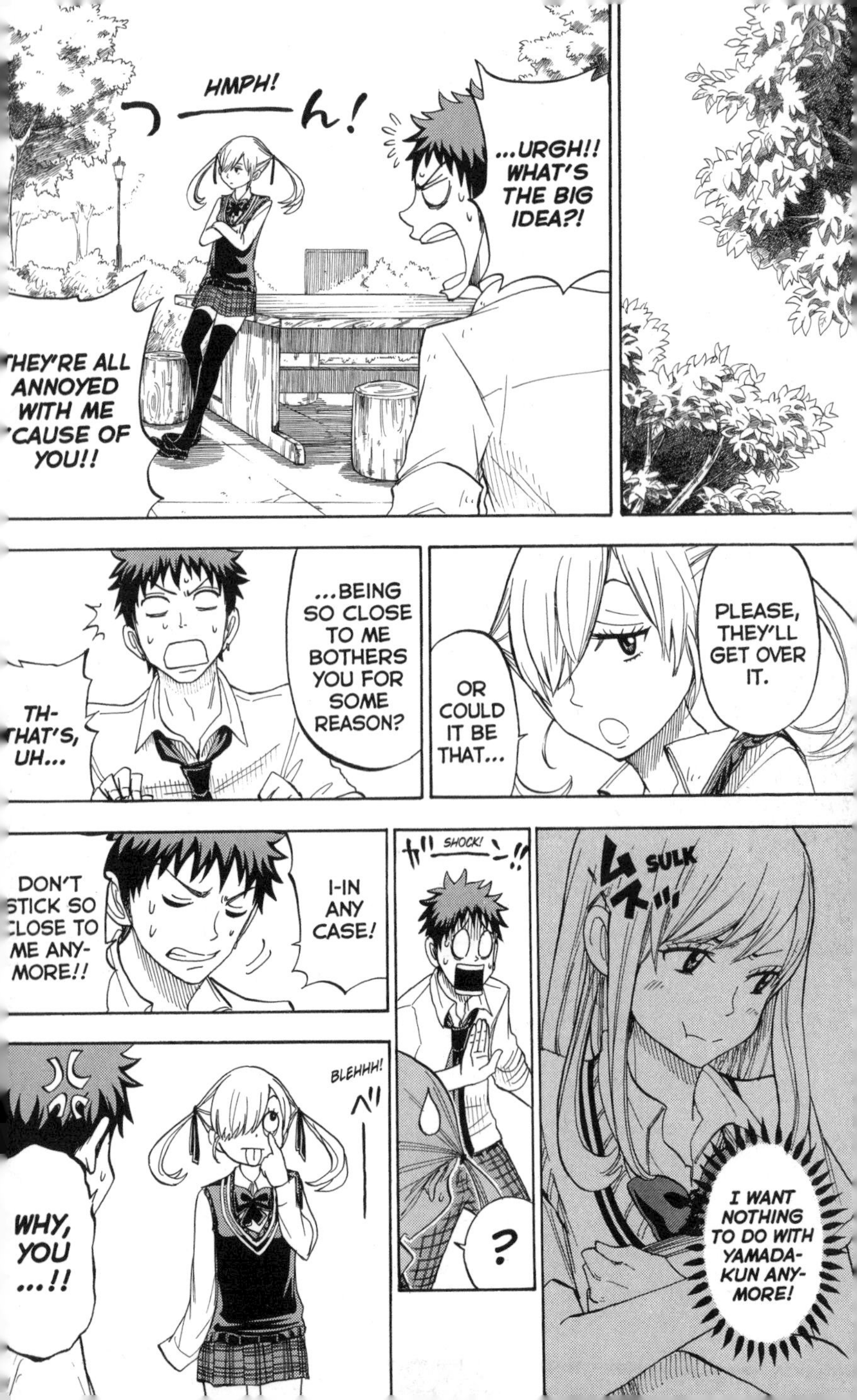

...URGH!! WHAT'S THE BIG IDEA?!
つーーん!
HMPH!
THEY'RE ALL ANNOYED WITH ME 'CAUSE OF YOU!!
PLEASE, THEY'LL GET OVER IT.
OR COULD IT BE THAT...
...BEING SO CLOSE TO ME BOTHERS YOU FOR SOME REASON?
TH-THAT'S, UH...
ムス"
SULK
I WANT NOTHING TO DO WITH YAMADA-KUN ANYMORE!
ガーン!!
SHOCK!
?
I-IN ANY CASE!
DON'T STICK SO CLOSE TO ME ANYMORE!!
べー
BLEHHH!
WHY, YOU ...!!

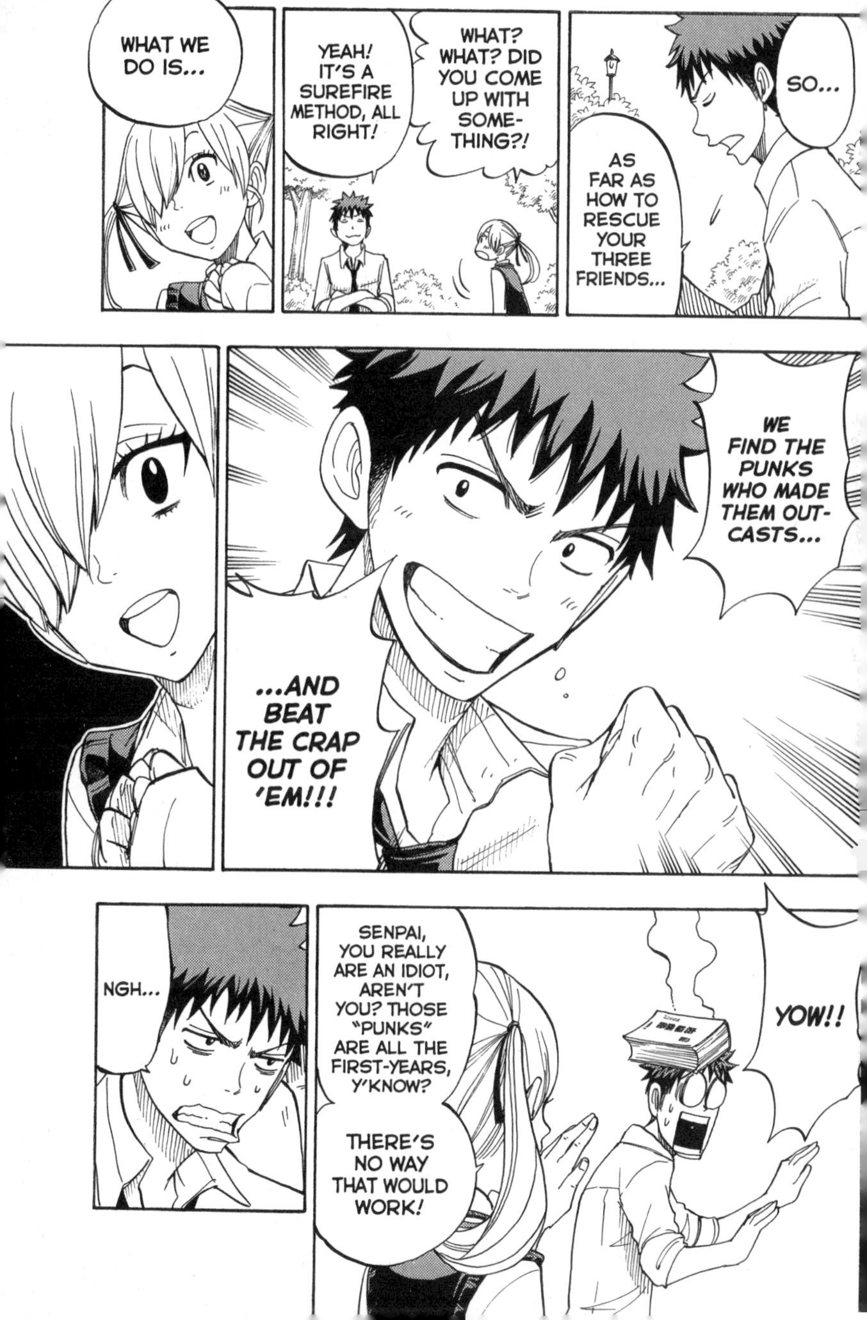
SO...
AS FAR AS HOW TO RESCUE YOUR THREE FRIENDS...
WHAT? WHAT? DID YOU COME UP WITH SOME-THING?!
YEAH! IT'S A SUREFIRE METHOD, ALL RIGHT!
WHAT WE DO IS...
WE FIND THE PUNKS WHO MADE THEM OUT-CASTS...
...AND BEAT THE CRAP OUT OF 'EM!!!
YOW!!
SENPAI, YOU REALLY ARE AN IDIOT, AREN'T YOU? THOSE "PUNKS" ARE ALL THE FIRST-YEARS, Y'KNOW?
THERE'S NO WAY THAT WOULD WORK!
NGH...

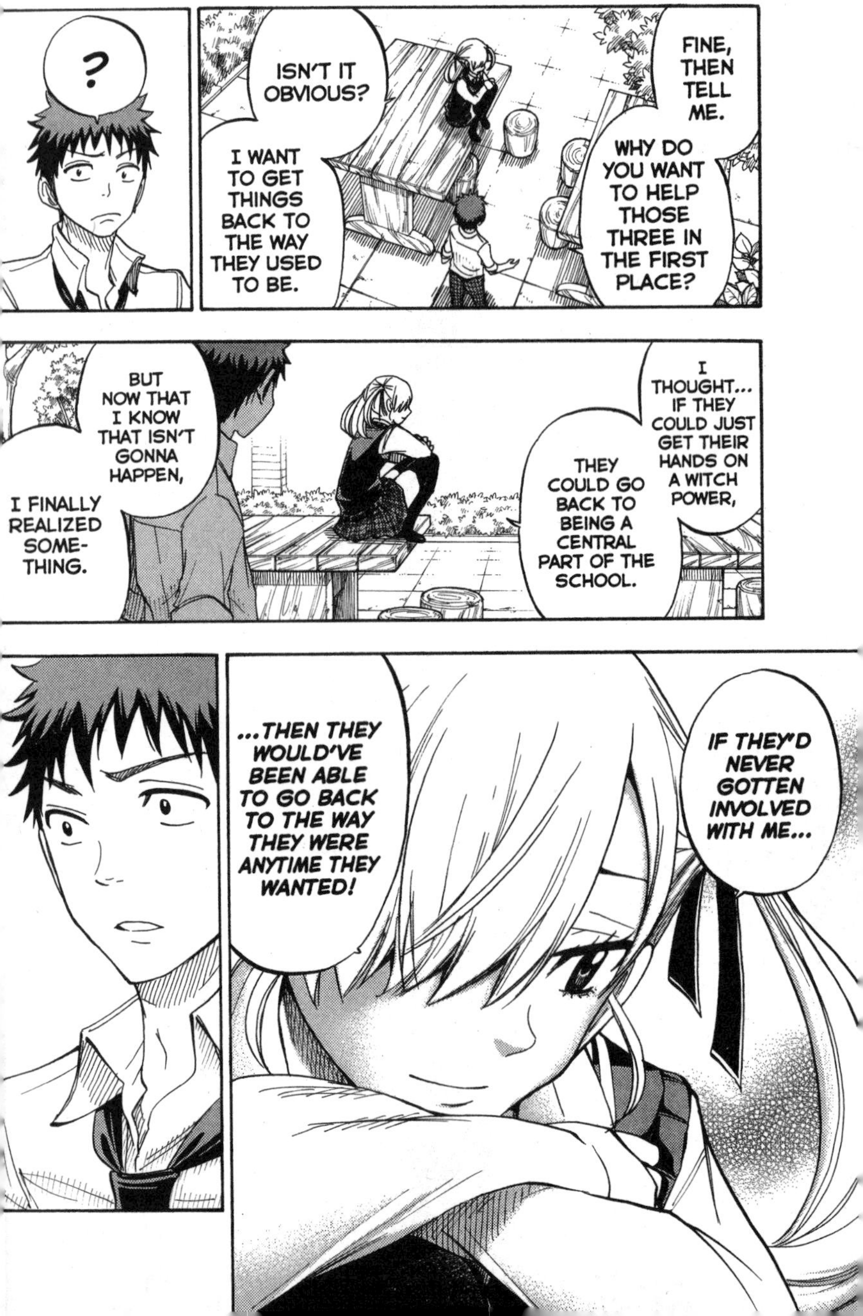
FINE, THEN TELL ME.
WHY DO YOU WANT TO HELP THOSE THREE IN THE FIRST PLACE?
ISN'T IT OBVIOUS?
I WANT TO GET THINGS BACK TO THE WAY THEY USED TO BE.
?
I THOUGHT... IF THEY COULD JUST GET THEIR HANDS ON A WITCH POWER,
THEY COULD GO BACK TO BEING A CENTRAL PART OF THE SCHOOL.
BUT NOW THAT I KNOW THAT ISN'T GONNA HAPPEN,
I FINALLY REALIZED SOME-THING.
IF THEY'D NEVER GOTTEN INVOLVED WITH ME...
...THEN THEY WOULD'VE BEEN ABLE TO GO BACK TO THE WAY THEY WERE ANYTIME THEY WANTED!

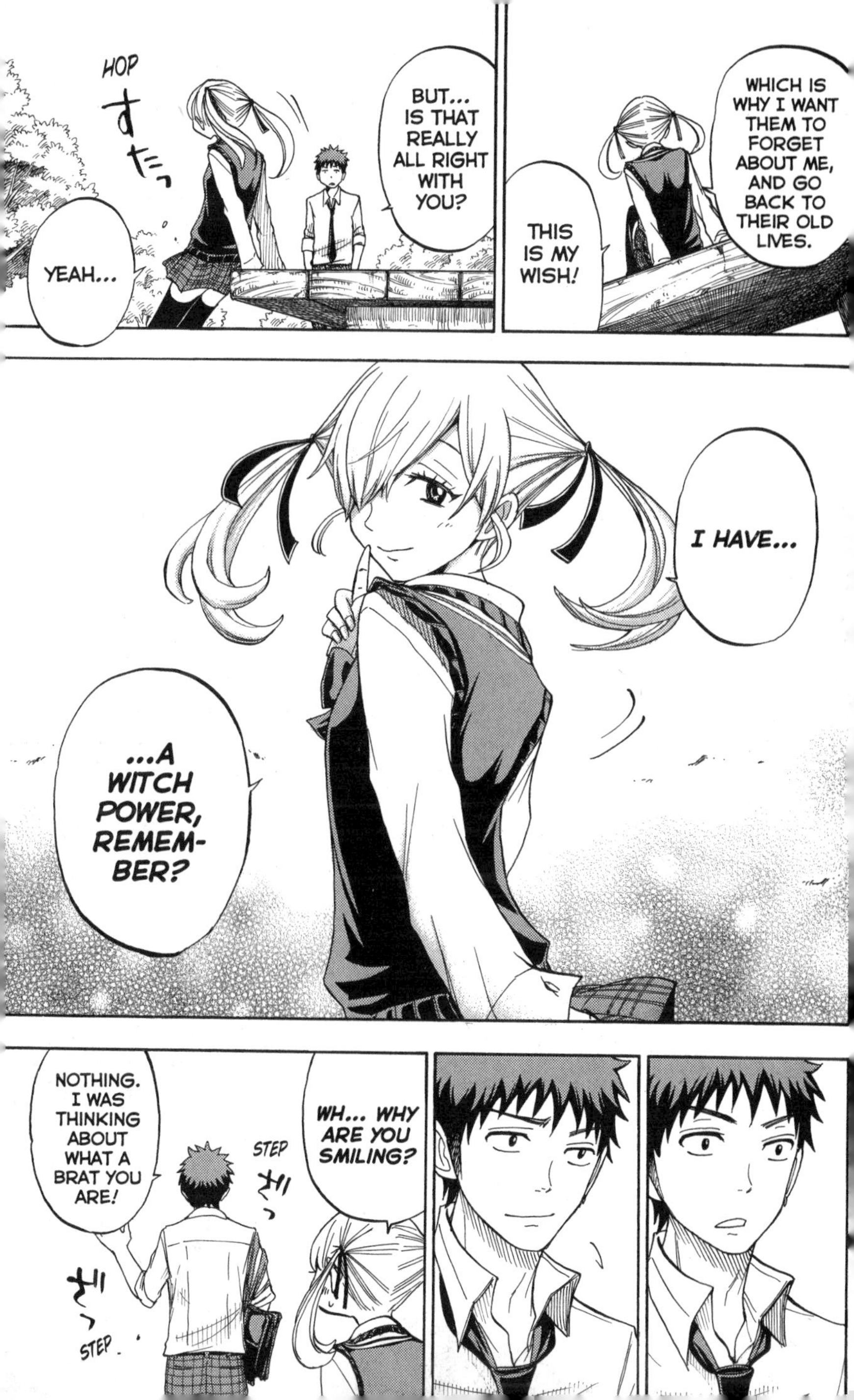
WHICH IS WHY I WANT THEM TO FORGET ABOUT ME, AND GO BACK TO THEIR OLD LIVES.
THIS IS MY WISH!
BUT... IS THAT REALLY ALL RIGHT WITH YOU?
HOP
すたっ
YEAH...
I HAVE...
...A WITCH POWER, REMEMBER?
WH... WHY ARE YOU SMILING?
STEP
ざっ
NOTHING. I WAS THINKING ABOUT WHAT A BRAT YOU ARE!
ざっ
STEP

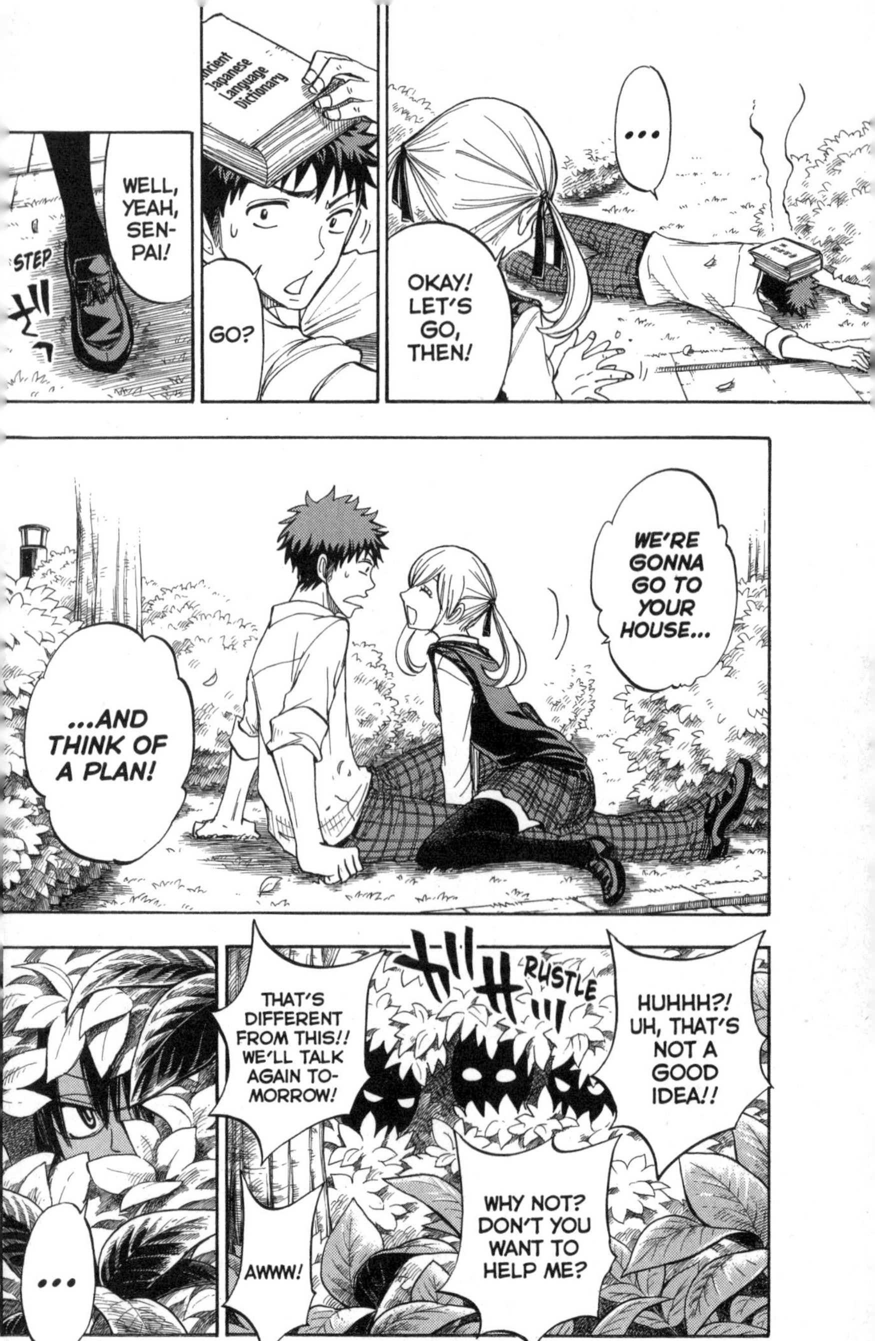
...
OKAY! LET'S GO, THEN!
Japanese Language Dictionary
GO?
WELL, YEAH, SEN-PAI!
STEP
WE'RE GONNA GO TO YOUR HOUSE...
...AND THINK OF A PLAN!
HUHHH?! UH, THAT'S NOT A GOOD IDEA!!
RUSTLE
WHY NOT? DON'T YOU WANT TO HELP ME?
THAT'S DIFFERENT FROM THIS!! WE'LL TALK AGAIN TO-MORROW!
AWWW!
...

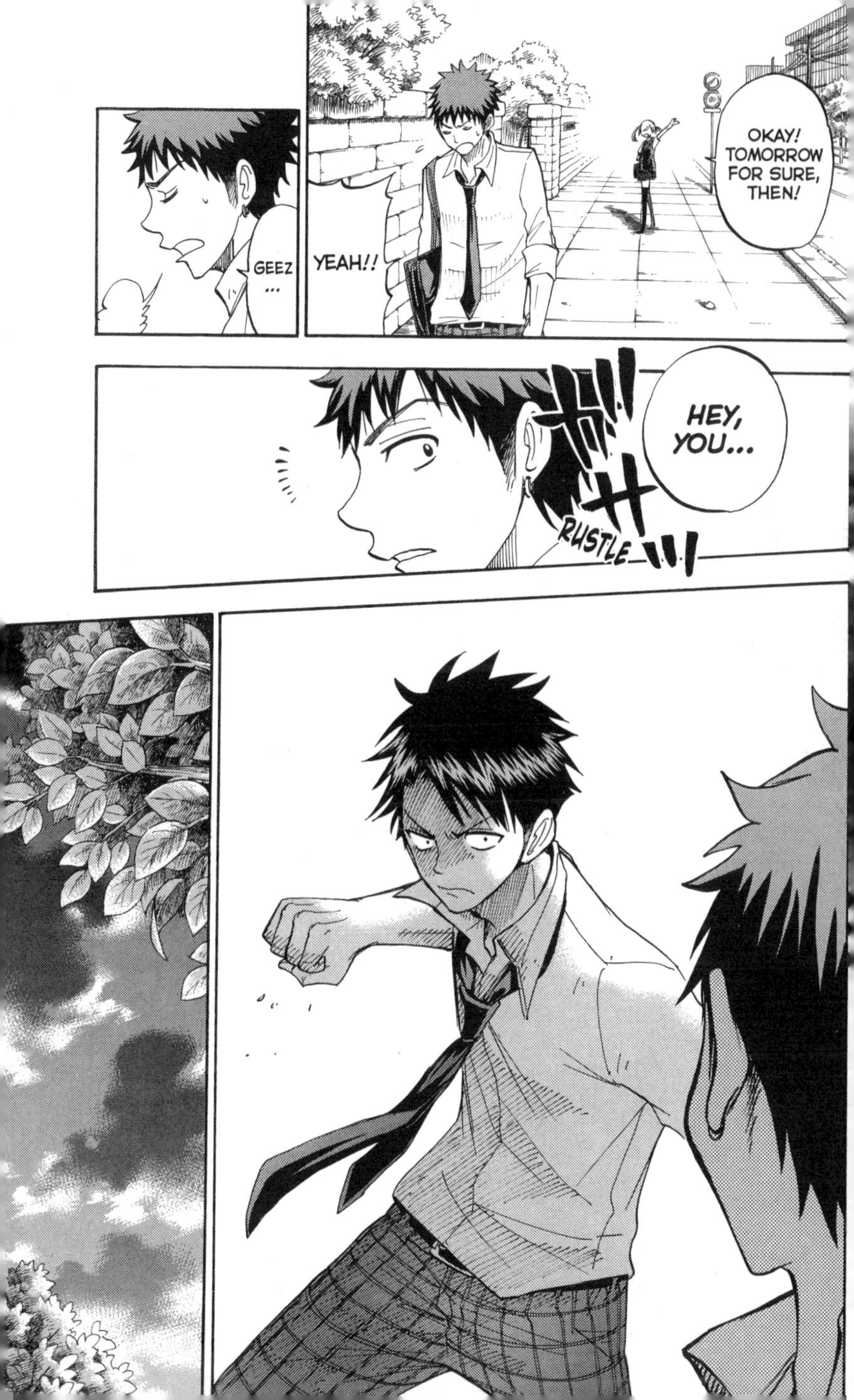
OKAY! TOMORROW FOR SURE, THEN!
YEAH!!
GEEZ ...
HEY, YOU...
RUSTLE

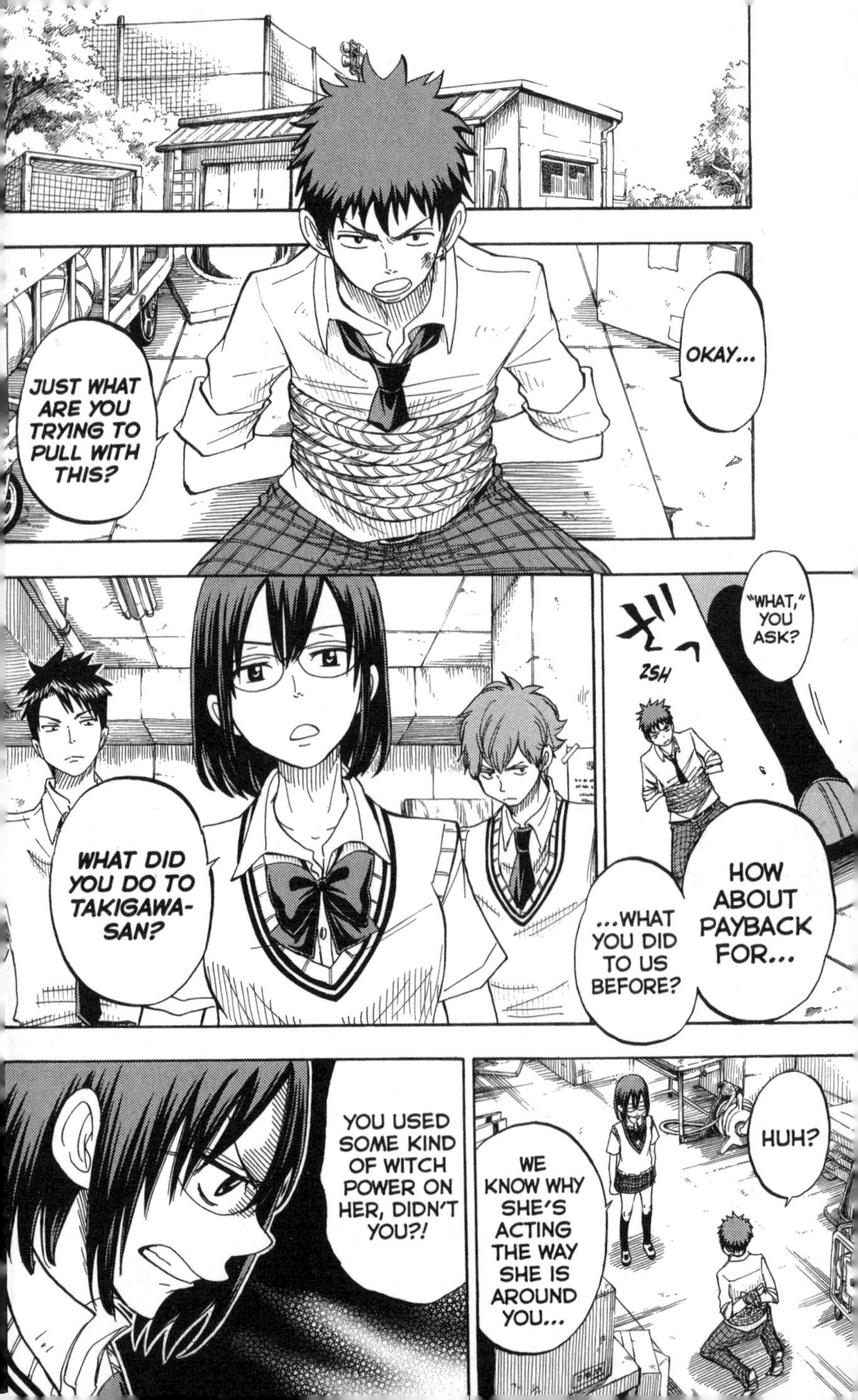
OKAY...
JUST WHAT ARE YOU TRYING TO PULL WITH THIS?
"WHAT," YOU ASK?
ZSH
HOW ABOUT PAYBACK FOR...
...WHAT YOU DID TO US BEFORE?
WHAT DID YOU DO TO TAKIGAWA-SAN?
HUH?
WE KNOW WHY SHE'S ACTING THE WAY SHE IS AROUND YOU...
YOU USED SOME KIND OF WITCH POWER ON HER, DIDN'T YOU?!

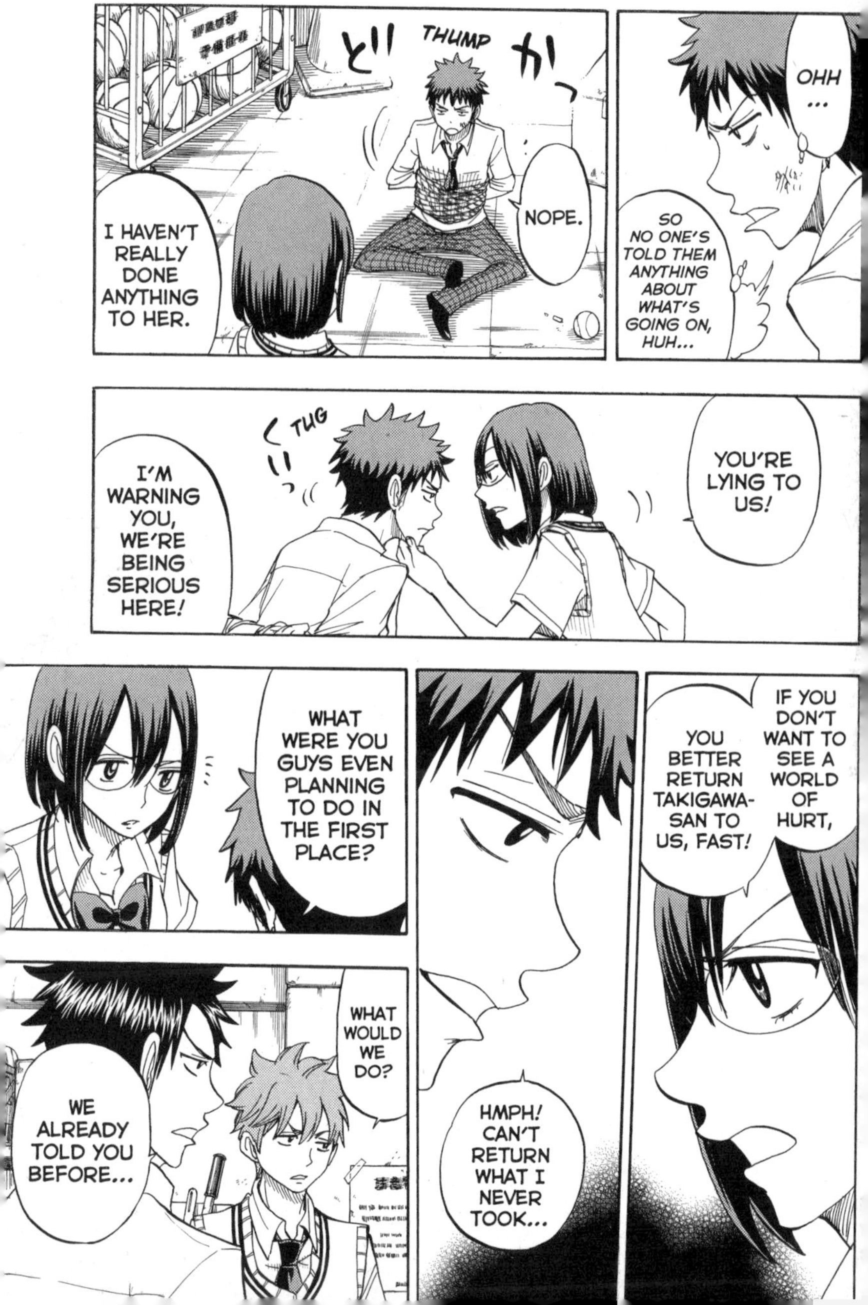
OHH ...
SO NO ONE'S TOLD THEM ANYTHING ABOUT WHAT'S GOING ON, HUH...
THUMP
NOPE.
I HAVEN'T REALLY DONE ANYTHING TO HER.
YOU'RE LYING TO US!
TUG
I'M WARNING YOU, WE'RE BEING SERIOUS HERE!
IF YOU DON'T WANT TO SEE A WORLD OF HURT,
YOU BETTER RETURN TAKIGAWA-SAN TO US, FAST!
HMPH! CAN'T RETURN WHAT I NEVER TOOK...
WHAT WERE YOU GUYS EVEN PLANNING TO DO IN THE FIRST PLACE?
WHAT WOULD WE DO?
WE ALREADY TOLD YOU BEFORE...

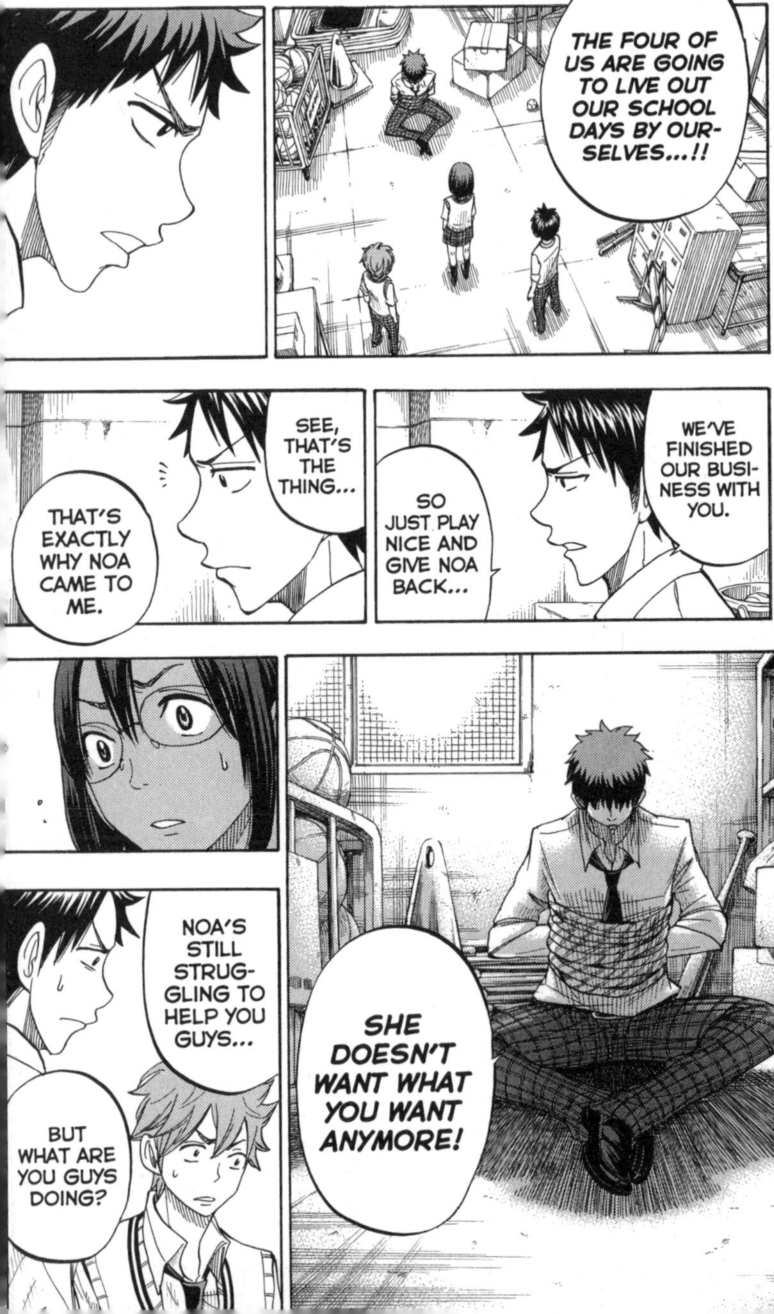
THE FOUR OF US ARE GOING TO LIVE OUT OUR SCHOOL DAYS BY OUR-SELVES...!!
WE'VE FINISHED OUR BUSI-NESS WITH YOU.
SO JUST PLAY NICE AND GIVE NOA BACK...
SEE, THAT'S THE THING...
THAT'S EXACTLY WHY NOA CAME TO ME.
SHE DOESN'T WANT WHAT YOU WANT ANYMORE!
NOA'S STILL STRUG-GLING TO HELP YOU GUYS...
BUT WHAT ARE YOU GUYS DOING?

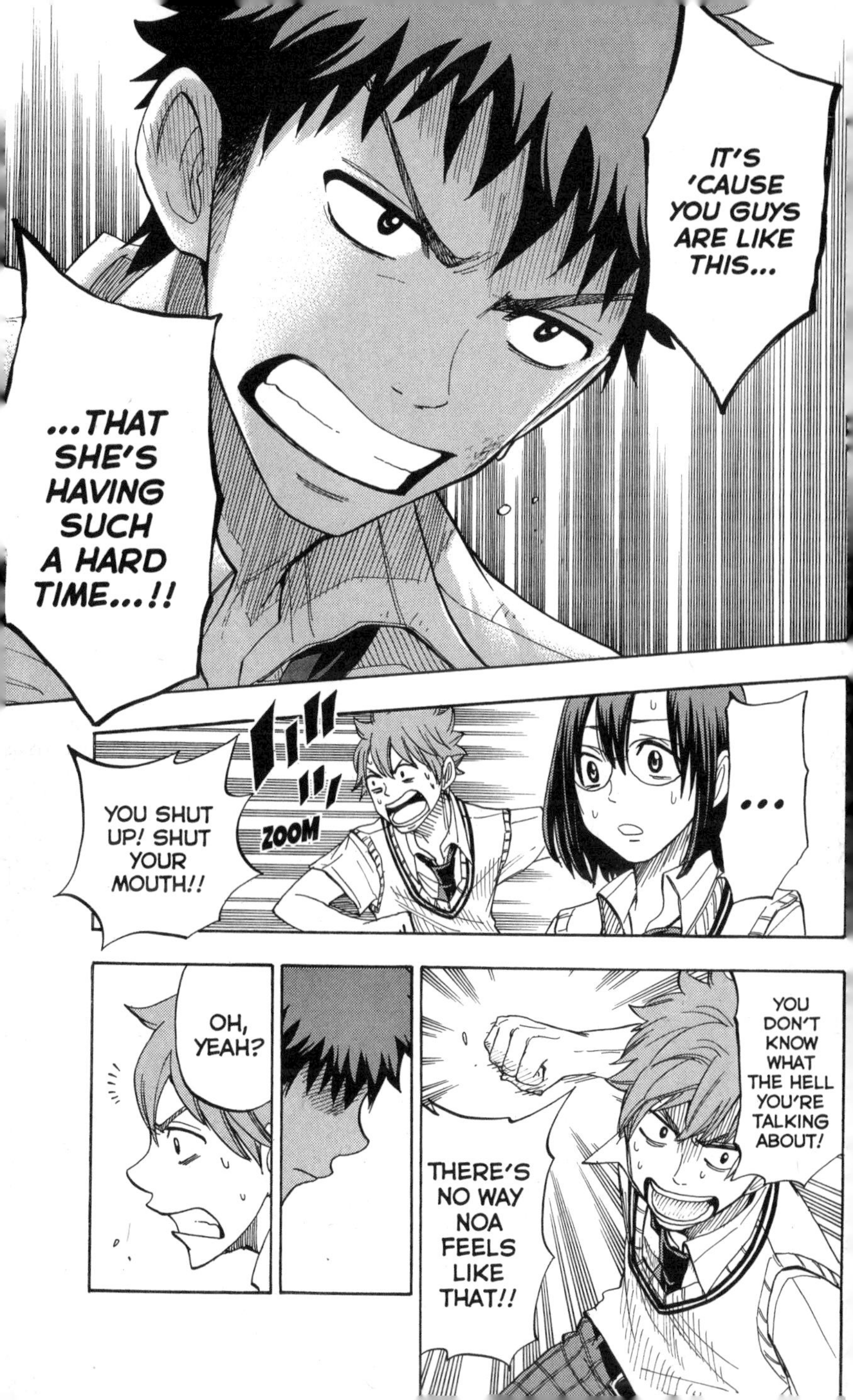
IT'S 'CAUSE YOU GUYS ARE LIKE THIS...
...THAT SHE'S HAVING SUCH A HARD TIME...!!
...
YOU SHUT UP! SHUT YOUR MOUTH!!
ZOOM
YOU DON'T KNOW WHAT THE HELL YOU'RE TALKING ABOUT!
THERE'S NO WAY NOA FEELS LIKE THAT!!
OH, YEAH?

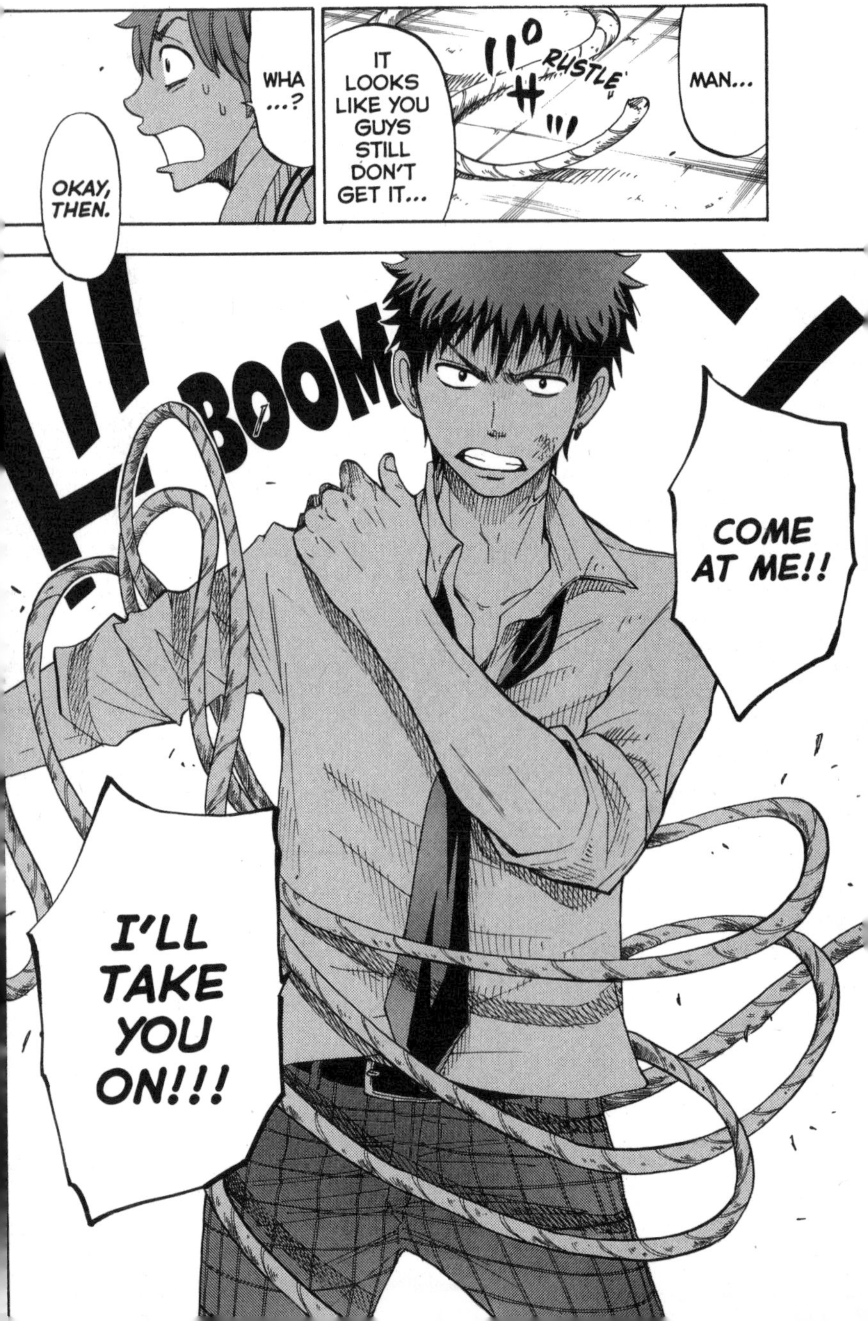
MAN...
RUSTLE
IT LOOKS LIKE YOU GUYS STILL DON'T GET IT...
WHA ...?
OKAY, THEN.
BOOM
COME AT ME!!
I'LL TAKE YOU ON!!!

CHAPTER 51: There is one condition.

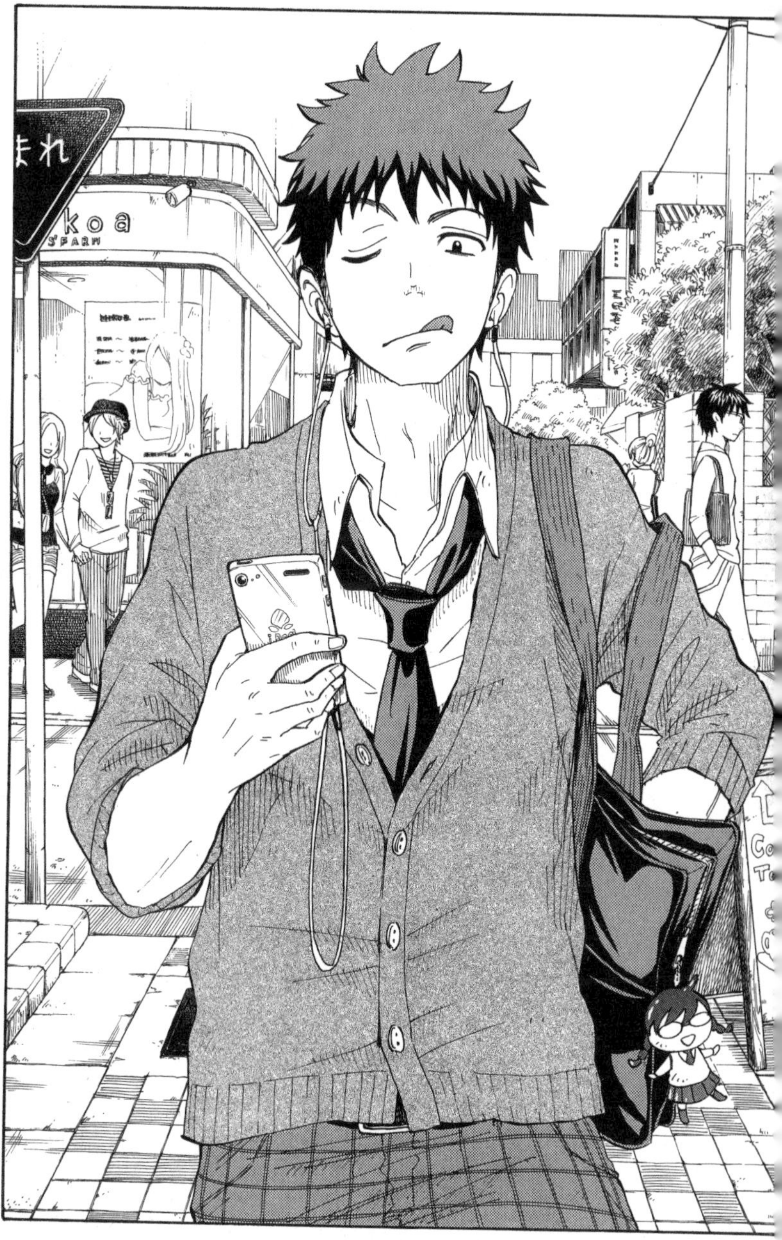

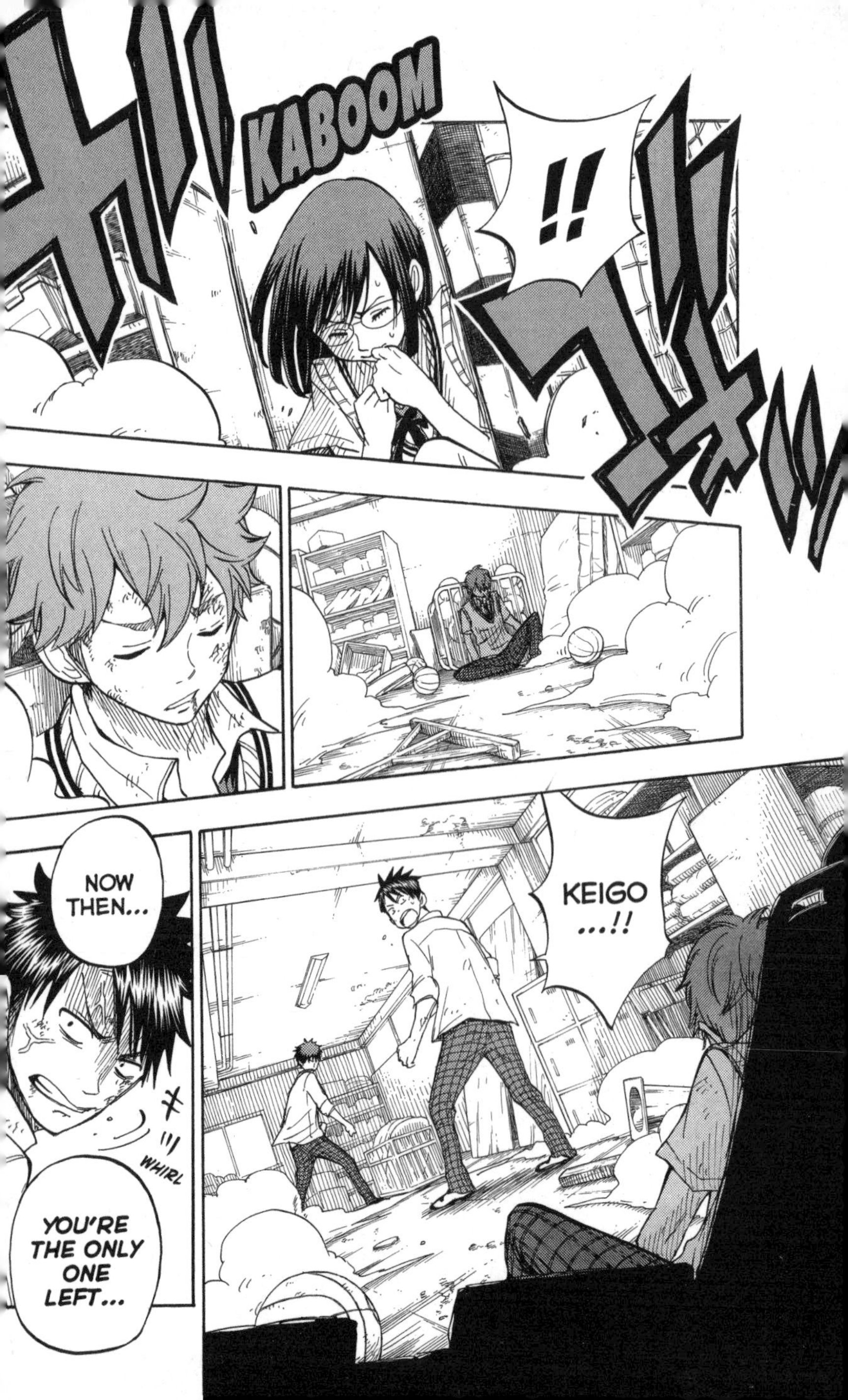
KABOOM
!!
KEIGO ...!!
NOW THEN...
WHIRL
YOU'RE THE ONLY ONE LEFT...

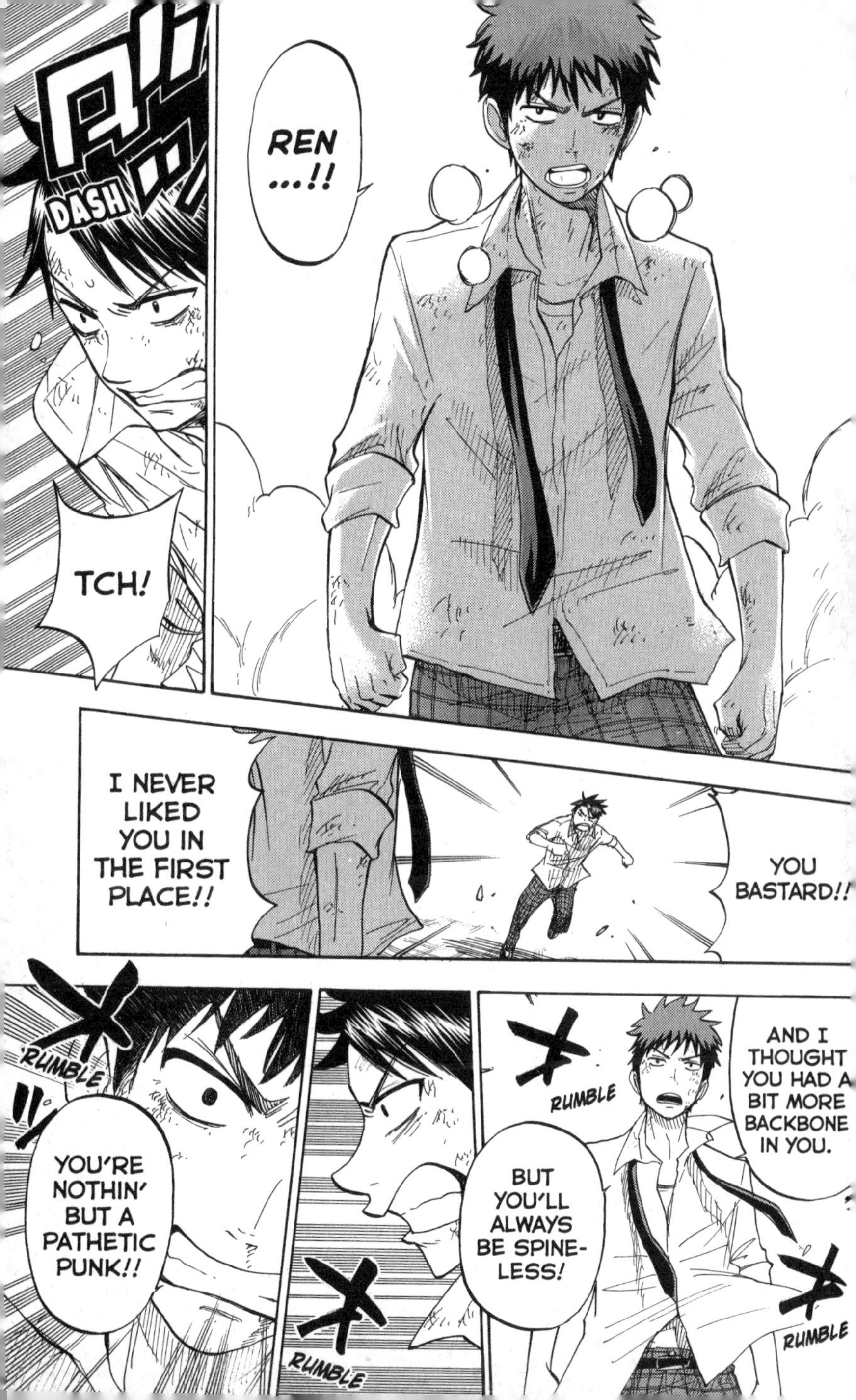
REN ...!!
DASH
TCH!
YOU BASTARD!!
I NEVER LIKED YOU IN THE FIRST PLACE!!
AND I THOUGHT YOU HAD A BIT MORE BACKBONE IN YOU.
RUMBLE
BUT YOU'LL ALWAYS BE SPINE-LESS!
RUMBLE
RUMBLE
RUMBLE
YOU'RE NOTHIN' BUT A PATHETIC PUNK!!

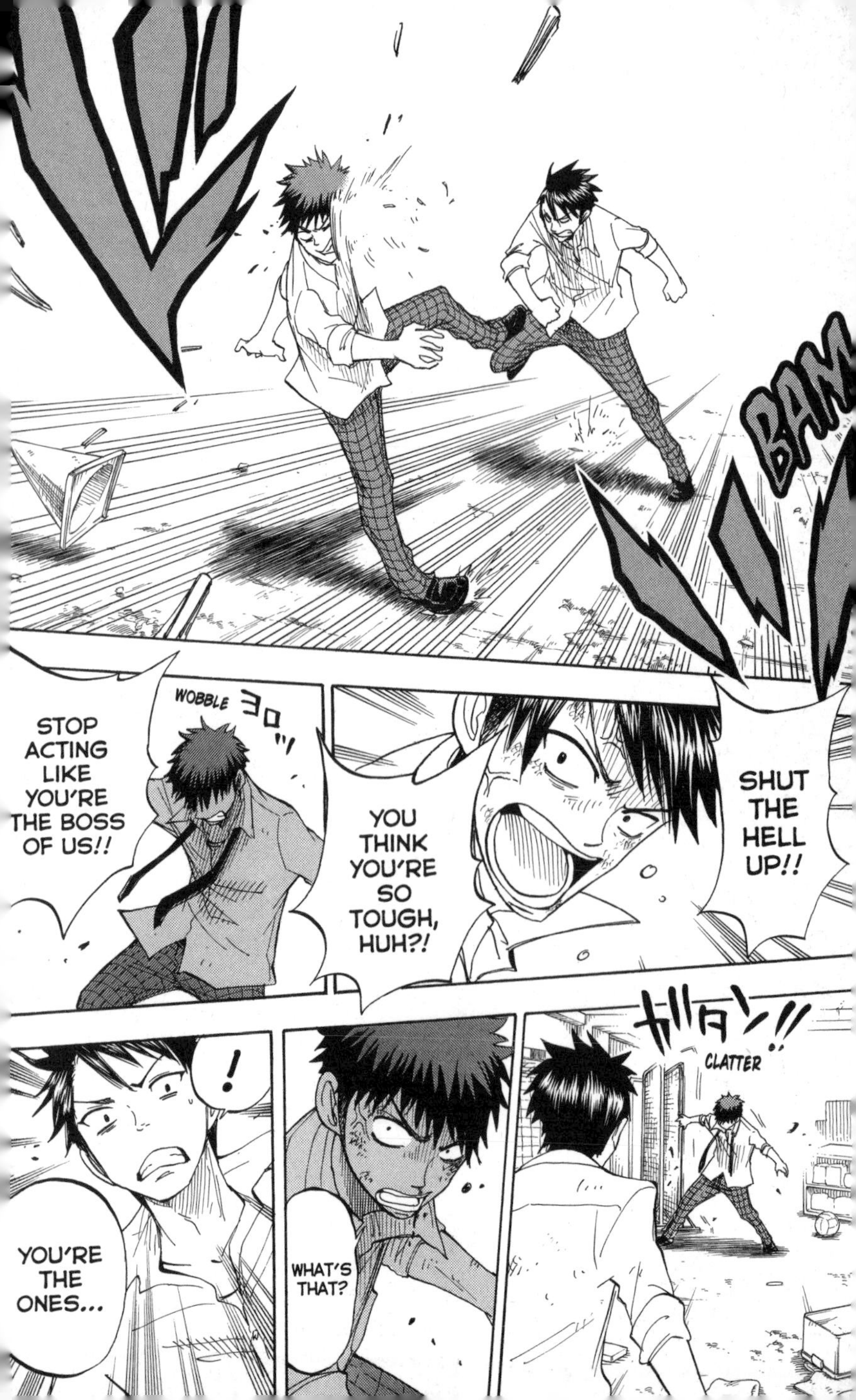
BAM
SHUT THE HELL UP!!
YOU THINK YOU'RE SO TOUGH, HUH?!
WOBBLE ヨロッ
STOP ACTING LIKE YOU'RE THE BOSS OF US!!
ガタン!!
CLATTER
WHAT'S THAT?
!
YOU'RE THE ONES...

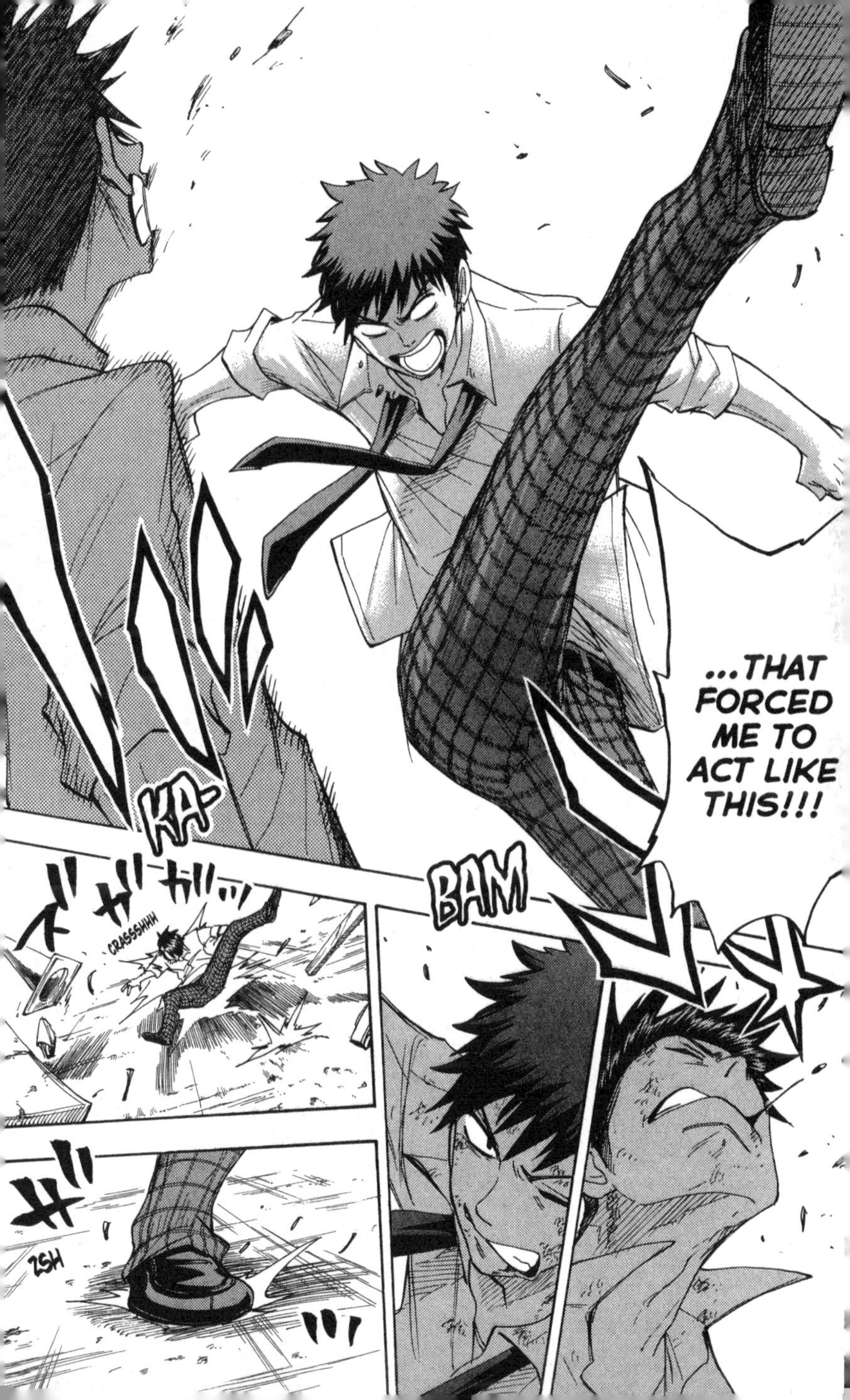
...THAT FORCED ME TO ACT LIKE THIS!!!
KA-
BAM
CRASSSHHH
ZSH

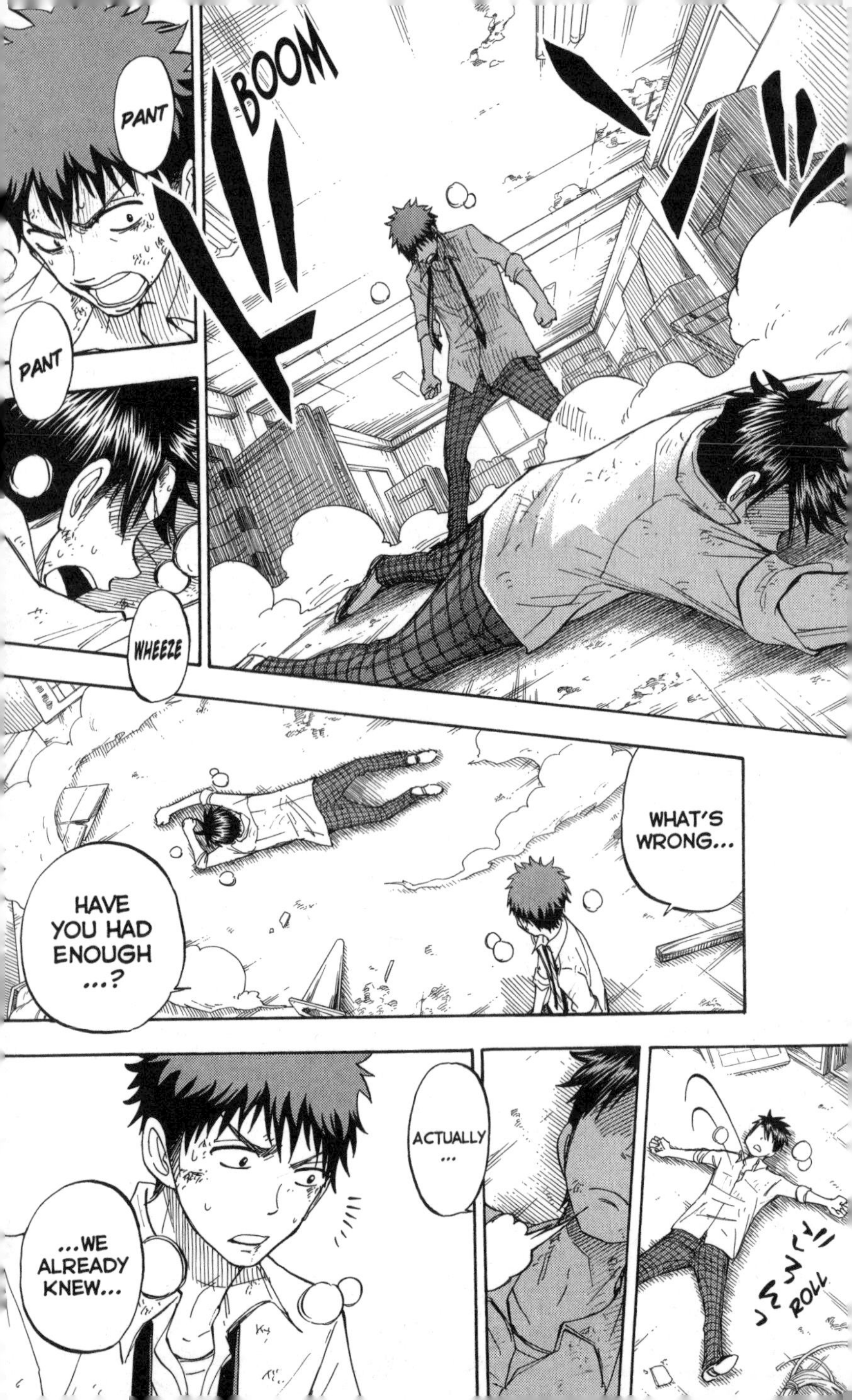
BOOM
PANT
PANT
WHEEZE
WHAT'S WRONG...
HAVE YOU HAD ENOUGH ...?
ROLL
ACTUALLY ...
...WE ALREADY KNEW...

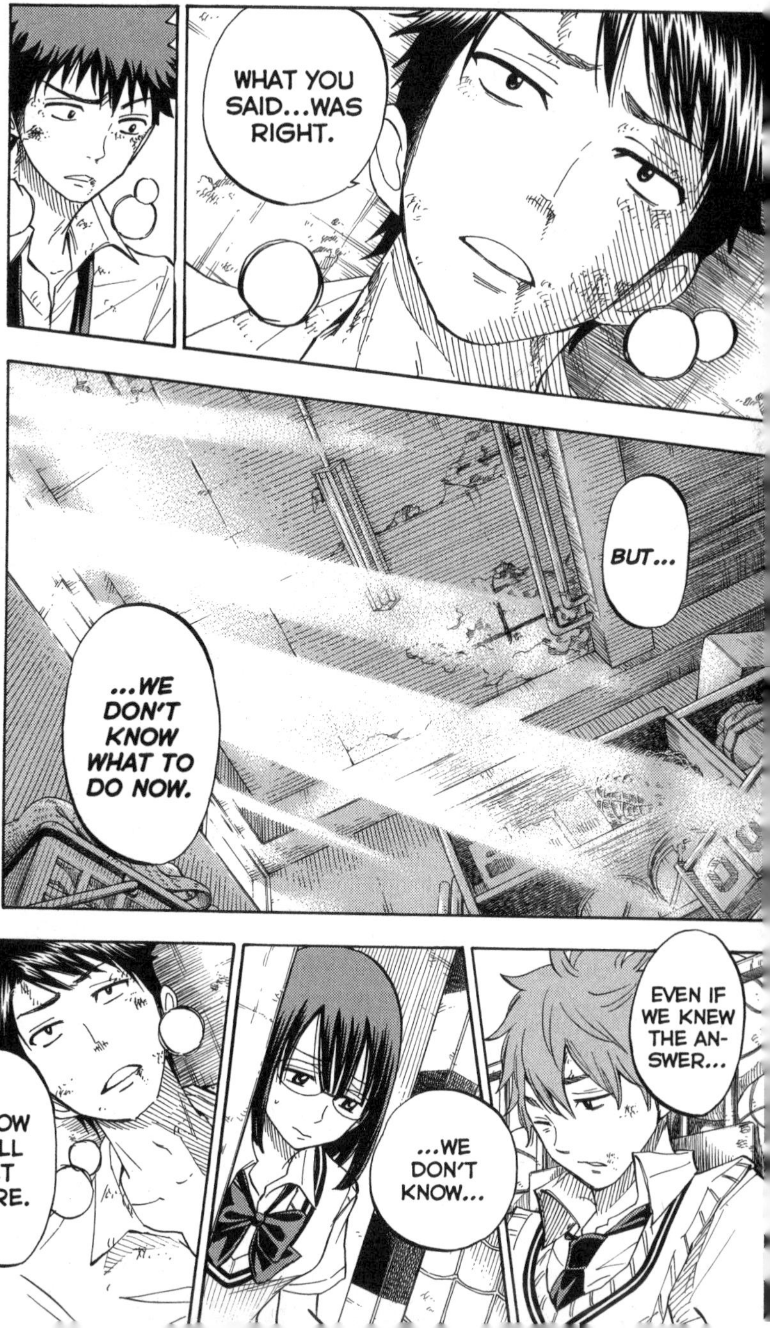
WHAT YOU SAID...WAS RIGHT.
BUT...
...WE DON'T KNOW WHAT TO DO NOW.
EVEN IF WE KNEW THE AN-SWER...
...WE DON'T KNOW...
...HOW WE'LL GET THERE.

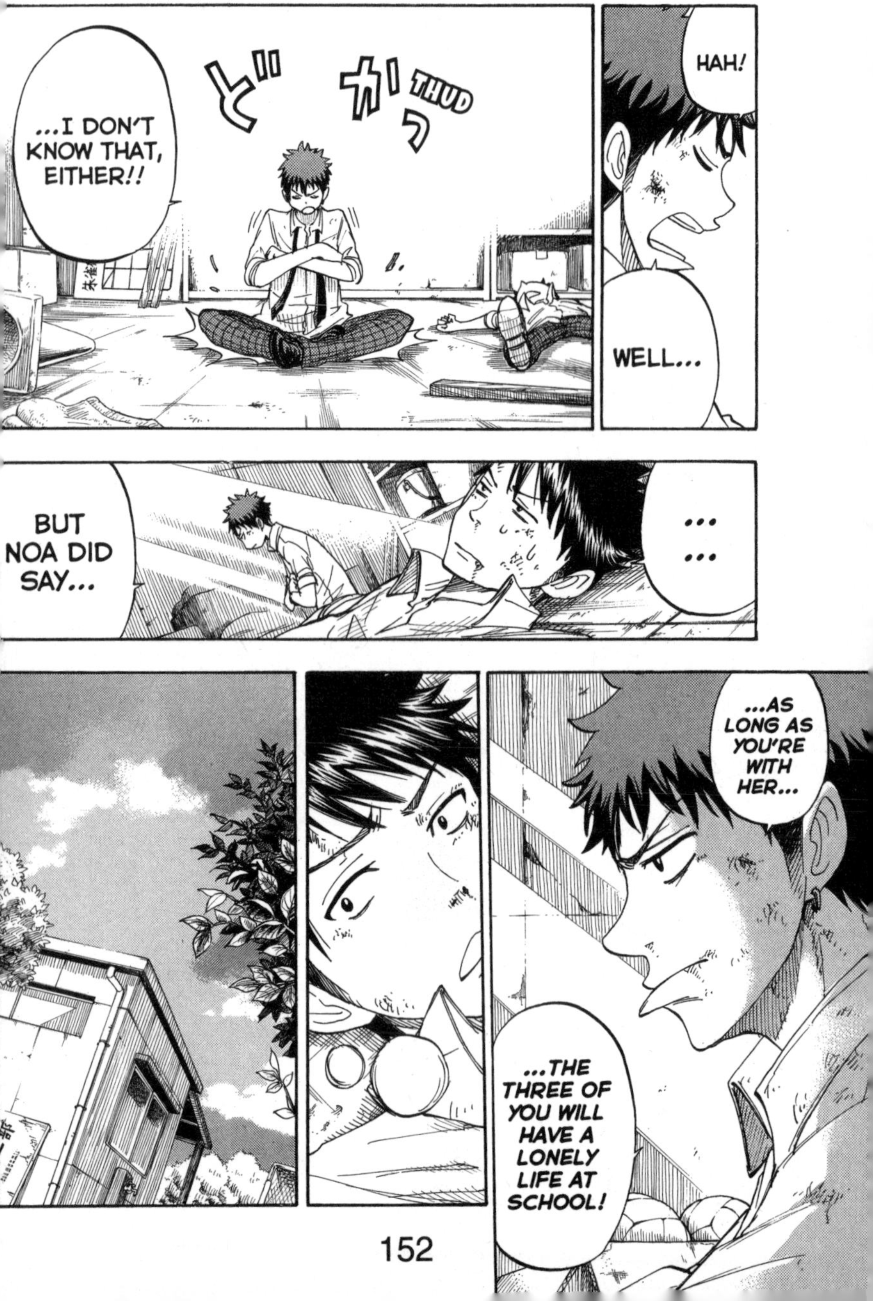
HAH!
WELL...
THUD
...I DON'T KNOW THAT, EITHER!!
...
...
BUT NOA DID SAY...
...AS LONG AS YOU'RE WITH HER...
...THE THREE OF YOU WILL HAVE A LONELY LIFE AT SCHOOL!

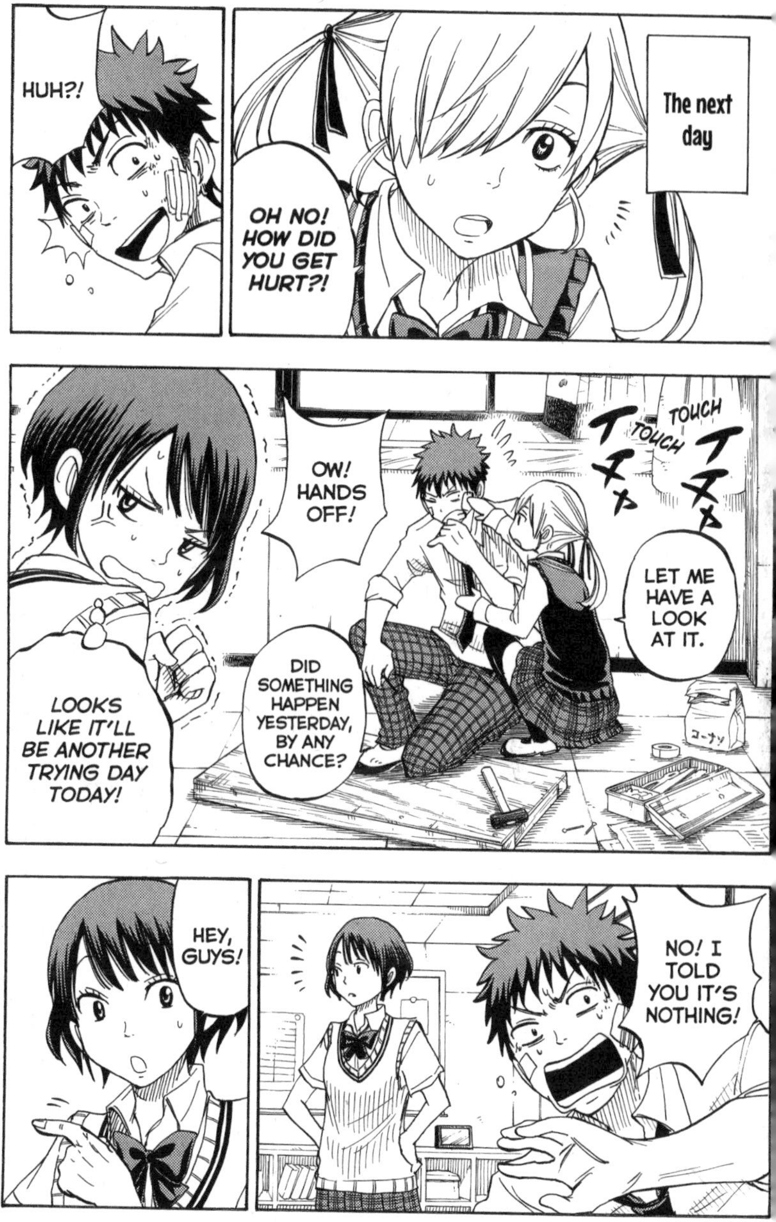
The next day
OH NO! HOW DID YOU GET HURT?!
HUH?!
TOUCH TOUCH
LET ME HAVE A LOOK AT IT.
OW! HANDS OFF!
DID SOMETHING HAPPEN YESTERDAY, BY ANY CHANCE?
LOOKS LIKE IT'LL BE ANOTHER TRYING DAY TODAY!
NO! I TOLD YOU IT'S NOTHING!
HEY, GUYS!

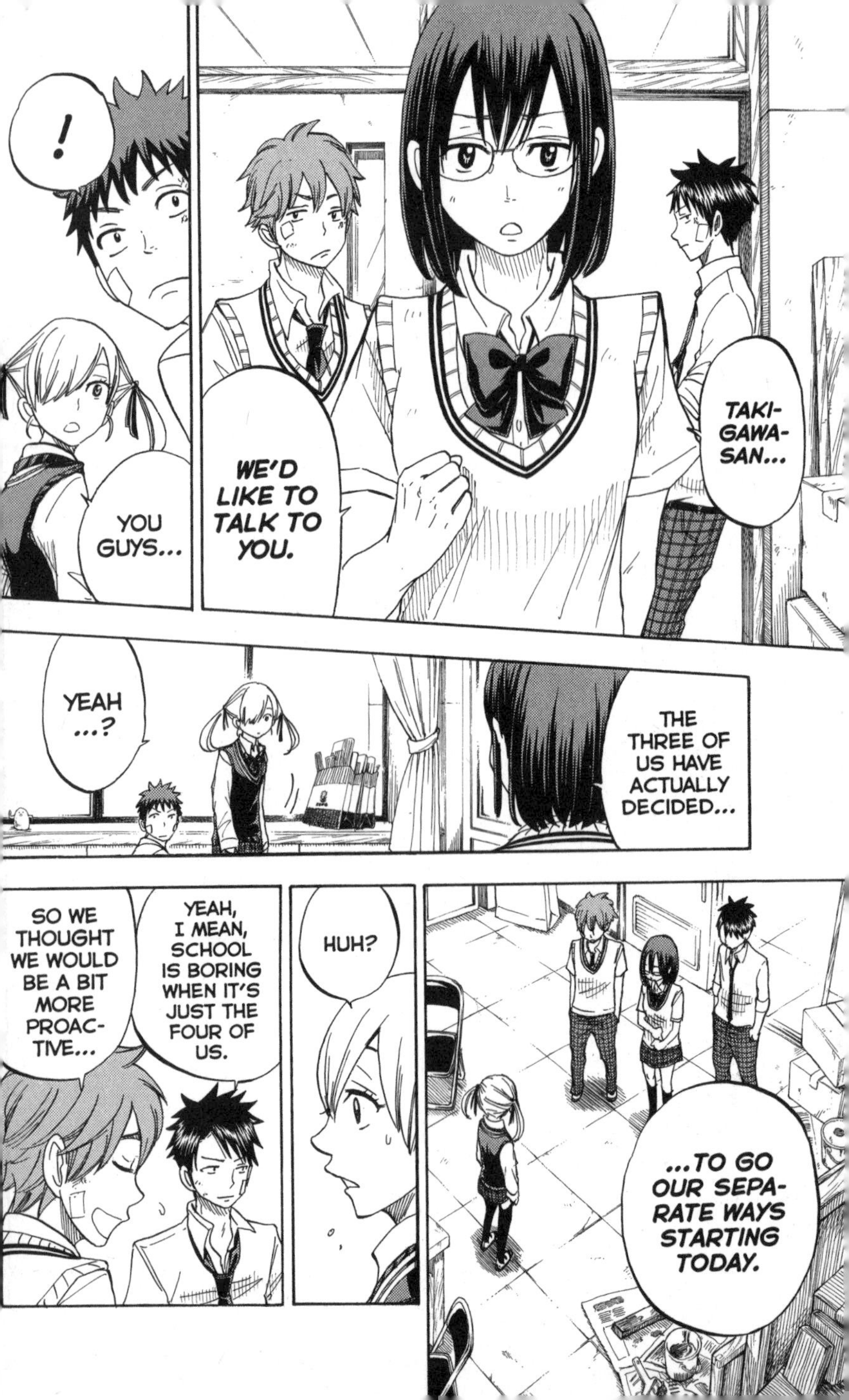
TAKI-GAWA-SAN...
WE'D LIKE TO TALK TO YOU.
!
YOU GUYS...
THE THREE OF US HAVE ACTUALLY DECIDED...
YEAH ...?
...TO GO OUR SEPA-RATE WAYS STARTING TODAY.
HUH?
YEAH, I MEAN, SCHOOL IS BORING WHEN IT'S JUST THE FOUR OF US.
SO WE THOUGHT WE WOULD BE A BIT MORE PROAC-TIVE...

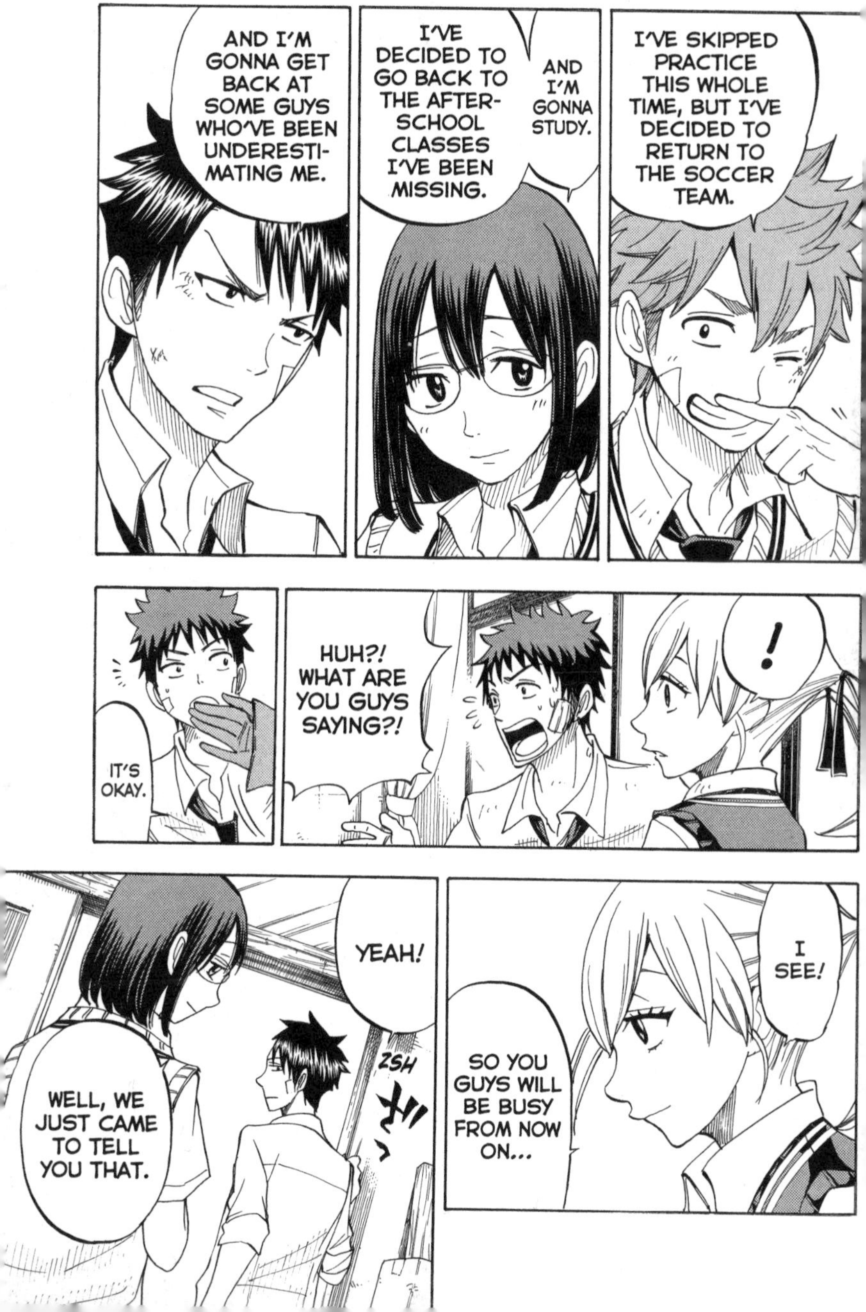
I'VE SKIPPED PRACTICE THIS WHOLE TIME, BUT I'VE DECIDED TO RETURN TO THE SOCCER TEAM.
I'VE DECIDED TO GO BACK TO THE AFTER-SCHOOL CLASSES I'VE BEEN MISSING.
AND I'M GONNA STUDY.
AND I'M GONNA GET BACK AT SOME GUYS WHO'VE BEEN UNDERESTIMATING ME.
!
HUH?! WHAT ARE YOU GUYS SAYING?!
IT'S OKAY.
I SEE!
SO YOU GUYS WILL BE BUSY FROM NOW ON...
YEAH!
ZSH
WELL, WE JUST CAME TO TELL YOU THAT.

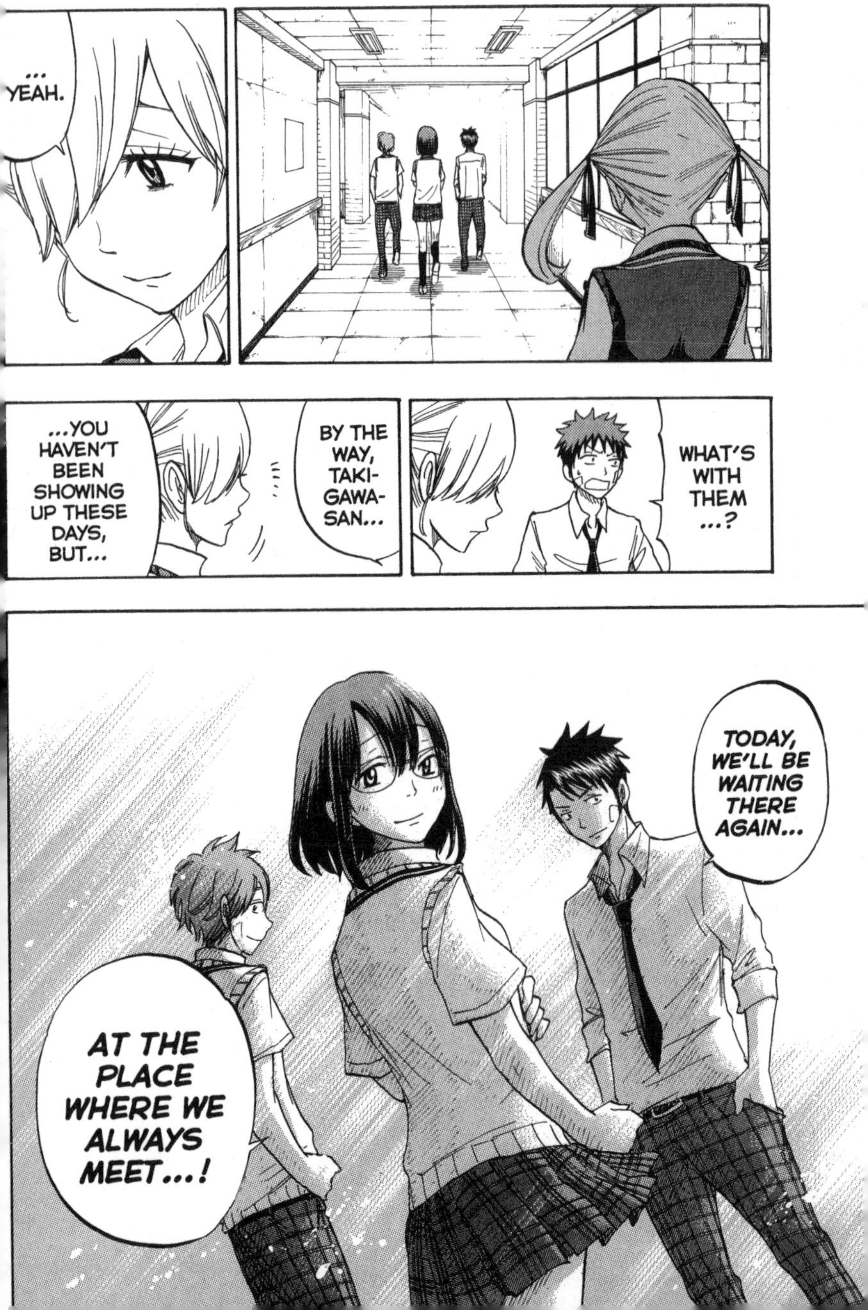
... YEAH.
WHAT'S WITH THEM ...?
BY THE WAY, TAKI-GAWA-SAN...
...YOU HAVEN'T BEEN SHOWING UP THESE DAYS, BUT...
TODAY, WE'LL BE WAITING THERE AGAIN...
AT THE PLACE WHERE WE ALWAYS MEET...!

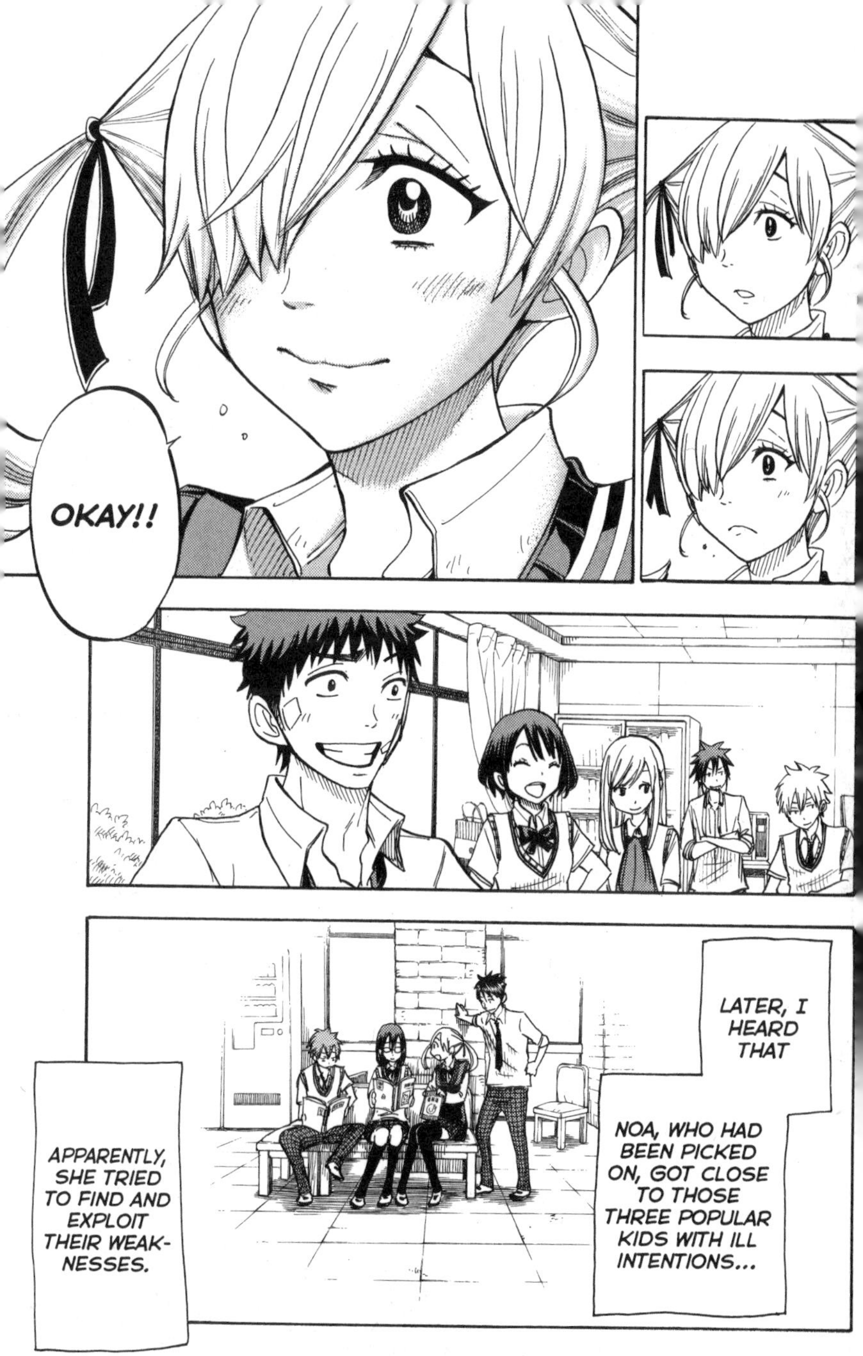
OKAY!!
LATER, I HEARD THAT
NOA, WHO HAD BEEN PICKED ON, GOT CLOSE TO THOSE THREE POPULAR KIDS WITH ILL INTENTIONS...
APPARENTLY, SHE TRIED TO FIND AND EXPLOIT THEIR WEAK-NESSES.

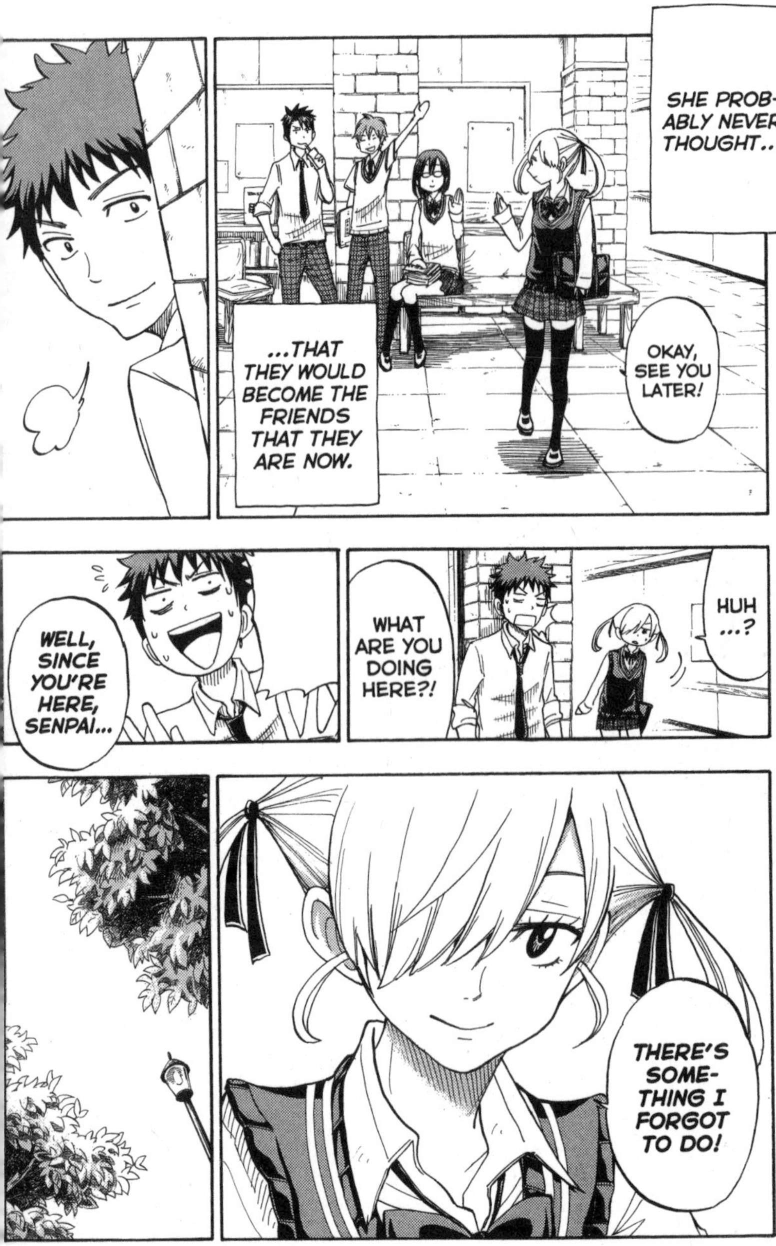
SHE PROBABLY NEVER THOUGHT...
OKAY, SEE YOU LATER!
...THAT THEY WOULD BECOME THE FRIENDS THAT THEY ARE NOW.
HUH ...?
WHAT ARE YOU DOING HERE?!
WELL, SINCE YOU'RE HERE, SENPAI...
THERE'S SOMETHING I FORGOT TO DO!

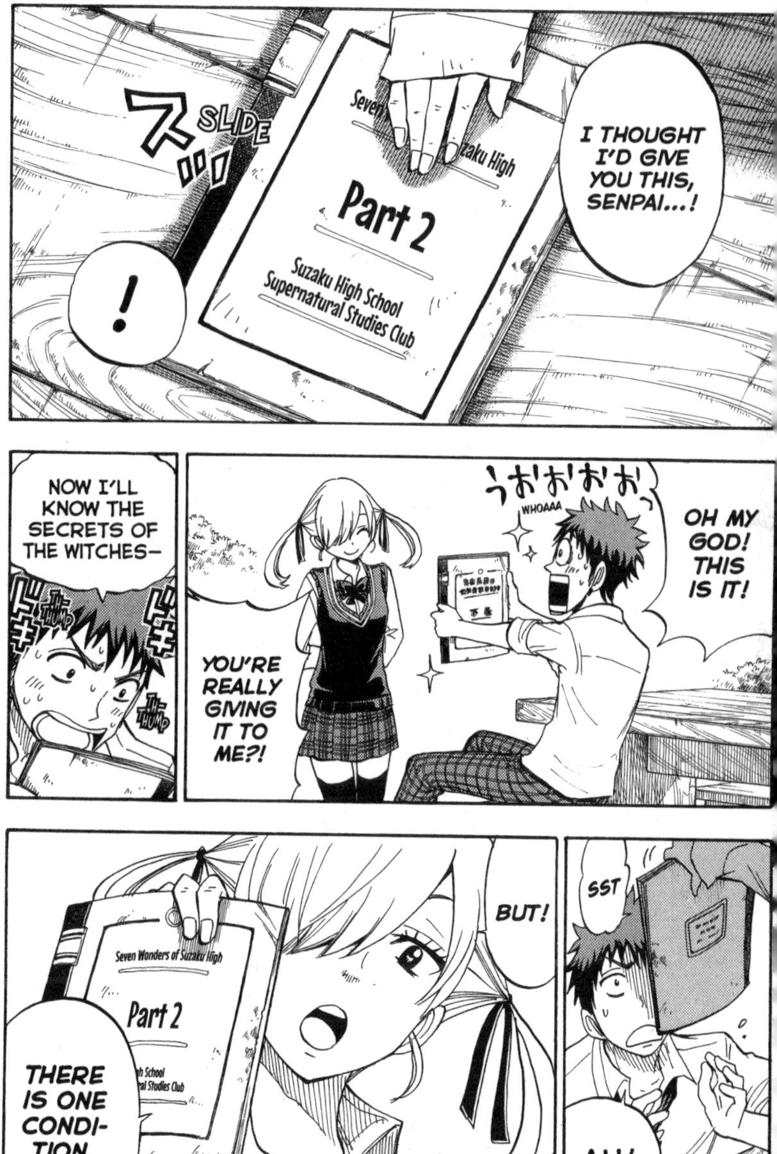
I THOUGHT I'D GIVE YOU THIS, SENPAI...!
Seven
zaku High
Part 2
Suzaku High School Supernatural Studies Club
SLIDE
!
OH MY GOD! THIS IS IT!
うおおおおっ
WHOAAA
YOU'RE REALLY GIVING IT TO ME?!
NOW I'LL KNOW THE SECRETS OF THE WITCHES—
THUMP
TH-THUMP
SST
AH!
BUT!
Seven Wonders of Suzaku High
Part 2
THERE IS ONE CONDITION.

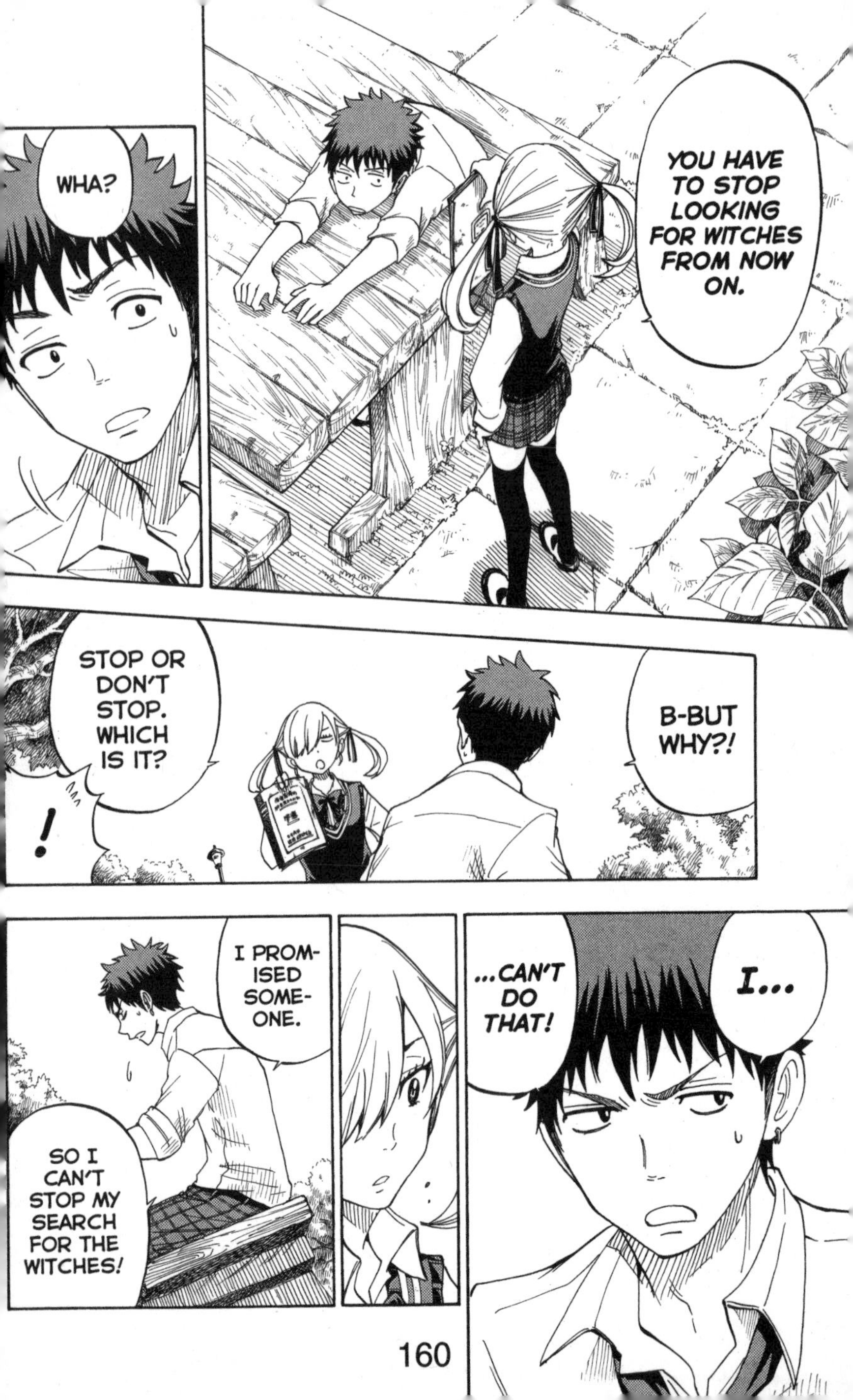
YOU HAVE TO STOP LOOKING FOR WITCHES FROM NOW ON.
WHA?
B-BUT WHY?!
STOP OR DON'T STOP. WHICH IS IT?
!
I...
...CAN'T DO THAT!
I PROMISED SOMEONE.
SO I CAN'T STOP MY SEARCH FOR THE WITCHES!

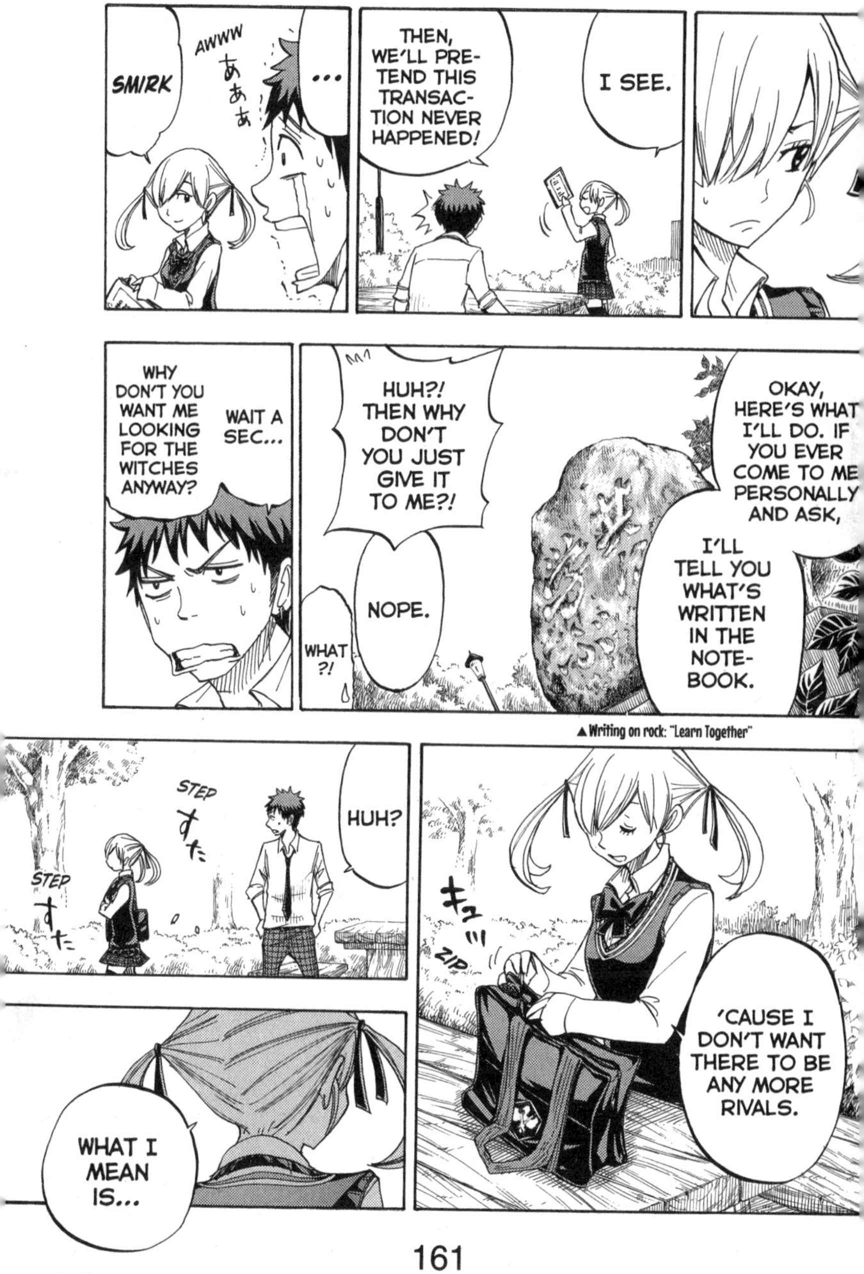
I SEE.
THEN, WE'LL PRETEND THIS TRANSACTION NEVER HAPPENED!
...
SMIRK
AWWW ああぁ
OKAY, HERE'S WHAT I'LL DO. IF YOU EVER COME TO ME PERSONALLY AND ASK,
I'LL TELL YOU WHAT'S WRITTEN IN THE NOTEBOOK.
HUH?! THEN WHY DON'T YOU JUST GIVE IT TO ME?!
NOPE.
WHAT?!
WAIT A SEC...
WHY DON'T YOU WANT ME LOOKING FOR THE WITCHES ANYWAY?
キュッ ZIP
'CAUSE I DON'T WANT THERE TO BE ANY MORE RIVALS.
HUH?
STEP すた
STEP すた
WHAT I MEAN IS...

▲Writing on rock: "Learn Together"

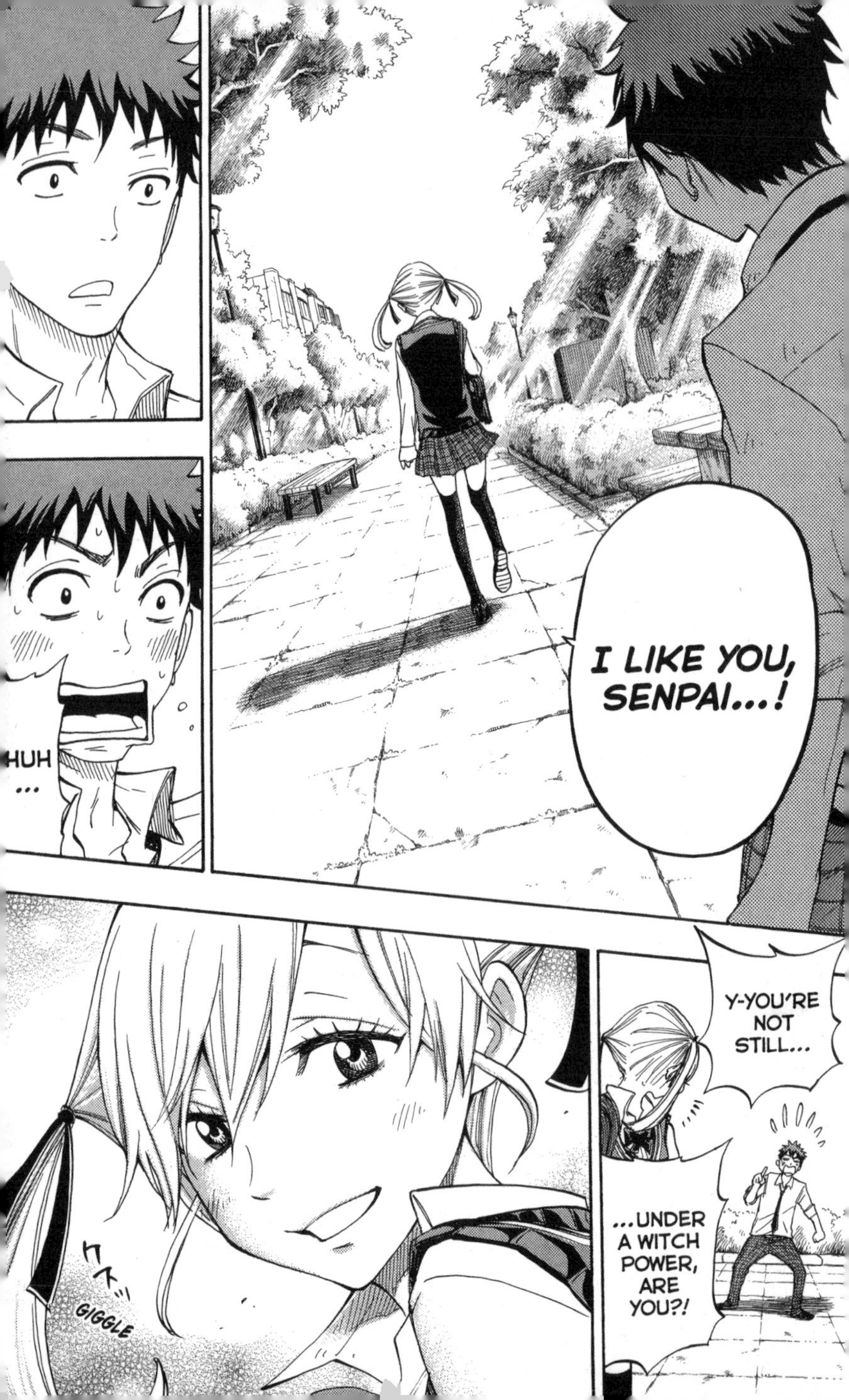
I LIKE YOU, SENPAI...!
HUH ...
Y-YOU'RE NOT STILL...
...UNDER A WITCH POWER, ARE YOU?!
クスッ
GIGGLE

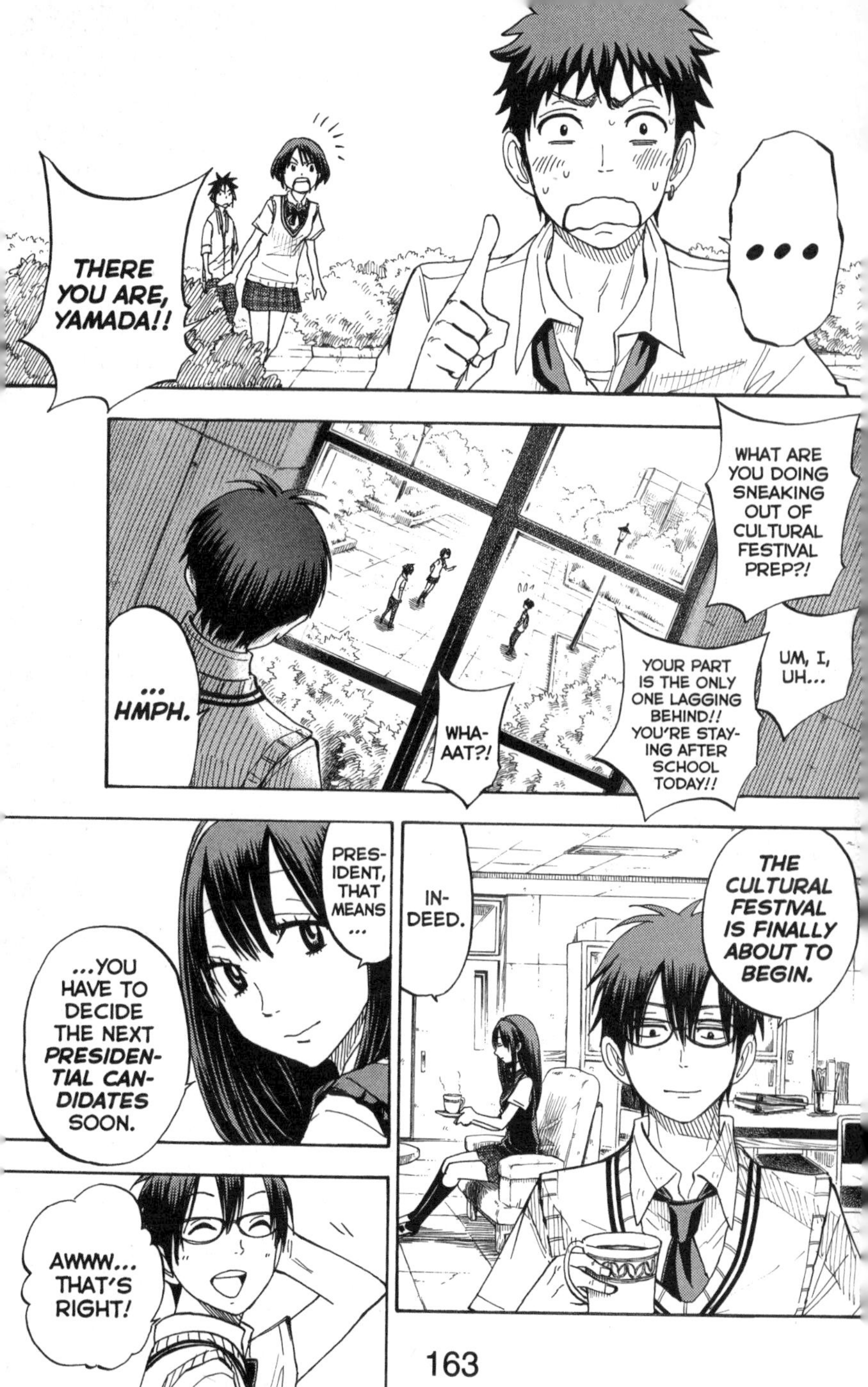
...
THERE YOU ARE, YAMADA!!
WHAT ARE YOU DOING SNEAKING OUT OF CULTURAL FESTIVAL PREP?!
UM, I, UH...
YOUR PART IS THE ONLY ONE LAGGING BEHIND!! YOU'RE STAYING AFTER SCHOOL TODAY!!
WHAAAT?!
... HMPH.
THE CULTURAL FESTIVAL IS FINALLY ABOUT TO BEGIN.
INDEED.
PRESIDENT, THAT MEANS...
...YOU HAVE TO DECIDE THE NEXT PRESIDENTIAL CANDIDATES SOON.
AWWW... THAT'S RIGHT!

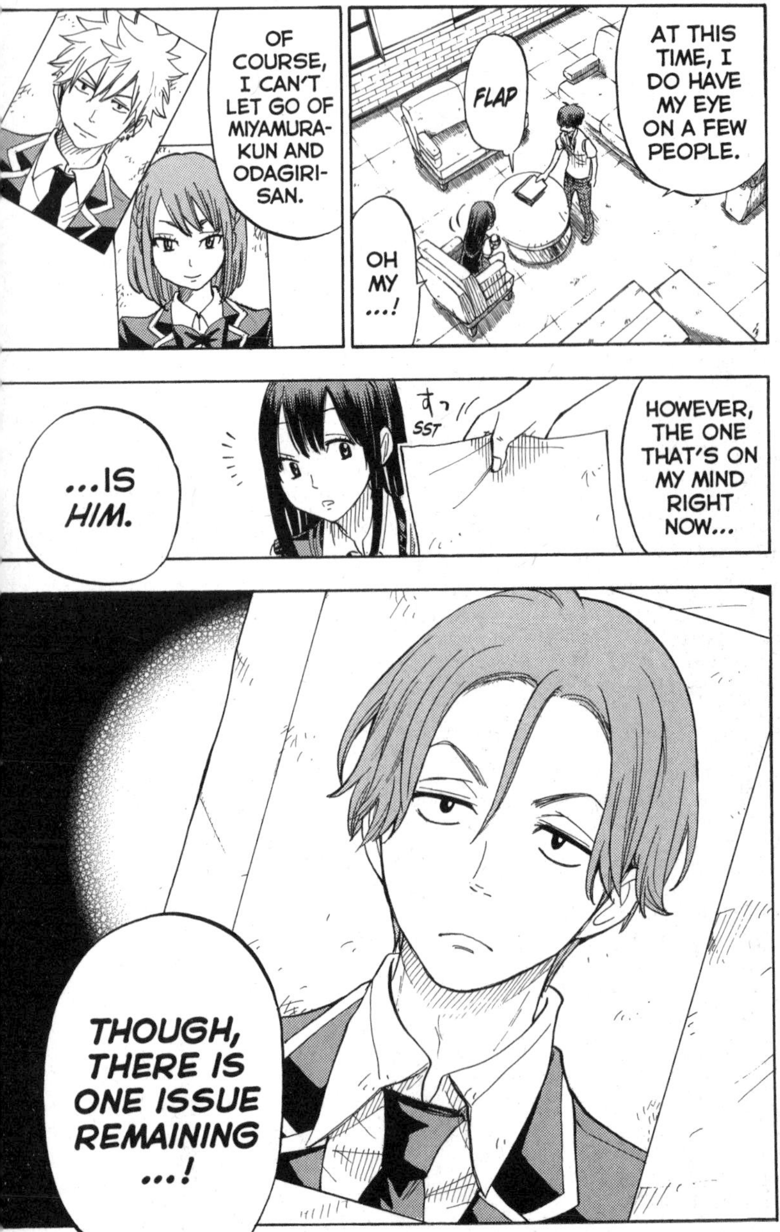
AT THIS TIME, I DO HAVE MY EYE ON A FEW PEOPLE.
FLAP
OH MY ...!
OF COURSE, I CAN'T LET GO OF MIYAMURA-KUN AND ODAGIRI-SAN.
HOWEVER, THE ONE THAT'S ON MY MIND RIGHT NOW...
すっ SST
...IS HIM.
THOUGH, THERE IS ONE ISSUE REMAINING ...!

To be continued in Volume 7

Yamada-kun and the Seven Witches

Yamada-kun and the Seven Witches **BONUS CHAPTER**

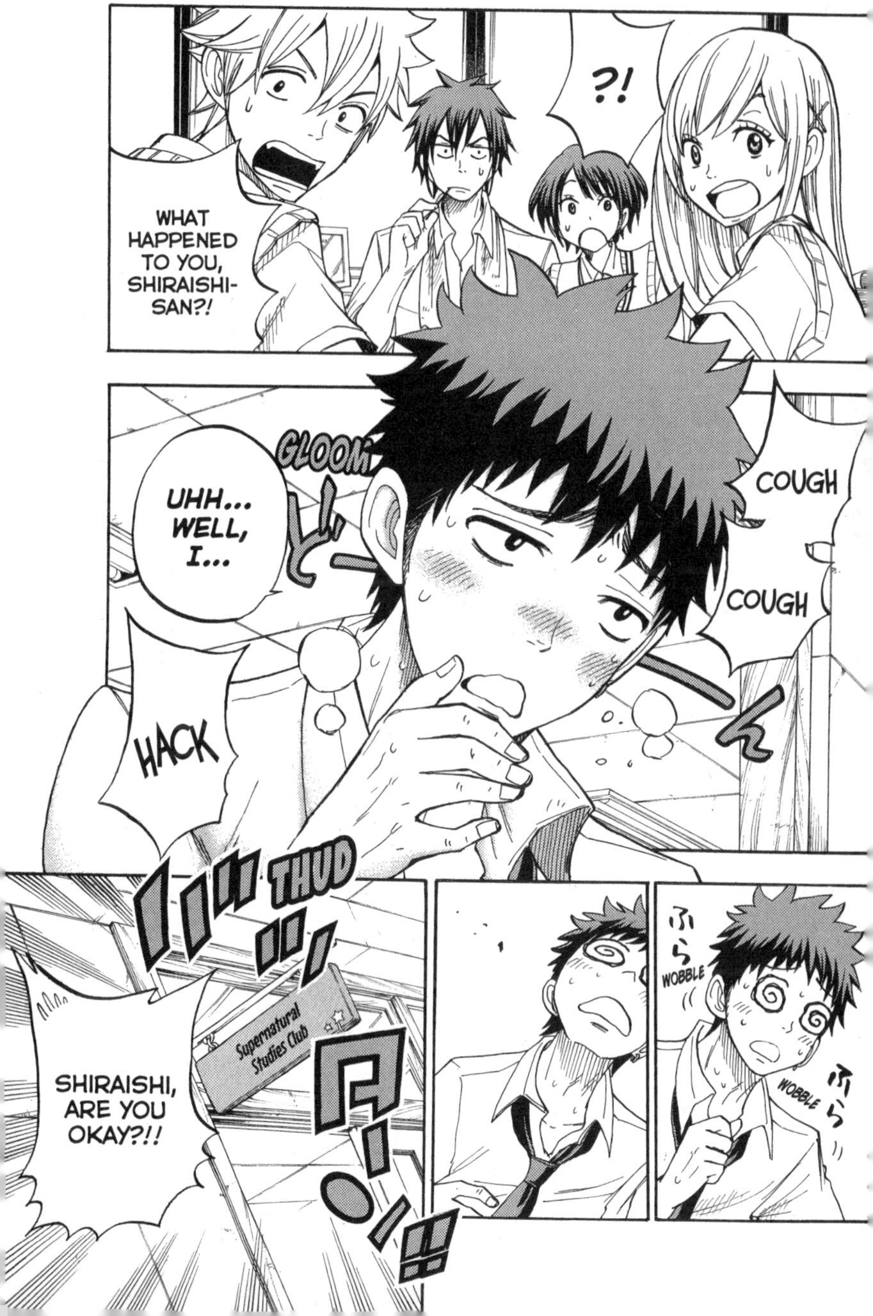
?!
WHAT HAPPENED TO YOU, SHIRAISHI-SAN?!
COUGH
COUGH
GLOOM
UHH... WELL, I...
HACK
ふら
WOBBLE
ふら
WOBBLE
THUD
Supernatural Studies Club
SHIRAISHI, ARE YOU OKAY?!!

BONUS CHAPTER: Turned on.

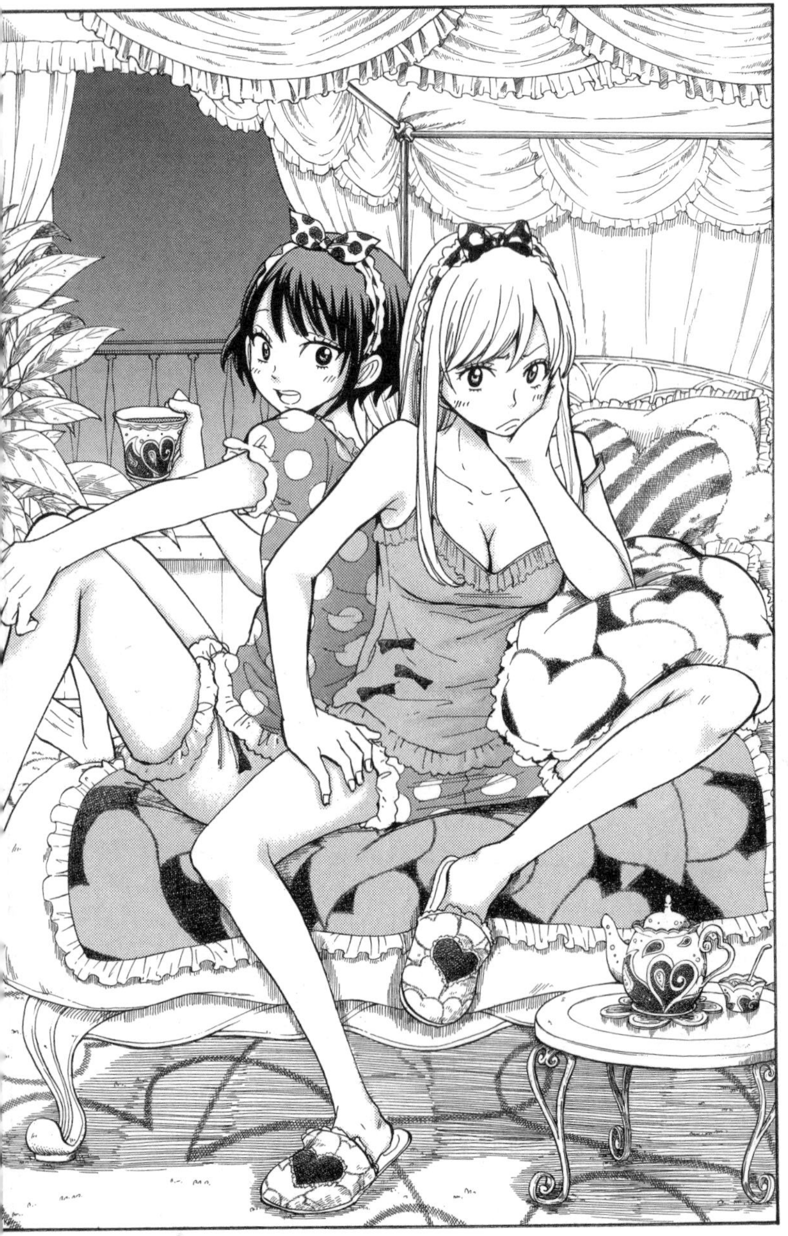

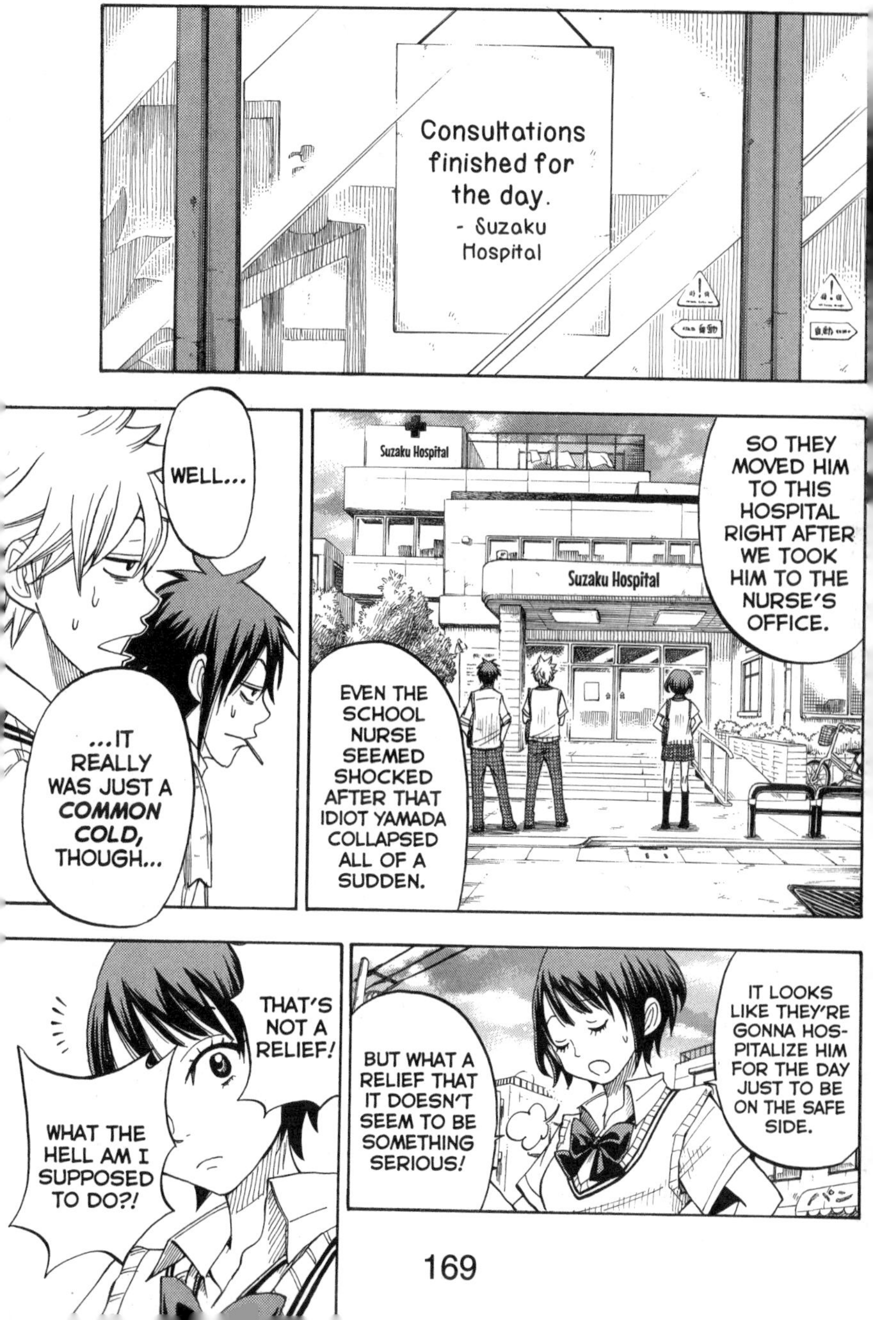
Consultations finished for the day. - Suzaku Hospital
Suzaku Hospital
Suzaku Hospital
SO THEY MOVED HIM TO THIS HOSPITAL RIGHT AFTER WE TOOK HIM TO THE NURSE'S OFFICE.
EVEN THE SCHOOL NURSE SEEMED SHOCKED AFTER THAT IDIOT YAMADA COLLAPSED ALL OF A SUDDEN.
WELL...
...IT REALLY WAS JUST A *COMMON COLD,* THOUGH...
IT LOOKS LIKE THEY'RE GONNA HOS-PITALIZE HIM FOR THE DAY JUST TO BE ON THE SAFE SIDE.
BUT WHAT A RELIEF THAT IT DOESN'T SEEM TO BE SOMETHING SERIOUS!
THAT'S NOT A RELIEF!
WHAT THE HELL AM I SUPPOSED TO DO?!

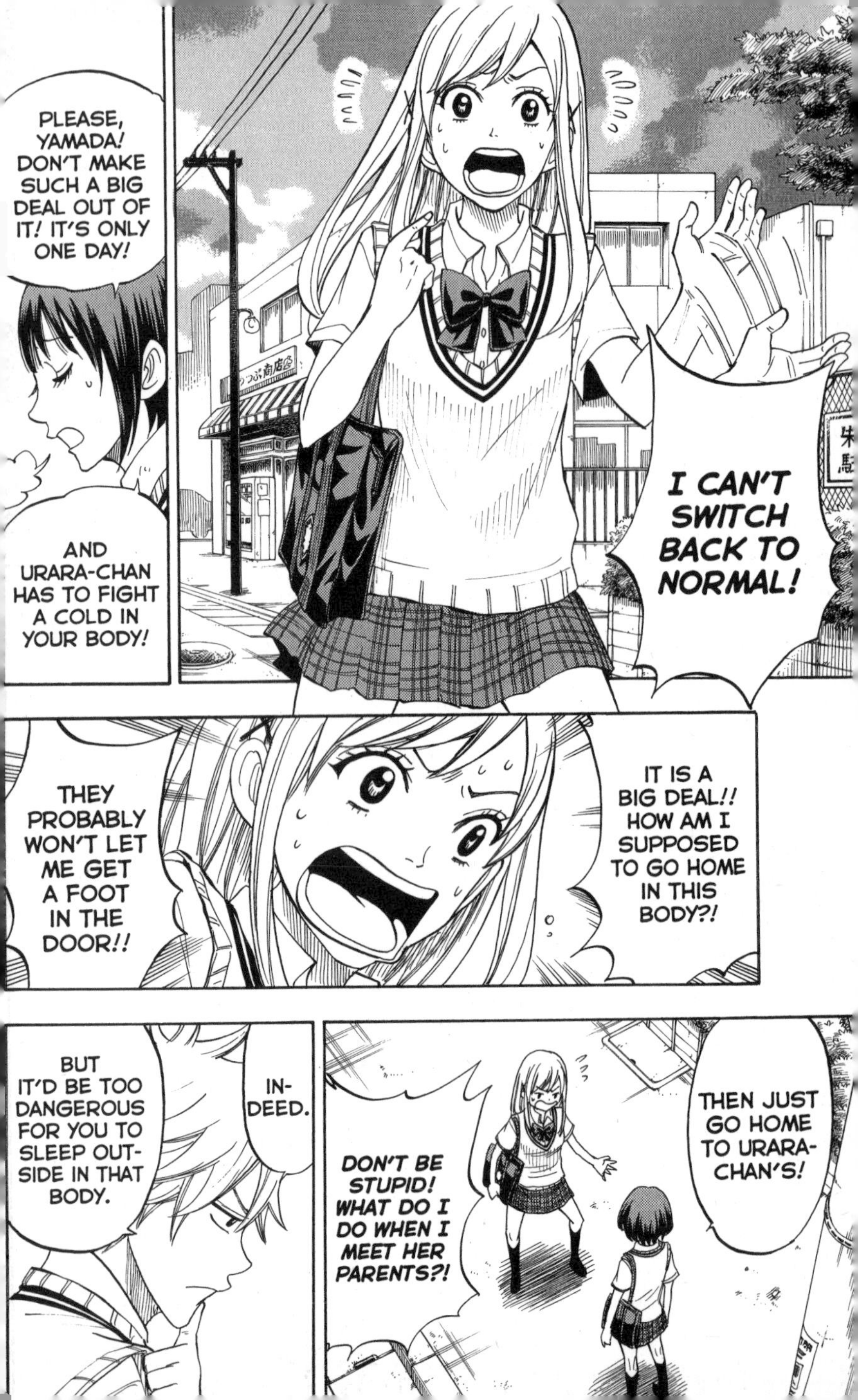
I CAN'T SWITCH BACK TO NORMAL!
PLEASE, YAMADA! DON'T MAKE SUCH A BIG DEAL OUT OF IT! IT'S ONLY ONE DAY!
AND URARA-CHAN HAS TO FIGHT A COLD IN YOUR BODY!
IT IS A BIG DEAL!! HOW AM I SUPPOSED TO GO HOME IN THIS BODY?!
THEY PROBABLY WON'T LET ME GET A FOOT IN THE DOOR!!
THEN JUST GO HOME TO URARA-CHAN'S!
DON'T BE STUPID! WHAT DO I DO WHEN I MEET HER PARENTS?!
IN-DEED.
BUT IT'D BE TOO DANGEROUS FOR YOU TO SLEEP OUT-SIDE IN THAT BODY.

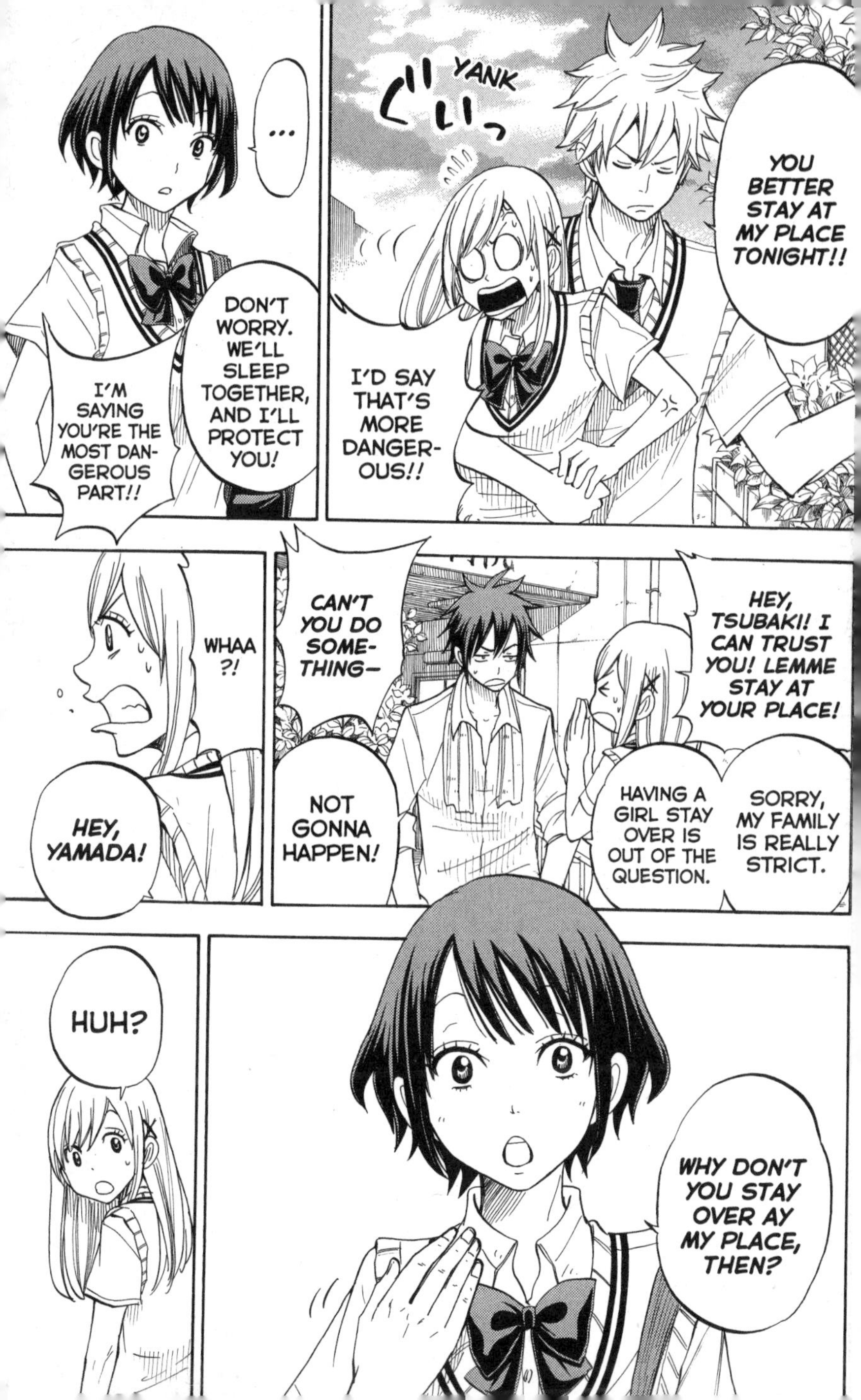
YANK
YOU BETTER STAY AT MY PLACE TONIGHT!!
I'D SAY THAT'S MORE DANGER-OUS!!
...
DON'T WORRY. WE'LL SLEEP TOGETHER, AND I'LL PROTECT YOU!
I'M SAYING YOU'RE THE MOST DAN-GEROUS PART!!
HEY, TSUBAKI! I CAN TRUST YOU! LEMME STAY AT YOUR PLACE!
CAN'T YOU DO SOME-THING—
SORRY, MY FAMILY IS REALLY STRICT.
HAVING A GIRL STAY OVER IS OUT OF THE QUESTION.
NOT GONNA HAPPEN!
WHAA ?!
HEY, YAMADA!
WHY DON'T YOU STAY OVER AY MY PLACE, THEN?
HUH?

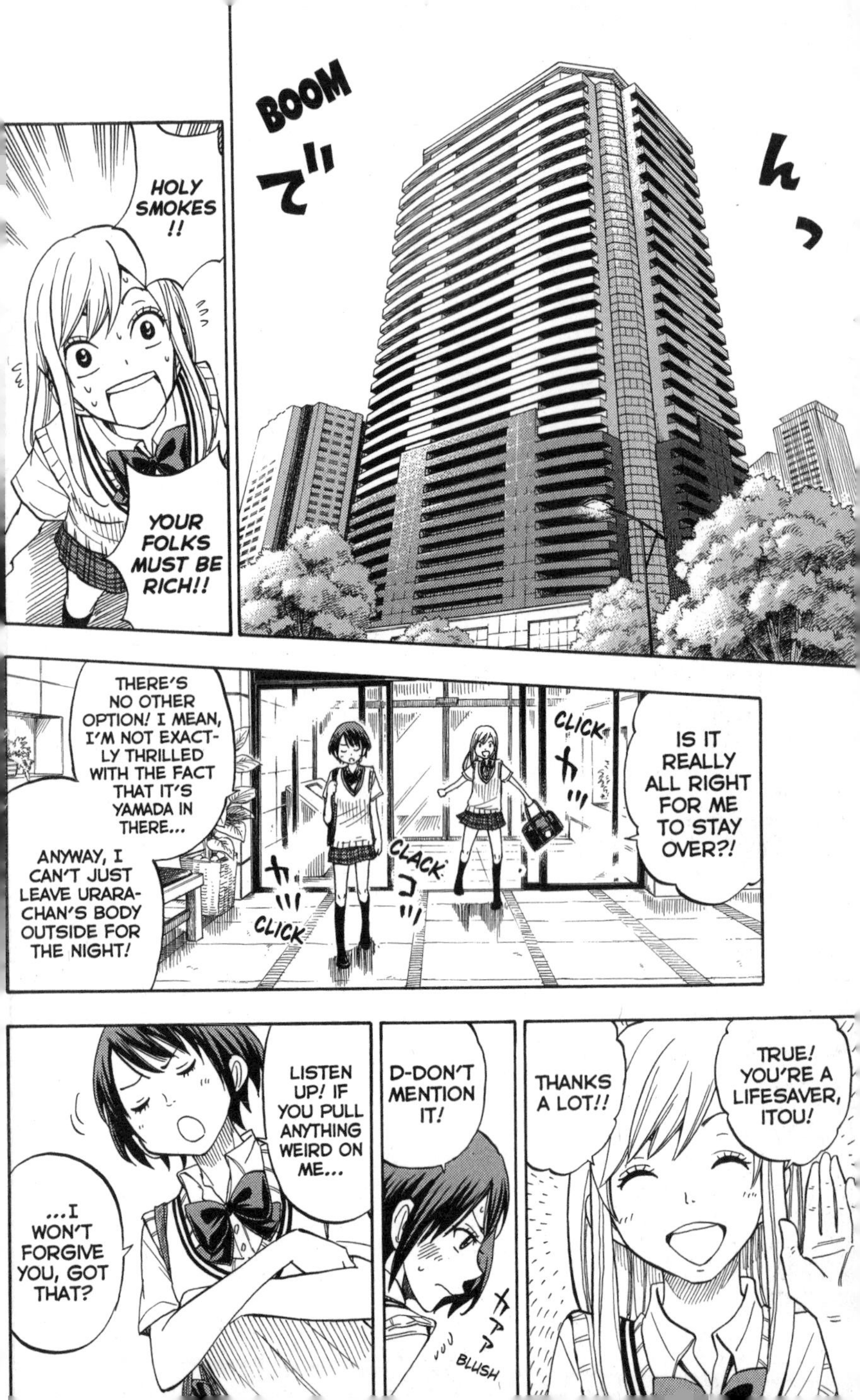
BOOM
で
んっ
HOLY SMOKES!!
YOUR FOLKS MUST BE RICH!!
IS IT REALLY ALL RIGHT FOR ME TO STAY OVER?!
CLICK
カッ
CLACK
コッ
CLICK
カッ
THERE'S NO OTHER OPTION! I MEAN, I'M NOT EXACTLY THRILLED WITH THE FACT THAT IT'S YAMADA IN THERE...
ANYWAY, I CAN'T JUST LEAVE URARA-CHAN'S BODY OUTSIDE FOR THE NIGHT!
TRUE! YOU'RE A LIFESAVER, ITOU!
THANKS A LOT!!
D-DON'T MENTION IT!
カァァ
BLUSH
LISTEN UP! IF YOU PULL ANYTHING WEIRD ON ME...
...I WON'T FORGIVE YOU, GOT THAT?

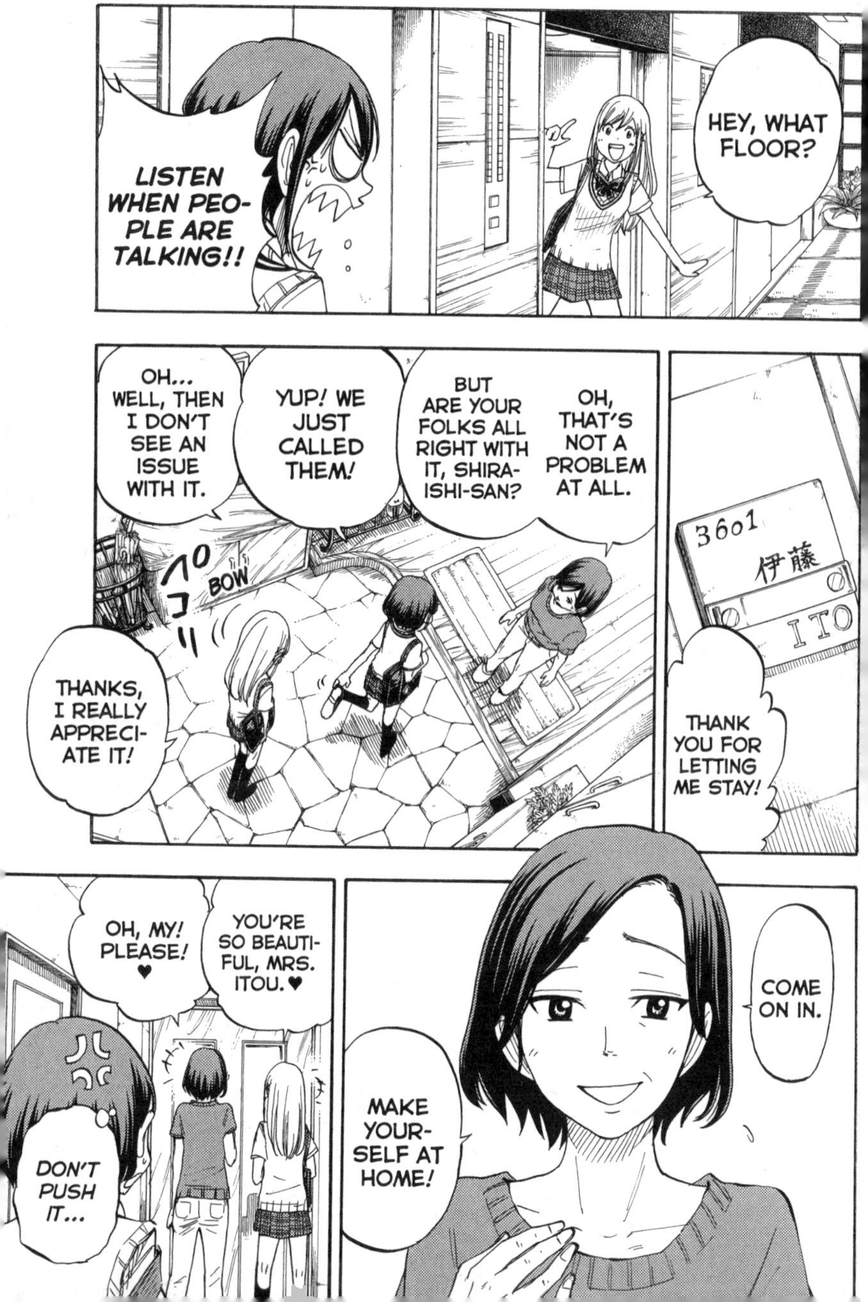
HEY, WHAT FLOOR?
LISTEN WHEN PEO-PLE ARE TALKING!!
3601
伊藤
ITO
THANK YOU FOR LETTING ME STAY!
OH, THAT'S NOT A PROBLEM AT ALL.
BUT ARE YOUR FOLKS ALL RIGHT WITH IT, SHIRA-ISHI-SAN?
YUP! WE JUST CALLED THEM!
OH... WELL, THEN I DON'T SEE AN ISSUE WITH IT.
ヘコ BOW
THANKS, I REALLY APPRECI-ATE IT!
COME ON IN.
MAKE YOUR-SELF AT HOME!
YOU'RE SO BEAUTI-FUL, MRS. ITOU. ♥
OH, MY! PLEASE! ♥
DON'T PUSH IT...

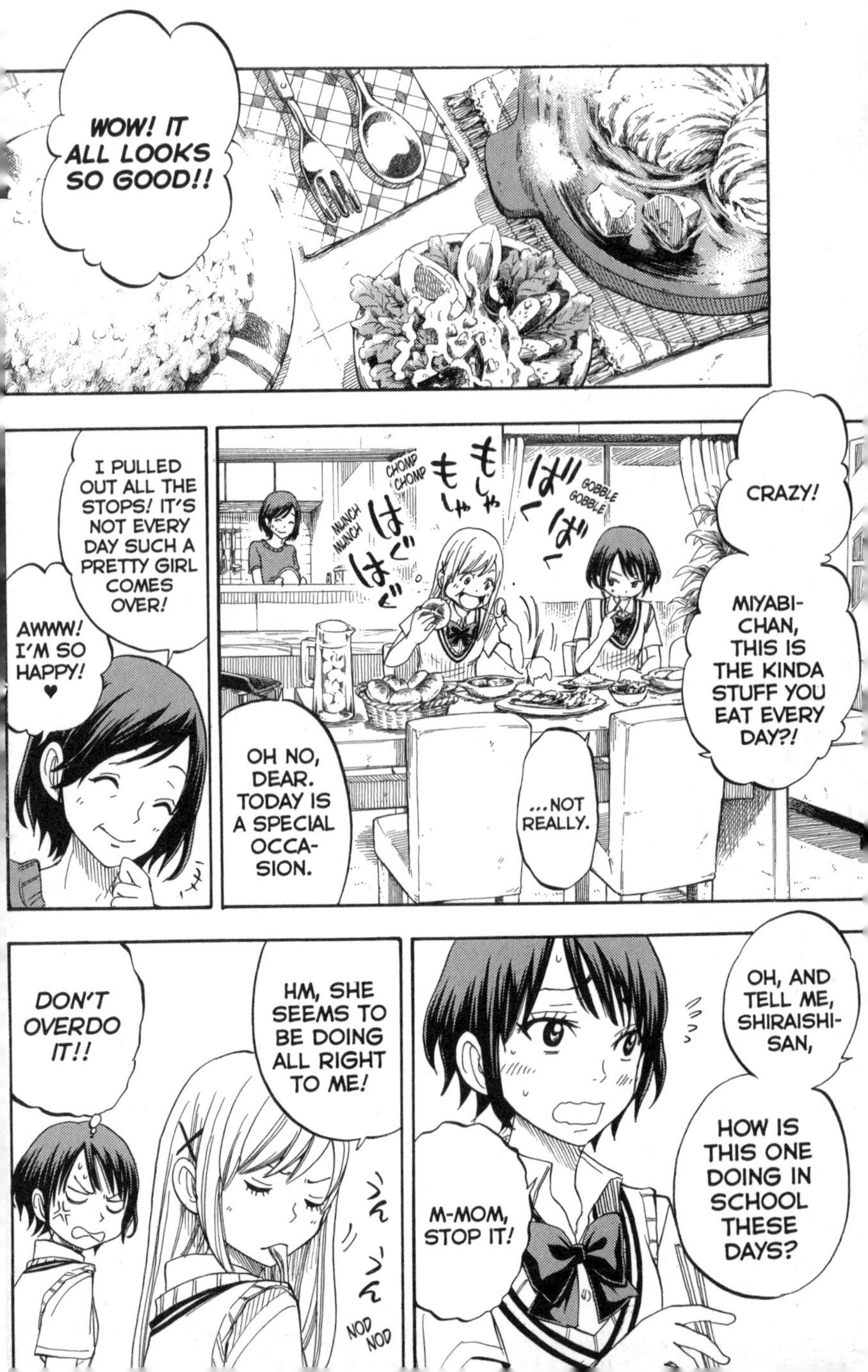
WOW! IT ALL LOOKS SO GOOD!!
CRAZY!
ばくばく
GOBBLE GOBBLE
もしゃもしゃ
CHOMP CHOMP
はぐはぐ
MUNCH MUNCH
MIYABI-CHAN, THIS IS THE KINDA STUFF YOU EAT EVERY DAY?!
...NOT REALLY.
OH NO, DEAR. TODAY IS A SPECIAL OCCA-SION.
I PULLED OUT ALL THE STOPS! IT'S NOT EVERY DAY SUCH A PRETTY GIRL COMES OVER!
AWWW! I'M SO HAPPY! ♥
OH, AND TELL ME, SHIRAISHI-SAN,
HOW IS THIS ONE DOING IN SCHOOL THESE DAYS?
M-MOM, STOP IT!
HM, SHE SEEMS TO BE DOING ALL RIGHT TO ME!
うんうん
NOD NOD
DON'T OVERDO IT!!

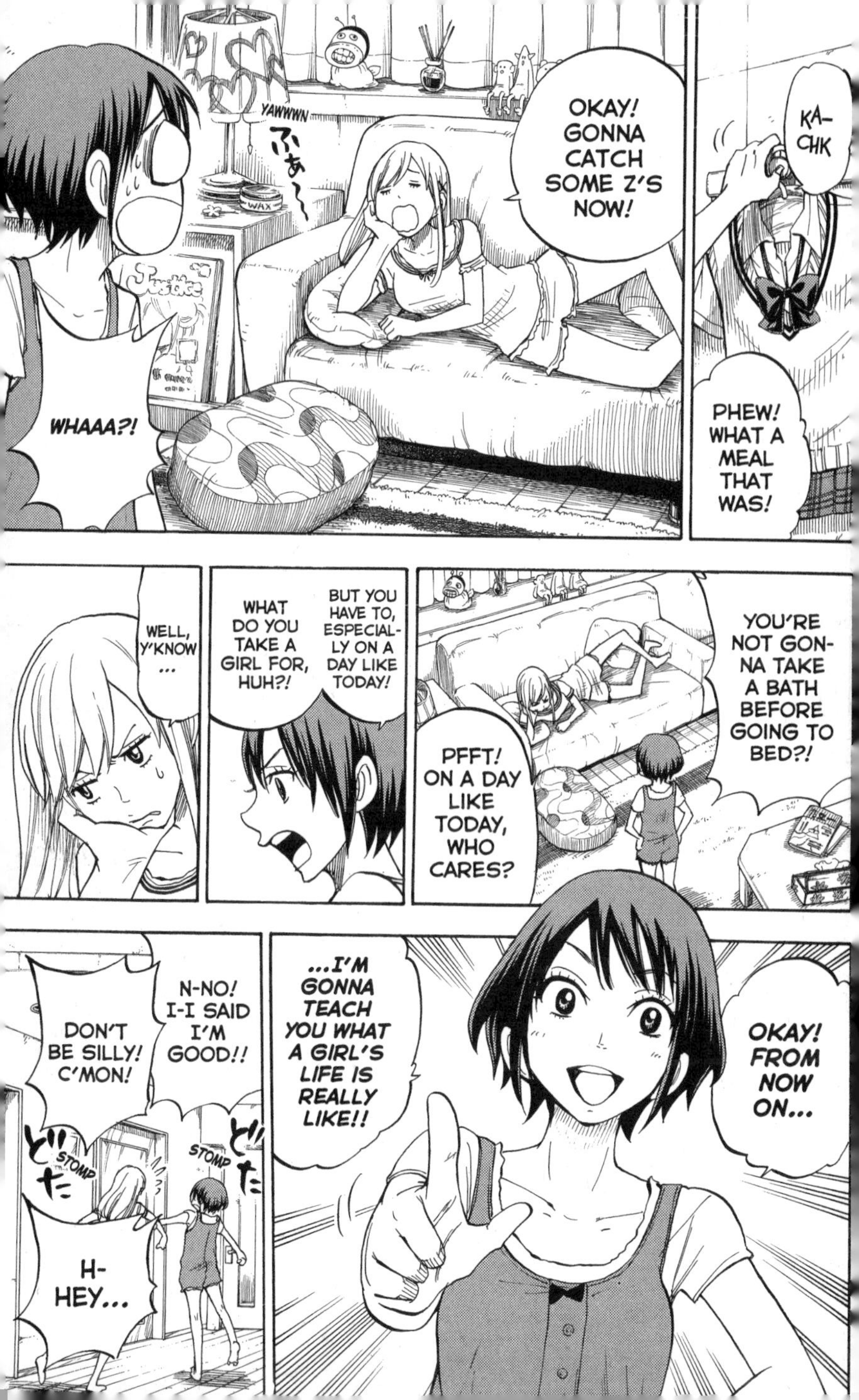
KA-CHK
PHEW! WHAT A MEAL THAT WAS!
OKAY! GONNA CATCH SOME Z'S NOW!
YAWWWN
ふぁ〜
WHAAA?!
YOU'RE NOT GONNA TAKE A BATH BEFORE GOING TO BED?!
PFFT! ON A DAY LIKE TODAY, WHO CARES?
BUT YOU HAVE TO, ESPECIALLY ON A DAY LIKE TODAY!
WHAT DO YOU TAKE A GIRL FOR, HUH?!
WELL, Y'KNOW...
OKAY! FROM NOW ON...
...I'M GONNA TEACH YOU WHAT A GIRL'S LIFE IS REALLY LIKE!!
N-NO! I-I SAID I'M GOOD!!
DON'T BE SILLY! C'MON!
どた
STOMP
どた
STOMP
H-HEY...

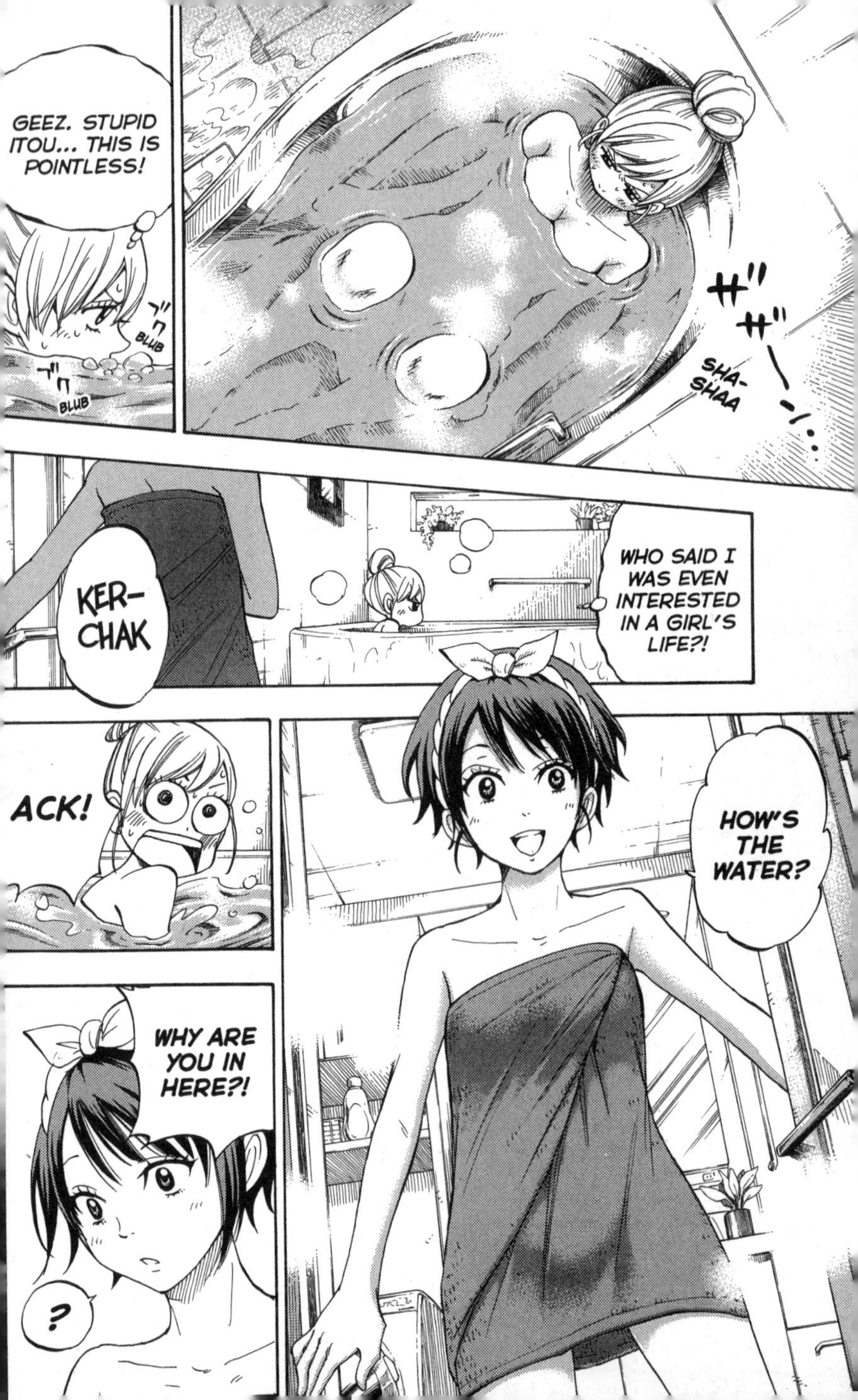
ザザーッ…
SHA-SHAA
GEEZ. STUPID ITOU... THIS IS POINTLESS!
ブク
BLUB
ブク
BLUB
WHO SAID I WAS EVEN INTERESTED IN A GIRL'S LIFE?!
KER-CHAK
HOW'S THE WATER?
ACK!
WHY ARE YOU IN HERE?!
?

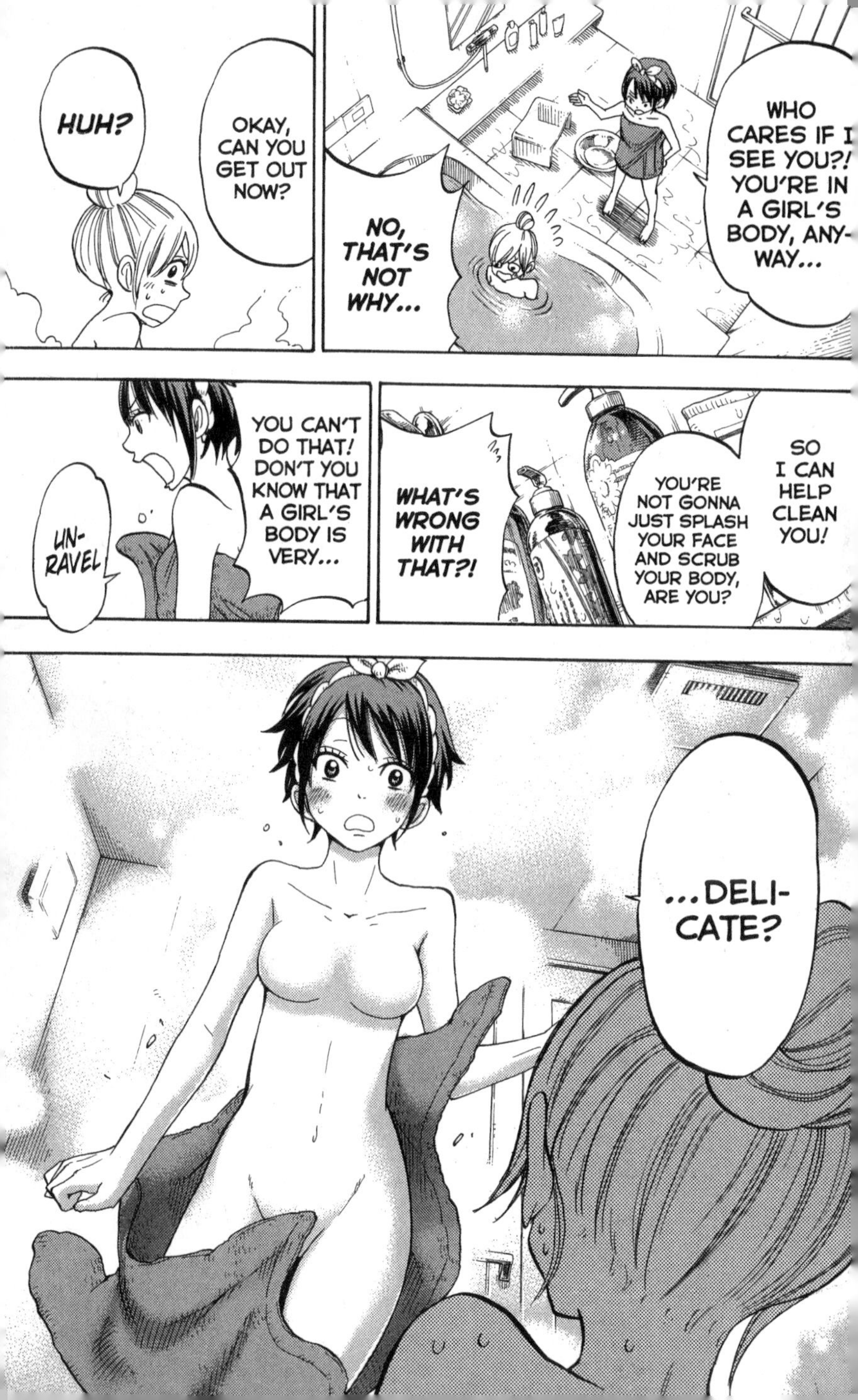
WHO CARES IF I SEE YOU?! YOU'RE IN A GIRL'S BODY, ANY-WAY...
NO, THAT'S NOT WHY...
OKAY, CAN YOU GET OUT NOW?
HUH?
SO I CAN HELP CLEAN YOU!
YOU'RE NOT GONNA JUST SPLASH YOUR FACE AND SCRUB YOUR BODY, ARE YOU?
WHAT'S WRONG WITH THAT?!
YOU CAN'T DO THAT! DON'T YOU KNOW THAT A GIRL'S BODY IS VERY...
UN-RAVEL
...DELI-CATE?

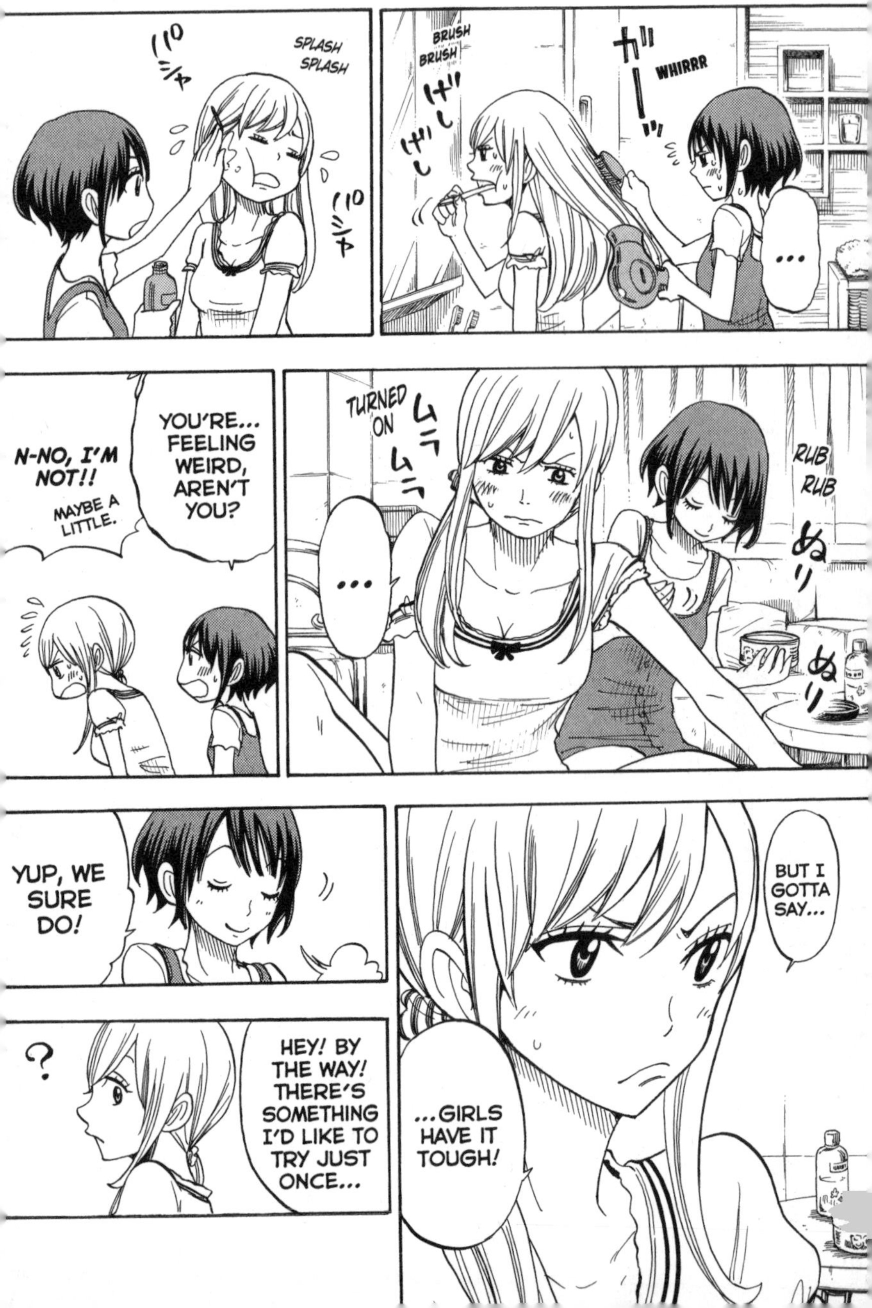

WHIRRR
ガーッ
BRUSH BRUSH
げし げし
...
パシャ
SPLASH SPLASH
パシャ
RUB RUB
ぬり
ぬり
TURNED ON
ムラ ムラ
...
YOU'RE... FEELING WEIRD, AREN'T YOU?
N-NO, I'M NOT!!
MAYBE A LITTLE.
BUT I GOTTA SAY...
...GIRLS HAVE IT TOUGH!
YUP, WE SURE DO!
HEY! BY THE WAY! THERE'S SOMETHING I'D LIKE TO TRY JUST ONCE...
?

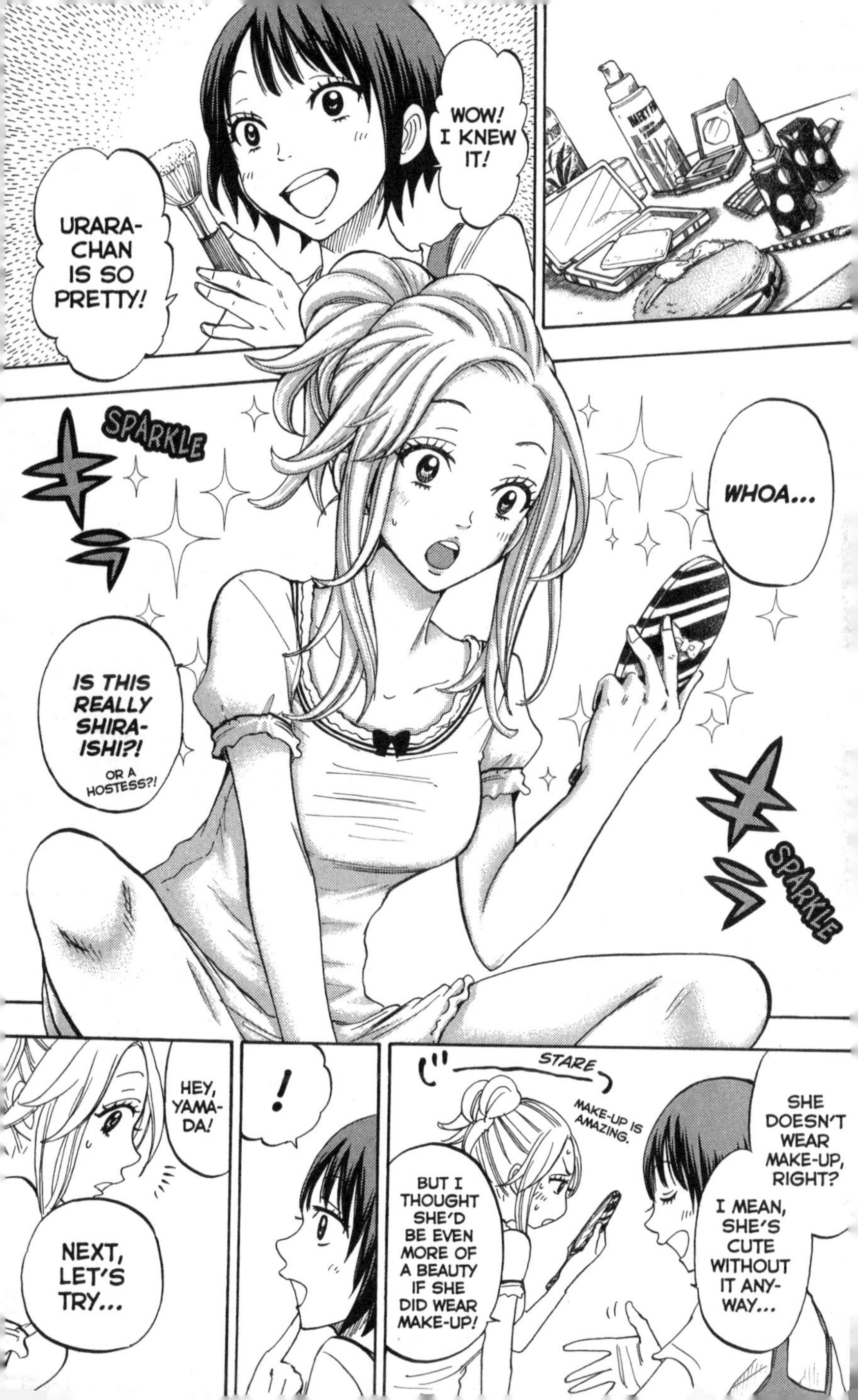

WOW! I KNEW IT!
URARA-CHAN IS SO PRETTY!
WHOA...
SPARKLE
IS THIS REALLY SHIRA-ISHI?!
OR A HOSTESS?!
SPARKLE
STARE
SHE DOESN'T WEAR MAKE-UP, RIGHT?
I MEAN, SHE'S CUTE WITHOUT IT ANY-WAY...
MAKE-UP IS AMAZING.
BUT I THOUGHT SHE'D BE EVEN MORE OF A BEAUTY IF SHE DID WEAR MAKE-UP!
!
HEY, YAMA-DA!
NEXT, LET'S TRY...

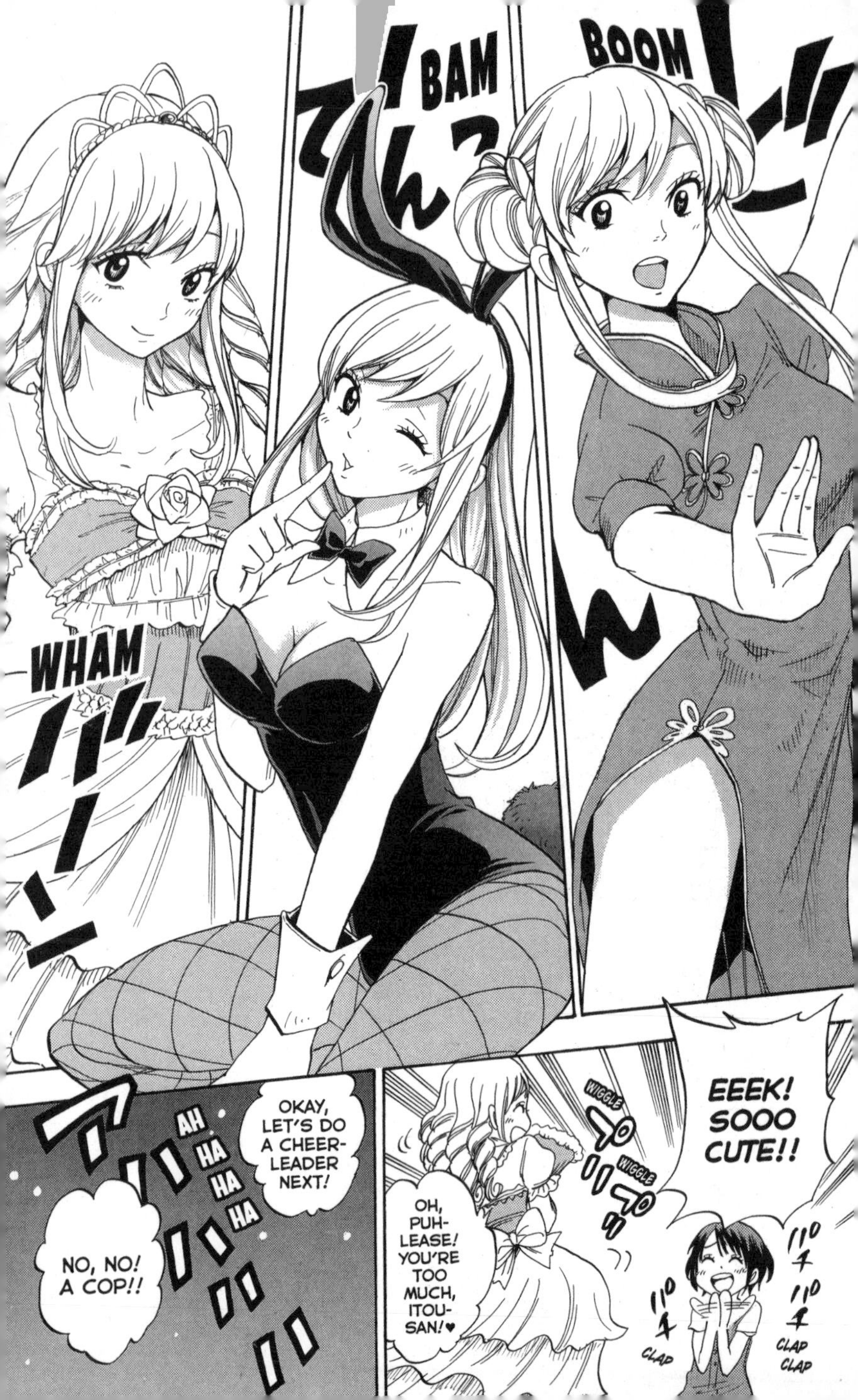
BOOM
BAM
WHAM
EEEK! SOOO CUTE!!
WIGGLE
WIGGLE
CLAP CLAP
OH, PUH-LEASE! YOU'RE TOO MUCH, ITOU-SAN!♥
CLAP
OKAY, LET'S DO A CHEER-LEADER NEXT!
AH HA HA HA
NO, NO! A COP!!

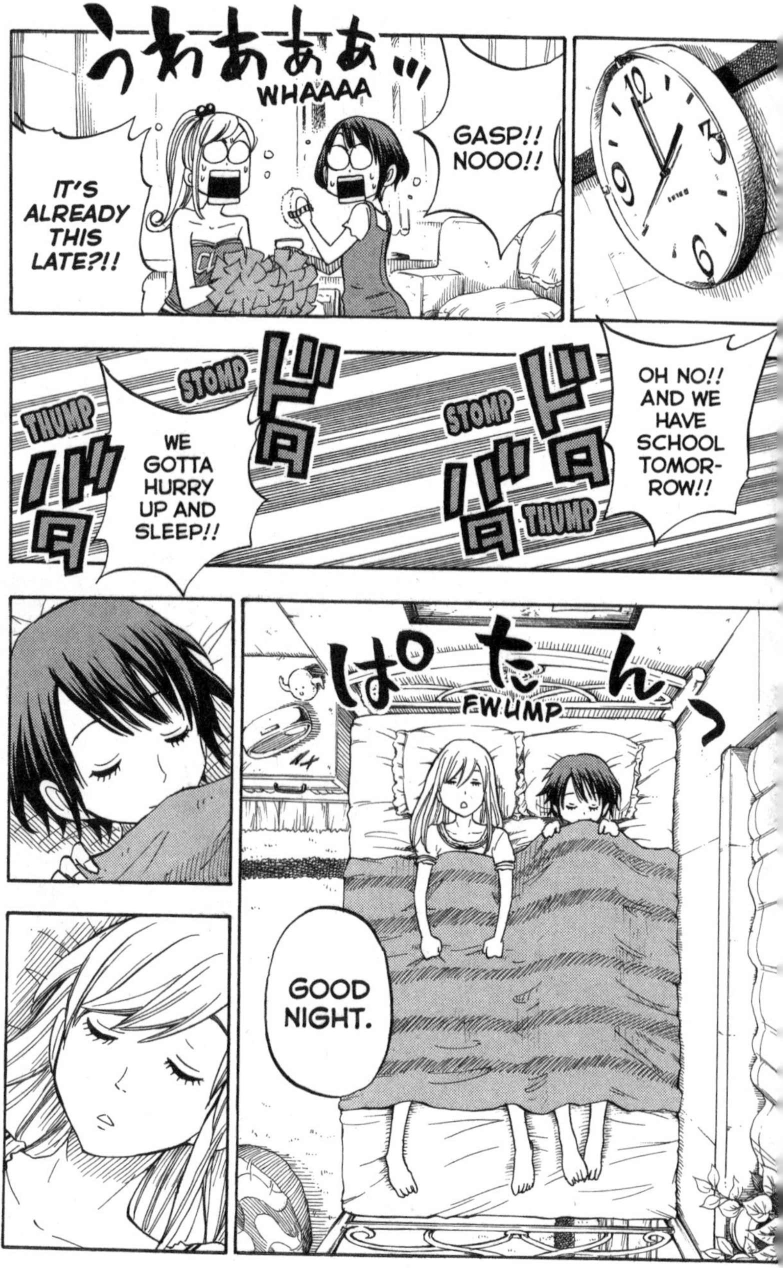
うわあああッ
WHAAAA
GASP!! NOOO!!
IT'S ALREADY THIS LATE?!!
OH NO!! AND WE HAVE SCHOOL TOMOR-ROW!!
ドド
STOMP
THUMP
ドド
STOMP
WE GOTTA HURRY UP AND SLEEP!!
ドド
THUMP
ぱたんっ
FWUMP
GOOD NIGHT.

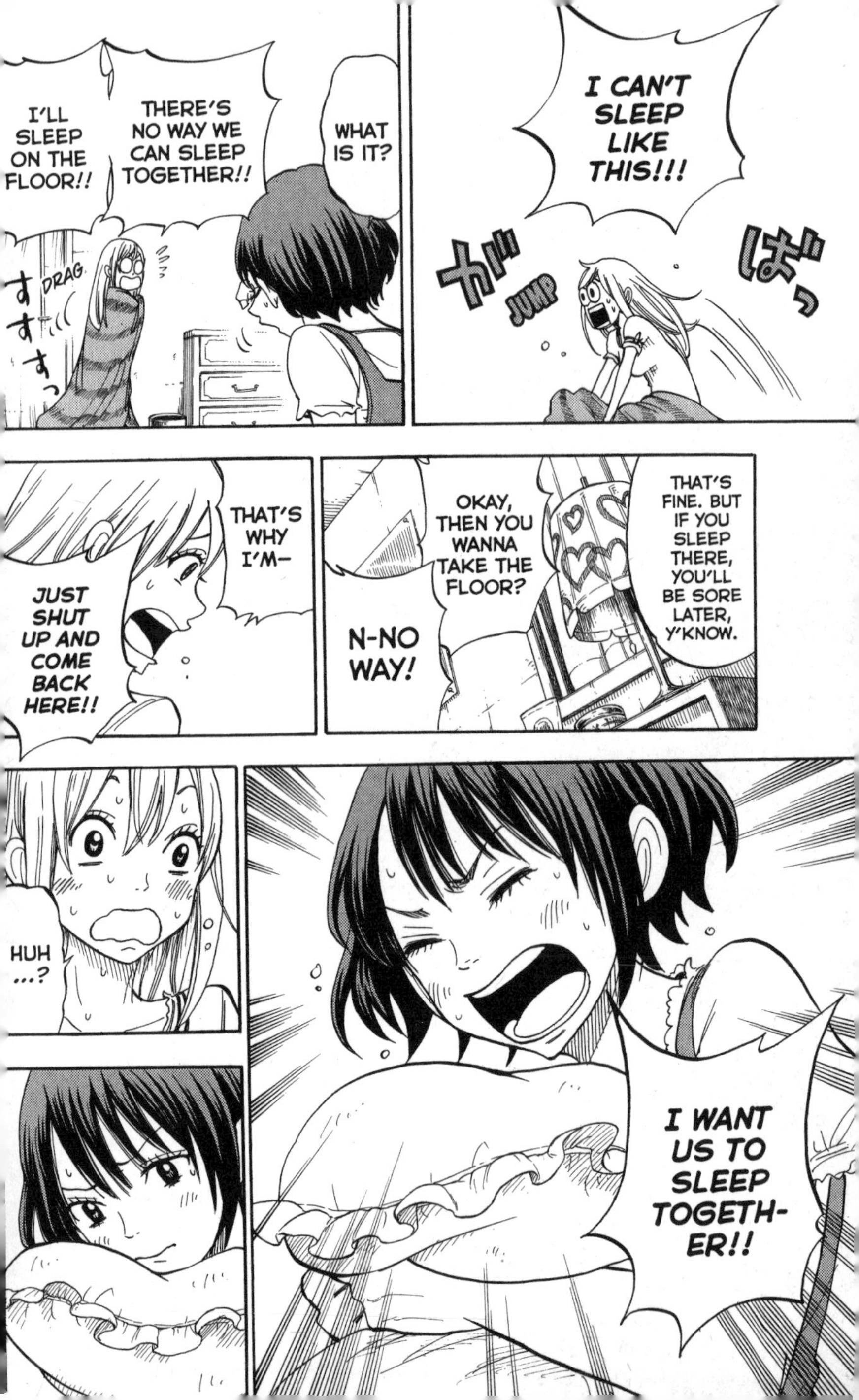
I CAN'T SLEEP LIKE THIS!!!
ばっ
JUMP
ガ
WHAT IS IT?
THERE'S NO WAY WE CAN SLEEP TOGETHER!!
I'LL SLEEP ON THE FLOOR!!
DRAG
すすすっ
THAT'S FINE. BUT IF YOU SLEEP THERE, YOU'LL BE SORE LATER, Y'KNOW.
OKAY, THEN YOU WANNA TAKE THE FLOOR?
N-NO WAY!
THAT'S WHY I'M–
JUST SHUT UP AND COME BACK HERE!!
I WANT US TO SLEEP TOGETH-ER!!
HUH ...?

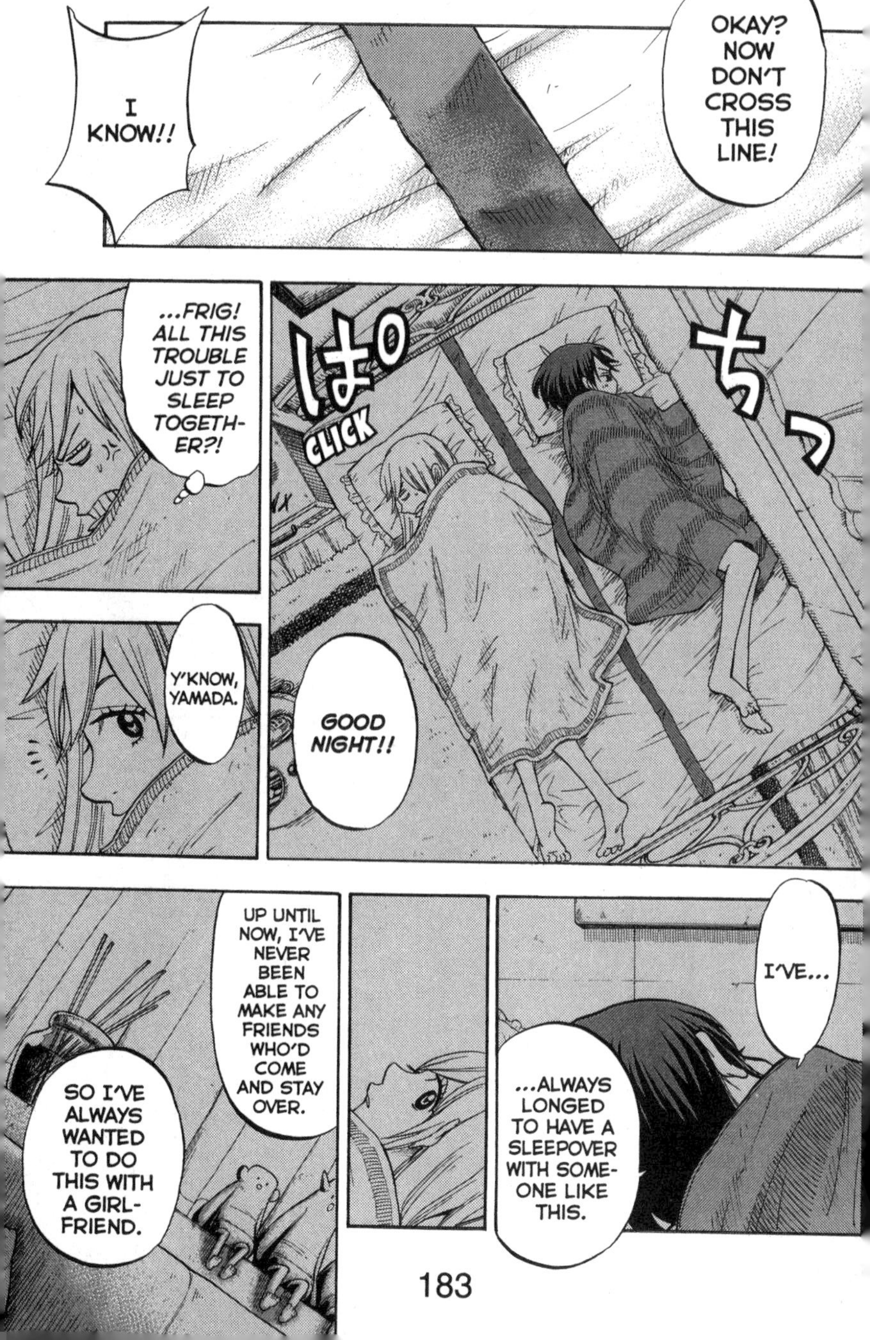
OKAY? NOW DON'T CROSS THIS LINE!
I KNOW!!
ちっ
はっ
CLICK
GOOD NIGHT!!
...FRIG! ALL THIS TROUBLE JUST TO SLEEP TOGETH-ER?!
Y'KNOW, YAMADA.
I'VE...
...ALWAYS LONGED TO HAVE A SLEEPOVER WITH SOME-ONE LIKE THIS.
UP UNTIL NOW, I'VE NEVER BEEN ABLE TO MAKE ANY FRIENDS WHO'D COME AND STAY OVER.
SO I'VE ALWAYS WANTED TO DO THIS WITH A GIRL-FRIEND.

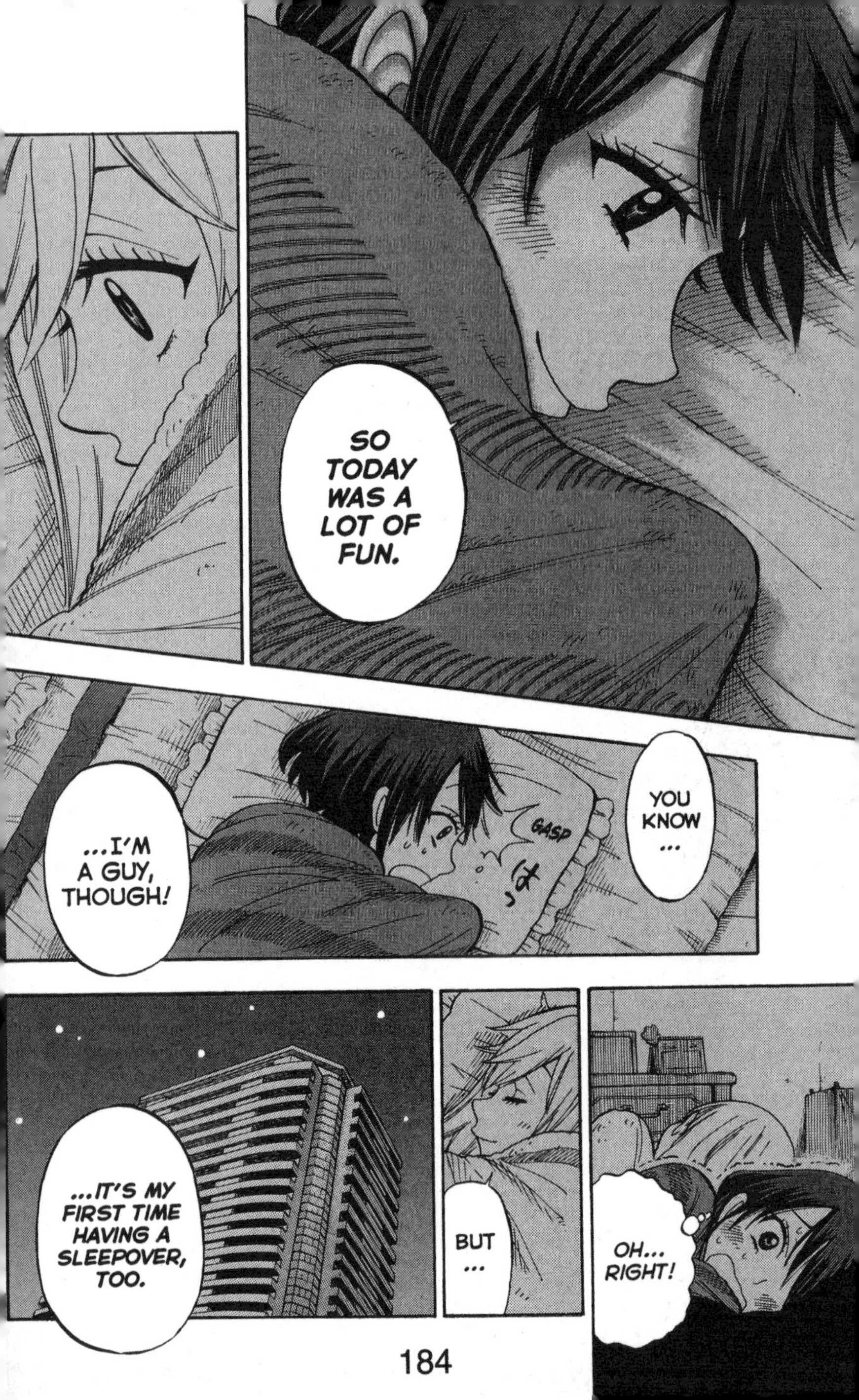
SO TODAY WAS A LOT OF FUN.
YOU KNOW...
GASP
...I'M A GUY, THOUGH!
OH... RIGHT!
BUT...
...IT'S MY FIRST TIME HAVING A SLEEPOVER, TOO.

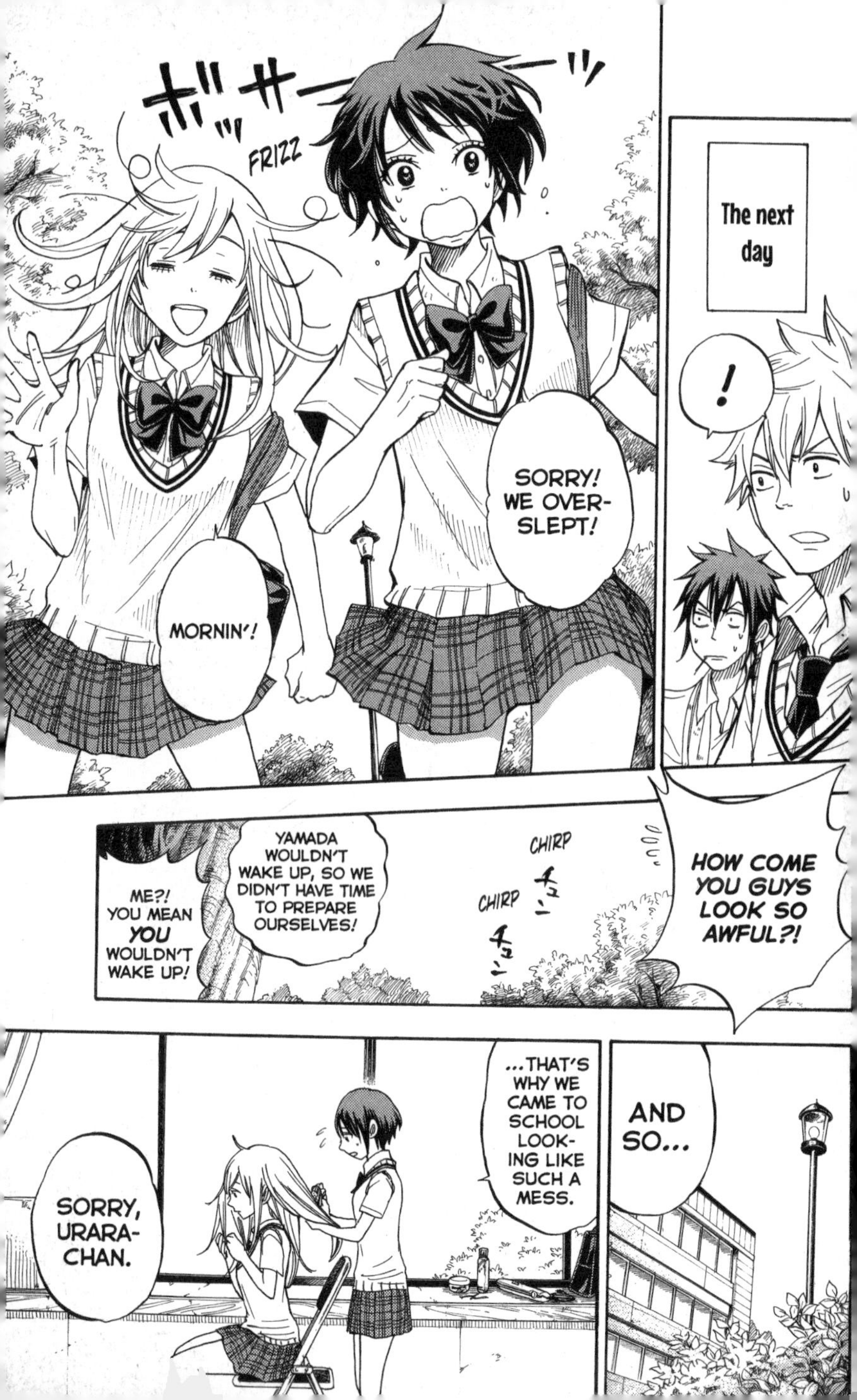
The next day
!
ボサーッ
FRIZZ
SORRY! WE OVER-SLEPT!
MORNIN'!
HOW COME YOU GUYS LOOK SO AWFUL?!
CHIRP
CHIRP
YAMADA WOULDN'T WAKE UP, SO WE DIDN'T HAVE TIME TO PREPARE OURSELVES!
ME?! YOU MEAN YOU WOULDN'T WAKE UP!
AND SO...
...THAT'S WHY WE CAME TO SCHOOL LOOK-ING LIKE SUCH A MESS.
SORRY, URARA-CHAN.

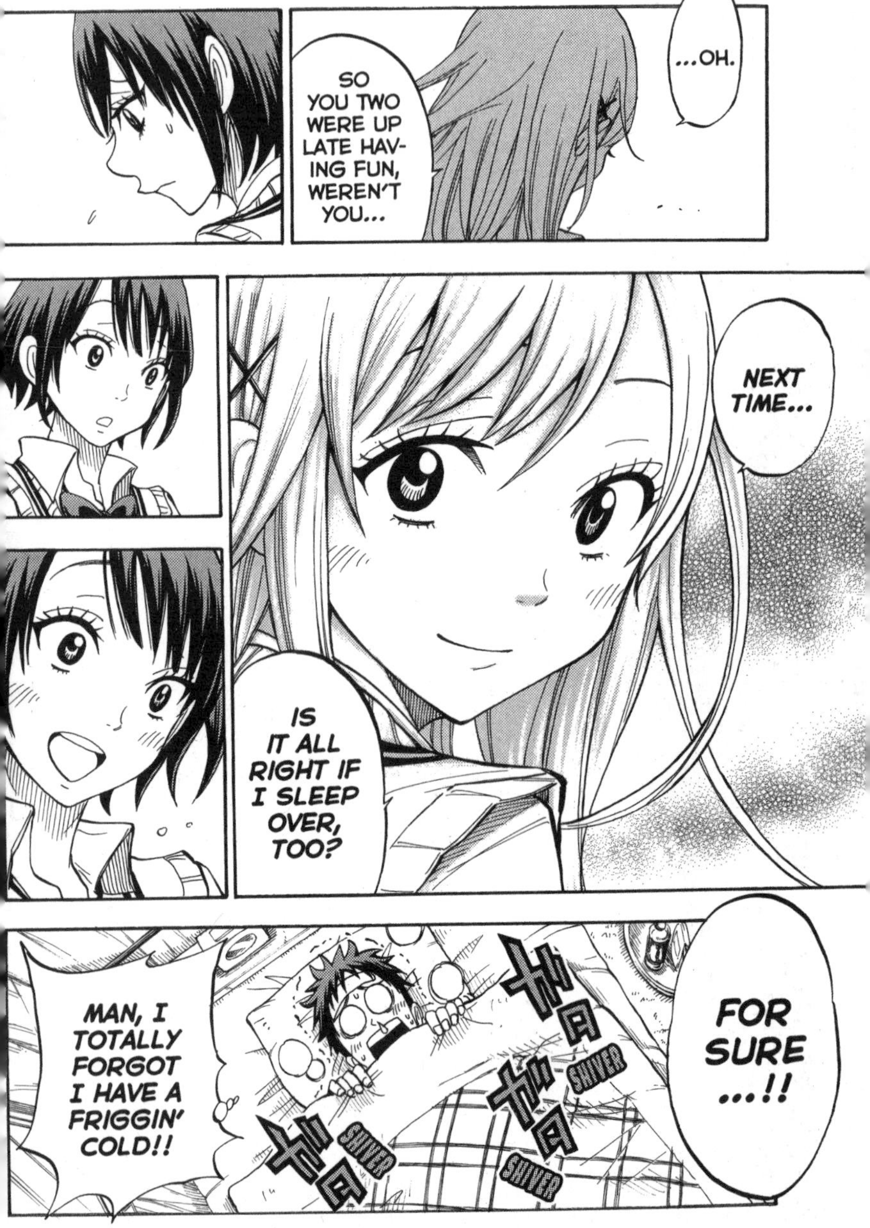
...OH.
SO YOU TWO WERE UP LATE HAV-ING FUN, WEREN'T YOU...
NEXT TIME...
IS IT ALL RIGHT IF I SLEEP OVER, TOO?
FOR SURE ...!!
SHIVER
SHIVER
SHIVER
MAN, I TOTALLY FORGOT I HAVE A FRIGGIN' COLD!!

End of Bonus Chapter

朱雀高等学校 裏ホームページ

SUZAKU HIGH SCHOOL UNDERGROUND WEBSITE

Well then, it's time for the fourth installment of this column! Shall we get started?!

That's right. Well, let's get right into it. So, about those fan letters to Itou that we requested last time…

Oh, come now! I told you to stop with all that (COY)

This is quite a shock!! **We didn't receive a single letter!!!**

Whaaaaaaaa?!! (SHOCK)

Oh well, it happens. Oh, but actually, we did receive one submission for this. Though, I'm not certain that it's a fan-letter…

Q1. With so many witches being large-chested, does Itou-san's flat chest have anything to do with her not being a witch?

Kagoshima Prefecture H.N. (handle name) Matsuko-san

Of course it has nothing to do with that!!!

Hmm. The mystery of the witches just keeps getting deeper and deeper…

I'm still looking for fan-letters…!!! (SNIFFLE)

Anyway, we've invited a special guest today! The idol of our school, heeere's Urara-chan!!

Hello. I'm not really sure what this is, but I thought I'd come by.

People have written tons of questions for you. Let's get right to it and answer some of those questions.

Q2. How many reference books do you have, Urara-chan?

H.N. Ohchan-san

Oh, yes. I don't really have that many. I periodically dispose of ones that I no longer use and I decide to dive deep into each book until I've completely mastered them.

Back when I went to your house with Yamada, I felt like I saw a bookshelf filled with reference books, though...

I can't believe you actually took in that much. You don't miss anything, huh.

Oh, sure. When that bookshelf gets full, I dispose of books in sequential order.

Q3. Tell me what your hobby is, Shiraishi-san!!

Hokkaido Prefecture H.N. Ippon-san

Collecting stationary.

I knew it! You must have a bunch of cute stationary, Urara-chan!

Using my favorite notebooks and writing utensils really makes my studying move along.

Q4. What's your favorite type of thing, Urara-chan?!

Saitama Prefecture H.N. Momo-san

Let's see... I love cute things!

You're at your cutest right now!!

I think the same thing!!!

Q5. It seems that you keep a black cat as a pet. Do you like cats? Tell me the name of your black cat. H.N. Kuracchi-san

That little guy just ended up living at my house one day. There are some days where it leaves and doesn't come back, so it doesn't have a name yet. But I do like cats.

I hate cats… They're scary…

But you have the word tiger (tora) in your name, Toranosuke… Just what happened between you and cats in your past?

Q6. What do Yamada-kun's lips feel like? H.N. Hotaruko-san

Hmm, well… I can't really describe the sensation.

Yeah. I can't really describe it.

Yup. Can't really describe it.

What is it with Yamada…? (DING)

Anyway, that's it for now! We're still getting more letters for Urara-chan than we have time to introduce to you guys but…we'll continue this another time!

Yeah. This was fun. Call me back sometime.

Next time, the supreme moron–**Yamada**–will be here! Send your questions and whatever else for Yamada to us! You can ask anything you want, so don't hold back!

Please send your correspondence here ↓

Yamada-kun and the Seven Witches: Underground Website
c/o Kodansha Comics
451 Park Ave. South, 7th Floor
New York, NY 10016

※ Don't forget to include your handle name (pen name)!

Translation Notes

BLEHHHH, page 134

The gesture that Noa is using is a taunt known as *akanbe* in Japanese. This taunt is often done by childish and *tsundere* characters. This is similar to the common American taunt of sticking one's tongue out while making a "blehh" sound.

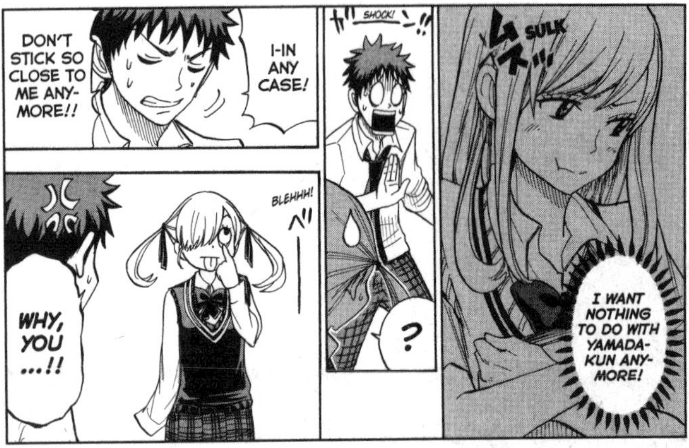
SULK
I WANT NOTHING TO DO WITH YAMADA-KUN ANYMORE!
SHOCK!
?
I-IN ANY CASE!
DON'T STICK SO CLOSE TO ME ANYMORE!!
BLEHHH!
WHY, YOU ...!!

Hostess, page 179

A hostess or *kyabajou* is a woman who works at a hostess bar. Hostess bars and the male-equivalent called host bars are places of entertainment where Japanese men and women pay to have conversation and drinks with beautiful people.

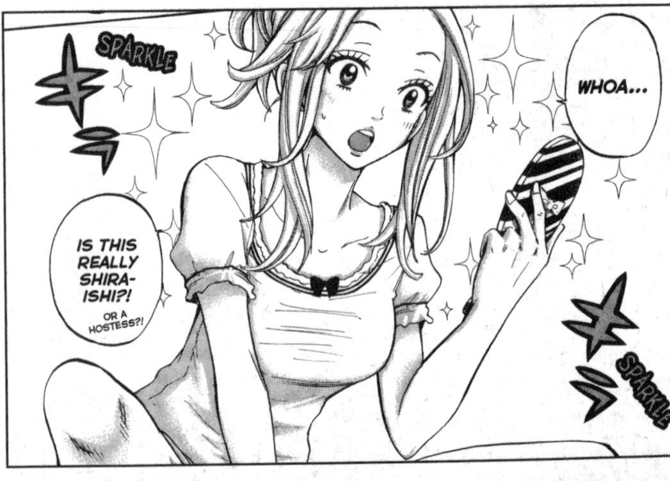
WHOA...
SPARKLE
IS THIS REALLY SHIRAISHI?!
OR A HOSTESS?!
SPARKLE

Yamada-kun and the Seven Witches volume 6 is a work of fiction. Names, characters, places, and incidents are the products of the author's imagination or are used fictitiously. Any resemblance to actual events, locales, or persons, living or dead, is entirely coincidental.

A Kodansha Comics Trade Paperback Original.

Published in the United States by Kodansha Comics, an imprint of Kodansha USA Publishing, LLC, New York.

Publication rights for this English edition arranged through Kodansha Ltd., Tokyo.

First published in Japan in 2013 by Kodansha Ltd., Tokyo, as *Yamada-kun to Nananin no Majo* volume 6.

ISBN 978-1-63236-073-1

Printed in the United States of America.

www.kodanshacomics.com

9 8 7 6 5 4 3 2 1

Translator: David Rhie
Lettering: Sara Linsely
Editing: Ajani Oloye
Kodansha Comics Edition Cover Design: Phil Balsman